THE QUESTION OF GOD

HEINZ ZAHRNT

THE QUESTION
OF GOD

*Protestant Theology
in the Twentieth Century*

TRANSLATED FROM THE GERMAN
BY R. A. WILSON

A HARVEST BOOK

A Helen and Kurt Wolff Book
Harcourt Brace Jovanovich, Inc.
NEW YORK

CONTENTS

In memoriam Edo Osterloh
Hans-Christoph Wasmuth

PREFACE

'The only possible new basis for theology is audacity'. This was said by Franz Overbeck, that strange professor of theology in Basle, and a friend of Friedrich Nietzsche. All his life he was a professor of theology, without retaining any personal belief; yet for this very reason he may have been more profoundly aware of the failings of the theology of his time than his believing colleagues. Overbeck's statement can serve as the motto for Protestant theology in the present century. In spite of all its hesitations and waverings, its erroneous apologetics and restorations, Protestant theology in this century provided a new basis, with audacity.

No matter how we describe the age in which we live – as an 'earth-shaking transition', as the 'age of the world wars', as 'the end of all certainty', as an 'age of crisis', an 'age of anxiety', or 'the end of the modern age' – in any case we are expressing the feeling that we experience a vast crisis and a transition of world-wide proportions. Faith in God is also drawn into this crisis and transition. The question of God is the interior obverse of our century, a century crowded with outward catastrophes, revolutions and discoveries; it is the deepest level of the earth-shaking transition in which we find ourselves.

A German poet, Christian Morgenstern, once made this note on his reading of Dostoievsky's *The Possessed*: '"Stop telling about that," cried Shatov, "we'll take it up later, let's talk about what really matters . . ." – and then they all talk about what really matters: whether there is a God or not; what man must do if there is no God; and whether indeed man can exist without God.' This passage sums up our present situation: we are concerned not with one or another aspect of Christian faith, nor with individual issues, the virgin birth, the divine sonship or the Ascension, but with the whole, the whole that really matters – with 'the question of God'.

The Christian proclamation, in its traditional form at least, no longer provides the majority of men today with a valid answer to the questions they ask about God, and consequently fails to provide them with an adequate way of understanding their position in the world and of mastering their lives meaningfully. The barb contained in the questions which most men are asking today about God is plainly this: the traditional Christian answers are no longer sufficient. Consequently, theology today must vindicate once again the language it uses about God, both in the sight of God and also in the sight of the world, if it is to continue to be, or is to become again, an appropriate language about God – appropriate, that is, both to God and to the world. Christian faith must be confronted in ruthless honesty with the changed reality of the world, and not only with the changed reality of the world, but also with the changed relationship of man to the reality of the world, with the whole consciousness of the truth and of reality in our time. This is the most important problem theology faces today.

Protestant theology has faced up to this problem in our century. As a result, it has come into flux again. From the First World War to the present day there have been more new developments, and indeed transformations and upheavals, in theology than in any other academic discipline except the natural sciences. It is the purpose of this book to give an account and an evaluation of them.

This will not be done in the form of a compendium. Both the theological situation and the personal involvement of the author in this situation prevent it. It is characteristic of this situation that a great dialogue is going on in theology today. It is this which has given the book its character and its form: it is an attempt to take part in this dialogue, by describing its main and decisive issues, and in this sense providing a 'guide line' through the often confusing richness of ideas.

In writing this book, I have never asked myself whether it is meant principally for theologians or non-theologians. I have been unable to draw any clear distinction between the two. I am not denying here that there must be in the Church a trained body whose task is the methodically ordered and conceptually clear consideration of the revelation of God to which the Bible bears witness. But I believe that here as elsewhere in the Church the principle of deputising must prevail, and that theology, more than any other discipline, must never become merely a field for experts. Just as in Switzerland there is only a small professional army whose sole task is to train a large territorial militia, so theologians should also form only a small professional army in the Church, with the task of creating a large body of theological territorials.

We have observed almost with dismay in recent years how the findings of theology are being kept from the community, and even consciously concealed, and how as a result there is today great confusion in the Christian community, simultaneously with a passionate desire for full information and honest discussion concerning the truths of the Christian faith. It is the purpose of this book to offer both, and in this way to provide a kind of 'first-aid'.

Hamburg, Easter 1966 Heinz Zahrnt

CHAPTER ONE

THE GREAT TURNING-POINT

God has spoken

Whoever attempts to give an account of Protestant theology in the twentieth century need not look long for a starting-point. It is identified with the name of Karl Barth. In the history of theology Barth dominates the beginning of the twentieth century as Schleiermacher dominated the beginning of the nineteenth century. From him we date a new era in the history of Protestant theology: the theology of the twentieth century began with Karl Barth.

From the historical point of view, the beginning of the twentieth century is not identical with the year 1900. Historically, the twentieth century began in August 1914 with the outbreak of the First World War. Nor did the theology of the twentieth century begin at the actual turn of the century. At that time, in the winter term 1899–1900, Adolf von Harnack was giving his famous lecture series to students of all faculties at Berlin university, *Das Wesen des Christentums* (The Essence of Christianity). Harnack's lectures – delivered extempore – were a great intellectual event, the highest expression and perfect manifestation of the age of bourgeois idealism, an age which was inspired by an optimistic faith in the human mind and in progress in history, and believed it could unite God and the world, religion and culture, faith and intellect, divine righteousness and earthly authority, throne and altar in a natural and almost unbroken harmony, and which therefore looked forward with confidence to the future.

In his seventh lecture Harnack said: 'We have received from the very foundation of our religion a lofty and noble ideal, an ideal which should be kept in view as our historical development proceeds, as its goal and lode star. Who can tell whether man will ever achieve it? But we can and ought to draw nearer to it, and today – as opposed to two or three hundred years ago – we are already aware of a moral obligation to proceed in this direction, and those among us whose experience is more subtle and therefore prophetic no longer look upon the kingdom of love and peace as a mere Utopia.'

Fifteen years later, on the evening of the 4th August, 1914, it was

Harnack who drafted the appeal of the German Kaiser to his people, and shortly after, together with ninety-two other scholars and artists, he signed the so-called 'Manifesto of the Intellectuals'. Apart from Harnack, this document was signed by the theologians Wilhelm Herrmann, Adolf Deissmann, Friedrich Naumann, Reinhold Seeberg and Adolf Schlatter, the philosophers Wilhelm Windelband, Rudolf Eucken and Wilhelm Wundt, the historians Eduard Meyer, Karl Lamprecht, Ulrich von Wilamowitz-Moellendorff, and the scientists Wilhelm Röntgen, Max Planck, Ernst Haeckel, and Wilhelm Ostwald. Max Klinger, Gerhart Hauptmann and Max Reinhardt also signed.

The manifesto of the ninety-three intellectuals signified the collapse of bourgeois idealist thought of the nineteenth century. Many of those who were to be the intellectual leaders of the next generation felt this to be so at that time; for example Karl Jaspers and Paul Tillich, Emil Brunner as well as Karl Barth. Forty years later Barth still recalls how 'one day in early August 1914 stands out in my personal memory as a black day. Ninety-three German intellectuals impressed public opinion by their proclamation in support of the war policy of Wilhelm II and his counsellors. Among these intellectuals I discovered to my horror almost all of my theological teachers whom I had greatly venerated. In despair over what this indicated about the signs of the time, I suddenly realised that I could not any longer follow either their ethics and dogmatics or their understanding of the Bible and of history. For me at least, nineteenth-century theology no longer held any future.'[1]

Theology could no longer go on speaking of God as it had done in the past. The attempt had to be made to do so in a new and different way, if what theology said about God was to remain, or was once again to become, responsible and worthy of acceptance. The question in fact arose whether and to what extent it was still permissible at all for theologians to speak of God. This was the question with which Karl Barth saw himself confronted at the beginning of his career.

At that time Barth was a young country pastor in the Swiss industrial township of Safenwil in the Aargau, and most of his early associates, Eduard Thurneysen, Emil Brunner, Friedrich Gogarten, and Georg Merz, were pastors like him. Looking back on their early days, Barth's most faithful friend, Eduard Thurneysen, wrote: 'This is how it all began. . . . Karl Barth as a country preacher took this office seriously and exercised it with a forcefulness and wholeness that was peculiar to him' – and it is as though Barth were replying to his friend when he writes: 'It was this miserable situation that compelled me as a pastor to undertake a more precise understanding and interpretation of the Bible.'[2] Throughout his life, when Barth has been asked what provided the impetus for the radical change in his theology, he has always derived it from the 'dilemma' into which he was forced by his ministry as a preacher. This was the beginning of everything for him, the source of all that followed, and the reason why in his theological thinking he has always displayed a partiality for preaching.

The renewal of Protestant theology in the twentieth century arose from the central task of the Church, that of preaching, or more precisely from the 'specific problem of the *pastor*, the sermon', from the 'familiar situation of the pastor at his desk on Saturday and in the pulpit on Sunday', from the 'position and problem of the Christian preacher with all its difficulty and promise'. How is it possible to preach with a news-paper open on one side of the desk and the New Testament on the other – where is the organic connection between these two worlds, and how can they be drawn together? Like every pastor, Barth is trying to come to terms on the one hand with the 'problems of human life' and on the other hand with the 'contents of the Bible'. He wants to speak to *men*, to the fabulous contradiction in their lives, but he has to do so as a pastor by means of the no less fabulous message of the *Bible*.[3]

Thus from the very first Barth is concerned with the question of *the proper understanding of holy scripture*, and therefore with the 'hermeneutic problem'. But within the limits of this problem he is concerned not with the methodological question: 'How is this *done*?', but solely with the fundamental question: 'How *can* this be done?' How, as a human being, can he venture to speak of God at all? How can the word of God be on the lips of man? It was this which oppressed those young pastors, and was the decisive issue in their 'theological existence'. What hitherto seemed the most ordinary and natural thing in the world – it had gone on in the Church for almost two thousand years, and every pastor did perform it in the pulpit every Sunday morning – all at once became something which was the very reverse of natural and self-evident; it became questionable, problematic, humanly impossible: 'As theo-logians we are obliged to speak of God. But we are men, and as such we cannot speak of God. We must be aware both of our obligation and our inability, and thus give God the glory. This is what oppresses us. Com-pared to this everything else is child's play.'[4]

Small wonder that, in the correspondence between the two friends Barth and Thurneysen during these years, the problem of preaching constantly recurs, and that we hear more of the oppression, burden and labour of preaching than of self-satisfaction and success. Barth wants to 'create', 'interpret', 'open up', 'show the way' with all his might. He feels 'an intense inner longing' to point out 'the essential' to himself and to others – and yet scarcely manages even a 'stirring sermonette, or lecture'. 'If only we were filled and driven, our sermons should appear simpler. Do you know, today I looked out of the window before the second sermon and saw how the Safenwil people went strolling happily instead of coming into the church again and I understood them very well, although theoretically I thought they ought still to hear about the sinners and the joy in heaven. I simply cannot as yet tell them – and who knows whether I ever will? – that they *must* hear. In the meantime they have full right to go strolling in their shirt-sleeves.'[5]

The difficulty of preaching made deep inroads upon Barth's previous theological convictions. Barth's background was that of liberal theology. He had learned it from his 'unforgettable' teacher, Wilhelm Herrmann, in Marburg, and Adolf von Harnack in Berlin, grafted upon the Reformed views of his native land, which he had adopted more or less unconsciously. Barth had connections with liberal theology not only from his academic background but also among his friends and his family. He had been editorial assistant of the *Christliche Welt*, the most influential journal of liberal Protestantism, and his brother Peter had married a daughter of Martin Rade, who was not only the editor of that paper but also the centre of the large circle of friends gathered around it. Now, however, in his parish, the questionable nature of this dominant theological tendency began to dawn upon Barth. This theology, he now realised, could not stand up to reality. It was no help when you had to go into the pulpit of Safenwil year in year out, Sunday after Sunday, 'conscious of the responsibility to understand and interpret, and longing to fulfil it; and yet utterly incapable'.[6]

What, then, did the university teach? Virtually nothing but the well-known 'awe in the presence of history'. This 'awe in the presence of history' does not merely signify a particular specialist method of sober historical and critical research into the Bible and Christianity, but implies a whole philosophy of life. This philosophy of life is backed by a specific conception of history, a vague historical pantheism, and this in turn is characterised by the gentle but obsolescent humanist idealism of the nineteenth century. It sees the divine goal of the historical process in the gradual victory of the powers of the spirit, which permeate history, and thus the progress of man, step by step, from the state of nature to civilisation. Each individual participates in the struggle by opening himself to the forces of the spirit, thus developing from the state of nature into a free personality. In the course of history individuals again and again appear who are the special bearers of spiritual and divine powers. One of those bearers of revelation, the highest and greatest, was Jesus of Nazareth. By following the example of Jesus and sharing in his inner life, man increases his consciousness of God and matures to become a free spiritual and ethical personality.

This is what 'awe in the presence of history' amounted to, as taught by the dominant theology of the time, as learned by Barth too from his theological teachers at the university. Now, in his parish, he came to recognise that it was quite inadequate for the understanding and inter- pretation of the Bible. This 'awe' rather signified the rejection of every reverent interpretation and understanding.

Thus Barth, impelled by the task and the needs of the preacher and disillusioned with the dominating theological method of the time, which offered him no help in his task and his needs, arrived at a com- pletely new starting-point for his theology. He opposed awe for the word of God to awe for history, and he opposed the theology of divine revelation to the theology of the human consciousness. This was a complete theological *volte-face*. Instead of making man, and the way he speaks and thinks about God, his starting-point Barth begins with God, and the way he speaks and thinks about man: 'It is not the right human thoughts about God which form the content of the Bible, but the right divine thoughts about men. The Bible tells us not how we should talk with God but what he says to us; not how we find the way to him, but how he has sought and found the way to us. . . . It is this which is within the Bible. The word of God is within the Bible.'[7] Thus in innumerable variations Barth repeats the thesis that the problem of theology is the word of God; it is its only problem, both pressing and insoluble.

Dominus dixit – 'the Lord has spoken!' This is Barth's starting-point. It is the one unique event of revelation, out of man's control, but decisive. It is the sole concern of the Bible and therefore of theology. Once it has pleased God to speak, all theology, being human speech about God, can only be a stammering repetition, a spelling out of what God has said, a thinking over of his thoughts. The theologian cannot derive the truth of God from historical study, nor can he deduce it psychologically from the pious consciousness of man, or by specula- tion from some philosophical concept of the infinite or the absolute. There is only one thing he can do, and that is to listen to the word of

God and expound it – in opposition to all history, psychology and speculation.

When, at the invitation of Georg Merz, Barth came to speak to a group in Munich which was studying social problems, he did not bring with him the usual lecture, but read the sermon he had preached two Sundays previously. The audience was astounded. Barth's publisher, Albert Lempp, looked him straight in the face and said, 'I have never heard the like of this before.'[8] What seemed so astonishingly new to him was basically the age-old theme of theology. But orthodox theologians had become accustomed to it, modern positivists had adapted it to the spirit of the times, and liberal theologians had weakened it completely. Here was someone who actually did not go beyond stating the Word as it was written, without the staleness of custom, without adapting or weakening it. But this meant that it had once again become astonishingly new, and was once again the 'fabulous thing' which according to the Bible no eye has seen, nor ear heard, and which is not known to the heart of any man. Because this theology was a theology of revelation and of the word of God, it began with fear and trembling, with astonishment and terror.

Barth draws attention to the 'extraordinary direction of vision' which can be seen in the biblical witnesses. As we observe them, we have the same impression as someone who is looking at people on the street from his window. He suddenly notices that they stop, throw back their heads, and, shading their eyes with their hands, look straight up, heavenwards, towards something which is hidden from the observer by the roof. Barth finds that in the same way the men of the Bible halt abruptly, redirect their attention, gaze directly upwards, and wait expectantly. 'Their eyes strangely open' and 'their ears curiously attentive', they all carry out the same movement. This implies that 'God has drawn the attention of these men to himself'. This explains the 'extraordinary direction of vision' which they all manifest.[9]

In opposition to every merely historical, psychological and speculative view of Christianity, Barth rediscovered the revelation of God as the decisive category of theological thought, and thereby restored to theology its own proper theme, which it had lost. He also placed the theologian in his proper place, 'beneath' holy scripture. Barth himself seeks to be nothing other than a scriptural theologian, a student and a teacher of holy scripture. The Bible forms the source from which alone his entire theology is drawn.

Thus at the end of the First World War, in his parish at Safenwil,

Barth wrote his first great theological work. Inevitably, it was the exposition of a biblical work, the Epistle to the Romans. The first edition appeared in 1918, and the second in 1921, in which, as he said himself, 'no stone remained in its old place'. The real effect of the book was due to this second edition. It was accompanied and reinforced by a series of essays and lectures in which Barth dealt simultaneously in theoretical terms with what he had carried out in practice in his *Epistle to the Romans*.

The 'Epistle to the Romans'

In the *Epistle to the Romans* Barth demonstrates what happens when someone, as he himself did, seeks to expound the Bible in a new way, understanding and expounding it more 'strictly' without the so-called 'awe in the presence of history'. Not that Barth basically rejected the historical and critical method which was dominant in theology at that time, as it is today.[10] He repeatedly acknowledges that he fully recognises its limited and relative place. The question is merely where the limit is drawn, and one must admit that Barth pushed it a long way back. However often he may protest in theory that he recognised and took seriously the problems of the historical and critical study of scripture, in practice he scarcely took it into account. He could not share the religious enthusiasm and scientific passion which others display in the struggle against 'rigid orthodoxy' and a 'dead literalist faith', but approached it 'coolly and attentively'. He once admitted to his friend Thurneysen that he was 'frightfully indifferent' to purely historical questions.[11]

The argument about the Bible in terms of history and comparative religion – positing the Bible as a human document, which contains the records of a Near Eastern tribal religion and a religion of Hellenistic civilisation – Barth regards as 'a battle which is over and done with', and which should be stopped as soon as possible. The really fruitful argument concerning the Bible begins *beyond* the understanding of its human, historical and psychological character, with the strange *content* of these human documents, their remarkable *matter*, and the theme, the biblical objective. Barth opposes to the fundamentally sceptical prejudice of others his own prejudice that the Bible is a good book, and that it is profitable to take its ideas at least as seriously as one's own.[12]

The background to Barth's criticism of the historical method is not merely distaste for the one-sided and barren way in which this method was widely applied in the theology of his time. He is afraid that man is once again attempting, largely with the aid of a fixed and rigid method, to seize hold of the text of the Bible and thus to bring the word of God under his own control. This would mean that the theologian's starting-point was once again man and not God.

Consequently Barth has never allowed the difficult historical questions and problems presented by the Christian revelation and its tradition to form a serious hindrance to him. He has always been interested only in the 'content' of the Bible, he has always pressed forward directly to its 'matter'. He seeks to know 'the Word in the words'. He desires to advance his understanding to the point where the enigma of the historical documents virtually disappears, and only the enigma of the theological matter remains: 'My whole energy of interpreting has been expended in an endeavour to see through and beyond history into the spirit of the Bible, which is the Eternal Spirit.'[13]

But does not this strict adherence to the spirit of the Bible demand a critique of its written text which is much more radical than any merely historical and philological critique? It looks as though Barth is ready to apply such a critique. He seems to wish to transcend the usual historical and philological criticism by a theological criticism on a higher level. 'The critical historian needs to be more critical,' he proclaims.[14] Once again, unfortunately, he goes no further than the assertion; nothing beyond it is visible in Barth's exegesis.

This led, as early as the beginning of the 1920's, to an interesting dispute with Rudolf Bultmann, which seems to anticipate later events. Bultmann had written what was on the whole a friendly review of Barth's *Epistle to the Romans* in the journal *Christliche Welt*.[15] He agreed entirely with Barth that the exegesis of the Bible should be concerned with the understanding of its 'matter'. But such a premise also demands that individual statements in the Bible must be measured by the yard-stick of its matter. No biblical writer, not even Paul nor any human being, always draws everything he says from his basic theme. Even in the Epistle to the Romans there are heights and depths, tensions and contradictions. Other voices speak in Paul besides that of the spirit of Christ: he draws from Jewish theology and popular Christianity, from Hellenistic enlightenment and Hellenistic sacramental belief. The matter with which the apostle is dealing is greater than the apostle himself. Thus it is not possible to avoid criticism, above all when one seeks to understand the matter with which the apostle is dealing.

To this theological criticism by Bultmann Barth replied with a kind of hypercriticism on the spiritual plane: when Bultmann invokes the 'Spirit of Christ' he is pointing to the crisis which is always that of the human spirit – and thus in Barth every criticism of the Bible, whether philological and historical, or theological criticism of its content, is overshadowed by the general crisis into which every human spirit is brought by the spirit of Christ.

Barth is willing, by this almost total renunciation of any criticism, to run the risk of identifying the text of the Bible directly with the word of God and so return virtually to the ancient orthodox doctrine of verbal inspiration. He replies to Bultmann's reproach that he is setting up 'a modern form of the dogma of Inspiration' by referring to what he had already said in the preface to the first edition of his *Epistle to the Romans*: 'Were I driven to choose between the historical-critical method and the venerable doctrine of Inspiration, I should without hesitation adopt the latter, which has a broader, deeper, more important justification.' Of course he was clever enough to add immediately: 'Fortunately, I am not compelled to choose between the two.'

What Barth gains by his method of interpreting the Bible is that the Epistle to the Romans once again genuinely begins to speak as though it had not been written 1900 years ago, but was a product of the hectic years following the war. The historical distance between the writer of those distant times and the reader of the present day is almost removed, so that the dividing wall of 1900 years becomes transparent and the dialogue between the document and the reader is concentrated entirely upon its content. The exegete has understood the author so well that he can speak in his name, and almost forgets that he himself is not the author. Barth's method of exegesis in the *Epistle to the Romans* has rightly been compared to the expressionist style in painting. The barrier between the artist and his object in real life, a barrier which is constantly present in both cases, is reduced to such a point that the two become a living unity. Barth's *Epistle to the Romans* seethes and rages like a volcano. He hurls forth his ideas and sentences as Van Gogh did his paintings.

The theology of crisis

Barth must be regarded not as a systematic theologian but as a prophet. The effect of his *Epistle to the Romans* was that of a violent explosion. Barth approached the text with a single assumption, 'that God is God'. His 'dogmatic presupposition' is that Paul knows this, and that he,

Barth, knows that Paul knows it. His objection to the dominant theology of his time was that it had forgotten this, and concentrated upon man and his belief, his piety, his religion, his culture, his mind and his emotion, instead of upon God and his revelation. And thus, like an Old Testament prophet, Barth is zealous for the deity of God, for his holiness and other-worldliness, and for the fact that God is *totaliter aliter*, wholly and absolutely different from man: 'If I have a system, it is limited to a recognition of what Kierkegaard called the "infinite qualitative distinction" between time and eternity, and to my regarding this as possessing negative as well as positive significance: "God is in heaven, and thou art on earth." The relation between such a God and such a man, and the relation between such a man and such a God, is for me the theme of the Bible and the essence of philosophy. Philosophers name this KRISIS of human perception – the Prime Cause: the Bible beholds at the same cross-roads – the figure of Jesus Christ.'[16]

There is an infinite qualitative distinction: God is in heaven and man on earth. This is the first and almost the sole principle which Barth, with his 'stricter understanding and exposition' of the Bible, derives from the Epistle to the Romans, and not only from the Epistle to the Romans, but from the whole Christian revelation. In order to exclude every confusion between the two, every irreverent assimilation of man to God, he forces God and man, heaven and earth, creator and creature asunder, by exalting the superiority of God and deepening the inferiority of man to their ultimate degree. No transition, ascent or building up of any kind, no development, bridge or continuity of any kind exists between one and the other. Between God and man lies a 'crevasse', a 'polar zone', a 'desert barrier'. Barth cannot pile up sufficient images and concepts, fresh starts, rolling periods and shattering anacolutha to describe this separation. One has to allow the effect on oneself of such a sentence as follows – and it is genuinely only a single sentence – in order to appreciate something of the passion of this theology, and of its champion. It is close to the style and language of the prophets: 'God, the pure and absolute boundary and beginning of all that we are and have and do; God, who is distinguished qualitatively from men and from everything human, and must never be identified with anything which we name, or experience, or conceive, or worship, as God; God, who confronts all human disturbance with an unconditional command "Halt", and all human rest with an equally unconditional command "Advance"; God, the "Yes" in our "No" and the "No" in our "Yes", the First and the Last, and, consequently, the Unknown, who is never a known thing in the midst of other known things; God, the Lord, the Creator, the Redeemer; this is the Living God.'[17]

Separation, distance, infinite qualitative distinction is for Barth the sole relationship between God and man. He can intensify this idea to the point of an assertion as paradoxical as: 'The vast *distinction* between God and man is their veritable *union*', or, 'When [men] perceive the utter *separation* between here and there [they] become aware of the only possible *presence* of God in the world.' Here all human thought, devotion and love towards God is so strictly excluded from faith that one can almost say that Barth's radical Christianity leads him to atheism. Certainly Barth can well understand the atheist: whether God exists is 'an entirely relevant and indeed inevitable' question. 'The cry of revolt against such a God is nearer the truth than is the sophistry with which men attempt to justify him.'[18]

The impression is sometimes given that Barth actually takes pleasure in despising man to the utmost. But he is sceptical to this degree for the sake of God alone. His sole purpose is to overthrow the false gods which man, man in his very piety, and above all man in the Church, has set up, so that God may once again be wholly God. Barth has rightly been compared with Samson, who pulled down the temple of the Philistines, even at the risk of being buried himself under its ruins.[19] Friedrich Gogarten, looking back on this gigantic work of demolition, this theological twilight of the gods, justly observed that this was not merely 'another way' of inquiring about God, but that it was 'a different God' who was the object of the inquiry. The God of traditional theology was the representative of everything true, good and beautiful in the world, the summit and consummation of human thought and life. By contrast, Barth's God forces open to an intolerable degree the problem, gulf and contradiction which pervades the whole of human life.[20]

The way in which Barth speaks of God in his early works makes it easy to understand why his theology has come to be known as the *theology of crisis*. In the *Epistle to the Romans* itself, the expression 'KRISIS' occurs on almost every page. But Barth does not use it in the sense Jacob Burckhardt does: to describe a transient historical moment, a ferment or upheaval within history, in which what has been comes to an end and something new begins. He understands it in a strict theological sense: the revelation of *God*, the crisis of the *world*. God, who is wholly other, who advances upon this world from beyond it like a 'wall of fire blocking the view in every direction', like a 'hostile fortress', like a 'clenched fist', like a 'cry of alarm' or a 'beacon' blazing into this world, acting to 'shatter', 'trouble', and 'undermine' everything here below. With the assertion of the infinite qualitative distinction between God and man, man moves with all that he is, has and can do, with his evil but also with his good, with his riches but also with his poverty, with his belief but also with his unbelief, under the lofty judgement of God, and for him and his world the judgement of God signifies nothingness, the end and death.

This theology was timely. Much that Barth said formed a theological counterpart to Spengler's *Decline of the West*. The 'earthquake zone', which the judgement of God brings upon every creature, seems to correspond exactly to the shock undergone by Western European man and his cultural optimism after the First World War. There has been some dispute as to how far the theology of crisis was influenced by the general crisis of the times. Barth's critics, such as the Swedish Lutheran Gustaf Wingren, have maintained that Barth was 'quite simply a modern man who uncritically adopted a particular emotional position in the cultural life of his time'.[21] Barth's supporters, however, such as the Dutch Reformed theologian G. C. Berkouwer, have vehemently denied that Barth's theology of crisis is a kind of theology of despair derived from the desperate situation of man in the post-war period, and have made great efforts to explain it in its own terms, or more precisely on its biblical basis.[22] Barth has uttered a judgement of Solomon on this matter: 'I cannot and really do not wish to demonstrate that we would have stood where we do now without the World War. But then who can demonstrate that it was the World War which led us to this decision?'[23]

Of course the theology of crisis was also nourished by the general feeling of crisis at that period, with its political and economic catastrophes, the collapse of its bourgeois idealist thought, its pessimistic critique of civilisation, and its atheism. All this provided its basis in experience; its representatives were personally involved in the crisis. Otherwise it would be impossible to explain the rapid success of the *Epistle to the Romans*. But the climate of the time provided no more than the background and distinctive note of the theology of crisis. It was born not as a result of the crisis of the time, but within the crisis of the time, as a result of a new encounter with the Bible in the midst of that crisis. It is this which led to Barth's critique, which was much more radical, less bourgeois and also less ecclesiastical than any secular criticism of civilisation which appeared at that time. It revealed the relativity and morality of every existent being in the world whatsoever

– 'from the microbe to the dinosaur, and even to the leader of a theological school of thought'.

By contrast to the vague idealist historical pantheism of the nineteenth
century, Barth presented a picture of history which seems almost
naturalistic or even materialistic: could not the history of humanity
ultimately be 'more honestly described if the stomach rather than the
head were adopted as the point of departure?' Cannot primitive
Christianity, the Crusades and the Reformation be more plausibly
explained in historical and materialistic terms than in any other way?
Certainly, man is distinguished by art, science, morality and a passionate
longing for fellowship with the infinite – 'Yes, but, God knows, we also
hunger and thirst, we digest our food, and sleep and lust. And where is
the boundary line between the two?' The history of man is 'unending
ambiguity . . . and in most of our activities manifestly so, but in fact,
ambiguous in all.'[24]

Crisis, division, separation, distance, infinite qualitative distinction –
all these concepts point in the same direction, towards a specific
theological tradition. When Barth had to address the 'Friends of the
Christliche Welt' shortly after the publication of his Epistle to the Romans,
he catalogued his theological 'family tree'. He mentioned Jeremiah,
Paul, Luther, Calvin and Kierkegaard. He specifically drew the attention
of his audience to the fact that the name of Schleiermacher was lacking
from this list. What united Barth's 'ancestors' was that their way of
speaking reduced man and his universe to nothing: 'A riddle, a problem,
and nothing more.' And precisely because Schleiermacher does not do
this, because unlike the others he does not speak to man in his irredeem-
able distress, his name is left out of this family tree. For at that time,
although for a different reason, Barth shared the conviction of
Nietzsche: Man is what must be overcome.[25]

When forty years later, in April 1963, Barth had to give the customary
speech of acceptance on receiving the Sonning Prize in Copenhagen, he
took the opportunity of explaining the influence of Kierkegaard upon
his theology.[26] First he enumerated those who influenced his theology
in his early period: Dostoievsky, Franz Overbeck, the two Blumhardts,
Hermann Kutter, 'the great Plato – yes, that is what I said, Plato!' To
these might be added, as Barth did on another occasion, Kant, or more
precisely neo-Kantianism, represented by the Marburg scholars Natorp
and Cohen. But Søren Kierkegaard was more important than all the
others. For Barth he was 'one of those whose cock-crow seemed to
herald the onset of a wholly new day'. Every page of the Epistle to the

Romans bears witness to how much Barth owes to Kierkegaard: the 'infinite qualitative distinction' between God and man, maintained in the face of all speculation that seeks to blur it, all aesthetic escapism and all cheap and undemanding Christian piety.

Here we must ask whether the content of everything which Barth says about God and man is not unchristian, or at least pre-christian, barely attaining to the level of the Old Testament. Does Barth know nothing of the revelation of God in Jesus Christ? The answer is that Barth believes that everything he says concerning God and man follows from the revelation of God in Christ, and from this alone. His interpretation of the revelation of Christ is also dominated by the infinite qualitative distinction between God and man, by the dialectic of time and eternity.[27]

In Christ the plane of human reality familiar to us is intersected, 'vertically, from above', by the wholly other, unknown plane of divine reality. But this point of intersection has no extension into the plane which is known to us; nowhere does it gain historical or psychological breadth. In the life of Jesus we can see only the 'shell-holes' formed by the unknown reality of God, and not that reality itself. The life of Jesus is essentially a 'passing-by', an 'exit', a 'bidding farewell', a 'transformation'. The life of Christ becomes tangible 'solely and exclusively' in 'his death on the cross'; his religious consciousness is the consciousness of his abandonment by God.

Of the incarnation of God Barth seems to know nothing. He does not see God as genuinely entering history; the divine touches this world only 'as a tangent touches a circle', 'without touching it'. The revelation of God is 'a mathematical point' and consequently has 'no secure standing place'. It is not one historical event among other events of world history, but 'the primal history', 'non-historical happening', 'time which is beyond time', 'space which has no locality', 'impossible possibility'. It is not a light shining in the darkness, but lightning flashing in the night, or rather, lightning which has already flashed. It is a 'submarine island' which as soon as a clumsy foot attempts to walk upon it, is immediately covered once again by the all-concealing water. All in all, revelation conceals more than it manifests; it limits rather than reveals. 'To us God is and remains unknown' – '"To be known directly is the characteristic mark of an idol."' (Kierkegaard)

Barth likes to quote the saying of Calvin, *finitum non capax infiniti*, the finite cannot comprehend the infinite, time cannot comprehend eternity. But if time does not comprehend eternity, and if the revelation of God is therefore 'time which is beyond time', the 'pure event' which flares up only in the 'moment' of which Kierkegaard speaks, without anything preceding or following it – how can it be expressed in words which imply permanence? Is it in any sense possible to 'draw a bird in flight'? This is to ask for speech about what cannot be uttered. This was the problem Barth was bound to see himself faced with as a theologian in regard to this 'permanent actualism': 'Does one single word of mine formulate the Word after which I am striving and which I long to utter in my great misery and hope? Does not each sentence I frame require another to dissolve its meaning?'[28]

The dominance of dialectic

Thus Barth was led to his *method of dialectic*, on the basis of which 'some onlooker', as he ironically puts it, has attached the name 'dialectical theology' to his whole theology. Concerning the dialectical structure of language about God, Barth offered the following definition: 'We can comprehend that we cannot comprehend God otherwise than in duality, in the dialectic duality in which one must become two, in order for two to be truly one.'[29]

It is not possible to give direct information concerning God and his revelation. The truth of God can never be expressed in a single word, but always only in *statement and counter-statement*. Every positive proposition has to be complemented and corrected at once by an opposing negative one. Affirmation must be clarified by negation, negation by affirmation. Thus for example whoever speaks of the revelation of God in creation must immediately speak of his concealment in creation. Whoever speaks of man as the image of God must immediately also speak of man's sin and frailty, and whoever speaks of death and of mortality has also and simultaneously to speak of the totally different life beyond death. Consequently man can only speak properly about God if he remains in constant dialectic motion. No matter where he begins, he is in a constant flux between the negative and positive position. The central point, from which affirmation and negation draw their significance and meaning, remains intangible and imperceptible. Positive and negative statements never form, as in thesis and antithesis, a synthesis which is a kind of higher unity. Only philosophers have the privilege 'to practise the art of synthesis'. The theologian is more like Moses, who gazed into the Promised Land, but never entered it. He is not allowed to utter a final word about God.

The purpose of the dialectic method is to express the inadequacy of all human statements concerning God, and to show that what theology says of God and what God himself says are incommensurate. By pointing to the ultimate irresponsibility of theology, it proves its responsibility. And while it is true that the dialectic method is 'far and away the best', it too cannot guarantee that the goal is reached. God himself only speaks when this way too comes to a stop.

Barth himself says that dialectics was meant only to be a 'corrective', only the 'touch of spice in the food'. But it certainly did not remain so. Barth turned dialectics into a method. The absence of a standpoint becomes his standpoint. Barth can pursue dialectics to the point of absurdity, until dialectics has cancelled itself out. But this by no means makes him free, receptive and flexible, rather it produces the very thing that Barth sought to avoid. The dialectic motion ceases and becomes static. By stretching all language concerning God upon the rack of the dialectic method, Barth actually attempts to 'draw a bird in flight'. He himself once compared the dialectic method to walking along a narrow rock ridge on which to stand still means to fall to either the right or the left. Barth himself did stand still, and did fall, to the left. His negation is stronger than his affirmation. This is what Urs von Balthasar called Barth's 'tragedy'. The final result is that Barth 'gesticulates in despair'.[30]

An early criticism of Barth by Paul Tillich points in the same direction.[31] Tillich makes the outright charge that Barth's dialectical theology is basically not dialectical at all. Everything is pushed into dialectic self-cancellation, to the point of cancellation of dialectics itself – but this infinite series of self-cancellations is not itself negated. It has become 'the position taken by the dialectic thinker, but is no longer itself dialectics'. As a result, crisis for Barth is not a state of continuous transition, but becomes fixed. This means that his theology once again takes on the interdicted 'mode of absoluteness'. Tillich sees the ultimate reason for this contradiction in a lack in Barth's theology: he misses the position which would provide the necessary basis for negation; Barth's theology does not encompass the affirmation which is the presupposition for negation. This is why Tillich postulates 'a return from the critical to the positive paradox'.

Of course the positive side is not wholly lacking in Barth. He too is concerned with man's salvation, and affirmation is clearly perceptible behind his negation; indeed affirmation is the hidden meaning contained in the negation. Judgement is a matter of grace. 'Judgement is not annihilation; by it all things are established.' 'If we believe . . . we perceive that men have been dissolved by God, and therefore exalted to be with Him.' 'Henceforward the negation in which we stand can be understood only in the light of the divine affirmation from which it proceeds. This means that the marks of human unrighteousness and ungodliness are crossed by the deeper marks of the divine forgiveness; that the discord of human defiance is penetrated by the undertones of the divine melody "Nevertheless".'[32] If God's grace in judgement, and his affirmation in negation, were not spoken of in this way, Barth's *Epistle to the Romans* would no longer be a commentary on the Epistle to the Romans! But the underlying tendency is stronger in the other direction: the emphasis is more upon judgement than upon grace; the dialectic motion does not swing evenly from negation to affirmation, but dwells longer upon negation. In Barth, as a result, crisis threatens to become an independent theme, and negation tends to dominate it. He confirms this himself when he describes the 'destined situation' of the Christian: 'We are more deeply committed to negation than to affirmation, to criticism and protest than to naïvety, to longing for the future than to participation in the present.'[33]

The consequence is that *faith* in Barth becomes almost entirely speechless, almost ceases to have any content, and invariably represents no kind of assertion on the part of man, but only his denial. Thus Barth's description of Christian faith is 'awe in the presence of the divine incognito . . . the love of God that is aware of the qualitative distinction between God and man', 'the affirmation of the divine "No" in Christ, of the shattering halt in the presence of God', 'of the restless persistence in negation'. Only 'those who stand in awe in the presence of God and keep themselves from revolt live with God'.[34]

Consequently faith signifies 'the end of all idealist assaults upon heaven', 'the end of all perceptibility and comprehensibility'. Faith is 'not a ground to stand upon, not a system to follow, not an air to breathe'. Rather it is, when it is true faith, nothing but a 'void' and 'vacuum', sorrow, waiting and deprivation, openness, a sign and a sign-post – 'a standing-place in the air'. This 'paradoxical character' of faith must in no way be disputed. In so far as faith attempts in any sense to be more than a vacuum, it is unbelief. *Credo quia absurdum* rings out from Barth almost like a note of triumph.

Everything Barth says about faith is barbed for a purpose. It is aimed against any attempt to proceed from the religious experience of man and to answer in this way the question of the certainty of Christian

faith. This was the way taken by Christian theology since Schleiermacher; it took its starting-point in man's religious awareness and sought
to describe it, arriving by this method at the contents of Christian faith.
Barth's objection is that in so doing theology turns faith into a human
attitude, and makes the problem of certainty the central issue of theological discussion. This was 'betrayal of Christ'! Faith has no historical
or psychological dimension in the life of man: 'There is ... no occasion
here for romantic experience, no opportunity for enthusiastic rhapsody,
no case for psychological analysis.' The believer's place is on the threshold, hoping and waiting. He cannot be sure that he believes; even that
he believes is only a matter of faith. The 'man of God' Luther died 'un-
edifyingly' with the word on his lips, that we are beggars and that this
is the truth. But woe to the man who turns his negations, his waiting,
sorrow and deprivation into an attitude, into a standpoint. This would
mean a new triumph of Phariseeism, more terrible than any which
preceded it.

In short, faith has neither form nor beauty. Rather than humanity it
reveals the limits of humanity. The borderline between faith and unbelief cannot be defined in human and sensible or historical and
psychological terms: 'The hands of all of us are and remain perceptually
empty.'

What is true of man's faith is also true of his acts. For Barth the sole
meaning of all *ethics*, as of all dogmatic theology, lies in 'a fundamental
assault upon man'.[35] Human actions are only 'good' in so far as they
bear witness to the 'overcoming of man', of his independence and his
own powers, his selfishness and his individual rights, and are therefore
demonstrations in honour of God, parables, signs and pointers to his
rule, to his coming, to his choosing and rejection – 'What is more than
this is of the evil one – even if it be the holiness and purity of a martyred
virgin.'

It is on this principle that the relationship of Christianity to civilisation is defined. Here Barth finds himself totally opposed to the 'cultural
Protestantism' characteristic of Protestant bourgeois culture at the turn
of the twentieth century. This type of Protestantism equated Christianity
with cultural progress, or even merged the two, whereas Barth saw the
attitude of Christianity to civilisation as 'a certain coldness'. Christianity's contribution to human civilisation and ethics does not consist in
confirming and strengthening them, but in protesting and questioning
them. Christianity moves the world, with its civilisation and lack of it,
into the light of the 'last things'; its purpose is not the transfiguration of

the present world; it brings the message of the world to come. Consequently it sees 'a great hand shaking' every achievement completed or
pursued; 'its comments always tend to slow down' the busy activity of
human construction; it recognises in all achievements 'a parable of
death'; and wherever mankind is building towers, it 'watches with some
discomfort'.

In the light of the ultimate, everything penultimate is brought into
question and submerged in the 'sphere of relativity': 'Perhaps – perhaps
not.' The Christian's awareness of the divine crisis in all history gives
him the freedom to decide sometimes in one way and sometimes in
another, and to apportion his affirmation and negation in different ways.
Because Christianity harbours a fundamental mistrust of all 'human
triumphs' it has a certain prejudice in favour of the oppressed and the
disadvantaged, and hence feels closer to the Russian than to his Western
European brothers. But when the levelling process set in, and critical
scrutiny of civilisation became the fashion, Christianity asked the opposite question: 'Whether the solidly Western agricultural labourer – the
Bavarian peasant, for example – is not nearer to the Kingdom of God
than the Russian man.' The Church keeps militarism at a distance 'with
a strong hand', but also rebuffs pacifism 'with a friendly gesture'.

The best example of Barth's cool aloofness towards any too positive
and unambiguous Christian activities is found in his exposition of
Romans 13, the famous chapter in which the apostle Paul exhorts the
Church at Rome to be obedient to the authorities.[36] For centuries this
has been the classic basis for a positive Christian doctrine of the state.
The Lutheran Churches in particular – but by no means they exclusively
– derived from this text the prohibition of any revolution and based
their political conservatism on it. At first sight Barth's arguments also
seem surprisingly conservative. Their tendency can be summed up in the
key word 'no-revolution'. But the heading which Barth gives to this
section should alert us. It says 'The Great Negative Possibility', and so
shows the completely different purpose which guides Barth in his
exhortation to 'no-revolution'. Whereas for example the conservative
Lutherans based the prohibition against revolution and the command
of strict obedience towards the authorities *positively* upon the God-
willed maintenance of the order founded by him, Barth justifies his
exhortation to 'no-revolution' *negatively* by God's abrogation of all
existing systems of order which is in constant progress. His 'precedent
judgement' is 'that the real revolution comes from God and not from
human revolt'. God is 'the great minus sign outside the bracket', which

cancels all operations within the bracket; to recognise this, and therefore to renounce the nebulous dreams of romanticism and to reject the semi-divine claim of the revolutionary, is, according to Barth, the teaching of Romans 13.

For that reason, Barth's concept of obedience to authority has a totally different emphasis than that of current Christian conservatism. He describes it exclusively in negative terms: as 'subjection', 'withdrawal', 'giving way', 'not-doing', as 'non-revolt', and 'no-revolution'. But in this way the Christian rids himself of all false 'credulity', of all 'army chaplain pep talk and solemn humbug', and recognises all politics as 'essentially a game'. He becomes a 'good citizen', 'remarkably well-behaved', who can now give consideration in practical terms to right and wrong within the world, because for him they are no longer a matter of ultimate assertions and accusations. But even this Christian practicality falls under the shadow of evil, and the proper advice can only be not to penetrate too deeply into this kingdom of shadows.

The kingdom of God reveals that all human activity is essentially a game, relative and irresponsible; it challenges man in all his institutions. Hence, for Barth the meaning of Christian ethics consists in the radical assault of God upon man: 'We cannot repair our damage. The disturbance affects the saints and the swine.'

The critique of religion

What Barth has to say about Christian faith and Christian action is a judgement of everything which has claimed throughout history to be religion and morality. It is simply a sentence of death. If it is possible to say that Barth's restless eloquence anywhere reaches a climax, it is at this point. Here the comparisons are at their most pointed, and examples and images occur in profusion. Here his tone becomes ironical and sarcastic, and he can become bitter and cutting.

Religion constitutes the most direct contradiction to faith.[37] It signifies the 'transgression of the fatal line laid down for us', the 'drunken blurring of the distance which separates us from God', 'our devotion to some romantic infinity', 'our investing of men with the form of God, and of God with the form of man', 'the divinisation of man and the humanising of God'. Religion is the 'shameless anticipation' of what can only proceed from the unknown God; it is the 'slave-revolt of man', who seeks to be like God and consequently confuses time with eternity and eternity with time. A religious man is 'that most obstinate species of the human genus', a 'sinner in the most obvious sense of the word'. But as the peak of attainment possible to man, religion is the high point of man's impossibility as against God. Everything that is called religion – 'from the grossest superstition to the most delicate spirituality, from naked rationalism to the most subtle mysticism of the metaphysician' – remains 'on this side of the abyss', distinguished only by a difference of degree from hunger, the need for sleep and sexuality. Some passages give the impression of being the work of a convinced psychoanalyst or an unteachable materialist.

The symbol of religion is Prometheus, who drew down the fire of Zeus upon himself; and it was the fire of Zeus and not the consuming fire of God. Consequently, it is not fire at all, but only 'a furnace from which a very peculiar kind of smoke pours off'. Barth sees all world views, religions and systems as rising up from this furnace, and their clouds of vapour and steam spreading out over the plain of humanity. He sees this mist and vapour as hanging over everything which proclaims itself as religion or world view, whether Christianity or atheism – 'All human activity, from the devotional exercises of a Benedictine monastery to the vigorous and comprehensive programme of the Social Democrats, is enacted on the rungs of one single ladder.'

How the tenor has changed from that of Schleiermacher and the Protestant theology of the nineteenth and even the twentieth centuries. Schleiermacher called religion 'a solemn music' accompanying all human action. In the name of religion Barth protests against such cheapening of religion.[38] He calls on the Psalmists, Moses, Job, Paul, Luther, Calvin and Kierkegaard. All these men 'had' religion, but a religion completely different from that described by Schleiermacher; it was not music and harmony, not the summit and fulfilment of true humanity, but its disturbance, cleavage and disruption.

Barth now draws a picture of religion which is virtually the opposite of what has just been described: religion is a 'heavy yoke' laid upon a man, that cannot be cast aside. It comes on man as a fatal necessity, as a 'misfortune'; under the weight of this misfortune John the Baptist went into the desert and Calvin's face took on the expression it had towards the end. Religion, therefore, should not be wished on anyone.

Thus religion stands in the 'twilight'; on the one hand it is the revolt of man who seeks to be like God; on the other hand it is the subjective side of the relationship to God, which exists of necessity (the 'unavoidable reflection in the soul . . . of the miracle of faith'). But even this subjective side of the relationship to God is as such necessarily subject to the law of death. There is no escaping this twilight.

Barth's critique of religion is aimed at every kind of religion, every step on the ladder. But its principal attack is directed against the highest step, that is, not against atheism, but against Christianity and against the Church.[39] Barth's fundamental comment upon religion, that it represents the culmination of human sin, is if anything intensified, multiplied when it comes to the Church: 'The abyss which is here disclosed is like to none other. Here breaks out the veritable God-sickness.' Even the Church sickens because God is God. The inescapable danger which threatens it is that of direct experience: the Church would like the revelation of God to be 'immediate and direct' and to possess it as such. As a consequence the Church becomes a place 'situated on this side of the abyss which separates men from God, where the eternity of revelation is transformed into a temporal, concrete, directly visible thing in this world; the lightning from heaven becomes a slow-burning, earth-made oven, loss and discovery harden into a solid enjoyment of possession . . . the "Beyond" is transfigured into "something", which . . . is no more than an extension of this world'. Barth contemptuously terms the Church 'organised religion' – an organisation to 'protect the proper interests of humanity against God' – the 'paraphernalia with which we erect, sustain and order the relation between men and God'.

It is small wonder therefore that Barth's *Epistle to the Romans* is in part a catalogue of ecclesiastical vices. The Church does not seek 'to be a stranger in the world' but wants to 'show off'; it does not like 'to wait' but 'is in great haste', it 'is hungry and thirsty for the concrete joys of the marriage-feast'. It is afraid 'of loneliness and the desert', and constantly unearths new 'hiding places' in which it can remain 'neutral'; 'it carefully pulls every live ammunition out of the barrel'. Since the beginning of time it has done more to 'put to sleep rather than to awaken inquiry concerning God'. Thus 'atheism' is revealed as the essential nature of the Church. This applies not to one Church or another, but to each and every one.

Yet the Church must exist, because the gospel exists, and because the gospel must be preached to man.[40] This is the dilemma: 'Here is the saving message of Christ, which is one thing, and there is the human work of the Church, which is something else.' This means that the Church, like religion, is an 'ambiguous fact': as a religious and ecclesiastical enterprise the Church is impossible, and as a religious and ecclesiastical possibility it is inevitable. The Church, 'from which we can never escape, is the canalization in history of that divine transaction in men which can never become a matter of history'. Consequently the Christian will not leave the Church, but 'fully aware of the eternal opposition between the gospel and the Church' he will remain in the Church 'miserable, hesitating, questioning, terrified' yet nevertheless not as a spectator alongside the Church, but as one who 'knows and suffers' in the Church.

Thus the Church is engulfed in 'an inevitable catastrophe', and the pastor is defending a 'lost position' – but 'all posts which men occupy as men are lost posts'. Summing up, one might say that the pastor's greatest fear must be that of 'stability', and his greatest care, that his post should remain lost. The image of the Church is that of the taber-nacle, the wandering tent in the desert, and it must not be turned into that of a temple or pagoda. 'A Church which is truly in earnest is itself bound to detonate the dynamite which blows up the pagoda.'

The Church is like the Grand Inquisitor in Dostoievsky. But the Grand Inquisitor is kissed by Christ upon his old and bloodless lips. Dostoievsky writes: 'This was His complete and only answer.' And Barth adds, 'It is just this complete and only answer which is the hope of the Church.'

The overturning of Schleiermacher

From the first page to the last Karl Barth's *Epistle to the Romans* is a sustained great protest against the theological era characterised above all by the names of Schleiermacher, Ritschl, Harnack and Troeltsch. Schleiermacher rightly heads this list, and not merely for chronological reasons. When his colleague August Neander announced his death to his students during his lecture course, he did so with the words: 'One day a new period in Church history will begin with him.' This prophecy was fulfilled. Though Schleiermacher did not found a theological school of his own, the words he himself once used in his academic address *Über den Begriff des grossen Mannes* (On the Concept of a Great Man) are applicable to him: 'He does not found a school, but an era.' In the field of theology, the nineteenth century became the era of Schleiermacher. He has rightly been called the 'Church Father of the nineteenth century'.

In order properly to assess Schleiermacher's theological achievement it must be seen against the background of the modern era, with its changed view of the world; once the discoveries of Copernicus had removed the earth from the centre of the universe, man was put in its place. Enlightenment and classicism, romanticism and idealism all accepted this view of the world as authoritative and Schleiermacher, in elaborating his theological system, followed suit. As a result, whether necessarily or not, the form it took was anthropocentric. The centre of Schleiermacher's thought was the religious self-consciousness of man. It formed the point of departure and the central object of his theology: the purpose of theology as he saw it was to describe systematically what the religious self-consciousness of a Christian 'expresses'. Consequently, the word of God and the gospel of Jesus Christ were replaced by religion or human piety. Of course Schleiermacher was also concerned with God and his relationship to man. But in describing this relationship, his point of departure was with his faith and religious experience; his way led from below to above. Man was the subject in his theology and God the predicate.

In a brilliantly written chapter on Schleiermacher in his *Protestantische Theologie im 19. Jahrhundert* (Protestant Theology in the Nineteenth Century) Barth agreed with the opinion of Heinrich Scholz that the essence of Schleiermacher's achievement could only be threatened by 'a corresponding counter-achievement, not [by] a cavilling criticism of detail'.[41] When Barth quoted this statement, he had already accomplished this 'counter-achievement'. The significance of Schleiermacher's lectures *Über die Religion* (On Religion) at the end of the eighteenth and the beginning of the nineteenth century was paralleled after the First World War at the beginning of the twentieth century by Barth's commentary on the Epistle to the Romans, and just as Schleiermacher's *Lectures on Religion* were followed by his *Glaubenslehre* (The Doctrine of Faith), so Barth's *Epistle to the Romans* was followed by the *Church Dogmatics*.

Barth literally stood the theology of the nineteenth century on its head, turning it upside-down. His way did not lead from below to above, but from above to below. God is simultaneously the subject and the predicate of his theology. Thus Barth carried out a vast rearrangement of the entire theological furnishings, provided one may call rearrangement a process which turns the whole house upside-down. But in spite of this radical reversal, we may still ask whether in his *Epistle to the Romans* Barth really found a completely new and original starting-point. In his previously mentioned account of Schleiermacher Barth himself wrote that today no one can say 'whether we have really overcome his influence, or whether we are still at heart children of his age, for all the protest against him, which now, admittedly, has increased in volume and is carried out according to basic principles'.[42] This sentence sounds almost like a personal confession: in spite of his vociferous and fundamental protest against Schleiermacher in his *Epistle to the Romans*, Barth shows that he is still fundamentally a child of that century; he continues to be dominated by nineteenth-century theological questioning. His answers go in the opposite sense, precisely the contrary of what Schleiermacher said, but he still allows the question to be dictated by his opponents. Because he reacts only to their questioning, he remains ensnared by it. And what happens to him as a result is precisely what roused his fundamental criticism of Schleiermacher: his assertion that it is in no sense man, but God alone, who is the subject of theology, is proclaimed with such intensity that attention is once again turned towards man. In the *Epistle to the Romans* also there is not merely a movement of God from above to below, but a great deal of motion on the part of man below.

The Catholic Hans Urs von Balthasar, who has pondered and understood Barth's theology more thoroughly and profoundly than many so-called 'Barthians', draws an interesting parallel from the history of philosophy: Schleiermacher was for Barth what Plato was for the thinkers of the Renaissance, Spinoza for Herder and Goethe, and Schopenhauer for Nietzsche: 'The die which impresses an ineradicable mark, the pattern from which one cannot break free in spite of all disagreement in substance.'[43]

Barth's *Epistle to the Romans* is the most important theological work yet written in the twentieth century. But like Schleiermacher's *Lectures on Religion* it is not merely an important theological work, but also a powerful source of religious ideas. Sometimes its effect is that of mighty prophecy, written with unparalleled energy, almost as though in ecstasy. Barth of course sternly rejects all 'virtuosity' in religion. But his own work contradicts him. Whether or not it may be ignored or even forbidden in his theology, Barth himself is a 'religious virtuoso', a creative religious genius. He plays the same instrument as Schleiermacher, but unlike him prefers the low notes, minor chords and sometimes even dissonances.

Two ways of speaking about God

Such a radical and almost violent prophetic protest against the dominant theology of the time could not long go without a counter-attack. This was led by Adolf von Harnack. In his person and his work he embodied everything which Barth was attacking. Barth had attended Harnack's lectures and seminars in Berlin. Now, in 1920, they met at a student conference in Aarau in Switzerland, Barth being thirty-four, and Harnack more than twice as old. It was an historic encounter. It was a meeting not merely of two men, but of two schools of thought, of two theological eras, of two different ways of speaking of God. It seemed that there was not a single phrase or a single thought which they might think or speak in common. Thus they parted without reaching an understanding.[44] This experience of total failure of communication was inevitably shattering in its effect upon such a person as Harnack. He could not forget it; the more he recalled Barth's lecture, 'the more it became disturbing, and in many respects offensive'. Three years later he addressed fifteen questions to 'those theologians who despise scientific theology'. Barth replied, and a public correspondence developed.[45]

Harnack was horrified by the new theology which was now gaining ground. The first thing he saw lacking in it was precisely what Barth had found in his work as a preacher to be the decisive weakness of liberal theology: awe in the presence of history, and therefore the scientific character of theology as a whole, derived from, and reflected in, the place it is accorded in the whole spectrum of academic study. 'Historical knowledge and critical reflection' is consequently the supreme requirement, which Harnack constantly stresses in his letters. Anyone who tries to understand biblical revelation without it 'replaces the true Christ by a figment of the imagination' and 'changes the chair of theology into a pulpit'. On the basis of his knowledge of Church history Harnack can only prophesy to Barth that the effect of such an enterprise will be 'not constructive but destructive'.

Barth firmly opposes these propositions in his tenet: 'The mission of theology is the same as the mission of preaching.' Only when theologians once again courageously devote themselves to their own cause, and base their theology once more on the scandalous testimony of the self-revelation of God, the representatives of other sciences, the lawyers, doctors and philosophers, will once again take notice of the theologians, instead of the theologians' taking notice of them as at present.

Harnack is incapable of separating the Christian revelation as radically from the whole history of civilisation and thought as Barth does in his theology of crisis. He regards as a single great unity what Barth strictly separates. He feels like Goethe that it would not have been worthwhile to have lived to seventy if all the wisdom of the world were only foolishness in the sight of God: 'How can one set up barriers between the experience of God and the good, the true and the beautiful, instead of linking them with the experience of God through historical know-ledge and critical reflection?' Anyone who, like Barth, breaks the link between God and civilisation will in Harnack's view be unable to offer permanent resistance to 'barbarity' and 'atheism'.

Once again Barth firmly rejects this view. 'No, God is simply not all this, as surely as the creator is not the creature, let alone the creature of the creature.' Statements concerning God which derive from the de-velopment of civilisation and its knowledge and morality do not in fact provide a defence against atheism, but demand it, because they them-selves originate in polytheism. As far as the fear of barbarism is con-cerned, it must be 'rejected as inessential and irrelevant, because the gospel has no more and no less to do with barbarism than with civilisa-tion'.

Harnack sees in Barth's dialectic method a 'most disturbing interpre-tation' of Christian faith and experience. It strikes down 'with a club' everything which presents itself as Christian experience. Instead of giving men love, joy and peace, the dialectic method leaves them torn in two, and 'prolongs their terrors'. Barth on the other hand seeks to preserve Christian faith from all contamination by human experience and 'sentimentality'. He persists in his dialectic method. It remains his firm principle that the direct opposition between God and the world is the only way in which man can arrive at unity with God.

The correspondence between Harnack and Barth was as fruitless as their debate in Aarau three years previously. It demonstrated once again how deep was the gulf which separated the two sides. Harnack added a postscript to it. In this he asked that the dialectic theologian might concede the validity of other theologians, and of their way of speaking about God, or that at least he might have some thought for his own children and friends who were incapable of walking, like him, on a 'tightrope'. He concluded with this question: 'Would he not do better, instead of proclaiming a strict Either-Or, to recognise that he plays *his* instrument, but that God has other instruments?'

Between two eras

Meanwhile, a vast theological symphony, in which everyone seemed to be playing one and the same instrument, was already under way. Like an alarm signal, Barth's *Epistle to the Romans* had summoned up friends and helpers who held similar views. Among these were Friedrich Gogarten, Emil Brunner, Rudolf Bultmann, Eduard Thurneysen, Heinrich Barth and Georg Merz. To use Thurneysen's words, they were like people who ran out on to the street shouting, because they had suddenly noticed that the house in which they were sitting at table was on fire.[46] Not that they were all simply disciples or imitators of Barth – though there were of course also such 'orthodox Barthians'; Barth himself always considered them as a 'punishment'[47] – but they had each arrived in their own ways at the same point as Barth, and yet each remained wholly independent. There was nevertheless extensive agreement and similarity between them. What united them was their position 'between two eras'.

'At last the way was open for inquiry concerning God. The gap between the eras has grown wider, and time now stands still. Will it be for a moment? For an eternity? Must we not now be able to hear the word of God? Must we not now be able to see his hand in his work? That is why we cannot and may not yet pass from one era to another. The decision must first be made here. Up to that moment we stand between two eras.'

These words come from an essay which Friedrich Gogarten published in 1920 in the *Christliche Welt* with the title *Zwischen den Zeiten* (Between Two Eras).[48] But it was more than an article, it was a manifesto, a call to battle, partly a diagnosis of the times and partly a sermon of condemnation. With prophetic passion Gogarten conducted a merciless and sometimes sarcastic reckoning with the past, with the bourgeois and liberal world of the nineteenth century, not only with its theology, but with its whole science and culture. The latter had been determined by man in every degree, 'right down to the most subtle ideas of God', and was a 'glittering confusion of divine and human' in all its thought, words and works. People had long suspected this and had come to 'mistrust it in their bones'. Now, when this world had received its 'death blow', and its 'disintegration', reaching into every hidden corner, was becoming visible, it was obvious that it had been essentially 'a work of man'. And as a result 'we can only be glad to see its decline . . . that is why we rejoice at Spengler's book'. Not that this means that God has come back. Nor is it either right or possible to rethink what God is. All that seems possible at the moment is what might be called a negative knowledge of God: what God is not and what he cannot be, with the recognition that no thought, not a single one, can reach out beyond the human sphere. Nothing would be more mistaken than to start now with a practical proposition or programme and to seek to do something. 'The great deliberation must come first, and must now begin. This is not a time for planning, but is the hour of repentance.' 'At this moment we stand not before our own wisdom, but before God. This hour is not our own hour. *We* now belong to no era. We stand between two eras.'

Gogarten's article is an impressive reflection of the dominant mood in the circle of 'dialectic theologians' at the time. It is no accident that its title *Zwischen den Zeiten* was adopted two years later, at Thurneysen's suggestion, as the name of the newly founded journal published by Barth, Gogarten and Thurneysen, with Georg Merz as editor. Within a single year, 1921–22, there appeared a second edition of Barth's *Epistle to the Romans*, Gogarten's *Die religiöse Entscheidung* (The Choice in Religion), Brunner's *Erlebnis, Erkenntnis und Glaube* (Experience, Knowledge and Faith) and Thurneysen's *Dostoevsky*. Though entirely fortuitous, it had the effect of a concerted theological assault. Other lectures, articles and books had already appeared or were to follow. Even their titles suggested a concerted programme; they all dealt with the same theme, and pointed in the same direction: *Religion und Kultur* (Religion and Civilisation, Bultmann, 1920); *Die Krisis unserer Kultur* (The Crisis of our Civilisation, Gogarten, 1920); *Die Grenzen der Humanität* (The Frontiers of Humaneness, Brunner, 1922); *Wider die romantische Theologie* (Against Romantic Theology, Gogarten, 1922); *Schrift und Offenbarung* (Scripture and Revelation, Thurneysen, 1924); *Die Mystik und das Wort* (Mysticism and the Word, Brunner, 1924); *Welchen Sinn has es, von Gott zu reden?* (What sense is there to speak of God?, Bultmann, 1925); *Die Offenbarung als Grund und Gegenstand der Theologie* (Revelation as the Basis and Object of Theology, Brunner, 1925). Not only are the titles and themes of these publications similar, but the views expressed in them – in spite of the independence possessed and maintained by their authors throughout – show such agreement that many passages in them are almost interchangeable. This can be seen from the following examples:

GOD AND REVELATION

'What we were concerned with was strictly that which alone can be the theme of an honest theology, that is, to give back to the word of God the place due to it, and to let it occupy this place in the carrying out of the work of theology.' (Gogarten)

'The knowledge of which all Christian theology consists is dependent upon the energy and clarity with which the idea of the deity of God or of the divine revelation is conceived or maintained. . . . Consequently revelation is not merely the content but also the basis of theology.' (Brunner)

'The object of theology is God, and the objection to liberal theology is that it does not deal with God but with man.' (Bultmann)

'We stand before the holy scripture and the claim it makes. Its sole and unique content is that God is truly God. . . . This God is wholly and completely outside our grasp. He is present where he reveals himself, he who is totally superior to us, whom we cannot grasp and comprehend, and who by the very act of revealing himself withdraws from us completely.' (Thurneysen)[49]

SEPARATION AND CRISIS

'At this point, where the divisions appear with terrible clarity, where the link between humanity and divinity is obliterated and a token of separation replaces it . . . here and here alone God is known.' (Brunner)

'Where the reality of God is recognised, there is no more room in the world for man, and the independent existence of man is done away with.' (Gogarten)

'God signifies the total abolition of man, his denial, the calling into question of man, a judgement upon man.' (Bultmann)[50]

RELIGION

'Of all man's presumptions, that which is commonly known as religion is the most monstrous. For it is the presumption of seeking to bridge over from opposite to opposite, from creator to creature, and to do so by starting from the creature.' (Gogarten)

'Like everything which man undertakes and which takes place within him, religion falls under the judgement of the absolute . . . religion in itself is the most untenable of all the manifestations of man's humanity.' (Brunner)

'The watchword "Yahweh *or* Baal!" has been uttered, and anyone who has heard it can no longer change this "or" into an "and". He may perhaps know these gods, but to him they are non-God, they are demons.' (Thurneysen)[51]

CIVILISATION

'Religion does not merely criticise one form of civilisation or another, but casts doubt upon civilisation itself and upon humanity, because it casts doubt upon man.' (Brunner)

'The judgement which religion pronounces on civilisation is not directed towards individual errors here and there . . . but towards civilisation as such.' (Gogarten)

'There is no action which can have a direct bearing upon God and his kingdom. Every form of human society, the worst and the most ideal, falls equally under his divine judgement.' (Bultmann)[52]

One can see that everything these theologians write echoes the shattering experience of the war and the post-war period. But they see the world war as merely a forerunner of the true convulsion. It did more than destroy the outward order. Everything that had been regarded as good, true and beautiful, as reasonable, civilised and liberal, as noble and humane, and which for more than a century had composed a whole world, had been destroyed. In its destruction, this world was revealed for what it was, the very delicate and skilful artifact of man. It is true that it was not a world without God, but its God had been a 'human God'.

In this situation the dialectic theologians suddenly found themselves overwhelmed by 'the insatiable need for the absolute'.[53] What is left, what endures, if the foundation of reality is collapsing everywhere? Man does not seek an answer to this question from the world, but from himself, as he stands before God. All these theologians look towards the crisis, the uttermost limits of human existential life, the judgement of God. That is why they utter constant warnings against suggestions for improvements or Church reform. The concern at present is not to provide instant satisfaction of the insatiable need for the absolute, but for man to wait upon God with empty hands, in total nakedness and total poverty. It is true that they all speak, in the language of Kierkegaard, a great deal of the 'Either-Or' and of the 'decision', but for them the decision consists in refraining from deciding, in enduring the situation and therefore remaining 'between the eras'.

The most radical of them all, the clarion caller among them, was undoubtedly Friedrich Gogarten. When Barth read his essay *Zwischen den Zeiten*, he immediately sent him his congratulations. Some time later Gogarten visited Barth in Switzerland. After his visit Barth wrote of him to Thurneysen: 'He is a Dreadnought on our side and against our opponents. He has quite the manners and also the equipment to be the very man who will be somebody,' and he wrote to Georg Merz: 'Gogarten, oh ho! A cruiser first class, sound currency, and unquestionably the man who will call you in Germany to battle.'[54]

Gogarten had been a pupil of Ernst Troeltsch in Heidelberg. But his background included more than the liberal school of theology. He had done work on Fichte as a religious thinker, and had written a book with the title *Religion weither* (Religion Abroad). When Tillich entreated him and Barth not to sever the link between theology and every other aspect of culture, he was able to answer that Tillich's words rang in his ears like a 'call to come home', because his 'home' had been in secular culture, but that he had consciously left this home and gone 'abroad', when 'after a long delay he entered a theological lecture hall for the first time'.[55]

Gogarten had already provided evidence of his renunciation of 'home' three years previously, when in 1920 he had given a lecture to the Friends of the *Christliche Welt* entitled 'The Crisis of our Civilisation'.[56] In this lecture Gogarten reduced everything to the 'Either-Or': 'Either we have a religion with the purpose of being the soul of this civilisation . . . or we have a religion which represents a perpetual crisis in this and every civilisation.' The first and last message which religion has to proclaim is that the kingdom of God is imminent, and this 'absolute other-worldliness' produces an absolute and permanent crisis of civilisation. What is manifested at the present time as a crisis of civilisation is only a minor anticipation and parable of this total crisis. Consequently nothing is gained by critical observations and proposals about individual details. There is only one way, and that is 'to return to the original creation, to the origin', 'to be born again by the spirit of God'. He quotes Luther: 'When God wants to bring us alive, he kills us', and the whole lecture closes with a call to repentance: 'The only way is for us to remain precisely where we have ultimately found ourselves: within the annihilating and creating act of God. We must remain at the point where Jesus Christ proclaims, today, as two thousand years previously: "Repent, for the Kingdom of Heaven is at hand."'

The lecture produced a great effect. Among those who heard it were Wilhelm Schäfer and the neo-Kantian Paul Natorp of Marburg University. Schäfer was reminded of Luther; in an article in the *Frankfurter Zeitung* he wrote of Gogarten: 'Divine power burned within him, as it did in Jesus when he overturned the tables of the money-changers in the temple.'[57] The reaction of Ernst Troeltsch was somewhat different. He discussed Gogarten's lecture in the Wartburg in the *Christliche Welt,* under the title *Ein Apfel von Baume Kierkegaards* (An Apple from Kierkegaard's Tree).[58] Troeltsch was the indefatigable champion, in the face of all historical scepticism, of a 'European cultural synthesis', and he felt that Gogarten, with his harsh dualism, took the easy way out by supposing that he could destroy with a single blow the 'mediation' with which others – and Troeltsch first and foremost – were concerned: 'Thus he cuts the knot just like Kierkegaard, the knot which thousands of years have tied for good reasons, which has become exceptionally tangled in the modern world, and which in truth too many people with bold but facile fingers are still complicating, without thought for the danger and difficulty of the task.'

Indubitably the radical repudiation of all the traditions of the bourgeois world by the dialectic theologians reflects the attitude to life of the 'lost generation' after the First World War. Klaus Scholder[59] stressed a particular aspect of this parallel. He raised the question whether the proclamations of judgement by the dialectic theologians, and by Gogarten in particular, might not be the theological equivalent of the ideas of the so-called 'conservative revolutionaries': in both cases there was the same passionate sentence of death upon the bourgeois world, the same rejection of all proposals and plans for partial improvement, and the same demand for heroic endurance. Scholder asks whether the struggle of the dialectic theologians against linking the word of God with any ideology did not leave the back door open to a new ideology, an ideology of crisis. The previous positive ideological ties, such as the ideas of a 'Christian civilisation', the 'Christian state', 'Christian society', etc., are merely exchanged for the corresponding negative ideological ties; radical acceptance of history is replaced by absolute refusal of history. These parallels between the theological development and the political situation cannot be dismissed. Gogarten himself accepted them to a certain degree when in 1937, in the introduction to his polemical work against Karl Barth's *Gericht oder Skepsis* (Judgement or Scepticism), he looked back upon his own theological past and wrote: 'This radical thought brought us dangerously close to the general crisis which shook human life to its foundation throughout the war and the postwar period, and to the feeling that there was no exit, and that the end had been reached, a feeling shared by many people at that time. There is no doubt that this general crisis was not without its influence upon the radicalism of our thought.'[60]

But in addition to the historical parallels, the critique must be extended to a fundamental theological issue. Dialectic theology is inspired by a passionate statement of the distinction between God and the world. It cannot sufficiently emphasize that there is no bridge, no continuity, no development leading from the world to God. By its very nature it

excludes any kind of *analogia entis*, that is, any and every attempt to
proceed from the being of the world to the being of God. But this
strict rejection of any positive *analogia entis* itself gives rise to the suspicion that dialectic theology in its turn is carrying out a negative
analogia entis. By stressing so forcibly God's negation in the midst of the
general misery of the time, and virtually snatching his judgement from
him, it runs the risk of surreptitiously making the historical situation,
and therefore something within time and within the world, a negative
point of contact for God's act of revelation.

But in spite of every legitimate criticism that can be made, dialectic
theology in its essentials is undeniably in the right. It brought about the
great change within Protestant theology which had become necessary
in the present century, the rediscovery of the deity of God. No one who
even superficially studies its testimony in its works will fail to see that
this is a genuinely new beginning; and whether he likes it or not, the
reader comes under its influence. The expression 'the golden twenties'
may have become a commonplace, but it applies to Protestant theology.
The years following the First World War were indeed its 'golden
years'.

The rediscovery of the deity of God

Naturally this great theological revolution did not take place all at
once; the new theology did not drop from the sky, was not propagated
by parthenogenesis. In fact it was prepared for and accompanied by a
whole series of new theological insights and discoveries. All these new
insights and discoveries went beyond liberal theology, by overcoming
it with the methods of critical research in the fields of history, philosophy, psychology and comparative religion, methods it had taught and
used itself.

First came the rediscovery of the holy by Rudolf Otto. His book
Das Heilige (*The Idea of the Holy*) appeared in 1917; twenty-five editions
were printed up to 1936, the thirtieth edition appearing in 1958. Thus
it is probably the most widely read theological work in German of the
twentieth century. Its significance lies in the fact that Rudolf Otto
defined the holy as an independent category, in contrast to the usual
identification of it with absolute moral good, and placed it beyond the
realm of the ethical and the rational. To describe the holy 'without its
ethical and without its rational element' he makes use of the term 'the
numinous'. The numinous has a two-fold character. In the first place

it is the *mysterium tremendum*. This includes everything which induces awe and terror in man: the strangeness and fearfulness, the majesty, the wrath and the energy of God, in short, the 'wholly other' which is not comparable with any human, earthly being. But at the same time the numinous is 'something uniquely attractive, and fascinating', something which 'confers blessing'. This aspect Otto calls the *fascinans*. Both aspects, the *tremendum* and the *fascinosum*, are inextricably linked; together they represent the content of the holy. The holy constantly produces a double reaction in man: he feels himself at one and the same time mysteriously repelled and attracted.

The numinous is present in all religions, from the cult of primitive people up to Christianity, as 'their real innermost essence', without which they would not be religions at all. It is this which produces the essential element of all piety, the 'creature-feeling'. This is the reaction which the numinous object provokes in the experience of the subject, the experience of sinking down and vanishing in one's own nothingness in the face of what is wholly superior to every creature.

The discovery of the numinous as an independent category did not merely lead to a new view of comparative religion, but also to what was in part a new view of the Bible and Christianity. At once new aspects of the biblical religion which had long gone unnoticed, or had been consciously overlooked, were brought back to life. In the Old Testament the demonic element was rediscovered, the wrath, the zeal and the anger of Yahweh, the fact that he is a living God and a consuming fire. In the New Testament the gospel ceased to be the all too plausible proclamation of a comfortable belief in the fatherhood of God; its content, the kingdom of God, was seen instead to be the 'most numinous object imaginable', 'greatness and marvel absolute' which, 'dark and menacing, approaches from the depths of "heaven".'[61] Otto also rediscovered the irrational elements in Luther, and the 'almost uncanny background' of his piety. In Luther he comes face to face with precisely what he recognises as the dual nature of the numinous: the *tremendum* in the terror of Luther before the anger of God, in his awe, his trembling, trepidation, fear and anxiety, and the *fascinosum* in his trust in the grace of God, in his boasting, dancing, leaping, strutting and merriment. These are not survivals from the Middle Ages, as had been supposed, but 'elementary and primitive feelings coming to the surface again'. Luther's theological successors, of course, did not preserve this religious legacy of the reformer. They forced his elementary religious experience into a theological system, and made his thoroughly

irrational faith into something rational, well-tempered and ordered.
'The Church became a school, and her communications, in truth, found
a more and more contracted access to the mind ... "through the narrow
clefts of the understanding".'[62]

Otto's interpretation of the nature of religion differs from the view
of Schleiermacher, and is in total opposition to that of Albrecht Ritschl.
Against the religious and ethical optimism of both he emphasises the
dark side of religion, lying beyond ethics. He rediscovered the anger of
God, which both had forgotten, and which from the first had nothing
to do with moral attributes, but acted 'like a hidden force of nature',
like 'stored-up electricity, discharging itself upon anyone who comes
too near'.[63] Consequently, for him 'sin' is in the first instance not a
moral, nor even a dogmatic concept, but a religious concept. It is the
feeling of total personal worthlessness which the profane person
experiences in the presence of the holy. The basis of the need for
'redemption' and for 'such strange things' as 'consecration', 'covering'
or 'atonement', is religious and not ethical. Typical of the difference
between the views of religion held by Rudolf Otto and Albrecht
Ritschl is their contrasting evaluation of Luther's work *De servo arbitrio*.
Whereas Ritschl describes it as 'an unfortunate botch', Otto regards it
as 'the psychological key' to Luther's religious feeling. It was this work
of Luther which impressed upon him the nature of the numinous by
contrast to the rational, long before he discovered it in the Old Testament and comparative religion.[64]

But Rudolf Otto did not merely recall to the theology of his time
certain aspects of religion which it had forgotten. He also asserted once
again the independence of religion as a whole, against the philosophical
view of his time, or at least against the encroachments of certain philosophers. By describing the category of the 'holy' as an *a priori* category,
he restored to religion its rights as an independent province of the
human mind and of human life: 'Religion is not in vassalage either to
morality or teleology, *ethos* or *telos*, and does not draw its life from postulates; and its non-rational content has, no less than its rational, its
own independent roots in the hidden depths of the spirit itself.'[65]

Rudolf Otto's book *The Idea of the Holy*, and especially his rediscovery
of the irrational and numinous aspect of the preaching of Jesus and the
faith of Luther, contains insights and discoveries which had also been
attained by the study of the New Testament and of Church history,
either earlier or about the same time.

The decisive turning-point in New Testament study had occurred one or two decades earlier, though the theological consequences were not immediately drawn. It was marked by the collapse of what is known as *Leben-Jesu-Forschung*, the study of the 'historical Jesus'.[66] Caught in a cleft stick between their duty as historians and their religious inclination, between the demands of historical and critical study and a genuine devotion to Jesus, scholars of this school had attempted to trace a path back from the biblical Christ to the historical Jesus. By working back critically in this way, they hoped to attain to a 'genuine' picture of the person and teaching of Jesus Christ, and thereby provide an historically unassailable basis for contemporary faith. But the picture that these scholars invariably produced of the historical Jesus was in point of fact not simply drawn from the historical sources, but was also largely inspired by the premises of the world view which they held themselves. The individual portrayals of Jesus they produced, although numerous and of considerable variety, were obviously almost all inspired by the neo-humanist myth of the twentieth century. 'The kingdom of God is within you' was the saying of Jesus to which they were partial, and on which they took their stand. Thus the kingdom of God proclaimed by Jesus became an inner kingdom of ethical values, of the true, the good and the beautiful. Supported by men who do the will of God in this sense, it develops as an entity immanent in the world, gradually progressing towards an ever higher consummation.

In the long run this portrait of the historical Jesus proved to be untenable. As soon as its hidden assumptions were revealed, it inevitably collapsed. Bringing this about was the achievement of Albert Schweitzer; his *Geschichte der Leben-Jesu-Forschung* (1906; 2nd ed. 1913; Eng. tr.: *The Quest of the Historical Jesus*) was the story of its collapse. As its 'negative result', this work uncovered the hidden self-deception of the liberal quest of the historical Jesus, and demonstrated the historical untenability of the portrait of the historical Jesus which it produced. The portrait of the historical Jesus which Schweitzer produced in his turn was completely different. According to him, Jesus was a man with strange, dark anxieties and ideas, an apocalyptic teacher remote from the world, who expected the imminent onset of the kingdom of God, but whose expectations and hopes came to nothing.

This picture of the person and the message of Jesus follows the lines laid down by the so-called *consistent eschatological* interpretation. This was initiated fourteen years before the publication of Albert Schweitzer's *Quest of the Historical Jesus* by the New Testament scholar Johannes Weiss, with his equally epoch-making book *Die Predigt Jesu vom Reiche*

Gottes (1892; 2nd ed. 1900; Jesus' Preaching of the Kingdom of God).
Weiss explained the career of Jesus on the basis of late Jewish apocalyptic, with its expectation of the imminent end of the world and its hope
of the coming of the Messiah, the Son of Man, who was to transform
the world and inaugurate the kingdom of God. He convincingly
demonstrated that for Jesus the kingdom of God was radically other-
worldly and belonged to the future.

It was at once obvious that Jesus was in no sense as close to us or as
familiar to us as, for example, Socrates, Plato, Kant or Goethe. The
kingdom of God, proclaimed by this curious stranger from Galilee, is
not the outcome of a development within the world but is an entity
wholly outside the world; it comes into being not through a continuous
progress within history, but is imminently awaited as a cosmic catastrophe from heaven. It does not signify the transfiguration of history,
but its end, and the demands which it makes upon man are so radical
and absolute that they create disturbance in our civilisation and morality,
rather than confirming them.

Contemporary theology was shocked by the discovery of the
eschatological and apocalyptic character of the person and message of
Christ. Even Johannes Weiss and Albert Schweitzer attempted to sidestep the consistent eschatology they had discovered by reinterpreting it.
Rudolf Bultmann quotes his professor of dogmatics in Berlin, Julius
Kaftan, as saying: 'If Johannes Weiss is right, and the conception of the
kingdom of God is an eschatological one, then it is impossible to make
use of this conception in dogmatics.'[67] But there too the historical truth
turned out to be stronger than all dogmatic doubts and objections.
Consistent eschatological interpretation prevailed, even in dogmatic
theology. The strange, remote, and wholly unworldly element in the
person and message of Jesus was once again brought to life. It concealed
the germs of a profound theological change, which was to take effect
in a way unforeseen by its originators, Johannes Weiss and Albert
Schweitzer.

This first turning-point in New Testament study was confirmed and
developed by a second new beginning, the study of literary categories,
'form-criticism', which is principally linked with the names of Karl
Ludwig Schmidt, Martin Dibelius and Rudolf Bultmann, and had its
inception about 1920.[68] These new critics sought to explore the tradition
about Jesus as far back as possible, even beyond our present gospels
and the sources still recognisable within them, to its oral stage, in order
to rediscover its earliest and original form. In so doing, they came to the

common conclusion that the motives and the laws underlying the development and shaping of the tradition concerning Jesus were intimately linked with the faith and life of the earliest Christian communities. The decisive motive power behind the development and shaping of the earliest traditions of Jesus is preaching in the broadest sense of the term. This means, however, that the tradition of Jesus owes its origin, form and preservation not to historical motives, but to those of faith, and that no portrayal of Jesus could be free from the concerns of faith. This means that the gospels are not historical accounts or biographies, but documents of faith, evidence of past preaching written for the sake of fresh preaching and to arouse new faith. Their intention is not to describe an historical figure of the past, but to proclaim the words and acts of the Lord who is present, as the decisive words of God spoken to man and demanding obedience. 'The Lord has spoken' means that the Lord speaks today. At all times we possess Jesus only in the *kerygma*, that is, in faith and in the preaching of the Church. But once the 'purely historical', as the ultimate standard of all divine truth, is reduced to a merely relative status, the gospel is given a new and urgent importance for the present day.

Finally, in the field of Church history, there was a renewal of *the study of Luther*. It might be said that only now was Luther properly discovered. Not the least reason for this was that in rapid succession the earliest lectures of Luther were found and published.

The first great step forward was taken by the Church historian Karl Holl of Berlin. In 1921, that is, almost simultaneously with the second edition of Barth's *Epistle to the Romans*, he published the first volume of his *Gesammelte Aufsätze zur Kirchengeschichte* (Collected Essays on Church History), entitled *Luther*. In a memorial lecture on Karl Holl, the Church historian Hans Lietzmann said of this book that 'it had the effect of a sudden and mighty revelation'.[69] The collection of essays was prefaced by the address which Holl gave at the University of Berlin on the occasion of the quatercentenary of the Reformation in 1917. Taking the significant theme 'What did Luther understand by religion?', he developed his new comprehensive view of Luther's theology. Holl interpreted Luther's religion predominantly as 'a religion of conscience'. Here he was still following in the footsteps of Kant and Ritschl, but he went beyond their rationalist and ethical interpretation of Christianity at the decisive point. By stressing conscience so strongly, he showed that for him the vital issue is not man, with his experience, enjoyment, desires, wishes and needs, who stands at the heart of religion, but God in his unceasing creation and activity, in his aliveness and holiness, his glory and majesty. Much that Holl says has Calvinist overtones. According to him the theology of Luther, and especially of the young Luther, is a continued, encompassing interpretation of the first commandment, 'I am the Lord thy God'. But for Luther the content of the gospel is precisely that God seeks to be the God and Lord of man; God manifests his glory by becoming in man what he is in himself. In this way Luther's doctrine of justification, with its profound antinomies of law and gospel, judgement and grace, the wrath and the love of God, and the justification and sanctification of man, is restored to its central position. What Holl once wrote concerning the rejection of the Wittenberg enthusiasts by Luther can be regarded as the theme of his whole interpretation: 'People who have once really encountered God, look differently and speak differently of God from those self-assertive persons who converse with him on terms of easy equality.'[70] This statement describes not Martin Luther only, but his interpreter Karl Holl as well.

Inspired by Karl Holl, studies of Luther began to abound. Most of them were purely historical in intention; they dealt mainly with the young Luther, with his student years and his early theology. But soon history did not seem enough. Luther ceased to be merely a part of past Church history, a figure of the late Middle Ages, an object of patriotic religious veneration; he became a source and focus of contemporary theology. We now speak of a 'Luther Renaissance' which coincided with the end of the First World War. In part it prepared the way for dialectic theology, and in part was nourished by it.

The rediscovery of the holy, initiated by Rudolf Otto, the rediscovery of the eschatological character of Jesus' preaching, by Johannes Weiss and Albert Schweitzer, the rediscovery of the nature of the gospel as documents of faith and records of preaching by the study of literary categories, and the rediscovery of the theology of Luther by Karl Holl and others, all imply a single massive shift of interest. But the hidden focus towards which all these several rediscoveries converge is the rediscovery of the deity of God. This is the central theme of Karl Barth and of dialectic theology.

CHAPTER TWO

DIVISIONS AND DISAGREEMENTS

Theological being in 1933

The influence of dialectic theology increased throughout the 1920's almost without opposition. It continued to gain adherents among theologians at the universities, but still more among pastors, and especially among younger men who had returned from the front. But it is probable that its effect in the history of the Church would not have been so great, had it not been for the challenge which, with the whole Church, it faced in 1933. A new contemporary urgency was unexpectedly given to its theme.

Dialectic theology had been concerned with the right knowledge of God. The content of its firm negation had been that God is God and man is man, and that man consequently possesses no faculty or ability of himself to know God; and it also affirmed, not quite so unambiguously, that God revealed himself to man in Jesus Christ alone, and that therefore the sole point at which man encounters the revelation of God is the holy scripture of the Old and New Testaments. This negation and this affirmation together formed its theme. Their reciprocal relationship gave theology its 'dialectics'.

Suddenly, everything that had been opposed so energetically, and which had been regarded as almost defeated, came to life once again. The question whether in addition to Jesus there might not be other divine sources of revelation, be it the living progress of history – and especially the contemporary moment of 'national revival' – the state, the people, the *Führer*, the race, or the nation, once again became of vital contemporary importance. Inevitably this led at once to the question of the nature and the mission of the Church: does the Church, with its mission of preaching the gospel of Jesus to all men, have its meaning and justification in itself and therefore form an independent entity apart from the people and the state, or is it simply intended, in its teaching and other works, to channel religious forces into individual and national life, and serve, as it were, merely as an ethical adjunct to the state, according to the slogan which many theologians at that time affixed above their desk or their bed: 'Germany is our task – Christ is our strength.'

Karl Barth saw himself faced once again with the problem of the 'theological existence' of the Church's preachers and teachers. As early as June 1933 he provided an answer in a brief work composed in a few days: *Theologische Existenz heute!* (Theological Existence Today!). It was the first of a series of writings in which Barth and the theologians of the Confessing Church conducted their campaign against their opponents in theology and Church politics during the struggle within the Church throughout those years.

'With regard to the great movement now sweeping through the nation'[1] Barth demonstrates as little reverence for history as he had previously shown to the hidden historical pantheism of his liberal theological teachers. Again, nothing has taken place in history which is able to transcend the word of God. The word of God has already conquered 'once for all' – the completed achievement of the history of salvation gives Barth confidence that it will also conquer in the future, and drive from the field everything that seeks to resist it. Consequently, 'theological existence' is to be found anywhere where anyone, while pursuing his life as a man, a father, a son, a German or a citizen, lets the word of God be what it is once for all, seeking it every day only in the holy scriptures of the Old and New Testaments, thus letting the holy scripture be his 'master', and God alone his *Führer*.

In a manner reminiscent of Luther's attitude to the enthusiasts in the Peasants' War, Barth responds to the political and religious excitement of many of his contemporaries by concluding his work with this warning: 'Friend, let us think both *spiritually*, and, consequently, *realistically*.' Barth himself had maintained this spiritual realism. He sought to teach his students in lectures and seminars 'only theology, now as previously, and as if nothing had happened' – 'perhaps in a slightly increased tone, but without direct allusions'. And here his mind travels from the University of Bonn to the near-by monastery of Maria Laach, where 'the chanting of the hours by the Benedictines . . . goes on undoubtedly without break or interruption, pursuing the even tenor of its way even in the Third Reich'. This sounds almost like passivity, but there are moments in history in which apparent passivity is the only attitude permitted to the Christian as the expression of his faith, his obedience and his trust. That this passivity must not be the same as inaction Barth demonstrated a year later, when he was the only German professor of theology who refused to take the state employee's oath of loyalty to the *Führer* without any qualification, and therefore lost his teaching post and was ultimately forced to leave Germany in 1935.

But in 1933 Barth not only immediately repudiated his opponents in theology and Church politics. There were also divisions and disagreements among the dialectic theologians themselves. They had of course never formed a completely united group, for from the first very diverse and independent minds of different theological origins had banded together. They were more agreed in what they denied than in what they affirmed. As a result, in the preceding years differences and contradictions of greater or less importance had repeatedly appeared, but had been constantly covered over by their unity in opposition. Now, however, they came out into the open. The group associated with the journal *Zwischen den Zeiten* broke up. In October 1933 Barth wrote the article *A Farewell*, in which he took his leave of the journal they had shared.

The fact that Gogarten in the late summer of 1933 had joined the 'German Christians'[2] was not the decisive factor for Barth. He saw in this outward event merely the conclusion of a long inner development.[3] From the very beginning, and in spite of the feeling that they were 'biting on the same bone', he had never been free 'at the bottom of things' of an 'element of distrust' of Gogarten.[4]

He now announced that the founding of a common journal had been a 'misunderstanding', a 'productive', 'perhaps even a necessary misunderstanding', but a misunderstanding nevertheless. Their common starting-point, the plan for a 'theology of the word of God', 'consciously based on the Bible and the Reformation', was shared only in appearance: in reality, however, Gogarten and also Emil Brunner had never seriously abandoned the 'anthropological tendency' in theology. Barth accuses them of no less than reverting to the natural theology of neo-Protestantism. The 'German Christians' whom Gogarten has joined are only the 'last, most consummate and worst offspring of the essence of neo-Protestantism'.[5]

As early as the autumn of 1922, that is, at the very time when they united to found the journal *Zwischen den Zeiten*, Barth, after a lecture by Gogarten, wrote to Thurneysen that 'the christological problem is dealt with and solved by him with the help of a speculative I-Thou philosophy . . . Heaven only knows where that will yet lead. Also in this respect I am really anxious about the future.'[6] With almost prophetic intuition Barth identifies in its very earliest stages the substance of the conflict which in 1933 was to lead to the breach between himself and Gogarten.

In contrast with Barth, Gogarten's interest was engaged from the very first in the discussion with modern thought. Troeltsch had introduced him to the problem of historicism, and throughout his life he had wrestled with it. Modern historical method subjects everything to itself; even theology cannot escape it. The consistent historicism of human thought is a fact which raises problems that theology must tackle in all their complexity; the only way for theology is to deal with the fundamental issues they pose.[7]

In carrying out this task, Gogarten made use of the work of Ferdinand Ebner. The latter, previously an unknown Austrian elementary school teacher, published in 1921 a book entitled *Das Wort und die geistigen Realitäten – Pneumatologische Fragmente* (The Word and Spiritual Reality – Pneumatological Fragments). He attacked German idealism in terms of linguistic philosophy; to the isolation of the self and the reserve of the non-self as conceived by idealism, Ebner opposes the I-Thou relationship as it occurs in speech, and which he sees as the deepest spiritual reality in human life. Man is a being who speaks, speech reveals him as a spiritual being. Thus Ebner regards all human existential life as conducted in a dialogue.

The effect of Ebner's book in the 1920's and beyond was extraordinarily fruitful, not least among numerous theologians. Gogarten too was influenced by it. He took over Ebner's philosophical categories in order to solve the hermeneutic problem in theology, the problem of how the historical word of God concerning man can be understood in man's concrete historical situation. The problem of reality begins for man at the point where he faces other men as his counterparts; all decisions concerning his relationship with reality are made in the sphere of his relationship to his fellow men. Man discovers himself as an I only when he is challenged by a Thou and becomes aware of reality as a sphere in which he takes decision and exercises responsibility. Only in this way does he obtain an understanding of himself and of his existence in history. It is on the basis of this dialectic in human existential life that Gogarten seeks to understand the Christian revelation and to conceive the historical reality of the word of God.

Barth, however, perceived in this 'anthropological underpinning' of theology merely an attempt to set up alongside the word of God, as the sole and sovereign court of appeal, a second human court of justice. The product of this procedure is 'lemonade', not worth the effort and the struggle which went into the renewal of theological thought and of the teaching of the Church throughout almost twenty years; and he counters Gogarten in unambiguous terms: 'From now on we go separate ways.' Barth repudiated Gogarten much as the Apostle John repudiated the heretic Cerinthus: John rushed from the baths when he learned that Cerinthus was also there – an anecdote frequently quoted during those years of numerous divisions in theology and Church politics.[8]

Eduard Thurneysen seconded his friend Barth. He too wrote his *Farewell to 'Zwischen den Zeiten'*.[9] As had been the case eleven years earlier, at the founding of the journal, he once again saw himself as a man called to sound the alarm. In a new, more urgent fashion battle was joined, as before, against the same enemy – in the cause of freedom of the word of God and of the Church. Georg Merz, the editor, had no choice but to announce in a valedictory statement the closing of the journal they had shared.

To Barth above any other is due the restoration of the central theme of Protestant theology after the First World War, and its preservation in 1933 against the new danger which threatened to overshadow and obliterate it. With the one-sidedness of genius he defended the truth he had seized upon, that there is no way from man to God, but only a way from God to man, and that God follows this way in Jesus Christ alone, and that man encounters God in the holy scripture alone. Barth will not listen to any other voice. Consequently, Emil Brunner compared him to a faithful soldier on sentry duty at night who follows his orders and shoots down everyone who does not give the correct password and so occasionally hits a good friend because he has not properly understood him.[10]

But does not Barth dismiss too hastily, and not for the first time, a problem which theologians had faced not merely since the days of neo-Protestantism, but from the very beginning of the Church, a problem legitimately theirs? This is the problem of what is known as *natural theology*. Barth, in his furious *élan*, has as it were run over it, overwhelming rather than solving it. The question remains whether God may not reveal himself in other ways and in other places than through Jesus and the Bible, ways anticipatory and therefore incomplete, tentative and therefore ambiguous. This at once leads back to the question of the so-called 'point of contact': how is it possible for man to perceive and comprehend the revelation of God in Jesus Christ as the revelation of God without some preliminary idea and knowledge of God with which the revelation in Christ can make contact? Among the dialectic theologians it was Emil Brunner who once again tackled the problem of natural theology; throughout his life it has remained a particular theme of his work.

Nature and grace

Emil Brunner also found that his optimistic belief in progress had collapsed during the First World War. From then on he regarded with suspicion any theology which appealed to the religious experience of man, and described it in negative terms as 'psychologism'. He considered Schleiermacher to be the typical representative of this psychologism and criticised him strongly in his probationary lecture in 1922 at Zürich; in a subsequent comment he refers to him in wholly unacademic language as a 'theological Paganini', 'the greatest theological virtuoso of the century'.[11] In 1924 Brunner wrote *Die Mystik und das Wort* (Mysticism and the Word), another attack on Schleiermacher. Brunner contrasts two modes of faith. Faith is either based on man's religious experience, or grows from listening to the word of God. Brunner terms the first mode 'mysticism'. In mysticism he sees the key word of the whole of neo-Protestant theology, of which he regards Schleiermacher as the 'classic example'. The second mode Brunner finds in the faith of the apostles and the Reformers; the task of the hour is to renew their theology of the Word. Thus Brunner's motto becomes 'Either mysticism or the Word!' He wrote his book in order to unmask the 'colossal self-deception' involved in the alliance between Christ and modern religion, between mystical immanentist philosophy and biblical Christianity.[12]

In his critique of Schleiermacher and neo-Protestantism, Brunner was wholly in line with Karl Barth. He had welcomed the first edition of Barth's *Epistle to the Romans* with 'enthusiasm'. But from the very first he kept his independence with regard to Barth, as became more and more evident in the years that followed, and quite particularly with the publication, in 1934, of his work *Natur und Gnade* (Nature and Grace). The sub-title, 'A contribution to the dialogue with Karl Barth', made it immediately obvious that Brunner was taking issue with Barth's views. While Barth makes nature and grace mutually exclusive and thus firmly rejects any kind of natural theology, Brunner sees the task of present-day theologians precisely in finding their way back to a 'proper', 'Christian natural theology'. Brunner does not intend to co-ordinate nature and grace as two parallel entities of equal value, but wants to bring them into a proper relationship, while completely maintaining the sole efficacy of grace. Barth criticised Brunner's theological views as unbiblical, Thomistic-Catholic, anti-Reformation, and tainted by the Protestantism of the Enlightenment. Brunner now demonstrated to him that he had the Bible and the Reformers on his side, while it was Barth who refused to follow them.

Within the Bible, Brunner appeals above all to the two passages in the Epistle to the Romans which have always been taken as the classic foundation of any natural theology: Romans 1:18–20 and 2:14–15. In the first passage Paul speaks of God's invisible being which, since the creation of the world, was made manifest in his works; and in the second, that God has written his law in the hearts of the Gentiles. Brunner further refers to passages from the missionary preaching in the Acts (14:8 ff.; 17:22 ff.). All these biblical texts concur in the view that God had revealed himself to men even before and outside Christ, and that for this very reason they have no excuse for refusing his revelation in Christ. The biblical view, which is clear on this point, is corroborated by the equally clear teaching of the Reformers, of both Luther and Calvin. These go even further in the direction of what Barth suspects to be 'Thomism' or 'neo-Protestantism', and speak more confidently of the revelation of God in creation than Brunner would ever dare. Within these limits, laid down by the Bible and the Reformers, Brunner establishes his Christian natural theology. His concern is on the one hand that theology should not go beyond these boundaries, and on the other that it should go to their full limits. Thus Brunner follows the Bible and the Reformers in teaching a revelation of God in nature through creation, which precedes his revelation in Jesus Christ through atonement.

As in every creation the spirit of its creator is 'in some way' recognisable, so also in the creation of God: 'He leaves the imprint of his nature upon what he does.' Consequently the creation of the world is at the same time his revelation. Brunner explicitly affirms that this proposition is not pagan but fundamentally Christian.[13] Though man immediately proceeds to distort God's revelation in creation into idols of his own, he could not do this if God had not in some way revealed himself in his creation. But precisely because God has revealed himself, and enabled man to know about him, man's disobedience is without excuse.

To the objective side of the natural revelation of God in creation corresponds the subjective side, the teaching of man as the image of God. But Brunner agrees to speak of man as the image of God only in the 'formal' and not in the 'material' sense. This 'likeness' he understands as based exclusively on the *humanism*, or that which distinguishes man, whether he is a sinner or not, from the entire rest of creation: that he is a subject, and that as a subject he possesses 'the power of speech' and 'responsibility'. Even as a sinner, he does not cease to be a subject, and therefore 'one with whom one can speak, with whom therefore also God can speak'.[14] Through human sin the recognisability of God in his works is 'marred', but is not 'destroyed'.

Here the 'point of contact' for divine grace in his human nature comes into play. It does not consist in any material residue of the image of God preserved in man but only in his 'purely formal accessibility to words', 'in the fact that men are not stones and clods', but human subjects, capable of being addressed, and themselves endowed with the power of speech and response. Only beings accessible to words are responsible, can make decisions, and can sin at all. Man's power of speech, which he has not lost even through sin, is the presupposition of his ability to hear the word of the divine revelation. But Brunner constantly stresses that this is the purely *formal* faculty of being able to hear. That man hears the word of God in *faith* is brought about solely by the word of God itself. Thus the sole efficacy of grace is not affected by this doctrine of the point of contact.

What Brunner has to say concerning the point of contact makes it clear why he is interested in natural theology. It is important for him not from a dogmatic, but from a methodological point of view. He has in mind the Church's teaching mission, particularly the dialogue with non-believers, with intellectuals and with modern youth. If this is to be pursued intelligibly, there is need of a natural theology. The method of teaching can never be separated from its substance: 'A pastor might – to put it somewhat strongly – go to heaven on account of the What but go to hell on account of the How.'[15] But experience teaches that wherever natural theology is despised, the question of the method of preaching is equally neglected. The neglect of natural theology must almost always bring with it a neglect of the pedagogic and pastoral element in preaching, and especially of the preliminary conceptual and intellectual work, which clears the way for the preaching, and seeks the form of expression most suitable for it at a given time. It is not a question of proving God's existence, but of the discourse which points to him. It is for this purpose that man's power of speech and his responsibility provide a point of contact. It is only possible to speak of God to those 'in whose vocabulary the word God is already present' and to preach repentance to those who already 'in some way' have a conscience. 'There are lots of orthodox preachers who have an extraordinary faculty of never coming to grips with conscience – in a manner apparently theologically correct.'[16] The ominous consequence of such contempt for natural theology and the point of contact which it provides will one day be the complete intellectual isolation of the Church.

The original revelation

In a broader and more comprehensive way, but also more radically and therefore less cautiously than Emil Brunner, Paul Althaus taught at the same time a 'general revelation' of God outside his special revelation. His purpose here, as in the rest of his theology, was to give expression to the Lutheran doctrinal tradition, of which, throughout his life, he felt himself to be the guardian in a special sense.

As Althaus once expressed it in a personal testimony,[17] he 'swam against the theological stream in Germany' from the very beginning of his academic career. What seemed 'unbearable' to him in the dominant theology in Germany was the 'narrowness' of its doctrine of revelation; he considered it 'unbiblical' and 'limited'. He was clearly aiming at Karl Barth and dialectic theology when he wrote, 'I could never understand how one could wish to be responsible to the Church and to theology for abandoning the whole world of nature and history to scepticism and secularism, and to parrot what atheistic philosophy has done towards taking God out of our life – and to claim at the same time that the glory of Christ was maintained by his being the only way to the Father.' Althaus sees the decisive reason for the one-sidedness and narrowness of dialectic theology in its rejection of a 'general revelation' of God. It is in conscious opposition to this that the general revelation of God became the determining theme in his own theology. He will not speak, however, of 'natural theology' – a concept he deliberately rejects – but of the original revelation of God. It is this doctrine of the 'original revelation' which is Althaus's distinctive contribution to the Protestant theology of the present day.

The 'original revelation' does not refer to a revelation given once only, in the beginning, to the first human generation, but to the original and ever-present testimony of God himself in the whole reality of man and the world. By virtue of this divine testimony, man stands 'in an ineluctable relationship to God even before the encounter with Jesus Christ, and without the biblical testimony'.[18] Althaus heaps proof upon proof, example on example from the vast scope of the original divine revelation: language, religion, laws, conscience, the standards of good, truth, beauty, and justice, the unalterable fact of existence, human life, but also human mortality, the ingenious ordering of nature, history and communal life in society, the vocation to tasks and offices, history, its mystery and meaning, its guilt and liability, its fate and responsibility. The whole of human historical reality is 'theomorphic'; it is in itself a testimony to the reality of God.

But this universal original revelation of God is by no means an independent and self-sufficient entity, but is strictly related to the saving revelation of God in Jesus Christ. This relationship is twofold. In a negative sense, the original revelation demonstrates the guilt of man's unbelief with regard to the gospel, and in a positive sense it shows his belief in the gospel as fulfilment.

The acceptance of the original revelation as knowledge of God by the natural man is never 'neutral'; it is always corrupted by him the very moment he receives it. He perverts it into idolatry, and becomes guilty of betraying it. As a consequence the manifestation of God is transformed for man into concealment. Althaus proceeds to contrast his first series of examples and proofs of God's testimony to himself in the total reality of man and the world with a second almost equally copious series of counter proofs and examples: that nature is dominated by a horrifying struggle for survival, that all life in history exists at the expense of other life, that we have fallen prey to evil and death, and that the problem of the meaning of life remains unsolved. Thus as we encounter the original revelation, we do it as men who at the same time stand under the wrath of God. Original revelation can make us aware of God, but it gives us no certainty of salvation: 'Homesickness is evidence that there is a home, but it is no guarantee of homecoming.' Constantly the original revelation cries out for the revelation of salvation. The natural knowledge of God cannot be 'complemented, but only amended' by the gospel.[19]

This leads to the positive side of the relationship between original revelation and the revelation of salvation. In the preaching of the gospel of Jesus Christ, the original revelation is 'fulfilled' and acknowledged by man in the right way. What takes place is a 'fresh recognition'. Since the original revelation, which is fulfilled in the revelation of salvation, happens in the total reality of man and the world, this means that the revelation of salvation does not take place in a vacuum, or create a separate sacral sphere, but is always related to the given reality of human existence and its experience of the world. It is not limited to the person and earthly life of Jesus Christ, but places in the proper light everything which was already present previously, nature, history, human society, the experience of conscience, and the self-knowledge of man in general. By relating the original revelation and the revelation of salvation to each other, Althaus succeeds in demonstrating that God is truly revealed in the world, and that the reality of the world is his reality. Thus the Christian belief in revelation does not have in mind a different and alien reality, but the present reality of our life and our world.

Unfortunately Althaus did not relate the original revelation to the revelation of salvation throughout as strictly as might be desired. Sometimes he is in danger of allowing the original revelation to break away from the revelation of salvation and to become independent. Thus for example Althaus mentions the 'direct certainty of the validity and holiness of ordinances', or says that 'even without the effect of the Christian gospel, the certainty of God constantly recurs as history is experienced'. As an example of this, he mentions the integration with the people, which many contemporaries have newly come to realise, thereby becoming certain that 'therein they are encountering the holy and the absolute'. He warns the preaching of the Church against breaking down 'the direct certainty of the validity and holiness of ordinances' and 'outlawing what proclaims to be an encounter with God as pagan deception, and calling contemporary men *away* from it to the God of the Bible'. If man resists this, it is not because of his 'sinful defiance of the word of God', but because of 'the sense of truth and reality which is given him by God himself'.[20]

Here an apprehension of the course of history has clearly broken into Althaus's theological assurance. He seems either suddenly to have forgotten that man never receives God's original revelation in a neutral way, but always turns it into idolatry in the very moment in which it is received, or he seems to have failed to understand the Germans of the 1930's. Accordingly it can with propriety be asked whether it was right at all to speak so emphatically at that time of the general revelation of God in the form of an original revelation. Was there not rather an obligation to emphasise more strongly the distinctiveness and exclusiveness of the revelation of God in Jesus Christ by contrast to what everyone was saying at the time – for what German citizen did not make some casual mention of God at that time? One of the highest principles in theology is that in everything it says it must keep the contemporary situation in mind. Consequently it cannot say everything with the same emphasis at every period. Even within theology, everything has its moment: the revelation of Christ and the natural revelation.

Barth's 'No'

For Barth not only was this not the time for natural revelation; according to him there never was time for it in theology. He abruptly asserts:
'No'. This single word is also the title of his retort to Brunner. The title
is characteristic of the work. It is an unrestrained work, unrestrained in
its polemic, unrestrained in its unwillingness to understand – and unrestrained in its Christianity. Barth asks whether the dialogue ought not
to be broken off as hopeless. On his lips this is a rhetorical question, as
he never even entered into any such dialogue. With regard to natural
theology he admits that he is 'ultimately uninterested'. In his eyes it is not
an independent theme and problem at all, but merely the 'great
temptation and source of error' in all theology. It comes from *Anti-
Christ*. Therefore it is 'to be turned away *a limine*, at the very threshold'.
It is a question which one must not even attempt, but one must turn
one's back at once and seek to bypass it as though it were an abyss. It
must be handled like a poisonous snake: 'You do not stare at the serpent,
with the result that it stares back at you, hypnotises you, and is ultimately certain to bite you, but you hit it and kill it as soon as you see
it!'[21]

Brunner had explicitly stated that natural theology did not form an
independent theme for him either, but Barth does not listen to this; and
that Brunner is not interested in it on dogmatic grounds, but for
methodological reasons, only makes the matter worse to his mind.
Here we come for the first time to those passages in Barth in which he
proclaims with passion and irony his lack of interest in the question of
the form and method of preaching. For him the method of preaching is
no more than a 'marginal question', the care of which one should cast
upon God. Barth is solely interested in the matter, in the substance of
the gospel, and he relies on this matter to make its point by virtue of the
'victorious power' which is founded upon it. The gospel is an event
which bears witness to itself as it is carried out. Anyone who, like
Brunner, is concerned with the point of contact and the form of
preaching, thereby betrays that he is seeking help elsewhere than in the
revelation of God; he has 'aimed at success' and made use of 'useless
bridges and tools', instead of simply listening to the command of God
and trusting his promise. Thus the question of the point of contact is
answered at once: the Holy Spirit himself provides the answer. Consequently Barth's advice for the approach to non-believers, intellectuals
and modern youth, with which Brunner is so concerned, is that one

must treat them 'quietly, simply (remembering that Christ has died and risen also for them), as if their rejection of "Christianity" was not to be taken seriously'.[22]

Here we find in Barth a Christian radicalism of which we are bound to ask whether it is still Christian. This 'unrestrained Christianity' seduces Barth into not taking history seriously. He trusts the Holy Spirit alone. No theologian will disagree with him in his trust, but would hope at best to surpass him in it. Yet even the Holy Spirit does not act in a magical way, but through concrete historical means. He acts upon living men, who have concrete experiences, problems and needs, also certain convictions, illusions and contradictions, and who think in specific categories. He does this through men, who before they speak must not only consider *what* they have to say, but also *how* they are to say it, with a loving regard for those whom they seek to save. Anyone who omits this step in exposition is ascribing magical power to the biblical word. And where magic begins, history ceases.

The 'No' which Barth hurled at Brunner was a symbol of his uncompromising attitude to the struggle within the Church. In the 'mediating theology' Barth saw the cause of all the misfortune of the Protestant Church in Germany. That is why he fights so passionately against every attempt to link up with nature, against the 'jolly little hyphens' between nature and grace, reason and faith, history and revelation, modern and positive, religious and social, German and Christian. In order to judge aright the attitude which Barth adopted, one must of course bear in mind that he had already begun the struggle before 1933, and continued it after 1945. That is why from the first his anger was aimed not so much against the enemies of the Church, who were working to destroy it from outside, as against its own representatives, who were in danger of hollowing it out from within by means of a massive ecclesiasticism.

He saw as the representative of such a too conscious and false ecclesiasticism the General Superintendent of Brandenburg, Otto Dibelius of Berlin. The latter had written a highly regarded book entitled *Das Jahrhundert der Kirche* (The Century of the Church). Barth spoke of it ironically as the 'purple' century. What he saw in Dibelius's book was the self-confidence and complacency of a Church which, like other human institutions, seeks, builds up and glorifies only itself, and consequently becomes unworthy of belief in its preaching – 'one stall in the market amongst others'. From this point of view, Barth gave a lecture in Berlin in 1931 entitled *Die Not der evangelischen Kirche* (The Distress of the Protestant Church). A week later Dibelius answered him in a

lecture entitled *Die Verantwortung der Kirche* (The Responsibility of the
Church). In it he asserted that there was no fundamental struggle
between himself and Barth. But Barth replied: 'No fundamental struggle? A *very* fundamental struggle, General Superintendent, be assured
of that!' Barth is of the opinion that in the German Protestant Church
'there is scarcely a word to be heard about Christ', but 'virtually only
alien, hostile, pagan words'. As by a 'poison gas', he is affronted by the
'evil odour of an abominable complacency and self-assurance'. Dibelius
concluded his address with the words *'Ecclesiam habemus*; we have a
Church'. Barth took up these words, but turned them against Dibelius:
'*Ecclesiam habemus* – how right you are, General Superintendent, but it
is for this reason that I can only oppose the dominance, unbroken to
this day, of your spirit and your attitude in the Church. I hope for a new
and different day in the German Protestant Church.'[23] For Barth, the
new and different day of the German Protestant Church has not come
to this day, neither in 1933 nor in 1945. His mistrust of Dibelius did not
disappear even when the latter took the side of the Confessing Church,
and as a result lost his office as General Superintendent; in fact after the
war this mistrust grew even stronger.

What Barth criticised above all in the German Protestant Church
was the 'hyphen between Christianity and the nation', between
'Protestant and German'. This seemed to belong to its 'permanent
stock in trade' and formed the 'true criterion of Church orthodoxy'.[24]
How right Barth was in his criticism was shown by the attitude which
the Church first adopted in 1933. That a part of the Church then had
second thoughts was due in a large part to Barth's unflagging 'No'. It
was he above all who gave the Confessing Church in Germany its
theological armoury. It was under his advice and influence that in 1934
the 'Theological Declaration of Barmen' was formulated. Barth was
rightly called its 'father'. The first thesis of the Declaration of Barmen
seems to present almost a summary of his theology: 'Jesus Christ, to
whom the Holy Scripture bears witness, is the one Word of God whom
we have to hear, and whom we have to trust and obey in life and death.
We reject the false doctrine that the Church can or must recognise as
the revelation of God other events and powers, forms and truths as the
source of its preaching, outside and parallel to this one Word of God.'

CHAPTER THREE

BEHOLD THE MAN!

Eristic theology

Barth's whole theological thought and work was determined by his concern for the identity of the Christian gospel, and by the determination with which he defended the purity of Christian doctrine and the independence of the Church against all attempts to weaken or fragment it. The demand made upon him by this task was so one-sided that he dealt inadequately with the other side of theology: the flexibility of the Christian gospel, the question of how the gospel can be preached in the contemporary situation of mankind and be appropriated by man. Emil Brunner devoted his whole interest to this aspect of the theological task. If we accept his own distinction between *credo* in the sense of the objective truth of faith and *credo* in the sense of the subjective approach to creation and faith, we can say that Barth in Basle was concerned above all with the *credo* as the objective truth of faith, while Brunner in Zürich was concerned above all with the *credo* as the subjective appropriation of faith.

'I was and am first and foremost a preacher of the gospel', writes Brunner in his autobiographical sketch. Barth could have said the same of himself. But what distinguishes Brunner from Barth, and gives his voice its distinctive note among the theologians of the twentieth century, is the pastoral and missionary responsibility which he has felt in a special way throughout his life, especially for those who dwell before the gate of the Church, for those who ask and who seek, as well as for those who are already silent and who no longer ask or seek. It is with these that Brunner seeks a dialogue. He takes seriously the coming of age of men, but is also aware of the dechristianisation which follows it like a shadow, and the growing lack of purpose and direction in every sphere of life. It is this which gives his theological work, again by contrast with that of Barth, its complexity and breadth. In addition to his specifically dogmatic works, he has written a whole series of books on political and social ethics. He is not merely interested in the Church's mission to the world, but in secular politics; not only in the encounter of Christianity with philosophy, but also in its confrontation with the totalitarian state; not only in the problem of other religions, but also in the question of social justice in the world. But for him the principal task of theology lies always in the kerygmatic and dogmatic spheres: 'The central issue must always be the struggle for a right understanding of faith in Christ.'[1]

Brunner likes to compare the task of the theologian with that of a front-line officer who finds himself under fire. He ought not to develop dogmatic theses in quiet self-sufficiency, concerned only with whether or not they are correct, but must adapt himself to the changing situation and always speak in direct confrontation. He is always in dispute and in dialogue: 'Every dogmatic statement is at the same time an apologetic and antithetical statement.'[2] To express the nature of this theology, Brunner speaks of *eristic theology*. He is clearly aiming at Barth when he writes: '*This* is the "touch of spice", *this* is the salt, without which any correct dogmatic theology goes rotten.'[3] Eristic theology is a kind of 'Christian Socratics'. It is distinct from the Socratic method of philosophy in that it does not draw the truth out of man by questioning, but worms out of him a confession of untruth. Its aim is to teach man to understand his own inquiry about God correctly, simply by 'bringing him to his senses'. Thus it reveals in him the ambiguity of his existential life; it attacks his cherished ideas and interrogates him about them until it shatters them for him; it drives human reason before it with its questions until it has it cornered at the point where, with its back to the wall, it either continues to utter a defiant denial or steps through the narrow gate of faith.

Man in revolt

Emil Brunner's concern is to reach modern man, who is largely dechristianised, with the message of the Christian gospel. This also lies behind his strong anthropological interest, shown in 1934 in his work *Natur und Gnade* (Nature and Grace), which aroused Barth's violent anger. A year later he enlarged the ideas laid down in that work into the comprehensive outline of a Christian doctrine of man. This was the first Christian anthropology since the theological revolution which came with the end of the First World War. Brunner entitled it *Der Mensch im Widerspruch* (Man in Revolt).

Brunner, like many Protestant and Catholic theologians of the present century, was also influenced by the I-Thou philosophy of Ferdinand Ebner and Martin Buber. Both sought to overcome the rationalist scheme of thought of subject and object, by understanding the human person in its relationship to the divine Thou, and therefore making a meaningful distinction between the realm of personal relationship, the I-Thou world, and the world of object relationship, the I-It world. Brunner admits that it led him to the 'quintessence of the biblical understanding of man',[4] and this all the more easily since Buber in particular derived his most important insights from the Old Testament and from the Christian philosophy of Sören Kierkegaard. Brunner himself holds that contemporary theology, Catholic as much as Protestant, owes more to Kierkegaard than to any other theologian or philosopher since Martin Luther.

In his anthropology Brunner proceeds from the fact that man asks questions, and that it is this which distinguishes him from all other creatures. This is shown not so much when man asks about the things which form his environment, but rather when he asks about himself. The questions man asks about himself reveal the fact that man is 'not merely what he is', but that he 'seeks himself in something higher', and that, whether he likes it or not, he must 'in some way or other reach out beyond himself' and 'measure his thinking, willing and acting by something higher than himself'. Essentially, this call to be truly himself comes to man not from the object, the It, which is opposed to the self, the I, but from the subject, the Thou, which is not merely opposed to the self, but determines the way the self is itself. Only when man discovers his relationship to another person, a Thou, can he know himself as a self and become a person. 'And were all human beings upon the earth to die and leave me alone alive: my life, in its impaired and solitary condition . . . would still be related to the "Thou" in remembrance, in longing and in hope.'[5]

If the nature of man is formed by this I-Thou relationship, then responsibility is evidently the 'nucleus' of all anthropology. This responsibility is not merely an attribute, but the substance of man: 'True responsibility is the same as true humanity.' But then the question arises, who the Thou is who calls to man and whom he answers. Is there really a relationship of call and response, or is man merely moving in a circle around his own self? It is at this point that the biblical message takes on for Brunner a decisive significance for anthropology. His thesis is that 'it is the understanding of man that divides faith from unbelief': thereon depends whether 'God or man is the centre'.[6]

Consequently, Brunner distinguishes between the 'true man' and the 'real man'. The *true* man is he who has his origin in the word of God, and therefore anchors his responsibility in a life lived by this word, in origin and destination. The *real* man is he who also has his origin in the word of God, but who denies this, and whose responsibility is therefore perverted. This real man is the theme of Brunner's book: he is *man in revolt*.

This revolt arises because man lives in opposition to his origin. The origin of man posits that God has created him in his image. But man opposes his creation: he relates not to God but to himself – not *sursum corda* but *cor incurvatum in se*! Consequently, his existential life runs in the reverse direction. Because he has removed God from its centre, his life becomes 'eccentric'. This has immediate consequences for his relatedness to his fellow men: by losing contact with the divine Thou, man also loses contact with the human Thou. Thus the real man lives in a revolt from his origin, and in opposition. This revolt is not something in man, but is man himself. Revolt is his 'constitution'.

As evidence of the existential life of man in revolt, Brunner demonstrates evident contradictions in the existential life of man. For example, man must form an idea of the absolute, he must conceive the absolute – in this God maintains a firm hold upon him, a hold demonstrating his relatedness to God, even though he has alienated himself from God. But he can only conceive of the idea of the absolute in empty and abstract terms, or fill it with a perverted content – it is this that shows that he has alienated himself from God, but that even in alienation he still remains related to him: 'Even the most horrible idol tells us something of the secret of the Holy, and the most abominable cultus tells us something of the fact that we have been created by God for God.'[7] This is true everywhere: the idea of God which the human mind forms, the idea of perfection for which it longs, the language in which it expresses itself, the idea of society which it creates, its moral consciousness and its striving for truth are all reflections of the same sick, divided man – the man who has his origin in God, but lives opposed to his origin, and has therefore perverted his life, yet cannot break away from his origin, but even in opposition and in perversion must bear witness to it; this is man opposing, in his revolt, his origin, creation and sin – the *rebel* against God, who yet at the same time is *God's* rebel, even in his rebellion pointing towards his creator and Lord.

This is Brunner's diagnosis of the 'real' man. What therapy does he offer? How can the real man win back his 'true' human nature? How can truth and the reality of man once again become united? For Brunner the answer is: through the revelation of God in Jesus Christ, and through man's faith in this revelation. Everything depends upon how this process is interpreted. And here we come to an idea of Brunner's which he had already hinted at in his anthropology, which he developed further in 1937, when he gave the Olaus Petri Lectures in Uppsala, and continued to explore in the years that followed, and which in his own judgement became his most important contribution to theological epistemology. This is the concept of *truth as encounter*, which he was the first to express and formulate.

Truth as encounter

The theses of a theologian often do not become truly alive and evident until it is realised what his aims are; and they in their turn are often best understood on learning what he is against. Brunner is against false 'objectivism' in theology, and is therefore against the intellectualist misunderstanding of Christian faith. If ever his lucid flowing style becomes passionate and emotional, it is in this context. To him, the shift from a personal understanding of faith to an intellectual under-standing is 'the most fatal occurrence within the entire history of the Church', the 'basic ecclesiastical evil', and the hidden cause of all other evils. Nothing, according to him, has put a greater strain on the testi-mony of the revelation of God in Jesus Christ, and so damaged the reputation of the Church.[8]

The intellectualist misunderstanding of revelation and of faith began very early, as early as the first centuries of the primitive Church. The cause of this was the intrusion of Greek philosophical thought into the Church. Under its influence, Christian theology applied the general rationalist concept of truth to biblical revelation, and consequently moved it into the pincers of subject-object opposition. The real evil and calamity was not the attempt to approach understanding of revelation either subjectively or objectively, but to force it into a category of thought which is alien to it. Whereas the Bible describes the history of the revelation of God entirely in verbs of movement, theology now speculated upon the Trinity and upon the person of Christ purely in categories of being and nature. Thus divine revelation became the supernatural imparting of doctrinal truths inaccessible to limited human reason, and faith accordingly became the unquestioning acceptance of these supernaturally revealed doctrinal truths.

Thus faith was turned into 'a matter of believing', with no distinction between dogma or the Bible as the object of belief. 'Fundamentally,

Bible-orthodoxy is precisely the same as dogma-orthodoxy.'[9] In both cases, there is a 'revealed truth', which *must* be believed. It is this obligation which destroys the nature of faith at its very root. It turns faith into a duty which man has to perform, and on the performance of which his eternal salvation depends. Thus 'orthodoxy' becomes the standard by which every Christian attitude is measured: 'If only your support of doctrine is clear and unequivocal, you are a Christian.'[10] Consequently it is no accident that orthodoxy has always been characterised by a notable lack of love.

Brunner seeks to overcome this imprisonment of theological thought in the subject-object dichotomy. The biblical revelation cannot be understood either from the point of view of the object, as merely an outward event, or from the point of view of the subject as merely an inner process. It lies 'beyond objectivism and subjectivism'. Brunner finds numerous parallels in modern thought to the overcoming of the traditional subject-object dichotomy, both in philosophy and in natural science. Examples in philosophy are provided by Dilthey, Husserl, Kierkegaard and Heidegger, who all have in common that they no longer make a sharp distinction between the subject which knows and the object which is known; the outstanding example in natural science is Einstein's theory of relativity, which makes the point of view of the perceiving subject part of the description of the world of objects. Brunner interprets this as the onset of a 'new Copernican revolution', the results of which are incalculable.[11]

The concept 'truth as encounter' heralds the overcoming of the subject-object dichotomy in thought. It very adequately reproduces the two decisive elements which are contained in the biblical understanding of truth: that it is *historical* and that it is *personal*. According to the biblical view, truth is not something which is inherently present in man or the world, and which man needs only to become aware of, but the divine truth *comes* to men from outside the world and *happens* among men in space and time. As a characteristic expression of this biblical understanding of truth, Brunner often quotes a verse from the prologue to the Gospel of John, although this was probably originally composed in Greek: 'Grace and truth became [*egeneto*] through Jesus Christ' (1:17). That truth 'became', that it is not eternal and timeless, that it is involved in history, and subject to historical change, is a self-contradiction to Greek ears. But for the Bible the whole question of truth hinges upon the fact that it is not something timeless, but something which comes into being, the act of God in space and time.

Because biblical truth is historical, it is also personal. God's revelation of his truth in an historical event in space and time does not signify that he originates an idea which is then taken up by human thought, or that he creates a series of facts which man has to take into account. It means that he himself, his *person*, is the content of this event. The revelation of God is 'the imparting of himself', what he speaks is 'addressed' to someone, and his word is 'a communicating word'. 'In his Word God does not deliver to me a course of lectures in dogmatic theology, he does not submit to me or interpret for me the content of a confession of faith, but he makes himself accessible to me . . . he does not communicate "something" to me, but "himself".'[12] Consequently the act of revelation and its content are identical. The fact *that* God has revealed himself to man includes *what* he has revealed: that he loves man and desires fellowship with him. Thus in the Bible the truth of God is always identical with the love of God. In the biblical understanding of truth the fact that truth is historical and the fact that it is personal are linked; together they define the nature of revelation as the self-imparting of God to man.

What is true of revelation from God's side is also true of its acceptance on man's part. His faith and knowledge are also a personal event throughout. Revelation as the sovereign self-imparting of God finds its counterpart in faith as the free self-giving of man. By revealing himself to man, God entices him out of 'the castle of the self' and enables him to open himself to God in his turn and to commit himself to him. Thus faith is seen to be not an object of knowledge, but an act of trust: man is now ready to receive his life from the hand of God and to exercise his responsibility in such a way that he responds to the word of God. And therefore Brunner describes the personal being of man as 'a responding actuality'. In this context, one of his favourite expressions for describing the biblical understanding of truth is once again drawn from the Gospel of John: 'to *do* the truth'. This expression is as far from Greek thought as the previous idea, that truth 'became'. But the two form an exact parallel. They signify that the truth of God is not an object, which lies before me and which I grasp, so that I then *possess* it, but that it is a movement, which comes to me, and by which I am possessed, so that I then *am* in it.

Thus the relationship which prevails between God and man is that of a *personal correspondence* – this concept sums up everything which Brunner has to say about truth as encounter, and indeed is a most pregnant representation of his fundamental theological concern. He sees in it the 'fundamental category', the 'basic ordinance', the 'original formal relationship', within which everything that the Bible says about God and man must be understood. The relationship of personal correspondence is a 'twofold but unambiguous relationship'. It is twofold, because it is concerned (primarily) with the relationship of God to man, and (secondarily) with the relationship of man to God; it is unambiguous, because whether it is that of God to man or of man to God, its meaning is always identical: it is that of the love with which God first loved man and with which man, as it were echoing this love, loves God in return. Therefore Brunner draws knowledge and fellowship into a unity: to know God means to be one with him.

Eighteen hundred years of misunderstanding of the Church

When faith is understood in such a personal way as in Brunner, certain conclusions necessarily follow for the concept of the Church. Moreover, Brunner is quite ready to draw these conclusions.

The question of what the Church is Brunner regards as 'the unresolved problem of Protestantism'. It comes from the fact that the connection between what the New Testament terms *ekklesia* and what we call the *Church* is not clear. Anyone today, regardless of whether he is Catholic or Protestant, Lutheran or Calvinist, who thinks of 'the Church' has in mind something impersonal, an institution, something which exists above individual men in the same way as the state. But in Brunner's eyes it is precisely this which is the 'eighteen-hundred-year-old misunderstanding of the Church'. It consists of understanding the Church as an institution and then simply identifying this institution with the *ekklesia*, the community in Christ of the New Testament.

The origins of this institutional misunderstanding of the Church are the same as those of the intellectual misunderstanding of faith, that is, they lie in the error of objectivist thought. In attacking one, Brunner simultaneously attacked the other. In his lecture on *Truth as Encounter*, he had already made a connection between the intellectual misunderstanding of faith and the institutional misunderstanding of the Church. In the years that followed, he worked out his ideas concerning the Church even more thoroughly and radically, and finally published them in a very individual and much criticised work entitled *Das Missverständnis der Kirche* (The Misunderstanding of the Church).

The author 'hopes to gain the concurrence of all those to whom Jesus Christ is dearer than their own church' – this sentence from the preface is characteristic of the approach of the whole book. The view that permeates it is the description of the Church as a personal fellowship with Christ, which means that the emphasis is on the personal element in the concept of the Church. The principal thesis which Brunner advances, which forms his starting-point and to which he constantly returns, is that the *ekklesia*, the community in Christ of the New Testament, is a 'purely personal fellowship', with nothing in the nature of an institution, and therefore not yet 'a Church'. It is brought into being only by men who are apprehended by the word of God, which is Jesus Christ himself, and so are brought into a personal relationship to him. Vertically, this relationship is realised as a fellowship with God, and in the horizontal sense as a human fellowship, a fraternity. Whereas it was later supposed that to describe what the Church is, it was sufficient to apply to it the two objective criteria of 'pure doctrine' and the 'right administration of the sacraments', the New Testament contains a whole series of other characteristics by which it was possible to tell whether one belonged to the community of Christ: a lively faith, the endurance of suffering, zeal for service, true brotherly love, mutual exhortation – all characteristics which distinguish the Church not as an institutional body, but as a personal fellowship. The proof of membership lies not in purity of doctrine, but in evidence of discipleship.

In this picture which Brunner paints of the New Testament *ekklesia*, there is something else associated with his powerful emphasis on the personal element, and this is a positive evaluation of the enthusiasm of the Spirit which prevailed in the earliest communities. The early Christians were conscious of possessing the *pneuma*, the Holy Spirit, and with this went powers of a non-rational nature. The Spirit seizes not merely the understanding, but also the heart, and through the heart penetrates into the deep unconscious levels of the soul, and indeed even into the body. Theology, which as its name implies is directed towards what is 'logical', is not an appropriate instrument with which to understand this activity of the Holy Spirit outside logic. Consequently the Holy Spirit has always been more or less the 'stepchild of theology' and his gift of inspiration a 'bugbear' for many theologians. Here again, Brunner utters a protest against the one-sided intellectualism of theology: from fear of a possible imbalance it despises the warning of the apostle Paul and 'quenches the Spirit'. In this way it becomes a 'hindrance' and even 'stifles' the Holy Spirit, at least with regard to the fullness of its dynamic and enthusiastic manifestation.

Now, of course, even for Brunner the New Testament *ekklesia* is not

solely a disordered mass impelled by the Spirit. Even as the purely
personal fellowship that it is it possesses offices and uses sacraments.
According to Brunner's reasoning, the Church in the New Testament
possesses institutions, but *is* not an institution; it *has* order, but *is* not
order. And the order within it forms 'something wholly spontaneous',
without a determining quality of its own, and is always merely 'pro-
visional', produced by the necessity of the moment and disappearing
with it. It is the messianic and spiritual element which prevents what is
spontaneous from hardening into institutions and thus leading to the
rise of a fixed Church law. Anyone who looks to the return of the Lord
in the future, and believes and loves at the present time by the power of
the Holy Spirit, has no need of Church law and cannot tolerate it. Thus
in Brunner's opinion, the Church in the New Testament is still unable
to be an 'institution' and therefore by definition still cannot be a
'Church'.

But the *transformation of the ekklesia into a Church* very soon began.
To the extent to which the messianic and spiritual elements disappeared,
and the attempt was made to protect and replace what was disappearing,
the New Testament *ekklesia* became an institution and therefore a
Church. This process of protection and replacement was threefold.
The word of God was protected and replaced by dogma, personal
fellowship by an institution, and personal faith by the doctrinal and
moral law. Moreover, Brunner constantly stresses that this was not
merely a development but a *transformation*: there was now pure doctrine
– but without the spirit of the word of God; right belief – but without
brotherly love; churches and offices – but without the link provided by
mutual service. Thus by gradual but constant stages the community
of Jesus as a purely personal fellowship turned into the Church as an
institutional organisation. Brunner's summary of this development
reads like the plot of a tragedy: 'Out of the "mystical" brotherhood
rooted in the Word and the Spirit, out of the Body of Christ whose
head is Christ Himself alone, and whose members therefore are of
equal status, out of the royal priesthood and holy nation has grown the
Church – a totality composed of individual communities, each of
which comes under the ecclesiastical jurisdiction of a bishop, who as
administering priest stands opposed to the receiving laity because he
controls the sacrament, the food of salvation, the sacral thing which
holds together the individual components and makes them into a solidary
collective.'[13]

The process by which the *ekklesia* turned into the Church was already beginning in the New Testament, and was completed under Constantine the Great. It is the beginning of the 'inflation of the Church on a grand scale'. The Church now stands ready-made as a sacred institution, as a sacramental and institutional source of grace, and as a hierarchical legal entity, in order to receive all who find their way into it.

The picture which Brunner paints of the New Testament community and its gradual transformation into the Church is not a new one. One may almost say that it is as old as the Church itself. From the very beginning of the transformation of the Church, there has always been present within the Church itself a powerful protest against the Church. The course of the 'Great Church' has been paralleled by the history of 'spiritualism', which has fought against all institutionalising and legalising, and sometimes against every concrete historical form of the Church, appealing against all mediations and sacraments, offices, ordinances and institutions to the direct and personal activity of the Holy Spirit. And this spiritualism has usually supported its polemic against the institutional Church by painting an idealised picture of the primitive Christian community, and contrasting it with the present-day Church, in order to call the latter back to the purity of its origins. Behind this romantic vision of the primitive Church lies a particular concept of history: the so-called idea of decline, which in contrast to the idea of progress places the highest achievement of history, not at the end, but the beginning, and consequently sees all historical development not as progress, but as a decline.

The idea of a decline was given a special application by the historian of canon law, Rudolf Sohm, to whom Brunner explicitly refers. According to Sohm, the Church of God is exempt from all law, and canon law contradicts the nature of the Church. Thus in the transformation of the Church into a legal institution Sohm sees a decline, as Harnack did in the development of Christian dogma.

From the historical point of view, Sohm's allegations have long been refuted by scholars. It is not possible to distinguish as he does *pneuma* on the one hand and law on the other. In fact, from the very beginning the Spirit in the Church always brought law into being. Thus, for example, when the apostle Peter was the first to be granted a vision of the risen Christ, this was unquestionably an experience in the Spirit. But this experience in the Spirit at once had legal consequences: it made Peter the head of the congregation of Jerusalem.

Yet one must ask whether Sohm's theory, apart from its inadequate historical foundation, is not of practical value and whether it contains not only the grain of truth which it is acknowledged to have, but even a considerable element of truth. A similar practical value and considerable element of truth also seems to me to be found in Brunner's exposition of the eighteen-hundred-year-old misunderstanding of the Church. This becomes clear at once when we see the theological consequences which he draws from his historical discussion of the relationship between the *ekklesia* and the Church.

His essential conclusion is that none of the existing Churches and sects is identical with the *ekklesia* of the New Testament, but on the other hand none of the existing Churches and sects is without some essential element of the New Testament *ekklesia*. In Brunner's view, nothing would be more false than for the present institutional Churches to attempt to transform themselves by purification or reorganisation into the *ekklesia* of apostolic times. Such an enterprise is impossible, because one cannot 'make' the *ekklesia*, any more than the New Testament *ekklesia* was 'made' in the first place. What can be expected of the present institutional Churches is only that they assist the coming into being of the *ekklesia*, or at least do not hinder it. In other words, the institutional Churches have to serve as instruments of the Holy Spirit, in order that through the preaching of the word of God men may come to believe in Jesus Christ and in this way the *ekklesia*, in the sense of a purely personal fellowship, would come into being. But the present institutional Churches place great obstacles in the way of the achievement of this aim. Brunner finds these obstacles expressed above all in two slogans.

The first slogan is: *Let the Church be the Church*. At the time of the Church's struggle in Germany against Hitler's programme of making the Churches political instruments, this slogan was deeply justified. But in isolation from the urgent needs of that period, it becomes a dangerous slogan, needlessly encouraging the Church in its already prevalent drive towards institutionalisation, and so leading to a new clericalism. Anyone who today insists on 'letting the Church be the Church' runs the risk of cutting himself off from the work of God, whose will is manifestly to destroy in our time the ancient vessels of the Church in which the *ekklesia* has been confined, or at least to supplement them by new vessels. In fact Brunner regards the existing Churches for the time being as indispensable from the point of view of the continuity of preaching and doctrine – but 'they have long since lost the monopoly of preaching Christ and still more that of creating Christian fellowship'.[14] Brunner regards the decisive purpose of the ecclesiastical transformations demanded by our age as 'the liquidation of the fatal inheritance from Constantine', and 'the replacing of the people's Church of Constantine by the pre-Constantinian church of those making confession'.[15] This indicates the direction to be taken in the development of new ecclesiastical forms. As a guiding principle, the false objectivism in the Church has to be overcome, and the reciprocal personal response in the relationship between God and man, which it made impossible, has to be restored. As a step in this direction, Brunner suggests the creation of 'living cells of fellowship' in which the nature of the New Testament *ekklesia* is realised: the unity of the fellowship of Christ in faith and loving brotherhood. Brunner does not discuss whether the national Church is still worth preserving today; what matters is that it should be understood merely as 'an institution for developing a believing congregation'.

The other slogan in which Brunner detects a dangerous tendency of present-day ecclesiasticism is the much-vaunted *rediscovery of the Church*. It is regarded, and no doubt rightly, as one of the most influential causes of the rise of the ecumenical movement in the twentieth century. In spite of this, Brunner has little use for it: this 'rediscovery of the Church' does not signify the rediscovery of the New Testament *ekklesia* which he longs for, but only 'the strengthening of that false ecclesiasticism' which results from setting too high a value upon the Church as an institution. The ecumenical movement should also proceed from the recognition that none of the existing institutional Churches is the *ekklesia* of the New Testament. To the extent to which this understanding gains ground in the Church, the way will be open for mutual respect and fraternal co-operation. And whereas the existence of numerous competing Churches is a scandal, the existence of numerous forms of fellowship in Christ is a necessity. Just as God spoke 'in many ways' in the Bible, so nowadays what is said of God, in view of the manifold varieties of human beings, must also be uttered in many ways: one person is best served by High Church liturgical worship, another by a Salvation Army gathering with hand-clapping and a band. Brunner asks: 'Should not the Lord be able to be in the midst of them in both cases?'[16]

Once again it is Brunner's concept of the Church in personal terms which is here in evidence. Thus for him the aim of the ecumenical movement consists not in the institutional *unity* of the Churches, but in their fraternal *fellowship*. Where the aim of ecumenical efforts is the organisational union of Churches which have come into being in the course of history, the false identification of the Church and the *ekklesia* is accepted, and in any Church unions which may take place, the 'more ecclesiastical' type will always prevail over the less ecclesiastical, so that one will ultimately arrive at the 'most ecclesiastical' of all Churches, the Roman Catholic. But where the intended aim is fraternal fellowship, the question of orders and forms becomes immaterial and one can afford to have a variety of them.

Everything that Brunner says about the form of the Church in the past and in the future has a touch of Utopianism. A tendency towards enthusiasm, so easily leading to a purely spiritualising belief, is visible in his one-sided emphasis on the personal and spiritual element in the Church, his contempt for its concrete and historical forms, and his disregard for the sociological conditions in which it exists. Yet one must ask whether the Church itself is entirely free from a tendency to Utopianism in the way it considers its future today. If it is possible for even a leading Lutheran bishop to complain of the 'craze for order' that has broken out in the Church, this is a sign that false objectivism, and therefore institutionalism, has made further progress. And this means that Brunner's work is of even greater contemporary importance than at the time when it was written.

In his struggle against the objectivism which has recently come to prevail in theology and in the Church, Brunner does not even spare his friend Karl Barth. He reproaches him with having lapsed into a 'new orthodoxy' and 'scholasticism'. He sees the reason for this 'change' in Barth in a shift that occurred in his understanding of faith, similar to that which took place very soon in the early Church, and repeated itself later in Protestant orthodoxy. Brunner believes that he can even pinpoint chronologically this shift in Barth's understanding of faith. In his view, it dates from the year 1924, when Barth took over the *natus ex virgine* – 'born of the Virgin Mary' – from the early Church. Here Barth replaced the truth of God, which encounters man and authenticates itself in man's conscience, by a 'supernatural fact, which "must be believed" on the strength of authority'.[17]

Since then, Barth has been attracted more and more strongly by what is objective, that is, by the object of faith. He has displayed less and less understanding of the identity of subject and object in faith, which was so important for the Reformers in their counter-attack on scholasticism. Whereas Luther never ceases to stress that 'God and faith are lumped together', in Barth the link between God and faith threatens to break apart. Instead of pondering the mystery of the threefold aspect of

Christian existential life, faith, love and hope, he cast aside the familiar warning of the Reformers and devoted hundreds of pages to the mystery of the divine Trinity. Once upon a time Barth was right in beginning the battle with an attack on the subjectivism of Schleiermacher. But he himself has now gone to the opposite extreme, and his own objectivism is as removed from the central position of the message of the Bible and of the Reformers as the subjectivism of Schleiermacher.

Is Brunner right in this criticism of Barth? Has Barth really undergone a theological *volte-face*? What happened in the meantime?

CHAPTER FOUR

GOD SPEAKS ABOUT HIMSELF

The humanity of God

In 1956, Karl Barth read another paper in the same room in Aarau in which almost forty years earlier he had disputed with his teacher Adolf von Harnack. The place was the same, but the theme entirely different; this time, Barth's subject was the 'humanity of God'.[1] This gave him the opportunity for a critical examination of the change which he and his friends had brought about in the theology of that time. Their theme had then been the deity of God.

Barth once again explicitly expressed his allegiance to the theological 'turning-point' which had been reached at that time. This 'campaign for an abrupt break', with its decided critical and polemical character, had been necessary in the face of a theological tradition two or three centuries old, which had forgotten the deity of God, and magnified man at the expense of God. The theology of that time was 'religionistic', 'anthropocentric' and 'humanistic'. What did it know and say about the deity of God? Its theme was not 'God in action' but 'the action upon man'. And when it spoke of God, this again simply meant that it spoke of man 'in a more solemn tone of voice'. An adequate response to this total perversion could not be provided by a further change of emphasis within the traditional pattern of theological inquiry; a complete change of direction was necessary if the Church was not to come to grief. Thus the deity of God was discovered as the theme dominating the Bible. It was a true word, and one which had to be maintained without qualification, but it was not the final word, nor the whole of the matter. Moreover, it was uttered 'without love'; people 'had their ears boxed' with the deity of God. *Senkrecht von oben* (perpendicularly from above), *totaliter aliter*, 'infinite qualitative distinction', 'vacuum', 'the barrier of death', 'mathematical point', 'tangent' – 'What expressions we used – in part taken over and in part newly invented! . . . How we cleared things away! And we did almost nothing but clear away. . . . Did not the whole thing frequently seem more like the report of an enormous execution than the message of the Resurrection, which was its real aim?' There seemed to be only one way in the

Bible, that from above to below, from God to man, and no way from below to above, from man to God. In retrospect Barth was able to understand the suspicion harboured by some of his contemporaries at that time, that here Schleiermacher was being stood upon his head for a change, and God magnified at the expense of man. It was 'all a bit too harshly inhuman'.[2]

At that time, some forty years ago, Barth and his friends would have been embarrassed if they had been required to speak of the *humanity* of God: 'We should have suspected evil implications in this topic.'[3] The divinity of God which had just been rediscovered had displaced the humanity of God 'from the centre to the periphery, from the emphasised principal main clause to the less emphasised subordinate clause'. That is, this insight was still too new and too recent; it had not yet been thoroughly thought out to its conclusion. This was the work which Barth carried out in the intervening years. He continued along the path on which he had set out after the First World War. And thus from the knowledge of the deity of God he arrived at the knowledge of the humanity of God: 'Who God is and what He is in His deity He proves and reveals not in a vacuum as a divine being-for-Himself, but precisely and authentically in the fact that He exists, speaks, and acts as the *partner* of man, though of course as the absolutely superior partner. . . . It is precisely God's *deity* which, rightly understood, includes His *humanity*.'[4] The divinity possesses the character of humanity!

This means that the theme of theology changes for Barth. It is concerned not with 'God in Himself' nor with 'man in himself' but with the 'man-encountering God' and 'God-encountering man', with the history 'in which their communion takes place and comes to its fulfilment', with their 'togetherness, their dialogue', their 'covenant'.[5] As early as in the *Epistle to the Romans* Barth described the 'relation between such a God and such a man, and the relation between such a man and such a God' as 'the theme of the Bible and the essence of philosophy'. But at that time he saw this relationship as consisting above all in the distance between God and man, whereas now he sees it as God's approach to man: 'To open up again the abyss closed in Jesus Christ cannot be our task.' Consequently, instead of speaking of 'theology', one must really speak of 'theanthropology'. 'For an abstract doctrine of God has no place in the Christian realm, only a "doctrine of God and of man", a doctrine of the commerce and communion between God and man' . . .[6] Thus in the theology of Barth 'diastasis' is replaced by dialogue, the abyss by partnership, and dialectics by analogy.

This raises the question whether a 'change', or even a 'break', has taken place in Barth's theological development. Barth himself commented on this question several times. The answers he has given have always been much the same: that he has remained basically faithful to the step he took after the First World War. All he has done is to pull out somewhat further the thread that he had tugged out at that time; in the process he has increasingly departed from his one-sided negations, and has 'gradually acquired more and more feeling for the affirmations by and with which we can live and die'.[7] But was not the very theology of crisis which Barth developed after the First World War of even greater contemporary significance after the Second World War? A friend once asked this question of Barth in precisely these terms. He told him how, at the destruction of Würzburg, he recalled the *Epistle to the Romans*, and continued, 'I seem to be like a sentry who has continued to guard the position of 1921, while you have moved beyond it.' Barth answered his friend by saying: 'There is no sense in pursuing such a theological bombardment. It is now time to say "Yes", and out of the same reasoning which obliged me to say "No" at that time.'[8]

A new note now enters into what Barth says about God and man. Everything is advanced more gaily and kindly, with humour rather than irony and sarcasm. Affirmation is everywhere stronger than negation. Other men, and especially Christians and theologians, withdraw in old age and become bitter, harsh and melancholy, but Barth's mood is now milder, kinder, more cheerful, more understanding and more loving. Affirmation has become more important to him than negation, and the message of God's grace more urgent than the message of God's judgement. Thus when Barth gave his last course of lectures in the winter term 1961–62 in Basle, he took the opportunity of this 'swan's song' to give a summing-up for himself and his contemporaries of what he had striven for, learned and championed in the field of Protestant theology, during his five years as a student, his twelve years as a pastor, and his forty years as a professor. He impressed upon the young students of theology that the object of theology possessed 'a definite gradient' and 'an irreversible direction', from 'No' to 'Yes'. And he exhorted them not to let the 'Yes' be overwhelmed by the 'No', not to be more interested in hell than in heaven, and not to be more concerned with the godlessness of the children of this world than with the sun of righteousness which has already risen upon them: 'The world knows that it lies in the power of evil – but not that it is upheld on all sides by the loving hands of God.'[9]

The question whether Barth's theology has undergone a 'change' or even a 'break' may be answered in this fashion: Barth's zeal for the deity of God remained unchanged, but the zeal of a prophet has become the zeal of an evangelist. The fire of the divine absolute which blazed in the *Epistle to the Romans* still burns, but it has now come to know the freedom of God as his 'freedom to love', and in this he has found a 'new task', that of 'rethinking and rewording everything I have said before in a new way, that is, as a theology of the grace of God in Jesus Christ'.[10]

The 'Church Dogmatics'

The second phase of Barth's theology has gradually found its final form in the *Kirchliche Dogmatik* (Church Dogmatics). It is Barth's most extensive work, containing his life's endeavour – the reflection and product of a process of thought encompassing half a century. With reference to this immense and consistent achievement of a lifetime, Urs von Balthasar has compared Barth to a climber who has 'unerringly taken one step after another, unobtrusively, with an energy usually displayed nowadays only by technicians, in order to present in the end his completed life's work'.[11]

In 1927, the first draft of his dogmatic theology appeared, under the title *Christliche Dogmatik*. But Barth immediately repudiated it, rewriting it completely; too often he had taken man as his starting-point and therefore, he feared, 'shown reverence to false gods'. In 1932, a new volume appeared, now entitled *Church Dogmatics*. Barth justified his change of title as an indication of his desire to anticipate the struggle against the indiscriminate use of the word 'Christian', he wanted to stress the fact that 'dogmatics is not a "free" science, but one bound to the sphere of the Church, where and where alone it is possible, and sensible'.[12]

Since then volume after volume of the *Church Dogmatics* has appeared, up to now ten volumes, 8,719 pages in all, some of them in small print (the other works and writings of Barth are of approximately the same bulk). But the work is not yet complete. It has long been a joke among theologians that God will not let Barth die before he has finished his *Dogmatics*, because God himself is curious to learn everything about himself. Barth, however, no longer expects to finish his work. Nevertheless, his *Church Dogmatics* cannot be considered an unfinished torso.

That the 'Barthians' praise it highly and make it the subject of lecture courses may be a foregone conclusion. But the Lutheran theologian Gerhard Gloege hails the *Church Dogmatics* as 'one of the greatest works of the modern intellect, and perhaps the most important achievement of systematic theology in the twentieth century', and the Danish theologian Regin Prenter, also a Lutheran, considers it 'perhaps the most powerful system which history has yet seen'.[13]

In *Church Dogmatics*, the author of the *Epistle to the Romans* has become a systematic theologian. He has mapped the design of a comprehensive dogmatic system. To a large extent it consists of biblical exegesis, combined with an astounding knowledge of the history of dogma and theology from every century of Church history. Everything is set out with broad strokes on a wide canvas, and expressed with exceptional eloquence, often in complex turns of phrase, elaborate sentences, and long rolling periods. If Bultmann and Tillich draw the reader into a clear and strictly ordered movement of thought, Barth seduces and carries him forward by the current of his work.

Barth's theology has frequently been described as 'beautiful' in the aesthetic sense, and not only with reference to the external features of his style. Its beauty derives from the passionate involvement of the writer in what he is describing. Untouched by any concern for modernity or success, Barth is solely and completely absorbed in the greatness of his subject. This subject is the universality and irresistibility of the revelation of God's grace. He seeks to testify to this before men, and so a triumphant note sounds in his style. It is the superabundance of the grace of God which makes Barth's language superabundant. Brunner once asserted that Barth must be regarded not as a 'systematic theologian' so much as 'a theological poet'.[14] It cannot be said, however, that Barth is not a systematic theologian; but it is true that there is something of the theological poet in him. Barth reiterates the revelation of God as in a poem. There is something 'playful' in his *Dogmatics*, not in the obvious sense of the word, but in the sense in which it is said of the wisdom of God that it rejoices in the earth and delights in the sons of men. The element of the purposeless, of the wholly gratuitous, in play approximates it to the praise of God.

Barth's style is the outward expression of his theological *method*. He arrived at his theological method between 1927 and 1932, between *Christian Dogmatics* and *Church Dogmatics*. During this period he wrote his book on Anselm of Canterbury's proof of the existence of God (1931); of all his books this one, he said, was 'written with the greatest

love', but would be 'read the least'; in this work, and not in his *No!
An Answer to Emil Brunner*, he sees his theology 'develop to greater
depth', and take a new departure after the first phase of his theological
development.[15] Barth's own view is that in his *Church Dogmatics* he
was merely following through the theological programme laid down
by Anselm of Canterbury and summed up in the sentence: *Fides
quaerens intellectum* – 'faith seeking understanding'. The origin and
object of faith and the understanding it seeks is the revelation of God
in the incarnate Son, to which holy scripture bears witness. This is the
divine reality which Barth seizes hold of and pursues, filling the
'vacuum' of his early period with a positive testimony. Clinging obediently to the witness of holy scripture, he seeks to match his thought to
the divine revelation, and to present it in its inner coherence and strict
intellectual necessity, in order to make it 'intelligible'. Barth's method is
deductive and descriptive, and has no apologetic purpose. It seeks only
to present and describe the word of God; of course he does examine and
criticise, not, however, the word of God itself, but only earlier theological presentations of it. In a television interview in Paris in 1964
Barth replied to a question about his work on *Church Dogmatics* by
comparing himself to a man who constantly goes round and round the
same mountain, observing it first from one side and then from the other,
and asking others to go round the mountain with him to be shown its
beauties.[16]

If the task of the theologian consisted solely of going tirelessly round
and round the revelation of God, as round a high mountain, and
showing its beauty first from one side and then from another, then his
proper place is always clear: he is always at the *foot* of the mountain,
beneath the scriptures of the Bible. And thus as a systematic theologian,
Barth seeks to be nothing more than a scriptural theologian. When in
1938 the American journal *Christian Century* asked him whether and
to what extent his thought had changed in the preceding ten years, that
is, in the years in which the early volumes of *Church Dogmatics* were
published, he answered: 'No, my thought has not altered, at least in so
far as I have been able to carry out my intention. Its object, its source
and its yardstick are now, as before, *not* what is called religion, but the
word of God, which speaks in the Holy Scripture *to man*.' And he went
on to say that he hoped to be found 'stubbornly unchanged' in this
matter to the end of his life.[17]

That Barth has remained 'stubbornly unchanged' in this matter up
to the present day will not be disputed. One must rather ask whether

he has not become even more 'stubborn'. The dangerous tendencies, which he displayed from the very first, of failing to distinguish strictly enough between the revelation of God and the words of the Bible, of simply identifying the two and taking them uncritically as 'word for word the same', have rather increased than otherwise in the course of his general 'more pronounced affirmation' in *Church Dogmatics*. Barth seems to be even further from the historical understanding of the Bible than in his early period. Admittedly, he repeats his earlier affirmation that the Bible is written by men, and that therefore historical criticism is fundamentally justified, but in practice he makes no use of this knowledge. Indeed Barth is perfectly capable of virtually withdrawing any justification for historical criticism which he allows in principle and of giving his support to an a-historical way of thinking: 'We must dismiss and resist to the very last any idea of the inferiority or untrustworthiness or even worthlessness of a "non-historical" depiction and narration of history. This is in fact only a ridiculous and middle-class habit of the modern Western mind which is supremely phantastic in its chronic lack of imaginative phantasy.'[18]

Barth also completely rejects not only historical criticism of the Bible, but also theological criticism of the content of the Bible. He ironically compares such critics with schoolteachers who look at their pupils' books over their shoulders, and give them good, fair or bad marks. Barth does not hesitate to assert that even 'the smallest, strangest, simplest, or obscurest' of the biblical writers has an 'advantage' over all later theologians, because he is placed 'in direct confrontation' with the object about which he is thinking and writing.[19] But is this really tenable? Can one seriously assert that the authors of the Pastoral Epistles, or of 2 Peter and the Epistle of Jude, for instance – and certainly not they alone – found themselves in a 'direct confrontation' and therefore in a fundamentally different situation from all who follow them? And should not what they and all biblical authors wrote be measured against the 'cause' that was their concern as well? Was it not consequently necessary to distinguish, not only between the revelation of God and the word of the Bible, but also between the words of individual biblical witnesses and that revelation? Anyone who, as Barth does (or at least risks doing), regards everything in the Bible as equally valid, should not be surprised if his contemporaries soon come to regard the whole Bible as equally invalid.

In the exposition of revelation, Barth's aim is so one-sided, and so unswervingly directed towards the object which he is expounding, that the expositor is disregarded, and to take him into account is even considered harmful. Barth rejects the extreme subjectivist principle of the nineteenth century: 'I myself as a Christian am the most proper object of knowledge to myself as a theologian.' He opposes to it the equally extreme objectivist thesis: 'I and my personal Christianity do not belong to the *kerygma* to be declared by me.' Excluding all subjectivity in this way, Barth appeals to the fact that with the exception of its first words, 'I believe', the Apostles' Creed says nothing about the subjective act of faith, and only speaks of the objective *credo*.[20] Yet in advancing this argument, Barth has recognised the importance of the position occupied by the words 'I believe' in the Creed. They are not merely 'the first words' in the numerical sense, but the sign outside the brackets, determining everything that comes within the brackets.

Anyone who has scant regard for the subjective side of the Christian faith must reject completely whatever goes by the name of *religion*. Thus one finds in the *Church Dogmatics* the same firm repudiation that we find in Barth's early period, at the time of the *Epistle to the Romans*: 'We begin by stating that religion is unbelief. It is a concern, indeed, we must say that it is the one great concern, of godless man.'[21] Nor is there a divine 'original revelation' as posited by Althaus; it is 'a purely empty concept, or one that can be filled only by illusions'. The God in whom Christians believe and whom they confess is 'not a particular instance within a class' – '*Deus non est in genere*' – but is '*a priori* the fundamentally Other'. Thus *before* revelation there is no general concept of the divine, and *after* revelation, there is only the 'most radical "twilight of the Gods" . . . Olympus and Valhalla decrease in population when the message of the God who is the one and only God is really known and believed.'[22] In Barth's critique of religion there is no room for what the modern age calls 'tolerance': apart from God, there are only false Gods, and apart from faith there is only superstition or unbelief. All this is by no mean expressed in abstract terms only, but made graphic with vivid details taken from the contemporary background, as in Barth's critique of religion after the First World War. Here, however, the background is different. Barth's comments on religion in *Church Dogmatics* were written mainly in the Hitler period. Thus there is the passage: 'It was on the truth of the sentence that God is One that the "Third Reich" of Adolf Hitler would make shipwreck.'[23] Here the dogmatic theologian Barth became a prophet, and his prophecy has been fulfilled before our very eyes.

In *Church Dogmatics* Barth's critique of religion is no less radical than in his earlier works, but its position has shifted: it is now only a by-product. While in the *Epistle to the Romans* the dialectical movement constantly threatens to come to a stop at the negative pole, negation is now merely the feebler obverse of the positive statement. The profound darkness which Barth sees surrounding religion is only the shadow within the excessively bright light radiated by the revelation of God. Barth's concern is to show that revelation is wholly and completely the word of God alone, and it is this assertion that he seeks to defend – to the glory of God and for the salvation of man.

It is at this point that the *virgin birth* finds its place in Barth's theology. It is given such preponderance because it documents the total elimination of man. Man of course also enters here, but only in the form of the *virgin Mary*; that is, of a 'non-willing, non-achieving, non-creative, non-sovereign . . . human being', 'not as God's fellow-worker . . . but only . . . in his readiness for God' and that only because God has already revealed himself to him. 'Behold, the handmaid of the Lord; be it unto me according as Thou hast said' – 'Such is human co-operation in this matter, that and only that!'[24]

Christological universalism

Anyone seeking to understand Barth's dogmatic system cannot proceed by the usual course from general principles to particular instances, but must follow the reverse process and begin with the particular – with a wholly concrete fact. This wholly concrete fact is the revelation of God in Jesus Christ: 'When holy scripture speaks of God, it concentrates our attention and thoughts upon one single point. . . . We may look closer and ask: Who and what is the God who is to be known at the point upon which holy scripture concentrates our attention and thoughts? . . . then from first to last the Bible directs us to the name of Jesus Christ. . . . When they are directed to Jesus Christ, then we see God, and our thoughts are fixed on him.'[25]

The beginning and the end of all knowledge of God consist not in a universal and abstract concept of the divine, but in the particular figure and concrete being of Jesus Christ. Who God is, and what is divine, and also who man is, and what is human, cannot be discovered by free inquiry, but can be learned only there where God has revealed himself. If God is called 'Father' and 'Almighty', our understanding of these terms must not proceed from our knowledge of fatherhood, power and love among men, deducing conclusions from human experience and applying them to the fatherly love and omnipotence of God. The reverse is applicable; that God is the 'Father' and 'the Almighty' is revealed to us in Jesus Christ alone, and everything that we know about fatherhood, power and love among men can be understood only by this reference, as an emanation and image of the omnipotence and the fatherly love of God revealed in Jesus Christ.

Thus there takes place in Barth's *Church Dogmatics* an unparalleled christological concentration,[26] unprecedented to this degree in the history of the Church and of doctrine. For Barth the concept of the 'Word of God' becomes increasingly identified with the concrete name of Jesus Christ. Barth's christocentricity is unparalleled. The whole of theology becomes christology – exposition, unfolding and commentary on what is contained in this name, in this single event in which God and man are united. For Barth, there exists no independent theme in theology outside christology, neither directly nor indirectly. Christology determines everything; not merely the doctrine of justification, atonement and redemption, but also the doctrines of creation, man, election, the Church and the last things, and indeed not merely all human knowledge of God and of his saving word, but also all human knowledge and wisdom whatsoever, the total reality of the world. If Barth is praised as a great systematic theologian, and his dogmatic theology is compared to a cathedral because of the coherence and beauty of its architectonic structure, this is due to its 'radical christocentricity': christology constitutes the centre of the whole edifice, and draws every detail into a single great unity. If ever *solus Christus* applied to any theology, it applies to Barth's *Church Dogmatics*; here we are as it were surrounded by Jesus Christ on every side.

But in making Jesus Christ the beginning and the end, Barth does not start with Christ's incarnation or with the events in Palestine in the years A.D. 1–30. His concern is with Christ's pre-existence, with the events that went before, in eternity, in heaven. In other words, in considering Jesus Christ, he does not begin as Luther advised 'below', 'in the flesh', with the man Jesus of Nazareth, but 'above', with the Son of God, who is the second person of the Trinity. Whereas we said earlier that God's fatherhood cannot be deduced from fatherhood as it is on earth, but only from God's revelation of himself to us as the Father, a more precise formulation is now called for: God is Father primarily by being the Father of his Son, and it is only as such that he is and reveals himself to be our Father. This implies also that the thought of Barth,

by being christological, is always and at the same time trinitarian. As
the doctrine of Jesus Christ his dogmatic theology is the doctrine of the
Trinity.

The point of view, then, which Barth adopts is set so high in heaven
that he can survey the whole panorama of the divine history of salvation. From this height Jesus Christ appears not merely as a point in
history, extending over thirty years, but as an event encompassing the
whole history of what has taken place between God and man, beginning
in eternity and extending into eternity. In him everything in heaven and
upon earth is concentrated, the beginning and the end, the first and the
last, not only time, but also eternity. In time and on earth, God merely
made known to man what he had consummated in eternity, by a decree
anticipating everything that is in time.[27]

This 'christological concentration' leads to that mode of thought in
Barth which he himself has termed *intensive universalism*. It is both
intensive and universal, because it sees the entire history of the world
and of salvation as comprehended in a single point, and develops it
from this point. That God and man are united in Jesus Christ is the
central fact, the basis and explanation of everything that is decreed in
eternity and takes place within time. We have already said that Barth
is unparalleled in his christocentricity; he is also unparalleled as a universalist. Both aspects may be summed up in the term *christological
universalism*.

Barth's christological universalism shows the bent of his theology:
it is dominated throughout by the freedom of God to love, and hence
is orientated towards grace. Barth asserts the absolute *priority of the
grace of God:* 'This is the place and the only place from which as
Christians we can think forwards and backwards, from which a Christian knowledge of both God and man is possible.'[28] This absolute priority of grace can be seen in the way in which Barth defines the relationship between *creation and covenant*, that is, between the order of nature
and the order of grace, which leads him to the recurring theme with
variations: 'Creation is the external basis of the covenant, the covenant
is the internal basis of creation.' Man is assigned the point of view from
which he is to contemplate the whole work of God: he is not to look
first on creation, turning his eyes to the redemption afterwards, but
from the start is to regard the creation from the point of view of the
grace of God in Jesus Christ. Barth opposes the concept of an independent creation; the mystery of creation can only be known and understood on the basis of atonement, of redemption. He never wearies of

describing the covenant of God with man as the goal of all history, emphasising the pre-eminence of grace over nature and creation: the history
of the covenant of grace is 'the scope of creation'; the aim of creation is
'the history of the covenant of grace instituted by God'; the creation is
'one long preparation'. Its nature 'is simply its equipment for grace';
creatureliness is 'pure promise'. This means that the world 'was created
and sustained by the little child that was born in Bethlehem, by the
Man who died on the Cross of Golgotha, and the third day rose again'.
Thus grace overshadows the whole of creation, and the whole of
history is 'a way under the sign of the man Jesus Christ'.[29]

In all this Barth reverses the conventional order in which redemption
follows creation and grace follows nature. In God's plan, redemption
was willed first, and creation second. God created the world for the
sake of grace, and did not institute grace for the sake of the world.
Barth can say first: 'The covenant is as old as creation itself,' and then
correct himself at once, within the same paragraph, stating: 'The
covenant is not only quite as old as creation; it is older.' Barth himself
calls this 'a wonderful inversion of our whole thought', and advises that
we should not allow ourselves to be put off by the difficulty in the
concept of time which may arise from it. It is true that within the realm
of created reality, creation is the first work of God, and redemption the
second, but measured by the eternal decree of God creation does not
precede redemption, but follows it.[30] Seen from above – and this will
always be Barth's viewpoint – creation only 'sets the stage for the story
of the covenant of grace': 'This was foreseen in the eternal election of
Jesus Christ, and specifically called into being in the beginning and as
itself the beginning of all things, to be the theatre and setting, the location and background, of the ordinary and extraordinary mediation of
his life and work.'[31]

Thus grace does not represent something which was later added to
creation, as though it were only the subsequent reaction of God to the
'incident' of sin which he had not provided for; rather, based on the
eternal purpose of salvation, the divine 'original decree', grace was
attendant to creation from the first as its goal, and is therefore antecedent
to creation. God does not first will and create the world and man, in
order to destine them afterwards to salvation; the reverse is the case.
Because God has resolved by his free love, before all time, to exercise
grace, and in order to provide an object and recipient of this grace and
a partner for himself, he creates, sustains and rules man and the world
for this reason alone, with this sole aim and for this purpose. The

revelation of God in Jesus Christ, resolved in eternity and already carried out, is the unique divine work, and all other divine works serve to prepare it, to accompany it and to bring it to its consummation.[32] Consequently, creation – nature, history, the universe and man – has no value or meaning in itself, but receives its value and meaning solely from the future revelation and redemption: 'And if we inquire into the *goal* of creation, the object of the whole, the object of heaven and earth and all creation, I can only say that it is to be the theatre of his glory. The meaning is that God is being glorified.' 'The meaning of the being and existence of the world created by God is to be the fitting sphere and setting of the great acts in which God expresses and declares himself, i.e. his overflowing love for man, establishing, maintaining, executing and fulfilling his covenant with him.'[33]

The aim of God's creation also guarantees that it is good. Whatever grievances and complaints it is possible to raise against the world, its goodness is unassailable: 'What God has created is good as such.' To recognise this, man must not only know from his own experience what is good or bad, but must also bear in mind for what purpose God has made the world. God has made the world to be the theatre of his glory, and man to be the witness of this glory. And 'for the purpose for which God made the world it is also good'.[34]

'The theatre of the glory of God' – this quotation from Calvin repeated here several times may virtually be regarded as the motto of the second phase of Barth's theology. The theme of the *Epistle to the Romans* was *finitum non capax infiniti* – the finite cannot comprehend the infinite, time cannot comprehend eternity. That of the *Church Dogmatics* is Calvin's description of creation, which Barth constantly repeats, as the *theatrum gloriae Dei*, the theatre of the glory of God. The two phrases are not mutually exclusive, but complementary. It remains true that the finite cannot comprehend the infinite, and that God does not descend into this world; but this world is the stage upon which God represents the drama of his revelation in Jesus Christ, which he has decreed in eternity – for his glory and for the salvation of man. The salvation, the task and the distinction of man consists in the fact that he is allowed to be present where God is glorified, as a spectator and witness of the majesty of God, affirming and repeating what God has said himself of his activity and his creation: 'Behold, it was very good.'

The same christological universalism which compels Barth to reverse the usual order of creation and redemption also enables him to define the relationship between the law and the gospel in a new and different way. He replaces the traditional order of the law followed by the gospel by a new order, that of *the gospel followed by the law*. Here again, the inversion is brought about by the pre-eminence of grace, which domin-ates everything. Because the 'special and direct content' of the gospel is grace, it is bound to take priority over the law. Just as redemption precedes creation, so that I must cling to this redemption in order to understand the mystery of the creation, I can likewise only perceive the law of God where his will is visible to me as grace: and this is 'in the carrying out of the will of God at Bethlehem, Capernaum, and Tiberias, in Gethsemane, on Golgotha, and in the Garden of Joseph of Arima-thea'. What happened in these places is pure grace. But when God's grace is *revealed*, the law too is revealed: for what God does *for us* is always and at the same time what God demands of us. Thus God does not speak to us first through the law and then in the gospel, but by speaking to us in the gospel, he simultaneously proclaims to us his law. Once again it is grace which is triumphant in this part of Barth's theology. Consequently his principle that 'creation is the external basis of the covenant, the covenant is the internal basis of creation', can now be rephrased as 'the law is nothing other than the necessary form of the gospel, the *content* of which is grace'.[35]

In his skilful interpretation of Barth's theology, Urs von Balthasar compares Barth's christocentric thought to an hour-glass.[36] Just as in the hour-glass all the sand has to go through a constriction in the middle in order to pass from the upper half to the lower half, so in Barth the whole reality of the world is related to the central event of the revelation of Christ. This is Barth's 'christological concentration', and apart from it he sees no link between God and man. And just as in the hour-glass the sand only runs from the top to the bottom, so the revelation of God moves only in one direction, from above to below. But just as in the hour-glass the movement from above to below starts off a movement *in the opposite direction*, since the sand in the lower half *rises*, so the revelation of God produces a movement in the opposite direction: it draws the whole reality of the world towards it and into it – this is Barth's 'intensive universalism'. But everything depends upon the one narrow passage in the centre. This is where things happen: everything must pass through it, but it also sets up a relationship, an analogy. Here we encounter analogy as the decisive new form of thought which is provided by Barth's christological universalism, and which in the *Church Dogmatics* takes the place of the dialectic found in the *Epistle to the Romans*.

The method of analogy

Analogy, equivalence, parable, image, likeness, impression, reflection, adumbration, allusion, correspondence, similarity, repetition, testimony, sign, demonstration – concepts of this kind are already to be found in the *Epistle to the Romans*, but as allusion only, vague and unclear. But in the *Church Dogmatics* they cohere, and receive an unequivocal and dominating meaning. They all point towards the same fact: the realm of creation does not confront the realm of grace indifferently, but everything contained in it is a symbol, figure, and sign. Between God and man, nature and grace, creation and redemption, prevails an all-embracing *analogy*: 'In great and little things alike, world-occurrence is a reflection and likeness [of the events of salvation].'[37]

It almost seems as though Barth has forgotten everything he previously thought and said, and that for a change he has stood himself on his head. But this is not the case. In the period in which he developed the method of analogy, Barth continued to insist that no way of any kind leads from man to God. Analogy is not based on some quality or disposition of man, or on any participation by God and man in the same being, from which man might derive the capacity to judge God by himself. To infer from the being of man the being of God on the basis of a pre-established general concept of being, is attempted by the so-called *analogia entis*. For this very reason Barth strictly rejects it, asserting that the *analogia entis* is the 'invention of the anti-Christ', and the determining reason why one cannot become a Roman Catholic (all other possible reasons for not becoming Catholic he considers as 'short-sighted and lacking in seriousness').[38]

If for Barth an analogy exists between God and man, it is only because God has revealed his divine essence to man; consequently, the analogy never leads from the creature to the creator, but always takes the reverse, irreversible direction, that of analogy from the creator to the creature. The reason why Barth uses the analogical method to an increasing extent, sometimes almost revelling in analogy, is that he is carried away by the concept of the grace of God. His firm repudiation of any *analogia entis* is based not so much on the negative assertion of the infinite distance between God and man, preventing any comparison between creation and creator, as rather positively on the revelation of divine grace, which opens the doors to the knowledge of God and of the world. If there is no path for human knowledge from below to God above, it is not because heaven is so high above earth but because God himself took the initiative and followed the path from above to man below. Whereas Barth earlier dreaded an encroachment on the part of man, he now praises the 'encroachment which has occurred, and still occurs from the side of God'.[39]

In order to stress the distinctive character of his analogical thought, Barth does not use the term *analogia entis*, but speaks of *analogia relationis* or *analogia fidei*, and also of *analogia revelationis*. All these expressions are intended to imply that while an analogy exists between God and the world because there is a *link* between them, it is God who *revealed* this link, and the analogy can consequently only be known in *faith*. The history of salvation cannot be seen and understood in itself, but only in relationship to the history of the world, and on the other hand the history of the world cannot be seen and understood in itself, but only in relationship to the history of salvation. Consequently, the history of salvation is the 'centre' and the 'key', while the history of the world is 'the circumference around that centre', and the 'lock to which that key belongs'.[40]

Barth makes ample use of this key; he handles analogy as a principle which opens the whole world to him. Between heaven and earth he knots as it were an enormous tapestry of correspondences and analogies, reminiscent almost of the medieval *ordo*, that universal divine order which reached from the throne of God down to the lowest regions on earth, and in which everything had its God-appointed place: 'But since within this world there really exists an above and a below confronting one another, since in every breath we take, in every one of our thoughts, in every great and petty experience of our human lives heaven and earth are side by side, greeting each other, attracting and repelling each other and yet belonging to one another, we are, in our existence, of which God is the Creator, a sign and indication, a promise of what ought to happen, in creation and to creation – the meeting, the togetherness, the fellowship and, in Jesus Christ, the oneness of Creator and creature.'[41]

But the full scope and the ultimate background of these analogies is only realised when we recall that Barth's doctrine of Jesus Christ is a doctrine of the Trinity, and that consequently his doctrine of the *analogia relationis* is a doctrine of the relationship of the three divine persons to one another and to the world, applying and perfecting the doctrine of the Trinity of the early Church. Everything that we say about God, all the words and concepts which we use in so doing, are defined by the relationship governing the being of the Trinity itself, and which is made known to us by revelation. By revealing his divine essence to man, God reveals to him the relationship between the Father, the Son and the Holy Spirit; and the relationship between God and man, and God and the world, forms an analogy to the relationship between the three persons of the Trinity. This trinitarian thought is not as new to Barth as it might appear. As early as 1924 – the same year in which according to Brunner he accepted the virgin birth – he wrote to his friend Thurneysen: 'At all costs, the doctrine of the Trinity! If I could get the right key in my hand there, then absolutely everything would come out right . . . [*Zwischen den Zeiten*] will become interesting only when *this* battleship shows its plumes of smoke on the horizon. All our present activities are just engaged in is as yet nothing but skirmishing.'[42]

Since then Barth has taken hold of the trinitarian key he was then longing for, and with its aid he is now able to speculate to his heart's desire. Thus for example, just as God is not dead, passive and inactive in his inner life and essence, but exists as Father, Son and Holy Spirit in an internal relationship and motion, which may well be described as a history, so equally what takes place upon earth as the history of God's dealings with man forms a correspondence and analogy to the historical being, essence and activity of God. Again: the distance between God and the world is nothing other than a figure, image and likeness of the distinction by means of which God is himself Father, Son and Holy Spirit – and the transition, mediation and communication which God allows to come about in the covenant with man is in its turn nothing other than the figure, image and likeness of the union of Father, Son and Holy Spirit. Again, what God does as creator of the world can be seen and understood in the Christian sense only as the reflected splendour of the inner divine relationship between God the Father and the Son, in that God the Father has 'begotten' the Son. Again, the relationship which exists within God himself as Father, Son and Holy Spirit is repeated in the relationship existing in the duality of man and wife; and this relationship and duality of man and wife is an image of the relationship between Christ and his Church.[43]

Thus as Barth's *Church Dogmatics* proceeds from one volume to another, the method of dialectics is replaced by the method of analogy. Guided by the stage direction in the Bible, 'On earth as it is in heaven', Barth draws a portrait of the world and of man which is analogous to his portrait of God.

The heart of all the analogies which Barth presents is the *analogy between God and man* – for in fact everything which God has done, he has done for the sake of man. The basis of the analogy between God and man is that Jesus Christ is present and revealed as true *God* in true *man*; the statements which theology makes about man must be made on the analogy of this fact. What true man is can only be derived from the human existence of Jesus Christ. The incarnation of Christ includes not only '"Behold your God!" but also *Ecce homo!*' It is not only 'the mirror of the fatherly heart of God' but is also and at the same time 'the mirror of the particularity of man'. That is why Christian thought about man must not proceed from the general concept of humanity, but from the concrete fact 'that one man among all others is this creaturely being, the man Jesus'. This is the *ontological determination of man*. It is from this that everything else follows: 'If in the midst of all other men, one is the man Jesus, then every man as such is the fellow man of Jesus.' It is part of the nature of every man, and therefore of human nature, that in Jesus he possesses his 'Neighbour, Companion and Brother'. He may not know this, or if he knows it, may not admit its truth, so that he protests against it; but 'he has no choice in the matter': 'We cannot break free from this Neighbour. He is definitively our Neighbour. And we as men are those among whom Jesus is also a man.'[44]

For Barth, the ontological determination of man by means of the human existence of Jesus is so decisive, and its effect as an analogy so universal, that he allows it to lead him to such dangerous theological paradoxes as: 'Godlessness is not, therefore, a possibility, but an onto-logical impossibility for man.' Barth's words here must not be taken at their face value. Obviously he knows that there is sin and godless human existence. But he arms himself against this objection simply by new affirmations: 'Sin itself is not a possibility but an ontological impossi-bility for man. We are actually with Jesus, i.e., with God. This means that our being does not include but excludes sin. To be in sin, in godless-ness, is a mode of being contrary to our humanity.' And if to this affirmation we once again advance the objection that sin and godless-ness do in fact belong to humanity, Barth points once again to the onto-logical determination of man, and assures us that 'the man who is with Jesus . . . is with God. If he denies God, he denies himself . . . He chooses his own impossibility.'[45]

Of course Barth's procedure here is not logical. He is even overstep-ping the limit laid down in the Bible, and is talking in a way which is theologically 'rash'. But it is when theologians speak 'rashly' that they utter their real message. They are known not by their words, but by the ideas that move them. The idea that moves Barth here, as everywhere, is the 'event' of Christ in everything that takes place. In the incarnation of Christ, God chose man to be his partner and companion in the covenant – for Barth this event is so determinative that he can see all human existence only as an analogy to it: 'The incarnation of Christ is the great glorification of man. In it, every man is ennobled in principle.'[46]

The analogy between God and man is continued in the relationship between one man and another. Our relationship to our fellow men must also be orientated solely in accordance with the ontological determination of man, which is that in the midst of all other men, one is the man Jesus, and that therefore every man as such is the fellow man of Jesus. At this point in Barth's work, the ethical test, as it were, follows from the dogmatic example. Just as he knows that every man, with no respect for persons, is regarded by God as one with whom he is united in Jesus Christ, he desires that every man, without regard for persons, should also be regarded in the same way from the human point of view: 'On the basis of the eternal will of God we have to think of *every human being*, even the oddest, most villainous or miserable, as one to whom Jesus Christ is Brother and God is Father; and we have to deal with him on this assumption. . . . On the basis of the knowledge of the humanity of God no other attitude to any kind of fellow man is possible.'[47] Barth's political ethics, with their sharp rejection of any anti-semitism, racial discrimination, or ideological double-think, are founded on this theological rock. This we shall discuss in another context.

Everything that Barth says about man, about the humanity of God, and about the fellowship of man, is summed up for him in the concept which has increasingly become a favourite of his, that of the *humanism of God*. At the *Rencontres Internationales* in Geneva, in late summer, 1949, where representatives of different faculties and schools of thought gathered to speak on humanism, Barth chose to speak of the 'humanism of God': 'The Christian gospel is the gospel of the humanism of God.' Against man's attempt to create his own humanity, Barth opposes the 'humanity of God', as 'the source and norm of all human standards and human dignity' – but for him the humanity of God does not present an attribute of God which is universal, immediately graspable and constantly available; rather it emanates from the self-revelation of the triune God in the incarnation of Christ: 'It is from this point of view that we look upon man.' In this lecture, Barth's friendly and triumphant tone is shaded by a touch of resignation. He does not really expect that his audience, largely agnostic or atheist, will accept the idea of the

humanism of God which he is propounding; while for his part he is not
able to regard what is nowadays put forward as the 'new humanism' as
anything really new at all – 'so far as it has made itself known up to the
present time, it displays a remarkably sceptical and sad countenance'.
Barth is probably right in both views.[48]

It is astonishing how positively Barth can think and write about man
– not *in spite of* his christological concentration, but precisely *because of*
his christological concentration. It does not reduce man's stature, but
reveals to him his true greatness for the first time; it does not see man
as swallowed up by the sheer divine absorption of God but maintains
man's independence with regard to God. That is why Barth is so fond
of the concept of 'partnership' and the biblical image of the 'game', in
which of course the creator has the first move, but the creature then
takes his turn: 'And so "man goeth forth unto his work and to his
labour until the evening" (Ps. 104: 23); to which it belongs that he can
use his senses and understanding to perceive that two and two make
four, and to write poetry, and to think and to make music, and to eat
and drink, and to be filled with joy and often with sorrow, and to
love and sometimes to hate, and to be young and to grow old, and all
within his own experience and activity, affirming it not as half a man
but as a whole man, with head uplifted and the heart free and the conscience at rest: "O Lord, how manifold are *thy* works (Ps. 104: 24)."
It is only the heathen gods who envy man. The true God . . . *allows*
him to be the thing for which he created him.'[49] There is hardly a single
Lutheran theologian who would write such words today – and it is all
the more remarkable that they come from the pen of a Reformed theologian. In this context, Barth can think of Calvin only with regret and a
note of criticism: 'Would that Calvin had energetically pushed ahead on
this point. . . . His Geneva would not then have become such a gloomy
affair. His letters could then not have contained so much bitterness.'[50]

Barth's personal experience during these years provides an interesting
parallel. The decade which brought not only the first volumes of the
Church Dogmatics, with their christological concentration, but also the
beginning of the conflict within the Church, and Barth's own dismissal,
was also that in which he found the time and the interest to concern
himself more than he had before with general intellectual history, to
become receptive to classical antiquity as never before in the course of
two journeys to Italy, to develop a new relationship to Goethe, to read
numerous novels (he does not fail to make special mention of 'the
splendid products of recent English detective literature') and to become

a bad but passionate horseman: 'Never in my life have I lived so happily in the world as in the very period that brought with it, in my theology, the concentration which to many people seems so monastic.'[51]

We must not invalidate all of Barth's theological and personal testimonies by a simple reference to Barth's undoubtedly optimistic attitude to life. Certainly this plays its part in Barth's theology, but the cosmic optimism of Barth's interpretation of the world and of man is not determined by psychological and biographical particulars, but by the substance of his theological understanding. Because Barth sees and understands the world and man from the highest and most central viewpoint, he succeeds in drawing the whole cosmos, both heaven and earth, into the process of Christ's revelation, weaving it into a net of analogies. In this process he portrays startling theological visions and religious landscapes of extraordinary beauty. It is at this point more than any other that Barth's theology can also be seen to be beautiful in the aesthetic sense. But Regin Prenter, himself christocentric, and profoundly in sympathy with the beauty of Barth's theology, rightly asks whether this is really 'the beauty of divine truth' or 'the beauty of the inventiveness of human genius'.[52] Without attempting to ascertain whether the beauty of divine truth may not also be present, we may be certain that Barth's universal analogical thought is the expression of the inventive power of a religious genius. Sometimes, on reading Barth, what comes involuntarily to mind is the scene in the Acts in which the Procurator Festus answers Paul, who has defended himself in a long speech: 'Paul, you are mad, your great skill is turning you mad.' This seems to be Barth's fate: he resists all religion and every assertion of religious genius in life, and yet he is a religious genius himself, both in the *Church Dogmatics* and in the *Epistle to the Romans*.

But the question is whether Karl Barth himself may not have been led astray by his 'great skill'. The perilously great skill of Barth lies in his unrestrained application of the analogical method. This is a consequence of his starting-point in christology, the rightness of which no one nowadays would challenge. Barth's error, however, lies in over-stressing his christological lever. The consequence is that he does not leave sufficient breathing space between the creation and the redemption, so that the reality of the redemption overwhelms the reality of creation – nature, history, the world and man – like a tidal wave, sweeping away any independent foothold it possesses. Barth himself asked: 'How will it stand with us when we are alongside Jesus Christ and follow him?' and 'Can the reconciliation of the world with God accomplished in him consist in anything but the dissolution of the world?'[53] Of course Barth is only speculating here, pushing an idea to its ultimate conclusion. But this ultimate conclusion reveals a fault, which, though concealed, is present from the first. No theologian who has studied the Bible will disagree with Barth when he asserts that the history of salvation is the 'centre' and that the history of the world is the 'circumference' around it. But every theologian who has studied the Bible will disagree with Barth when he considers the history of the world as devoid of any meaning or value of its own, serving only as the analogy, image, sign, correspondence and adumbration of the history of salvation, and that this is so from all eternity. The same Barth who in his struggle against natural theology, with its general concept of the divine, emphasises so strongly the concrete and historical figure of Jesus Christ, makes use of Jesus Christ in his analogical thought as a universal and supra-temporal principle which can reveal to him the reality of the whole universe – with the result that the reality of the universe evaporates.

Two examples can be adduced in what Barth says about suffering and what he says about marriage. Barth sees all *suffering* in the world as an analogy to the suffering of Christ: '*Here* there was suffering.' By comparison with it, all other suffering is 'unreal suffering'. 'Only from this standpoint, by sharing in the suffering He suffered, can we recognise the fact and the cause of suffering everywhere in the creaturely cosmos, secretly and openly.'[54] Certainly in pastoral exhortation one may venture to place human suffering in the light of the suffering of Christ, and to interpret it as a participation in that suffering. But has one the right to turn this into a universal truth and to assert that all suffering in the world, past, present and to come, is, apart from Christ, 'unreal'? Like the whole of creation, all suffering in creation has its own dignity and claims our respect. There is a Christian excess which threatens to turn into inhumanity.

The second example is that of *marriage*. Barth interprets the duality of man and wife as a repetition of the facing positions within the Trinity, and as an image of the relationship between Christ and the Church. The question is, which is the first here and which is the second? Did God create marriage because he wanted marriage as a duality between man and wife, or did God create marriage because he willed an analogy to the relationship within the Trinity and to the history of salvation? In the first case, marriage is an earthly ordinance willed by God, the meaning and glory of which lies in itself, and whoever pleases may in addition speculate about it as an analogy to the heavenly order. In the second case, marriage is merely an earthly material thing, fashioned by God for the purpose of adumbrating the heavenly order.

By carrying us up to heaven in his trinitarian speculations, Barth takes away the ground from under our feet. Here again, more markedly than before, it is evident that the basic fault of the whole of Barth's theology is that it is unhistorical.

God's election in grace

Barth's theological purpose, the Christian impulse which inspires him, urges his thought on, and never permits him to pause and stand still until it has reached the farthest point and has passed the limits of what is permissible, finds forcible expression in his doctrine of *predestination*. This is the apex of his theology, if one can name as apex what in fact is the root of everything. It is the origin of Barth's christological concentration and his intensive universalism, it is the point from which everything else is illuminated; here the light becomes very bright, even glaring. Barth himself calls his doctrine of election the 'common denominator' of his theology.[55] Everything that he says about God and the world, creation and redemption, providence and atonement, the Church and the end of time, has its starting-point and corner stone in this. Urs von Balthasar rightly called the volume of the *Church Dogmatics* which deals with the doctrine of predestination 'the heart of Barth's theology, a kind of dithyramb of almost six hundred pages'.[56]

When we hear the word 'predestination' darkness descends and we stumble into the infinite abyss of the hidden God, who, before all time, even before the Fall, and in fact before the beginning of creation, beyond good and evil, was pleased to destine some to eternal blessedness and others to eternal damnation. And we think of the obscure game of question and answer which men have played with the eternal decree of God, by seeking anxiously for signs, like theological astrologers, in order to read from them the will of God concerning their eternal destiny. Barth puts an end to this game: 'For our part we can no longer agree to such a procedure – [It is a false, stultifying and in any case a profoundly unchristian mystery play].'[57]

Barth attacks the 'architectonic symmetry' of election and rejection; for him predestination signifies not darkness *and* light, but light only. Definitions abound by which he affirms the nature of predestination as radiant light: it is 'the sum of the gospel', 'the gospel *in nuce*', 'good news, the best news, the wholly redemptive news', 'the very essence of all good news', a witness 'that all the ways and works of God have their origin in His grace'. Thus when Barth speaks of predestination, he also speaks of God's 'election in grace'. Just as God's freedom is his freedom to love, and God's deity includes his humanity, as the creation is merely the external basis of the covenant, and the law merely the mode of the gospel, so God's election is only the expression of his grace. The phrase 'election in grace' expresses the fact that at the beginning, and before the beginning, of all God's dealings with his creation there lies a basic and original decision, and this decision is that God 'is gracious and not ungracious'.[58]

Barth derived the necessity for this 'total revision' of the dogma of predestination from his christological concentration. The eternal election does not form a sub-chapter of the doctrine of the *hidden* God, but is the principal chapter and indeed the sole chapter of the doctrine of the *revealed* God: 'There is no will of God which is different from the will of Jesus Christ.' In the beginning there was not an obscure, independent and abstract divine original decree, becoming gradually illuminated as it was carried out. In the beginning there is, here also, the clear, concrete manifestation of God in Jesus Christ, placing everything at once in a clear, bright light: 'In the beginning with God was One, Jesus Christ. And precisely that is predestination.' Therefore: 'If we would know what election is, what it is to be elected by God, then we must look away from all others, and excluding all side glances or secondary thoughts, we must look only upon the name of Jesus Christ.'[59]

Jesus Christ is both the subject and the object of the divine election. Here again, Barth's thought is wholly trinitarian; his doctrine of election is also an application and consummation of the doctrine of the Trinity: Jesus Christ is simultaneously 'God who chooses' and 'man who is chosen'. In him God chose himself, but in the form of man.

In Jesus Christ both aspects of predestination become visible, not only who is chosen and what it is to be chosen, but also who is rejected and what it is to be rejected – but the decisive emphasis is on the fact that God in Jesus Christ makes himself responsible and bears the blame for man's disobedience, and takes upon himself the whole consequence of his actions, his rejection and his death: 'In the election of Jesus Christ which is the eternal will of God, God *has ascribed to man the former*, election, salvation and life; and *to himself he has ascribed the latter*, reprobation, perdition and death.' Because God made the rejection a matter of his own, rejection no longer matters to us. The only truly rejected man is now God's own Son! And thereby double predestination has ceased to exist for man: 'In so far, then, as predestination does contain a No, it is not a No spoken against man. . . . So then belief in predestination signifies in itself and *per se* belief in the non-rejection of man, unbelief in his rejection.'[60]

In this way Barth becomes the systematic theologian of grace. Because he concentrates everything upon the single issue of election in Jesus Christ, he succeeds in breaking the power of double predestination and creates a closed system of grace: 'If indeed God has opened his heart to us in Jesus Christ, there is no higher will in God than the will of his grace.' Consequently all the ways and works of God are determined by grace 'from the beginning'. This term 'from the beginning' constantly recurs in Barth. It makes grace the sign outside the bracket which includes the works of God. Henceforth – that is, from eternity – everything which God does is 'without exception' grace. There is nothing which is not grace. 'God is gracious and continues gracious even where there is no grace. And it is only by grace that the lack of grace can be recognised as such.'[61] It is the divine choice which for Barth makes Christianity so triumphant an affair, and gives his theological language its note of victorious passion. The whole of his *Church Dogmatics* is a single great hymn to the grace of God.

For Barth the triumph of grace is so mighty and universal that he is driven by it to the edge of heresy. It is not difficult to compile from almost every volume of the *Church Dogmatics* and other works by Barth, written during the same period, an increasing number of statements which do not merely contain a tendency towards the so-called '*apocatastasis*', that is, the universal reconciliation of the world to God, but appear to proclaim it quite openly: God's decision to be gracious, made in eternity, is irrevocable; man cannot alter or reverse it; he cannot bring into being any fact which would abrogate God's election in grace. Here faith is the sole possibility, and unbelief 'the excluded possibility'. After the One, Jesus Christ, has been rejected, rejection is no longer a possibility for the many: 'They may choose as they do. They may proceed as far as they are able. But the situation and reward of the rejected for which they stretch out their hands in their folly when they reject God, will assuredly not be secured by them. . . . They can, of course, dishonour the divine election of grace; but they cannot overthrow or overturn it.' Barth does not deny that there is unbelief in the world, any more than he denies that there is sin and godlessness in the world. But unbelief cannot prevail against God's original decision, that he will be gracious and not ungracious. Thus in the ultimate sense Barth cannot take unbelief seriously. Barth answers the objections of unbelief with a parable. If a king awards a decoration to a subject, and the person it is intended for does not accept it – does this mean that the recipient has not received the award from the king? Whoever does not believe in the grace of God is like someone who is behind the times, whose subjective knowledge has not yet caught up with the objective reality. Barth does not deny that God punishes man, but grace prevails over the punishment: 'Even the wrath and judgement of God which may overtake man do not indicate any retraction, but only a special form, and in the last analysis the most glorious confirmation, of the permission and promise given to him.'[62]

A whole series of similar examples can be adduced. Whether Barth is speaking of man, his sin, his unbelief, his godlessness, or of the election, the atonement, the redemption, and the Church, a *universalist tendency* is evident throughout his theology. It is never made clear how Barth makes this universality of grace compatible with the possibility of human decision, and therefore the possibility of damnation, so avoiding the consequence of apocatastasis, universal redemption. But he attempts to do so. Whenever he comes to speak of apocatastasis, he denies it. He skirts it by appealing to the same freedom of God which makes his grace so unlimited. Grace forbids faith to turn the *open* number of the elect in Jesus Christ into a closed number, on the pattern of the classic doctrine of predestination. But to reckon with the redemption of *all* men would equally result in a *closed* number. The freedom of divine grace precludes the drawing of any limit, for we have no control whatsoever over it, and are unable to reduce or widen its limits.[63]

The fundamental openness of the number of the elect has to be reflected in the 'open situation of proclamation'. Consequently, Barth answers the charge that he teaches an apocatastasis by constantly referring to preaching: The Church's mission is not to define and contemplate the divine choice, but to preach it, thereby perfecting the destination of the elect. Predestination is not an object for inquiry and discursive description, but for faith and personal address: 'It is meant for you!' Outside this existential context the grace of God becomes isolated from faith and is turned into a general world view. Hence the Church must not preach an apocatastasis, but neither must it preach a 'powerless grace of Jesus Christ', nor 'a wickedness of men which is too powerful for it'. Of course in practice a preacher will distinguish between believer and unbeliever, but he will start from this distinction, not exalt it into a principle, but will always call together those who are so divided, preaching to believers the rejection they have deserved, and to non-believers the election they have not deserved, but to both the One, in whom they are elected and not rejected.[64]

It is touching to observe how Barth himself is constantly overwhelmed by the triumph of divine grace and is led into extending the open number of the elect in the direction of universal redemption, turning it thereby into a closed number. At any rate he is more concerned to avoid too strict a limiting of grace than to prevent it from extending too widely. He prefers the danger of an apocatastasis in the Church's preaching of the life-giving gospel to preaching the deadening law and avoiding this risk, but turning Christianity into a 'gloomy' affair. Consequently, he can even ask 'whether the concept [of universal redemption] could not perhaps have a good meaning'. It might serve to remind theologians that they have no right 'to set any sort of limits to the loving kindness of God made evident in Jesus Christ. Our theological duty is to see and understand it as being still greater than we had seen before'. Even 'what is apparently overbold' is 'normal, the only thing possible' – 'a strange Christianity whose most pressing concern seems to be that divine grace might lean too far in this direction, and that hell, instead of being filled with a lot of other people, might prove to be empty'.[65]

Small wonder that Barth's bold abolition of the symmetry of divine judgement sparked off a violent theological attack. Fortunately Barth did not allow such criticism to influence his praise of the universality of divine grace. There is undoubtedly a tension in his thought between universal election and human decision, and this tension is not resolved. But even if Barth had taken his doctrine of predestination to the ultimate consequence of universal redemption, he would have found himself in exalted theological company. Origen and Schleiermacher also shared in this 'heresy'. These are presumably the last theologians with whom Barth would want to be associated, let alone consigned to the same hell. But to charge Barth with heresy would be to underestimate divine grace and the theology of Karl Barth. The tendency towards universal redemption should not be made the reason for a critical attack upon Barth. It calls for our full understanding, especially in a theologian for whom Christianity is 'nothing but radiant good news', who therefore varies the theme of divine grace with unfaltering perseverance, and whose entire life and work forms an unequalled great hymn to the love of God. If a critical objection is justified at this point, then only in so far as his tendency towards a doctrine of universal redemption is another symptom of a fault that goes deeper and runs through all of Barth's theology: the fact that it is unhistorical. It is a fault we have repeatedly encountered and now, towards the end, it stands fully revealed.

Monologue in heaven

A notable contradiction prevails in Barth's theology: he seeks to be a theologian of revelation, more strictly than almost anyone else. He recognises only a single assumption for theology: *Dominus dixit*, 'the Lord has spoken'. Yet he, the strict theologian of revelation, adopts a point of view not beneath but *above* revelation, not in time but in eternity. Of course the incarnation of Christ is the central factor of his theology, as the cross and the resurrection are for Bultmann, and Pentecost for Tillich; no one excels him in his praise of 'the miracle of Christmas', and for him the virgin birth is a fundamental tenet of Christianity. Yet his point of departure is not the event of the incarnation, but the pre-existence of Christ, the being which is Christ's before all time in eternity. A commemorative article on Barth's seventieth birthday was rightly entitled 'The Rediscovery of Heaven'; no other title would have characterised Barth's theology more accurately. Indeed, at the very time when other theologians were rediscovering, in the context of the world's total secularisation, the worldliness of Christianity, Barth rediscovered heaven.

But did Barth really, as he intended, remain at the *foot* of the mountain? Instead of going constantly around the mountain and showing men its beauties from below, first from one side and then from the other, has he not rather climbed the heights of the mountain, so that he now wanders upon its broad summit and shows men all the splendours of the divine revelation in a single all-embracing view from above? In other words, Barth, instead of seeing into the glass, as is ordained for men, has strayed *behind* the glass. He is peering into the script destined for the persons of the Trinity, and sometimes one even feels that he is prompting them.

It is not Barth's christological concentration which is responsible for this theological 'high flying', but the transference of this christological concentration into heaven. He doubles as it were his christological concentration, concentrating it on an operation within the Trinity. Thus the process of revelation is reduced to a monologue conducted by God with himself as three persons, as Father, Son and Holy Spirit.

Henceforth Barth remains captive within this triune circle. Consequently everything is anticipated, has already happened in this original perfect tense, which one is tempted to call a pluperfect tense. Everything is not merely decreed in eternity, but already perfected; what takes place in time is merely the carrying out of the original divine decree, a repetition of the original and eternal pattern. Reduced to a formula, we might say that the divine Trinity devised a drama in eternity, and gave its first performance within itself, played by the three persons. Now this drama is to be re-enacted on earth, as it has been in heaven. To this end the world is created as the stage, and man as the spectator.

It is this 'eternalisation' within the Trinity of the christological concentration which first brings about what Paul Althaus calls Barth's 'christomonism' and Urs von Balthasar his 'christological construction'. The whole creation – nature, the world, man and history – is now forced into the christological pattern and so deprived of its own meaning and status. Everything takes place from Christ and for Christ. This summing up of the beginning and end of all things in Jesus Christ becomes the real driving force of the whole of the historical process that lies in between. No one will object to the way Barth draws together the beginning and end of the whole historical process in Jesus Christ. But the question is whether in Barth it is still a matter of an historical *process*: does he present anything in history as still *happening*?

For how can anything still happen when everything has already 'happened' in eternity? The eternalisation of the divine revelation necessarily leads to an abstract pietism. The basing of the events of salvation upon a timeless event in the perfect tense results for Barth in an irreparable loss of concrete historical reality. He no longer sees the revelation of God as a drama enacted between God and man, full of tension and change, with moments of progress, moments of retrogression and turning-points, with gradations, phases and epochs, but only as 'enlightenment' about an event which has long since taken place. Historical perspective disappears in the dimension of eternity. Virtually no other theology talks so much about events, happenings and history as Barth's, but there is virtually no theology with so little action, because all the action has already taken place in eternity. Thielicke is right when he states: 'Here is only the motion of waves in a semblance of history, over a foundation which is timeless or belongs to the beginning of time.'[66]

The denial of the historical nature of revelation becomes particularly evident in Barth's teaching on the incarnation. It is here that Barth pays the heaviest toll for having placed his starting-point in eternity. Since, unlike the New Testament, he does not begin in history, with the event of the incarnation itself, going back from there to the pre-existence of Christ, but proceeds instead from the pre-existence of Christ as something perfected at the beginning of time, deriving from it everything that has followed after, he sees Christ as equally and permanently present at every stage of the history of redemption, so that for him the incarnation is not a really new event, a new intervention of God, the turning-point of history, but only a new mode of something that had been permanently present. 'The Word became flesh' means for Barth: 'The Word took on flesh.' The incarnation of Christ merely recapitulates, clarifies and reveals what has always been. Thielicke translates this in the following image: 'Christmas has turned into an Advent, perhaps a particularly luminous Sunday of Advent, with five candles on the wreath, but it is no longer the feast of Christ as the turning-point between two aeons.'[67]

By developing everything that happens, both the history of revelation and the history of the world, from a single point, Barth runs the risk of arriving at an abstract *monism*. He has been under this threat from the first. To begin with, the *monon* that determines everything in his thought was the crisis with its dialectic of time and eternity; later it became grace, concentrated into the divine choice from eternity, but both are equally abstract and timeless. This monism brings Karl Barth close to Hegel, however strange this fellowship may seem in a theologian such as he. His affinity with Hegel is betrayed by his sharing with Hegel a difficulty in fitting sin into his monist system. Without sin there is no redemption – but how, when and where does sin enter into an historical process which is wholly and completely determined by what was already perfected at the beginning of time?

Barth encounters great difficulty when it comes to the reality of *sin*. He has to indulge in extensive speculation, on the one hand in order to maintain the priority of grace and not slip into dualism, and on the other hand in order not to do away with the reality of evil and so to slip into monism. His thought is 'supralapsarian'; that is, he once again adopts a point of view 'above the fall', in eternity, and makes no fundamental distinction between the situation before and after the fall. According to Barth evil is 'the possibility which God in his creative decision has ignored and despised, like a human builder when he chooses one specific work and rejects and ignores another'. Consequently Barth calls evil nothingness: 'It is from the very first that which is past. It was abandoned at once by God in creation. . . . It has no substance. . . . It has only its own emptiness.' But this does not reduce evil simply to nothing, and make 'nothingness' equivalent to 'nothing'. Even with his left hand, God does nothing in vain, and his negative will also is mighty, creating a real counterpoint. That which has been voided by God lives by the fact that God does not will it. This, precisely, gives it life. It is 'not created but posited' – posited by the fact that God has 'opposed' himself to it. This nothingness is the 'impossible possibility', an 'awkward reality', but a reality nevertheless, 'the reality behind God's back, which he passed over when he made the world and made it good'.[68]

Thus evil is the product of a rejection by God, concomitant with the creation. But fundamentally, this rejection of evil as nothingness is the repetition of a first rejection. Its first rejection – if one may use the concept of time at all – had already taken place in the election of Jesus Christ. But since this election took place before all time, in eternity, one must really say that the rejection of evil had already taken place before it came into being. Barth says as much: 'In the first and eternal Word of God the sin of man is already met, refuted and removed from all eternity.' Seen from this point of view, nothingness has in Barth no longer any 'objective existence'. The priority of grace takes away the historical significance of evil. It is now only a 'shadow'. Barth compares it to a wasp without a sting. Man is only frightened of the movements of the wasp so long as he does not know that it has no longer any sting.[69]

The priority of grace takes away from evil its real historical significance. But in proportion as evil loses its historical reality, the redeeming act of Christ also diminishes in historical reality. If Jesus Christ precedes everything, then he also precedes sin. But if this is so, then his cross is 'not really brought about by sin, but only by his self-sacrifice, decreed from eternity', and the fall is therefore merely an act necessarily created as a framework for this. Even the cross becomes ultimately only a monologue of God the Father with himself as God the Son, and therefore 'a ghostly apparition without reality'.[70]

In Barth there is not a really effective struggle on the part of God against evil, no assault by his love upon the world, but only a manifestation of his love, enlightenment about it, the symbolic demonstration and imparting of a state of things in eternity: 'It is not that something takes place – something becomes evident.'[71] This is why *knowledge* and *understanding* are of such great importance in Barth's theology. Believers and unbelievers are distinguished from one another by the fact that believers already possess knowledge of a given matter, which is still unknown to unbelievers, and consequently missionary activity consists of imparting this particular matter and making it known. The Swedish Lutheran theologian Gustaf Wingren, one of the most acute critics of Barth (who is, however, not always wholly just), once described this shift of emphasis in Barth's theology in the following image. If someone receives a postal order for 100 marks, the important thing for him is that he gets the money; but for Barth the important thing is that he receives the knowledge that he is getting 100 marks.[72] To put this in plain terms, the nature of revelation as an event is reduced by Barth to the realm of knowledge; the revelation no longer *takes place*, but all that happens is that the knowledge that a revelation has already taken place is *imparted*; what has always been is simply made known.

The same indifference to history permits Barth to soar in his enthu-siasm above the concrete historical situation of man. If everything has already been completed in heaven, then nothing really threatening can happen on earth any more, and one can even allow oneself to have a sense of humour. But Barth's much vaunted humour also has its sus-picious aspect. Many are annoyed by the way in which the remnant of our earthly burden, which must be borne, is so lightly shuffled off; they cannot resist the impression that the cares and troubles which threaten them are too rapidly lifted up into the light of eternity, and that their questions and problems are given too ready and easy an answer. Thus they give up the dialogue with theology in disappoint-ment.

Nothing reveals the lack of contact with the contemporary historical situation in the theology of Barth so much as the fact that the problem of the *language of preaching* plays virtually no part in it. When Barth discusses this, he does so almost entirely in a negative way, criticising and rejecting the idea. This is all the more surprising, since the point of departure of Barth's whole theological thinking was the difficulty of preaching, and since then, as he himself has assured us, he has constantly had the task of preaching in mind in the course of his dogmatic work. In the first volume of his *Church Dogmatics* he writes: 'The normal and central fact with which dogmatics has to do is, very simply, the Church's Sunday sermon of yesterday and tomorrow, and so it will continue to be.'[73] And when Barth was asked in the television interview in Paris in 1964, mentioned above, what was his main concern when he taught theology, he answered, referring to his own experiences as a pastor, that fundamentally his theology was no more than an attempt to answer for what he had to do in the pulpit, and to find a better method for this than he had learned in his time at the university – and he continued: 'When I now face the students, I see them in the position of future pastors. And I imagine them in their robes in the pulpit, facing the open Bible and the congregation. The great task of theology is first to find the way into the Bible and then the way from the Bible into life. Basically this is my very simple recipe.'[74]

Unfortunately, Barth has only provided the first part of this recipe: he has certainly shown theology a way into the Bible, but he has not shown it the way from the Bible into life with the same determination. He has always given the question of the substance of preaching precedence over the question of the form of preaching, in the conviction that once the substance was rightly understood, the form would appear of itself. As though it were as obvious as that! As though one could distinguish so simply between the substance and form! As though the substance ever existed without the form! Barth's theology is lacking in a relationship to the concrete existence of man and the actual development of the world. Not sufficient account is taken, in this theology of the word, of the fact that the situation to which the word of God has to speak possesses theological relevance, and that, as Martin Buber once expressed it, 'situations have a word to add as well'.

Once again this is a consequence of the fact that his theology is unhistorical, which is true both of its negative and its positive aspects. In the negative sense, when Barth hears of the 'relating' of the word of God to human existence, this at once provokes in him the old fear that God and human existence may come to be placed upon the same level, so that the creature is confused with the creator. Consequently he declares: 'It is not the case that theology has to give a theological answer to the question of existence . . . the theme of dogmatics is always the Word of God and nothing else.'[75] In the positive sense, anyone whose starting-point is on such a lofty level as that of Barth either ignores completely the task of building a bridge from heaven to earth, or fails to carry it out from the first. How theology can maintain a constantly renewed responsibility for what it says about God not only in the sight of God himself, but also in the sight of the world, is a question which has never seriously disturbed Barth. And there is no reason why this question should disturb one who can go back to something that has already been carried out at the beginning of time, and who is convinced that everything has already been perfected in eternity, and has simply to be revealed here in the world. Because God's cause in the world has already triumphed, all the Church needs to do is to bear witness to this victory; because the word of God has already 'come' among men through its own freedom and power, the Church no longer needs to be concerned how it is to come among men with the word of God. All it has to do is to 'sow the seed just as it is', unmixed 'with the seeds of its own thoughts'. The only way in which Jesus Christ can be preached is for him to preach himself. Where this happens, it is Barth's conviction that a proper relation to the actual situation comes about as it were automatically.[76]

Barth does not deny that because the Christian gospel is addressed to an audience, some consideration must be given to its language, but when he speaks about this, his tone is largely ironical, and almost contemptuous: 'A little "non-religious" language from the street, the newspaper, literature, and, if one is ambitious, from the philosopher may thus, for the sake of communication, occasionally indeed be in order. However, we should not become particularly concerned about this.' Assertions like this reveal that Barth has never genuinely recognised the problem involved in the language of preaching in its full profundity. For him the question of language remains ultimately merely a question of words and technical terms: 'How do I make the child see reason?' For him it belongs not to biblical exegesis or dogmatics, but to practical theology.[77]

Lessing's question, which has been so constant a preoccupation of theology during the modern period, right up to the present day, how the historical distance, the 'dreadful gulf' of 1900 years between the revelation once given and present-day preaching may be overcome, has never seriously been touched upon by Barth. He regards it as merely an unreal technical problem, and not a genuine spiritual or theological question. Lessing's question is only genuine in so far as it betrays man's attempt to flee, an attempt like Adam and Eve in the Garden of Eden to hide from 'Jesus Christ as he makes himself present and mediates himself to us' and to find a place of safety: 'In any other sense than this the question of Lessing, the question of historical distance, is not a genuine problem. . . . It is the product of . . . fear of the truth.'[78]

There is no question that preaching in Germany today, and not only in Germany, would be very different without Karl Barth and his theology. But the effect of Barth's theology has been twofold. On the one hand, without it present-day preaching would not be so pure, so biblical, and so concerned with central issues, but on the other hand, it would also not be so alarmingly correct, boringly precise, and remote from the world. Barth certainly turned the preaching of the Church from the defensive to the attack, but he did not at the same time provide it with adequate weapons for its attack. He increasingly emphasised the unchanging message of preaching, rather than its flexibility; the question of bringing the Christian gospel up to date so that modern man can understand it has never been one to which he has devoted any special consideration in his theology.

The consequence has been that in Barth's theology and in the Confessing Church which was influenced by him, 'the restoration of the Church' and 'a positivist doctrine of revelation' have become increasingly predominant. Barth must have been particularly hurt by the fact that this reproach was deliberately made against him by the most important of his disciples, Dietrich Bonhoeffer. In his *Letters and Papers from Prison* Bonhoeffer writes: 'Barth was the first theologian to begin the criticism of religion, and that remains his really great merit; but he put in its place a positivist doctrine of revelation which says, in effect, "Like it or lump it".'[79] Similarly, Paul Tillich had written some years earlier from his observation post in America: 'The development of the German Confessing Church in the last two years proves how necessary the struggle remains. The Grand Inquisitor is now entering the Confessing Church wearing the strong but tight-fitting armour of Barthian supranaturalism.'[80] Whether the term used is 'the positivist doctrine of revelation' or 'supranaturalism', what these critics are objecting to in Barth is that he simply presents the truths of the Christian revelation without making clear their relevance to life in the mature world of the present day.[81]

But this cannot be called a false development of Barth's theology, for its roots go back to the very starting-point of that theology. Barth has repeatedly said that this theology was born out of the 'distress of pastors in their preaching'. Consequently, from the very first, it possessed the character of a 'theology for the clergy', which was more concerned that preaching should be correct than with the direction in which it was aimed. It is true that the Confessing Church was able, with the aid of this 'theology for the clergy', to survive in the Church's struggle under the Third Reich, but it would hardly have been successful in this if it had not been fortified by an infusion of the kind of pietistic lay devotion which this theology itself had once condemned as 'the brushing aside of distinctions', 'romantic immediacy' and 'mysticism'. It is true that pietism itself was ruined by this alliance: its longing for a 'pure heart' became a concern for 'pure doctrine'.

Thus the rediscovery of the revelation of God after the First World War became, after the end of the Second World War at the latest, an ecclesiastical system, and awe at the infinite distance between God and man became a concern for orthodoxy. Barth of course also introduced powerful new ideas within orthodoxy itself, but on the whole he contributed more to the strengthening than to the breaking down of ecclesiastical orthodoxy, and more to the widening than to the bridging of the abyss between Christianity and the world. Barth must take part of the blame for the invention of the esoteric language now spoken by theologians, which is barely comprehensible to a single non-theologian. In Barth's own work this rigidity is constantly relaxed and brought to life by his religious genius. But many of his disciples give the impression that they are sitting in the Garden of Eden under the tree of knowledge showing each other the fruits that they have plucked, which are good to look at and good to eat, while Adam and Eve are gathering vegetables for the market by the sweat of their brow.

It was after the Second World War that an event took place in which both Barth's theological outlook and the criticism made of it were subjected to a powerful blaze of light. The occasion was the first Assembly of the World Council of Churches in Amsterdam in 1948. Barth had to give the introductory lecture on the whole theme of the conference: *The Disorder of the World and God's Plan of Salvation.* In his very opening words he turned the theme 'back to front'. The conference, he said, should not begin below, with the 'disorder of the world', nor with the deliberations and measures with which it was hoped to deal with this disorder, but 'above' with 'God's plan of salvation', with 'his kingdom which has already come, is already victorious, and is already set up in all its majesty', with 'Jesus Christ, who has already taken away the power of sin and death, of the devil and hell, and has already given due honour to God and to man in his own person'. Once again, it is what is already completed and accomplished before time which dominates Barth's thought here. It led him to make this criticism: 'The material presented to us here gives me the same strange impression as garments of deep mourning.' It also gave his words a note of triumph: 'Let us come out of this mourning!' But it also lifted him dangerously high above the earth! 'We must be God's witnesses. He has not called us to be his barristers, engineers, managers, statisticians and directors.'[82]

After the conference in Amsterdam a sharp controversy took place between Karl Barth and the American theologian Reinhold Niebuhr. The theme of Niebuhr's criticism of Barth's lectures was that 'We are men and not God'. He recalled the starting-point which Barth's theology had first adopted. It had begun with the warning that God is in heaven and man upon earth. In the meantime, the wheel had turned by 180 degrees: 'This theology is now in danger of offering a crown without the cross, a triumph without a battle, and a faith which ignores the confusion of human existential life instead of transforming it.' The consequence is that it skates over the circumstances of human existence, avoids concrete difficulties and tragic decisions by retreating before them, deprives the historical responsibility of Christians of all meaning, and allows them to forget that – however justifiable it may be to bear in mind God's ultimate victory and to warn against trusting in one's own powers – they are meant to co-operate with God. 'Christian faith knows a way through this suffering, but no way round it.'[83] The charge Niebuhr is raising against Barth here concerns precisely that which we have deplored as the unhistorical nature of his theology.

In Amsterdam Barth asked how we could have hit upon the 'perverse idea' of 'basing our evangelical relationship to modern men upon our ability to come to a tabulated agreement with their infamous axioms: as though we had a right to regard secular man of today from any other point of view than that for them also Jesus Christ died and rose from the dead, becoming their divine brother and redeemer'. The question Niebuhr poses in turn is: 'Does this mean that the apostle Paul has no right to analyse the longing of his time for the "unknown God" and to prove its importance for the gospel? For example, if Mr Julian Huxley writes a book entitled *Man in the Modern World* . . . is the apologist's only task to assure Mr Huxley that Christ also died for him, even though, with the belief he holds at the present moment, Mr Huxley probably cannot understand why anyone should die for us at all?'[84]

In spite of all his assurances to the contrary, Barth's theology is not concerned with a true dialogue, but is as much a monologue as the revelation of God with which it deals. What is lacking in this theology of the word of God is any attempt to relate the word of God to a situation, either to the concrete existential life of individual men or to the historical development of the world in its totality. Consequently it lacks any correlation between man's questions and God's answers. What is missing in this theology of God's turning towards man is man in his concrete situation. Barth merely recites the words of holy scripture, and with his impassioned style carries them triumphantly into the present day, but he does not really translate them into the terms of our present-day existence.

Surprised by the effect of the *Epistle to the Romans*, Barth once wrote: 'If I look back upon the path I have followed, I seem to be like someone who is groping his way up the steps of a dark church tower and suddenly seizes the bell rope instead of the hand-rail, and hears to his horror the great bell striking above him, heard by others besides himself.'[85] In the meantime, the sounding of this bell has turned into a trinitarian peal, ringing out the triune love of God, to the glory of God. But this divine peal of bells rings out over an earth which constantly grows more godless. God is in heaven and man is on earth – while this gap was reduced in Barth's theology, in the reality of the world it was growing greater. Above in heaven the eternal peal of the Trinity rings out, while on the earth below more and more men ask: 'Where are you, O God?'

CHAPTER FIVE

FROM THE WORLD BEYOND
TO THIS WORLD

The modern age takes stock of itself

Luther asked at the end of the Middle Ages, 'How can I get a gracious God?' At the time this was a purely personal question asked by a single lonely Augustinian Friar. But in this purely personal question, the single lonely Augustinian Friar asked the decisive question of his age. Yet who today would seriously ask whether God was gracious to him? Most modern men – and who, whether he be a Christian or not, is not a modern man in this respect? – are anxious not about their salvation in the world to come, but about their well-being in this world. What is at issue is not the eternal salvation of their soul, but their temporal destiny. And if they still have any interest in God at all, it is not that he should exist in a beyond, in 'heaven', but that he should show himself in the world, in their lives. If he is gracious, eternal and omnipotent, what matters above all is that he should be so *here and now*! Thus at the end of the modern age, if we inquire about God at all, our question is different from that posed at the end of the Middle Ages. We no longer ask whether God is gracious, but whether God is there at all. Our question is, 'Where are you, O God?'

Long ago an answer was given to this question: 'Have you ever heard of the madman who on a bright morning lighted a lantern and ran to the market place calling out unceasingly: "I seek God! I seek God!" As there were many people standing about who did not believe in God, he caused a great deal of amusement. Why! is he lost? said one. Has he strayed away like a child? said another. Or does he keep himself hidden? Is he afraid of us? Has he taken a sea voyage? Has he emigrated? – the people cried out laughingly, all in a hubbub. The insane man jumped into their midst and transfixed them with his glances. "Where is God gone?" he called out. "I mean to tell you! *We have killed him –* you and I! We are all his murderers! But how have we done it? How were we able to drink up the sea? Who gave us the sponge to wipe away the whole horizon? What did we do when we loosened this earth from its sun? Whither does it now move? Whither do we move? Away from all suns? Do we not dash on unceasingly? Backwards, sideways, forwards, in all directions? Is there still an above and below? Do we not stray, as through infinite nothingness? Does not empty space breathe upon us? Has it not become colder? Does not night come on continually, darker and darker? Shall we not have to light lanterns in the morning? Do we not hear the noise of the gravediggers who are burying God? Do we not smell the divine putrefaction? – for even Gods putrefy! God is dead! God remains dead! And we have killed him! How shall we console ourselves, the most murderous of all murderers? The holiest and the mightiest that the world has hitherto possessed, has bled to death under our knife – who will wipe the blood from us? With what water could we cleanse ourselves? What lustrums, what sacred games shall we have to devise? Is not the magnitude of this deed too great for us? Shall we not ourselves have to become Gods, merely to seem worthy of it? There never was a greater event, and on account of it, all who are born after us belong to a higher history than any history hitherto!" Here the madman was silent and looked again at his hearers; they also were silent and looked at him in surprise. At last he threw his lantern on the ground, so that it broke in pieces and was extinguished. "I come too early," he then said, "I am not yet at the right time. This prodigious event is still on its way, and is travelling – it has not yet reached men's ears. Lightning and thunder need time, the light of the stars needs time, deeds need time, even after they are done, to be seen and heard. This deed is as yet farther from them than the farthest star – and *yet they have done it!*" It is further stated that the madman made his way into different churches on the same day, and there intoned his *Requiem aeternam Deo.* When led out and called to account, he always gave the reply: "What are these churches now, if they are not the tombs and monuments of God?"[1]

This is the famous passage from Friedrich Nietzsche's *The Joyful Wisdom*, which he entitled 'The Madman'. Nietzsche clears away the smoke-screen that covers the reality of our religion, and reveals the uneasy situation in which we live. This passage, therefore, must unquestionably form part of any stocktaking of Protestant theology in the present century.

There was a precedent of a kind for Nietzsche's famous proclamation that God is dead. This is Jean Paul's *Rede des toten Christus vom Weltgebäude herab, dass kein Gott sei* (Speech of the Dead Christ from the Universe, that there is no God), which has come to be more and more

frequently quoted in recent years.[2] It has rightly been called an 'apo-
calypse of atheism'. It reads: 'Now a lofty and noble figure with an
everlasting sorrow descended from the heights on to the altar, and all
the dead cried out, "O Christ, is there no God?" He answered, "There
is none" . . . I voyaged through the worlds, I climbed into the suns and
flew along the Milky Way through the wastes of heaven; but there is no
God. I climbed down as far as the shadow of being is cast, peered into
the abyss and cried out, "Father, where are you?" But all I heard was the
eternal storm which no one governs, and the shining rainbow from the
west hung over the abyss without a sun to make it, and rain fell from it.
And as I looked up at the immeasurable universe to find the divine eye,
an empty and bottomless socket stared back at me; and eternity lay
upon chaos and gnawed at it and chewed upon it . . . and everything
grew empty. Then came a heartrending sight. The dead children who
had come to life in the graveyard came into the temple and cast themselves down before the lofty figure at the altar, and said, "Jesus, have we
no father?" And he answered, his face streaming with tears, "We are all
orphans, I and you, we are fatherless." . . . Then, as great as the highest
finite being, he raised his eyes towards the nothingness and the empty
immensity, and said, "Dumb, unbending nothingness! Cold and
eternal necessity! Senseless chance! . . . How solitary everyone is in the
vast tomb of the universe! I am alone with myself – O Father! O
Father! Where is thine everlasting bosom, that I may rest upon it? Ah,
if every self is his own father and creator, why cannot everyone be his
own avenging angel?"'

Jean Paul introduces his *Speech of the Dead Christ* with these words:
'If ever my heart were so sad and dulled that all the feelings within it
that affirm the existence of God were destroyed, I would startle myself
with this essay of mine and it would heal me, and give me back my
feelings.' Thus for Jean Paul the *Speech of the Dead Christ* is no more
than a dream, an atheist's nightmare, and this dream ultimately leads to
a joyful awakening: 'My soul wept for joy, that it could once again
worship God – the joy and weeping and faith in him were prayer. And
as I arose, the sun shone low behind the full, purple ears of corn . . .'

For Jean Paul atheism is still no more than a threatening possibility,
but for Nietzsche it is already a reality. He takes stock, as it were, of the
modern age. God is dead – for him this is the 'greatest new event' of
history. It is impossible to conceive of this event in terms which are too
universal or too sweeping. Nietzsche's declaration that God is dead does
not mean merely that belief in God has disappeared and that questions

are no longer asked about him, but also that in the course of an irresist-
ible movement *from the world beyond to this world*, all metaphysics
whatsoever come to an end.

This interpretation of Nietzsche's phrase 'God is dead', an interpretation which takes it beyond everything merely Christian and religious,
is given by Martin Heidegger in his *Holzwege*.[3] According to him
Nietzsche's statement that God is dead describes the fate of Western
metaphysics as they developed after Plato, in the form of a distinction
between a world of the senses and a world beyond the senses, where the
world beyond the senses is regarded as the one which is real and true in
the proper sense, sustains and determines the world of the senses, and so
prescribes its limits. Admittedly, when Nietzsche speaks of the death of
God, he is thinking in the first instance of the Christian God, but at the
same time he is using the name of God to refer to the world beyond the
senses as a whole, the world of ideals, standards and values, of the true,
the good and the beautiful, the attributes of the final goal poised above
earthly life like the light of the sun, and as such determining it from
above and outside itself. When Nietzsche now proclaims that God is
dead, this does not merely signify that there is no more God, but that the
basic structure of being as a whole is shattered. The world beyond the
senses, which was hitherto regarded as the only one which was true and
effective in the proper sense, has now become unreal and ineffective;
it has lost its power and no longer brings life; all metaphysics has come
to an end.

Thus it is not man who becomes arrogant and simply puts himself in
the place of God. That would be an over-simplification, expressed too
much in the language of Christian apologetics. Rather, at the very
moment when the world beyond the senses, which previously determined the standards, aims and values of earthly life, has become powerless and lifeless, man finds himself unexpectedly faced with the task of
taking over domination of the earth. His autonomy is a kind of self-
defence. Now he is obliged to act upon the world, which is the object of
his knowledge and plans; he must impose his own values, standards and
aims upon it, and so supply the light which previously shone down on
the world from above. It is this which leads to the total secularisation of
the world, and its consequence is atheism.

In the modern age, *secularisation*, the ordering of the world on its own
terms, has overwhelmed every province of life like an avalanche. This is
the greatest and most extensive process of secularisation which has ever
taken place in the history of Christianity, or indeed in the whole history

of religion. Something implicit in the very origins of the modern age is being fulfilled in our own time: the process of secularisation has largely been completed, and is the accepted characteristic of our whole life and existence.

Its origins can be found as early as the seventeenth century, during the wars of religion. The struggle between denominations forced men to ask what was their common ground, beyond what was in dispute, so that they could base the truth upon it. This search for an undisputed basis of truth led towards human reason, common to all, and equally binding upon all. As time went on, reason became increasingly certain of itself, and increasingly independent of the claims of theology and the Church. It became increasingly free of the tutelage of the Church and theology. It claimed increasingly, as its own proper concern, what had hitherto been regarded as divine revelation and therefore accessible to faith alone. And its success seemed to provide a brilliant vindication of its claim.

The beginning and the completion of the process of emancipation which led towards the autonomy of human reason and therefore towards the secularisation of the world can each be characterised by a contemporary quotation. The quotation which characterises the *beginning* of this process is from the Dutch jurist Hugo Grotius. At the beginning of the seventeenth century he wrote a major work on international law, the first of its kind. In it he said that law possessed validity *etsi Deus non daretur* – even if God did not exist! For Grotius God still existed, but he had already excluded him from the world. The state and justice live according to their own laws, which derive from human reason; they are a law unto themselves. Here the way was opened to the autonomy of man. Secularism is present here in outline: the self-contained world which no longer understands itself as the creation of God, or derives its life and law from the creator, but which contains its truth and justification within itself.

This outline was developed and extended by the Enlightenment. In the Enlightenment, according to Kant's famous definition, what took place was that 'man left behind the immaturity he had brought upon himself'; increasingly, man had come to learn, as Kant demanded, 'to use his understanding without being guided by another'. But in our own days this movement towards the autonomy of man has been brought to completion. The metaphysical foundations have everywhere been destroyed: science, politics, society, economics, justice, art and morality are understood in their own terms and follow their own laws. There are no longer any reserved areas which follow some kind of extraneous 'metaphysical' or 'divine' laws. Man manages without 'God' as a working hypothesis; he also copes with the world and with his life without God. He has carried out the advice given to him by Zarathustra: he has turned away from all 'worlds beyond the world', and has remained faithful to the earth; he has broken with all powers outside the world, and has firmly established himself within this world.

Just as man has become adult, the world has changed from God's world to man's world. And man in his turn is quite ready to accept full responsibility for his world, not only for its individual parts, but for the whole of it, for its progress and its meaning. In fulfilling this task, he develops a seriousness of purpose, a stern discipline, a clear-eyed vigilance and a lofty responsibility. At least these virtues are more characteristic of him than the moral defects and weaknesses which the preachers of ecclesiastical and secular morality deplore in him in sermons and exhortations. It is true that his ethics have changed. Man was previously responsible *to* an order which was given to him, and he had to take care to maintain this order as he received it; today man is responsible *for* the order of his world, and must at any rate be concerned to create the new order which is necessary to maintain that world in being. With an unerring, unswerving and almost stubborn loyalty man clings firmly to the earth, and attempts to preserve it from possible catastrophe. Previously his watchword was *extra ecclesiam nulla salus*, 'outside the *Church* there is no salvation'; now it is *extra mundum nulla salus*, 'outside the *world* there is no salvation'.

The final outcome of this development has been summed up by Werner Heisenberg in one brief sentence: '*For the first time in the history of mankind, man everywhere is faced only with himself.*'[4] This is the second quotation, which characterises the *completion* of the movement towards the autonomy of man. It began with *etsi Deus non daretur*; it is completed in our own time with 'Man everywhere is faced only with himself'.

The consequence of this total secularisation is *atheism*. The secularisation of the world and the exclusion of God from the world are one and the same process. When man comes to conceive of the world and deal with it as an object, then in his hands it becomes secular, finite and godless from the very earliest stages of history and on to the uttermost reaches of the universe. The experience of modern man is the same as that of King Midas. Everything he touched turned to gold; and everything which modern man touches, works upon, knows and experiences – nature, history, the life of the soul, inward and outward things – becomes 'the world'. It is a world which is understood solely and completely in its own terms, so much so that there seems to be no more room in it for God. At the present day it is becoming more and more evident that to all appearances human life can be understood and lived in purely immanent terms, on its own basis, and that it can be described and comprehended without ever being touched, let alone disturbed, by the question of God. It is as though we no longer had any practical basis in experience for what Schleiermacher once described – in an admittedly inadequate definition of religion – as the 'utter dependence' of man. Thus, for example, if we do not celebrate harvest thanksgiving with as much enthusiasm as previous generations, this is due not merely to our ingratitude, but also to the fact that we possess artificial fertilisers. Bertrand Russell once expressed this situation in an epigram: fishermen with sailing boats believe more easily in God than fishermen with motor boats.[5] Man's increasing ability to fabricate anything and everything corresponds to the increasing absence of God in the world. The more man succeeds in making himself master of the world, the more the consciousness of the absence of God from the world becomes widespread. The reverse is also true: the more the consciousness of the absence of God in the world becomes widespread, the more man considers himself obliged to take the world into his own possession, as his own responsibility.

We seem already to have gone beyond what Nietzsche asserted. All he could say was that the monstrous message of the death of God was still on the way, and was still far off, and that it had not yet reached the ears of men. In the meantime, however, it has long since reached the ears of men, and men have grown used to it. Whereas atheism was previously the concern of a small *avant-garde* group, it has now become a mass phenomenon. It is no longer the abstract and intellectual conception of a handful of individuals, but characterises the existential attitude to life and the mentality of innumerable people. It is not merely the theoretical view of a minority, but the unthinking practice of the majority. But although it has become apparently so superficial, it has at the same time put down much deeper roots. Atheism determines the intellectual and spiritual climate of our age; it is in the air we breathe. It no longer constitutes a denial, but is an assertion in its own right. Nowadays people no longer come to atheism through what may be a severe inward struggle or through dangerous conflicts with society, but treat it as their automatic point of departure. Our modern secular atheism is as far removed from Nietzsche's passionate denial of God as is the present atheist in Eastern Europe from the passionate unbelievers

in Dostoievsky. People are no longer concerned to refute God, but have
passed beyond the problem of God. Atheism itself has become secularised at the present day.

This is what theology finds when it takes stock of the modern age.
Faced with these facts, it must vindicate anew what it has to say about
God, if the churches are not to become in reality the graves and tomb-
stones of God. Henceforth, there can be no responsible way of speaking
of God which from first to the last does not keep constantly before it,
in all its seriousness and with all its force, what Nietzsche termed 'the
greatest new event' of history. An honest theology is only possible in
the future if it goes cheek by jowl with atheism.

Naturally, life in the modern age does not go on without religion.
But the growing movement towards the autonomy of man is linked
with a tendency to push religion more and more towards the edge of
life. It is tolerated at best only as an enlargement of reality by God.
Religion is placed like a golden frame about the dark and dismal land-
scape of the world, in order to make the appearance of the world a little
more tolerable. The world is allowed to take its course, and life is left
to follow its own laws, but on the edge of it a quiet enclave, sheltered
from the wind, is set up, in which it is possible to take refuge and try
as in the past to soar into an untroubled world beyond this world. But
such pious activity has no longer any relation to the wide field of
secular reality in which the most intensive part of most people's lives is
led today. This religious 'provincialism' is reminiscent of an attempt to
preserve a tiny allotment garden in the middle of a wholly industrial
area. The attempt may succeed for a while, but only as long as it suits
the owner of the industrial land. As soon as he lays hands on it, life in
this religious garden is finished.

Thus Christian faith runs the risk of being driven by secularisation
into a dangerous schizophrenia, consisting of the division of one reality
into two realities, the reality of God and the reality of the world. Viktor
von Weizsäcker expressed this threatened dichotomy in two questions:
'How can a scientist tolerate the admission that God intervenes in our
experiments? But how can a religious man tolerate the idea that at the
moment he enters his laboratory, he hangs his God on the hook with
his hat and stick?'[6] The dangerous dichotomy which Viktor von
Weizsäcker refers to here does not affect merely the natural sciences, nor
even scientific study in general, but the whole of life. The old danger
which has always threatened Christianity, that of the Christian heart
and the pagan mind, has come to a head with the total secularisation of

the world. Theology seems to have reached an insoluble dilemma. If theology means speaking about God, it must necessarily be universal; that is, it must testify to the rule of God over the whole world, if it is not to disobey the first commandment. But how is this still possible? How can one still speak of God in a secularised world? How can one still be a Christian in a secularised world? How can one still be 'religious' at all in such a world? This is the question posed for Christianity by total secularisation. Here is the real challenge to faith and theology in the present age.

Intellectual honesty

The problem of total secularisation has been posed in honest terms by many Protestant theologians in the recent years, but above all by Friedrich Gogarten and Dietrich Bonhoeffer.

As far as the style and the setting of their thought is concerned, these two theologians are very different. Gogarten is a typical academic theologian, a strict systematic thinker whose thought possesses a penetrating and almost violent power, and who develops everything inexorably from a single point. Since the last war he has published one book after another, all dealing with the same group of problems. Bonhoeffer was also, of course, an academic systematic theologian of high rank, but the powerful influence of the background of personal experience is more evident throughout his work. With an implacable refusal to compromise, he took part in the Church struggle, helped to provide illegal theological training in the Confessing Church, and finally, as a soldier in the counter-espionage service, became a political conspirator. His final and significantly new theological ideas were written in prison, not as a complete and mature work, but as tentative essays, fragments and sketches, deriving perhaps from this very fact a particularly compelling and direct persuasive power. Their effect is that of prophetic warnings, and sometimes almost of a single cry, sealed by martyrdom. Consequently, Bonhoeffer's friends and admirers must guard against trying to link his later writings from prison too closely with his previous thinking and writing, and making the whole into a theological system, canonising its author according to their taste as a saint or a doctor of the Church. It is true that from first to last there are consistent features in the whole body of Bonhoeffer's work, but they cannot be reduced to any theological common denominator. It is equally wrong for an unrepentant official Church Christianity to claim

Bonhoeffer's martyrdom for itself, without regarding itself bound by his statements. Only someone who has understood Bonhoeffer's words can rightly interpret his death.

In spite of their differences in style, and sometimes also in the content of their thought, there is a close link between Gogarten and Bonhoeffer. They are both impelled by the same question, and working towards the same understanding. The thought of both is concerned with the same complex of problems: the confrontation of Christian faith with the changed reality of the secularised world. Gogarten formulates the task as follows: 'It has become necessary to pose the question of Christian faith in a completely new way – that is, with respect to the secularisation of the whole of human existence which has in fact taken place.'[7] And Bonhoeffer writes: 'What is bothering me incessantly is the question what Christianity really is, or indeed who Christ really is, for us today. . . . The question is: Christ and the world that has come of age.'[8] The following statement of Heidegger is true of the theological efforts of Gogarten and Bonhoeffer: 'Only where the consummation of the modern age ceases to be alarmed at its own proportions, is future history being prepared.'[9]

Gogarten and Bonhoeffer are impelled towards the confrontation of Christian faith with the changed reality of the world by their respect for the requirement of intellectual honesty. To be intellectually honest means to keep one's thought in accordance with reality. But our reality is determined by the fact that the process of secularisation which has gone on since the beginning of the modern age has by now enveloped our whole life: 'Anyone who will not accept this is trying to live in a world which no longer exists.'[10] The requirement of intellectual honesty results from the discovery of the autonomy of human reason in the modern age. The extent to which it is also required by Christian faith can only be shown by a more profound theological understanding of the process of secularisation.

Gogarten and Bonhoeffer see an honest encounter of Christian faith with total secularisation as all the more urgent, in that the process of secularisation poses difficult and perilous questions which concern both faith and the world itself. There is a danger that through secularisation faith will wither away, by becoming imprisoned within the framework of a private morality, by concerning itself merely with the salvation of the individual soul, and thus isolating the Church more and more from the world. But the stability of the world is also threatened by secularisation. Every day it becomes more questionable whether man is adequate, with his ethics and his passions, to the task he has taken upon himself in the modern age of being lord of himself and of the world. This double threat, to faith and to the world, raises the question whether there can be any limit to secularisation, whether there is anything in the world which can escape its onslaught, whether it can be limited and restrained at all, and where, if there is a limit, it is to be drawn. Thus the question of the limits of secularisation leads on to the question of its meaning; for I can only limit something when I have understood its meaning. Gogarten and Bonhoeffer seek not merely to understand secularisation better than it has hitherto been understood by theology, but also better than it has understood itself. They appeal as it were from a secularisation which understands itself wrongly to a secularisation which understands itself aright. Associated with this in their works is the attempt to understand Christian faith in such a way that it no longer needs to hide in fear from the changed reality of the world.

By attempting a new and better understanding of secularisation and Christian faith, by seeing each in the light of the other, they take theology back into the open arena of intellectual confrontation with the world. In this process, they find themselves driven back to the very first principles of the understanding of traditional Christian words and concepts, while at the same time they are also guided by a presentiment that there is something new and revolutionary in them. Gogarten and Bonhoeffer acknowledge ungrudgingly the maturity of human reason, and the secularisation of the world which results therefrom. They do not defend themselves against it in the manner of the mistaken theological apologetic which frantically seeks to reserve for faith what faith has long ago handed over to the good offices of reason, and which, as though stupefied by the hopelessness of this procedure, persists in it with even greater obstinacy. Nor do they see the development of the modern age, like traditional Catholic or Protestant histories, as a falling away of man from God or from Christ, with the result that this development has increasingly come to regard itself as anti-Christian. Finally, they do not indulge in a romantic longing for a return to an imaginary Middle Ages. Rather, they accept the maturity of human reason, and the secularisation of the world which results from it, for what they are: the outcome of a necessary historical process. There is no escape from this process, at least not by renouncing intellectual honesty, but only by conversion and repentance. But conversion and repentance are something quite different: they do not lead out of reality, but into reality. Consequently, by coming to grips, radically and selflessly, with

the changed reality of the world, Gogarten and Bonhoeffer have set in
motion in theology more than a new mode of thought: they have
inspired a movement of repentance, a conversion in theological thought.
One cannot exist without the other: there is no intellectual honesty
without conversion and repentance. Here too it is true that 'whoever
loses his life shall find it'. Whether Gogarten and Bonhoeffer have also
found the reality of the world in a new way by the conversion they
have brought about in theological thought remains to be seen.

The end of religion

Many Protestant theologians, those among them at least who are
sensitive to the present age, and sincere, follow Gogarten and Bonhoeffer
in acknowledging the coming of age of the world as an established
historical fact which cannot be reversed by any Christian artifice. But
among them all Dietrich Bonhoeffer occupies a place of his own: more
radically than the others, even than Gogarten, he focusses his analysis
of the historical situation upon the phenomena of religion, and so arrives
at his famous thesis of the *end of religion*. Here he is following his master
Karl Barth, under whom he never studied, but whose works, as he
admits, he read in their entirety. He accepts Barth's critique of religion,
with its radical distinction between human religion and divine revelation, and yet goes decisively beyond this. Whereas Barth largely
restricts his criticism of religion to the field of dogmatics and fundamental theology, Bonhoeffer draws from it practical conclusions,
relating it to the concrete historical situation. He puts his criticism to a
practical test, by confronting Christian faith with the changed reality
of the world. Here his theological knowledge is combined with the
practical experience which he gained as a conspirator, co-operating with
politicians and diplomats, and as a prisoner, in his association with his
guards and fellow prisoners in military and Gestapo prisons. Thus he
arrived at the following radical judgement: 'The time when people
could be told everything by means of words, whether theological or
pious, is over, and so is the time of inwardness and conscience – and that
means the time of religion in general. We are moving towards a
completely religionless time.'[11]

As an example of the fact that men are already 'in reality radically
without religion' Bonhoeffer points among other things to the Second
World War. By contrast with the First World War, and indeed to all
previous wars, it no longer provoked any kind of religious reaction.

Even the Western pattern of Christianity can now be regarded only as a 'first stage towards complete religionlessness'. Bonhoeffer regards the secularisation that has already come about, and the state of religion-lessness which accompanies it, as so final and complete that he is no longer able to share the view so widely held at the present day, that modern man compensates for the loss of his traditional religion by at once setting up a substitute for religion: 'Idolatry implies that people still worship something. But we do not now worship anything, not even idols. In that respect we are truly nihilists.'[12]

Bonhoeffer sees in religion only an historically conditioned and there-fore transitory expression of Christianity. It is like a garment which the Christian revelation has worn up till now, whether rightly or wrongly, but which is now at last completely worn out. Different ages regard this garment differently. It is true that Bonhoeffer never gives a precise and comprehensive definition of what he understands by 'religion'; but the individual statements which he makes on the subject are so unequivocal in their sense that it is not difficult to obtain from them at least an approximate picture of what he has in mind. This picture is no doubt one-sided, and is to some extent a polemical caricature. A number of terms are characteristic of it: 'metaphysical', 'individualist', 'anthro-pocentric', 'pietistic', 'mystical', 'this world and the next', *Deus ex machina*', 'the eternal salvation of the soul', 'salvation in the world to come'. Drawing these terms together, we find in them an accurate representation of that Western transcendental metaphysics, the end of which was proclaimed by Nietzsche, as Heidegger interprets him.

Bonhoeffer considers the decisive characteristic of all 'religion' to be that of thinking in two separate spheres: God exists in a world above and beyond, while man exists here below. Like the *Deus ex machina* in ancient tragedy, God reaches down from above into this lower world, while man longs to rise out of this world to the world above and beyond, where he will be redeemed in a new and better life. The premise upon which this metaphysical thinking in two spheres depends is the acceptance of the necessity of religion, that is, the endowment of man with a religious faculty, in such a way that religion is rooted in the structure of the human mind.

As long as Christianity has existed, it has lived in partnership with this kind of 'religion'. But the age of religion is now at an end, and religion is no longer accepted as a necessity. As the autonomy of human reason and the secularisation of the world advanced during the modern age, so God was forced out of the world. In a kind of reaction, Christianity, its thought still confined in the same two spheres, has anxiously sought in its turn to preserve some room for God and religion within the world, or against the world. The attempt is made, by returning to the so-called *ultimate questions* of knowledge and life, to demonstrate to a world that has come of age that it still cannot exist without 'God' as its guardian. This might be described as a search for an 'emergency exit' for God out of the increasingly narrow space in which he has been confined.

In order to save the existence of God from the continual encroachment of scientific *knowledge*, an attempt is made to find gaps and flaws in the continuous chain of causality in nature, into which God can be reintroduced; a search is made for gaps which still exist in the sphere of scientific study, and God is then used to fill these gaps. Thus God is equated with what has not yet been discovered. But this is nothing more than to use God to plug the holes in the incomplete fabric of human knowledge. As an attempt to rescue God, this is as unworthy as it is hopeless. By using this proof of God, religion has thrown away its case. For since it is of the nature of human knowledge never to be content, but constantly to reach beyond itself into what is still unknown, unexplored and unexplained, God is subjected to a 'continuous retreat' and is forced into an ever stricter confinement. The further science advances its frontiers, the more 'God loses ground'. If once he filled the whole cathedral of the world, he is now as it were forced back into the sanctuary, or has even taken refuge upon the altar, where he dwells like the deity of some heathen religion.

As a working hypothesis of science, or even of politics, art, or morality, God has been defeated, and must be abandoned. 'A scientist or physician who sets out to edify is a hybrid.'[13] This dawned upon Bonhoeffer when he read in prison Carl Friedrich von Weizsäcker's book *Zum Weltbild der Physik* (On the World View of Physics). Von Weizsäcker's words, spoken twenty years later, in his Gifford Lectures given at Glasgow University in 1959–61, sound like an echo and a confirmation of this: 'Modern scientists in general find it very difficult to think of a religious interpretation of natural law as anything but an additional tenet, probably mythical and certainly not logically connected with the concept of the laws of nature.'[14]

The other attempt of Christian apologists to demonstrate that God is indispensable is based on a return to what are called the *ultimate questions* of life. God having been excluded from the public aspects of human existence, an attempt is made to retain him at least in the realm of personal inner and private life, and to make room for him there. Man is reminded of his limits – sickness, suffering, distress, care, sin, guilt, and death – and an attempt made to demonstrate to him that in such extreme situations he cannot endure by his own power, but is dependent upon God, the Church, and the priest. Thus the 'secrets known to a man's valet' – the realm of his intimate life, from his prayers to his sexual life – have become 'the hunting-ground of modern pastoral workers'. Bonhoeffer compares their activities to those of 'the dirtiest gutter journalists': just as the latter drag the intimate lives of other people into the light of day, to ruin them socially, financially or politically, so the clergy do the same, in order to practice 'religious blackmail'. Bonhoeffer describes this 'sniffing-around-after-people's-sins' as 'clerical'; he holds it in total contempt. But he finds the same unchaste and clerical sniffing-around-after-sin among the 'secularised offshoots of Christian theology', existentialist philosophy and the psychotherapists, and he derides them as he does Christian theologians: 'Wherever there is health, strength, security, simplicity, they scent luscious fruits to gnaw at or lay their pernicious eggs in.' They try to persuade man, when he is secure, contented and happy, that he is really unhappy and desperate, and is simply unwilling to admit it; they set themselves to drive people to inward despair, and when they have succeeded, the game is in their hands – 'That is secularised methodism.'

Thus an attempt is made to 'fall upon a few unfortunate people in their hour of need and exercise a sort of religious compulsion upon them'. Bonhoeffer's aristocratic sense of style revolts against this effort 'to exploit man's weakness'. He regards it as no more than a 'revolution from below, a revolt of inferiority': it is as though 'the vulgar mind is not satisfied until it has seen some highly placed personage "in his bath"', or 'as if you could not know a fine house till you found a cobweb in the furthest cellar', or 'as if you could not adequately appreciate a good play till you had seen how the actors behave off-stage'.[15]

But cannot both Christian and secular 'methodists' appeal to the central message of the gospel? Did Jesus himself not say that it was not those who are well who need a doctor, but those who are sick, and that he came to save sinners? Bonhoeffer's reply to this objection is: 'When Jesus blessed sinners, they were real sinners, but Jesus did not make everyone a sinner first. He called them away from their sin, not into their sin. . . . Never did he question a man's health, vigour or happiness, regarded in themselves, or regard them as evil fruits; else why should he heal the sick and restore strength to the weak?'[16]

Bonhoeffer is much too permeated by the power of the healthy, simple and natural goodness of this world to give any chance in a world that has come of age to a clerical, unchaste, and pietistic 'methodism', whether Christian or secular, whether practised by theologians, existentialist philosophers or psychotherapists. For who are reached by such an outlook? Only a 'few "last survivors of the age of chivalry" or a few intellectually dishonest people', 'a small number . . . of degenerates, of people who regard themselves as the most important thing in the world, and who therefore like to busy themselves with themselves'. But one must not imagine it possible to convince the normal healthy man in the street, 'the ordinary man, who spends his everyday life at work and with his family, and of course with all kinds of diversions', by reminding him of the limits of his existential life, that he is dependent upon God, and so to affect him religiously. Secularised man can manage – even without God. But when he has managed to resolve the extreme situation in some 'natural' way, then faith in God is once again shown to be superfluous, 'and the theologians are at the end of their Latin'.[17] Since it is the nature of secularisation that it never comes to a halt, but constantly advances, seeking to take possession of the whole world, it also forces God out of his hidden refuge in the intimate corners of human life, and finally conquers the very last strongholds of religion, when it does not simply leave them to wither away.

Bonhoeffer regards the whole attack by Christian apologetics upon the adulthood of the world, whether it deals with the 'ultimate questions' of knowledge or those of life, as pointless, ignoble and unchristian: 'Pointless, because it seems to me like an attempt to put a grown-up man back into adolescence, i.e. to make him dependent on things on which he is, in fact, no longer dependent, and thrusting him into problems that are, in fact, no longer problems to him. Ignoble, because it amounts to an attempt to exploit man's weakness for purposes that are alien to him and to which he has not freely assented. Unchristian, because it confuses Christ with one particular stage in man's religiousness, i.e. with a human law.'[18]

Different motives combine in the way Bonhoeffer takes the part of those without religion, and turns against Christian apologists: his intellectual honesty, his insight into the spiritual situation, his recognition of the adulthood of the world, his respect for the freedom of others, his predilection for what is simple and healthy, his hatred for everything that is mere pious talk, his exquisite sense of style and his conviction of the mighty power of the word of God, which needs no ally. He once summed this up in a letter, and at the same time made clear the positive nature of his theological purpose: 'I therefore want to start from the premise that God should not be smuggled into some last secret place, but that we should frankly recognise that the world, and people, have come of age, that we should not run man down in his worldliness, but confront him with God at his strongest point, that we should give up all our clerical tricks, and not regard psychotherapy and existentialist philosophy as God's pioneers. The importunity of all these people is far too unaristocratic for the Word of God to ally itself with them. The Word of God is far removed from this revolt of mistrust, this revolt from below. On the contrary, it reigns.'[19]

One must judge more cautiously than Bonhoeffer whether it is really the case, as he asserts, that the end of religion has come, and that we are coming to an age which is wholly without religion. The matter has not yet been decided. Protestant theology itself, now that Karl Barth has begun with a complete *tabula rasa*, must think out once again in fundamental terms whether there is really any *a priori* necessity for religion, and whether one may continue to look for a 'point of contact', a 'prior understanding', or a 'readiness to be called' on the part of man. But we must wholly agree with Bonhoeffer that we find ourselves in a completely new situation with regard to religion. Gerhard Ebeling was right to speak in his systematic interpretation of the theology of Bonhoeffer, with regard to total secularisation, of a '*novum* without parallel' within the whole of the history of religion.[20] What is new in our position in the history of religion is that what is taking place is not the disintegration of one particular religion, accompanied as in the past by the transition from an old religion to a new, but the destruction of the very essence of religion. Something has really come to its final end in our times. Things will never again be as they were. Religion as the supplementing of reality by God, as a particular province on the edge of life, has disappeared for ever. Something new is making itself known, something that at best we can only see dimly, but of which we can as yet have no proper conception. All one can say so far is that there will either be no religion any more, or else that religion will be a power affecting and determining the whole reality of life.

The justification for this view is the fact that a causal, historical and logical connection exists between total secularisation and Christian faith. The end of religion asserted by Bonhoeffer, and indeed the 'death of God' dreamt by Jean Paul and proclaimed by Nietzsche, are only the ultimate consequences of the way in which the Christian belief in God itself deprives the world of divinity. Here we come to the decisive realisation which at the present day determines all theological consideration of secularisation, wherever it seeks to be more than a lament or an attack. Here we come to the decisive issue in the theme we are studying. Total secularisation has not simply come upon Christian faith in the modern age as a calamity from outside, but is rather the ultimate outcome of something inherent and essential in the attitude to the world of Christian faith itself.

Man between God and the world

This brings us to the great systematic achievement of Friedrich Gogarten. More than anyone else, he has made the autonomy of man and the worldliness of the world the object of his theological thought. His principal thesis, repeated in many varied forms, is that the starting-point of the process of secularisation lies in Christian faith itself; without Christian faith the world as it is today would have been impossible. Secularisation is 'a post-Christian phenomenon, that is, a phenomenon brought about by Christian faith'; it is, 'regardless of what it has become at the present day, a legitimate consequence of Christian faith'; 'the first mighty step towards giving form to the world and to reality by using the forces of Christian faith'.[21] Consequently, anyone who seeks to call a halt to secularisation, supposedly in the interests of faith, is acting against faith. And for the same reason, secularisation is a task which faith must take upon itself.

The whole of Gogarten's theological thought is concentrated upon this *connection between secularisation and Christian faith*. In interpreting this connection, he begins with the central point of all Protestant theology, and Lutheran theology in particular, the justification of man in the sight of God through faith alone. When we think of the word 'justification', we think at once of the personal relationship of the individual to God, his eternal destiny, and his salvation in the world to come, and we are inclined to ask whether there could be anything more remote, more unworldly, and more intimate than that, and whether it is not the very expression of the individualistic longing for redemption in a better world to come which for Bonhoeffer is the characteristic of everything he dismisses as 'religion'. But Gogarten now shows that inherent in this very act of justification, so remote, so intimate, and apparently so unworldly and individualistic, is a completely new attitude of man towards the world. The dominating aim of his theology is with remorseless logic to deduce this new attitude of man to the world from the original premise of justification. Consequently, the theme of his theology is not 'man in the sight of God', but man 'between God and the world'.

The existential being of man is essentially determined by the fact that he stands between God and the world. He is not man without God, but neither is he man without the world. He belongs *to* God, but he belongs *in* the world. The peculiar and burdensome problems of his existence are those of attaining a right attitude to both, to God and to the world, and of adopting a right position between God and the world. This relationship is a right one when God is truly God for him, and the world is truly the world. But he is open to the grave danger of confusing God and the world, so that God becomes the world for him, and the world becomes God.[22]

Gogarten's thought takes Luther's doctrine of justification to its ultimate conclusions: he deals with *the doctrine of justification in relation to the world*. For him, justification and creation are inseparable. For him, the justification of man in the sight of God, and the understanding of the world as the creation of God, are one and the same act. Man obtains his salvation by understanding his own self, and also the world, as what they are originally and essentially – God's creation. That theology has not related justification and creation in this way, but has separated them, is regarded by Gogarten as one of the most unfortunate theological developments of the modern period. This is why it has been possible for theology to overlook the genuinely Christian purpose in the process of secularisation, and to take arms against it.[23]

Secularisation and Christian faith are so closely linked that in the history of human thought secularisation is only a by-product of Christianity, one of the many which it has produced in the course of its history. But in addition to this, secularisation derives originally and directly from the very heart of the Christian revelation. However surprising it may sound, the coming of age of man and the worldliness of the world are a direct consequence of the fact that Jesus Christ is the 'Son' and that as the Son he has revealed the 'Father'. Of course in order to understand this, one must understand the divine sonship of God in the right way, that is, not metaphysically, as was done in the christological dogma of the early Church with the aid of Greek philosophy, but historically, in accordance with the thought of the Bible and the historical method of the modern age. In the earthly and human sphere itself sonship is not in the first instance a category of natural causality, but a personal and historical category. Someone is a son only through and by his father – but this he understands not by learning of his bodily origin, but only by knowing his father, and recognising himself as a son by so knowing his father. Similarly, Gogarten interprets the way in which Jesus is the Son of God not through the category of natural causality, 'begetting', but in the personal and historical category of 'sending'; the Father sends and the Son obeys. But this means that Jesus is not the Son on the basis of a particular physical parentage and constitution, but on the basis of a particular historical attitude. He is the Son, because he lets God be completely his Father. Jesus 'has nothing of himself', but by having nothing of himself, he has everything from God, and it is in this way that he shows himself to be the Son. But by showing himself to be the Son, he proclaims and reveals God as the Father – for someone is a son only through and by his father. Thus in the way Jesus is the Son, fatherhood and sonship form a single living movement.

Through the revelation of the Father by the Son man is placed in a new relationship to God and to the world. Gogarten sees this as the decisive event which determines the whole subsequent history of mankind. It broke down the mythical world order which had endured for thousands of years. The essence of this ancient mythical world order, as Gogarten sees it, was that the cosmos was understood as being brought into being and governed in all its parts by eternal primeval forces. They constituted the law which kept the world and life in proper order. Man knew that he was dependent upon these forces, and timidly conformed himself to their eternal rule. He regarded the cosmos as good, divine and sacred. But as a result man venerated as divine the primeval forces of the cosmos, although they were powers existing within the world itself. This was what the Bible described as the original sin of man, the worshipping of the creature instead of the creator. Hence the cosmos was sealed off from God, while man was imprisoned in this sealed cosmos. Instead of drawing his life from God, he drew it from the world. It is true that even before Christ man distinguished himself from the cosmos, by reflecting upon it. But the decisive problem which confronted him was once again how he could conform himself in his thought and action to the rule of the eternal world order. Thus even man's reflection upon the cosmos did not break down the barriers which held him within it. Even in his thought he remained imprisoned within the world.[24]

It was Christian faith which finally set man free from his imprisonment by the world. By giving man a new access to the Father, Jesus

Christ broke the bonds of the cosmos which imprisoned him. Through his obedient sonship he restored our lost sonship. Consequently Christ is referred to in the Bible as the 'first-born of many brethren': he is the first member of a new race of sons.

According to Gogarten, man has attained his profoundest knowledge of himself in the concept of *sonship*; in it man has finally found himself. Gogarten sees sonship as including both a new relationship to God and a new relationship to the world. Man has once again become what he is intended to be by God's eternal creative will: the *son of the Father* and *lord of the world*. In this way he stands in his right place between God and the world, in which God is God to him, and the world is the world.

God is God to him – this implies that man no longer derives his life from the world, but from God; and he receives from God not merely the various things which he actually needs in order to live, but his whole self, his existence as a person. He manifests his sonship by relying with utter trust, in his whole being, upon him who has revealed himself to him as the Father, and by attributing everything that he is, that he possesses and that he can achieve to the Father. Thus he once again becomes God's creature, and is once again whole and sound; or as Paul puts it, and Luther, following Paul: 'righteous in the sight of God': 'The true and highest honour with which the son can honour the Father is that of being his son from his very heart.'[25]

But because man has once again come to regard God as God, he is also able once again to regard the world as the world. Through his sonship, his relationship to the world has fundamentally changed. He is no longer a part of the world, no longer imprisoned by the world, fearfully worshipping the forces that rule in it, but is now *free* with regard to the world. From henceforth the world is no longer an object which he venerates as divine, but the sphere in which he exercises his reason. As the son of the Father he is an heir, and as an heir he is lord of the world. Just as a son receives his heritage from his father when he comes of age, so the world is given to man by God as a heritage. Because he has been pronounced to be of age, he has an independent responsibility for ruling the world.

Man's new position with regard to the world is summed up in the phrase of the apostle Paul: 'All things are lawful' (1 Cor. 6: 12). Gogarten regards these words as one of the most important statements in the whole of the New Testament: he sees them as the hidden seed and starting-point of a vast movement in world history which nothing can halt: 'However slight the outward cause which led Paul to make this statement that "all things are lawful", it is nevertheless one of the most powerful sayings which has ever been uttered. For because a completely new relationship of man to the world was revealed in it, it has fundamentally changed the face of the world. It laid the foundation of the domination over the world and its forces which the human mind was later to achieve.'[26]

'All things are lawful' – these words proclaim that the world is *secular*. They take away the distinction between the sacred and the profane, and so hand over every province of life and the world to the free action of man. If 'all things are lawful' for man, then there can no longer be in the world any distinct areas of piety, any separate religious spheres, any specific sacred acts, or anything at all which possesses an enhanced relationship to God and is therefore capable of mediating divine salvation to man. Instead, everything is profane, and at man's free disposal.

But this does not signify that he can do whatever he fancies with it! The statement of Paul quoted by Gogarten, that 'all things are lawful', continues, 'but not all things are helpful'. This means that distinctions must still be made, for the good order of the world has to be maintained. But these distinctions are not a matter of faith, but of *reason*. Man must use his reason to decide what may or may not be helpful at any given time in maintaining the good order of the world. According to Gogarten, the same distinctions between life and death, sacred and profane, good and evil, useful and useless, proper and improper, which are present in the world, and which reason can perceive in any given case, apply to human activity in the world, including that of Christians. Consequently all human action in the world is subject to reason, and in fact it is faith itself which subjects to reason man's activity in the world, so that this activity may preserve its purely secular character, while faith itself remains pure faith.

The purpose of man's lordship over the world is not to redeem the world; it is not for him to bring about the salvation of the world through his activities. Salvation always comes from God alone, and man can receive it only in faith. God has not made man the saviour of the world, but its guardian, in order to preserve its secular existence by his works, so that the world may remain the world. We can paraphrase Gogarten's meaning by saying that it is the duty of a politician to establish order and not to set up the kingdom of God; of a doctor to heal the body and not to save the soul; of a judge to pronounce judgement, and not to carry out the last judgement; of an historian to study what has happened and not to investigate the will of God. The reason why, in considering man's responsibility for the world, Gogarten stresses so strongly the distinction between 'faith' and 'works', is not in order to divide man's existential life into two parts, that of a Christian and that of a man, but only in order to reduce human activity to its proper proportions, so that it remains a genuinely earthly and secular activity, and thus does not take the form of a religious claim upon God or upon the world.

Thus by starting with the central essence of Christian faith, the justification of man in the sight of God, Gogarten succeeds in providing a new relationship between man and the world. In this way he unites again justification and creation, which in his view modern theology has separated, with damaging results for both faith and the world. It is understandable that Gogarten does not find the current Christian concept of 'God's children' adequate to describe the new relationship of man to God and to the world which is implicit in faith. It is too limited and too naïve. It lays too much emphasis on mere childlike submission to the fatherly rule of God, and does not make sufficiently clear that in addition to all the boundless trust a son has to show, maturity, independence, freedom, responsibility, decision and authority are also required of him. It is in order to emphasise this 'manly', 'regal' character of man's responsibility for the world, against all false Christian naïveté and childishness, that Gogarten speaks of 'sonship' instead of being 'God's child': 'It is the son, not the child but the grown man, who must take responsibility in the sight of God the Father for his relationship to the world, of which God has made him Lord.'[27]

Secularisation and Christian faith

'If we have faith in God we are no longer the slaves of the gods . . . God himself has deprived the world of its divinity.' Carl Friedrich von Weizsäcker, who follows Gogarten in his interpretation of secularisation,[28] sums up in this short sentence the change which took place with the entry of Christianity into the world. It set in motion an historical process which has continued ever since, which is still at work today, and of which the consequences are incalculable. The essence of this process is as follows. By delivering the world of its divinity, God has brought about a profound and fundamental change in the relationship of man to the world. Man has become independent with regard to the world, and has taken responsibility for it. Gogarten sums up this new

freedom of man in the words of the apostle Paul: 'All things are yours
. . . whether the world or life or death or the present or the future, all
are yours' (1 Cor. 3:21 ff.). But with the change in the relationship of
man to the world, the world itself has also changed. The mythical world
has become historical; it has ceased to be worshipped as divine, and has
become the sphere in which human reason is exercised. And this has
opened the way to the secularisation of the world and the autonomy of
human reason, and so to the domination and manipulation of the world
by modern science and technology. Everything that has happened since
has been a development and consequence of this one single original
event, the secularisation of the world by God in the revelation in Christ.

By comparison with this revolution, Gogarten regards all the other
changes which the world has undergone as 'insignificant', and 'partial'.
For however much they may have shaken the world, they all took place
within the world and acted upon it. But in the revolution that took
place in Christ, another world came into being. It is as though the world
has received a new 'constitution'. It is true that before Christian faith
came into the world, the Greeks had also looked objectively at the
world and practised philosophy and science, but in spite of all their
enlightenment they never completely gave up the religious veneration
of the world. It was Christian faith which first brought about a radical
change, and so introduced a 'new era', a 'new aeon', to the extent that
we can legitimately reckon our calendar from that time and distinguish
between B.C. and A.D.[29]

But the coming of age of man and the secularisation of the world,
which from the very first were potentially implicit in Christian faith,
were not immediately realised in the history of the Western world.
At first, and indeed very soon after Paul, a back-lash occurred.
The Middle Ages repeated in a Christian form what had previously
existed in a heathen form. The hierarchical and sacramental world
of the Middle Ages, as a single and unified totality, once again
imprisoned man and deprived him of his independence. Then came
Martin Luther, who destroyed the unified world of the Middle Ages,
which had lasted for a thousand years, by translating into reality what
from the very first was implicit in Christian faith with regard to man's
relationship to the world. He had to do this if, as he asserted, he had
truly rediscovered the pure gospel; for it was this very gospel which
contained within it man's freedom from the world. Gogarten considers
that Luther was faced here with a wholly new task, never before
recognised for what it was, not even at the time of the New Testament.[30]

Luther dealt with this task by his *distinction between the two kingdoms*, the kingdom of God and the kingdom of the world. This distinction was to affirm that in the kingdom of the world God has subjected all things to human reason. Gogarten quotes numerous passages in Luther as evidence of this. Here are only two examples: 'In the kingdom of the world one must act from reason, for God has subjected such temporal rule and bodily matters to reason, and has not sent the Holy Spirit from heaven for this purpose . . . for this reason too, God does not teach in the holy scripture how to build houses, make clothes, marry, make war, sail ships, and so forth; for the natural light is sufficient for this.' Luther even goes so far as to say: 'God does not need Christians for secular rule. Consequently it is not necessary for the Emperor to be holy; he does not need to be a Christian in order to rule. It is sufficient for the Emperor to possess reason. It is in this way that God the Lord also maintains the kingdom of the Turks and Tartars.'[31]

Luther is saying two things in these statements. First, that man has to take care of the things of this world in accordance with his reason; and secondly, that in this way God is exercising his rule over the world. This means that man is lord of the world, but that he exercises this lordship in the service of God, as his son. By this means, as a consequence of Christian faith, Luther brought about the secularisation of the institutions of earthly life, or at least advanced it to a considerable extent. One has only to consider the impact on culture, politics, society, economics, science and art of one of Luther's statements which is frequently and casually quoted: 'The Christian is a free lord over all things and subject to no one.' Gogarten is right to assert that 'at this point everything must change' and to continue 'as everything has in fact changed in the centuries since the Reformation'.[32]

Luther himself was not concerned here with the autonomy of human reason. He was not interested in that at all. His exclusive concern was the gospel. All he desired was that the gospel should remain the gospel. It was for this reason alone that he handed over the kingdom of the world to human reason. But by so doing, whether he wished or not, he was opening the door to the modern age, and paving the way for the autonomous culture of our age, with its abundant powers to change and control the world.

The result was different from that anticipated and desired by Luther. For Luther the coming of age of man, and with it the secularisation of the world, was a consequence of Christian faith and the freedom of man for God which it brought with it. By contrast, the essence of the modern

process of secularisation which was beginning at this time is that the
freedom of man with regard to the world has broken away from Christian faith and freedom for God. Modern man no longer derives his
responsibility for the world from God the creator, but from himself.
This does not imply, however, that the process of secularisation has
ceased. While Christian faith cannot exist without secularisation, it is
quite possible, once the process of secularisation was set in motion by
faith, for it to continue without faith. For it contains a genuine possibility inherent in human nature; and therefore the freedom of man can
endure even without faith, through its own power.

Consequently, the modern process of secularisation has an 'ambiva-
lent' character. The world which it brings into being is no longer
properly speaking Christian, yet neither is it wholly unchristian. Carl
Friedrich von Weizsäcker has an image which clearly typifies the
'ambivalence' of the modern world: a secularised monastery is still the
same building as before; its rooms still have the structure of monastic
cells, a refectory and a chapel, even if they are now used for other
purposes. Similarly, the modern world still has the structure of a
Christian world; it forms as it were a 'photographic negative' of the
older Christian world. The original drawing is still the same, and it is
only the colours which have changed: black has changed into white,
and white into black. This explains why the concepts in which we have
described the process of secularisation all sound 'ambiguous'.[33]

Man's 'sonship' continues, but because it is separated from faith, it
takes on another form. Modern man still remains the 'heir to the world',
more than ever before, but he now seizes the heritage which has been
bestowed upon him as his own possession, without feeling any kind of
further obligation to the 'Father'. He pleases himself; he is self-sufficient.
He no longer relies upon God, and in fact it seems that God now relies
upon him. This is the only explanation of the rapidity with which
secular thought in the modern age has been able to develop into atheistic
thought. Hegel, of course, sought no more than to retrace the ways of
the divine spirit – but where would the divine spirit be without Hegel?
Ludwig Feuerbach drew the ultimate consequence from Hegel's presumption: man creates God according to his own image.

Nor does 'freedom' cease to exist in the modern age, once it has
broken away from Christian faith and therefore from its source. But
whereas man is in principle free from the world, he allows himself to be
imprisoned once again, together with his freedom, by the world. His
domination of the world makes him dependent upon the forces which

control it, and which his intellect itself has released. In losing his freedom
for God, therefore, man runs the risk of losing his freedom altogether.
Every genuine historical test of strength to which the idea of freedom
has been subjected has shown how unsure in its foundations and feeble
in its resistance it is in the modern age. In fact at the present day the
final period of the modern age, which began with so arrogant a belief
in freedom, is now drawing to an end in fear and doubt about that
freedom.

Gogarten does not make any moral judgement on this situation, but
rather a theological, or more precisely an historical judgement. In
Gogarten's view nothing is achieved by trying to determine whether
what has taken place has been right or wrong. All pious theories of a
'fall' are inadequate. Gogarten perceives in the whole process of secularisation something which approximates a tragic necessity. He certainly
sees the presence of guilt, of a great deal of guilt. But in the modern age
man has virtually no choice but to continue on the way upon which he
has set out, once he has taken on responsibility for the world. The
essence of the world is its unity and coherence of meaning, and this unity
and coherence and therefore its meaning derive from its being God's
creation. But what happens if man now no longer believes that God is
the creator of heaven and earth? The unity and coherence of the world
cannot simply cease, allowing the world to sink into chaos and into
meaninglessness. So Prometheus must climb up into heaven. Man himself must be God. He himself must take over responsibility for the unity
and coherence of the world, for its order and for its future. He himself,
with his thinking, his plans and his creative activity, with the totality of
his life and intellect, and with the ultimate and highest thoughts of
which he is capable, must attempt to give the world a meaning derived
from himself, in order to justify the world in his own eyes. The only
way in which he can do this is to aim for perfection, and he cannot cease
until he has brought history to an end, and made the world into a self-
contained cosmos. But in this striving for the perfection of the world
man himself is destroyed. For the consequence of perfection is the
abandonment of humanity. Wherever man seeks to build a perfect
world, he abuses man by making him his means and his tool, a slave of
the world which he plans.

Thus once man has ceased to understand himself and the world as
God's creation, he is ceaselessly driven on 'into a titanic struggle without
remission or ending'. No sooner does he believe that he has attained to
his ideal, than he must set out once again. His attempt to give meaning

to the world only leads him deeper into meaninglessness. By owing his
responsibility for the world to himself, instead of to God, man has
overreached himself: 'How can he, who must derive his life from himself, fill the infinite and boundless universe with his own life and
meaning! Its meaninglessness only increases with every drop of blood
and spirit which he spends upon it . . . here man is basing his life upon
the horrible lie of a responsibility which does not exist and which,
however seriously it is taken, cannot exist, because it is empty. For a
responsibility which is not a response, and which therefore does not
come about by listening in obedience to a word which invokes it, is
empty and is a phantom. Wherever life is based upon it – and in the
modern age man bases his life to an increasing degree on such a responsibility – life is drawn from a vacuum and expended in a vacuum, drawn
from nothingness and expended in nothingness. Where this goes on
continuously, it will some day become visible, and *then* everyone will
become aware of it.'[34]

Theology and the Church share the guilt for the absence of any
Christian meaning in secularisation and therefore for the 'catastrophe of
the modern age'. The unmasking of this guilt is the polemical purpose
of Gogarten's interpretation of secularisation. His polemic is not
directed, as is normal elsewhere, against the claim of science to domination, but against the failure of theology. The Church and theology have
failed to understand the process of secularisation in the modern age, and
instead have dreamt as before of a world which is a unity in itself. Consequently, in spite of the step in the right direction taken by Luther, they
have failed to respond to the challenge of secularisation in a selfless way.
Instead they have sought to oppose it by endeavouring, without right
or title, to withhold from reason what God himself had long ago
entrusted to its care. It seems as if they had grudged man the freedom
which Christian faith has revealed to him, and which he may properly
claim to the full. He was to remain the child of the Father, instead of
becoming his son. Thus modern man, abandoned by theology and the
Church, has misunderstood his freedom and brought it to realisation
without faith, or even in opposition to faith. But as usually happens in
such cases, the very hopelessness of their efforts caused theology and the
Church obstinately to persist in their error – 'and things went from bad
to worse'.[35]

Hence secularisation in the modern age has got on the wrong track.
Justified at its outset, the mode of its realisation has gone awry. As a
result, Gogarten distinguishes between two kinds of secularisation. The

one continues to be linked with Christian faith, so that the world is
delivered of its divinity through the revelation of Christ, the other
becomes separated from Christian faith, so that the world is delivered
of its divinity by man. The first case Gogarten describes as *secularisation*,
and the second as *secularism*. Thus secularism is a 'degenerate form of
secularisation'.

Secularism can appear in two different forms. The first is that of a
doctrine of salvation or *ideology*. This represents an overt or concealed
attempt by man to give the world a meaning based upon himself, to
restore its unity and coherence, and so to bring salvation to it. He is not
content to put forward what is only a partial view of the world, but
consciously or unconsciously elevates this partial aspect to the status of a
total interpretation of the world. All the phenomena of life are sub-
sumed into one ultimate theme, and this is presented as a unified formula
capable of informing with meaning the life of the totality of the world,
and so also of the individual. There is hardly anything in the world
which has not been made a symbol and fountainhead of the meaning of
the life of the individual and of the whole of history. This always leads
to an attempt at creating a perfect world. The result is not the liberation
of man, as was the intention, but an increase of his servitude. Man, who
is imperfect, is made the slave of a system alien to him.

The other form of 'secularism' is *nihilism*. Man becomes weary of the
constant meaninglessness to which he is exposed, and comes to regard
all questions which concern the world as useless in their totality, ultimately renouncing any attempt to find meaning, unity and coherence
in the world. He gives up the struggle or falls into despair. But at this
point the second form of secularism tends to become confounded with
the first. Exposed to the meaninglessness of chaos, and in order to have
at least something to hold on to, even if it is only an illusion, man
seizes the next best ideology at hand and subjects himself to it.

Faced with this two-fold danger present in secularisation – the lapsing
into an ideology or the falling into nihilism – the task of Christian faith
is to protect secularisation from degenerating and turning into secularism. Faith cannot carry out this task by reversing the process of secularisation and rechristianising the world, but only by helping it to remain
secular: 'Christian faith and civilisation have not so much to do with
each other that the latter must be christianised. The opposite is the case:
Christian faith plays its part by keeping civilisation secular.'[36]

The best test of the extent to which Christian faith takes seriously its
responsibility for secularisation is its relationship to *modern science*: for

no manifestation of the process of secularisation that has taken place in the modern age is so pure and so remote from faith as this. According to Gogarten, the right relationship between faith and science is maintained when both faith and science remain themselves. But he is convinced that only Christian faith can make this possible.

The purity of faith is demonstrated by a resolute recognition that science is independent of faith. It is this issue more than any other that decides whether Christian faith seriously intends to be faith and nothing more, and to hand over all earthly and human action without reservation to reason. If Christian belief in the creation is a genuine faith in God the creator, and not a philosophical interpretation of the world, it must set modern science free to pursue its studies of natural causation and its control of the world and cease to consider that anything in the sphere of science might serve as theological proof and should therefore be excluded from causal observation. Any conflict arising in this sphere would indicate that faith still has certain concealed reservations about the scientific study and control of the world by the use of reason, and is therefore still permeated by elements of a particular world view.

The purity of science must be manifested in the same way as the purity of faith by its remaining within the world, and enduring the fact 'that the world is only the world'. Its task is to study that part of the reality of the world which is accessible to rational experience, part by part, and piece by piece. But science would inevitably be broken down into separate specialisations, and ultimately fall into ignorance, if it did not ask the question of the meaning within the totality of the world of every phenomenon, however insignificant, and of every event, however unimportant. Yet only by asking, in this way, questions directed towards the 'partial totality' of every individual fact, can science become conscious of its responsibility for the whole of being, of the world and of mankind. Its knowledge of the totality of the world can only be a knowledge that poses questions, and therefore a knowledge that remains ignorant. Science can never transcend this 'inquiring ignorance', if it is not to go beyond its own inherent limits. Consequently, science must constantly be ready to submit to experiment, without reservation, the knowledge of the world which it believes it possesses. Otherwise it ceases to be science, and becomes a philosophical world view.

But this does not imply, for example, that Christian faith should have an answer ready for the inquiring ignorance of science, at least not in the sense that it should provide science with the philosophical world view which science itself cannot supply. It is not the task of faith to provide a Christian covering for the gap which science by definition leaves open or at least ought to leave open. Rather, faith ought to remind science of its essential openness, of its secular character. Otherwise belief in God as the creator of the world would be turned into a 'Christian world view', the most disastrous form of Utopianism that could be imagined. Christian faith, instead of preserving secularisation from degenerating into secularism, would itself degenerate and become 'Christian secularism'.

To sum up the relationship between faith and science in a few words, one may say with Gogarten that science is without faith, or else it ceases to be science; but only where faith exists can science be without faith.[37] We cannot escape this dialectic relationship between faith and science. Since the process of secularisation has come into being, in essence since the coming of Christian faith into the world, the unity of knowledge and faith has been destroyed once for all, and cannot be restored by any device, however ingenious, on the part of faith or on the part of knowledge. Since that time, knowledge and faith have no longer been able to exist in a unity, but only in a duality, or more precisely in a juxtaposition which preserves the identity of both. Faith must not subject knowledge to itself, nor must knowledge attempt to eliminate faith. Instead, knowledge and faith, like the law and the gospel, must remain until the last judgement unconfused but unseparated: 'Their unity is the affair of God, and their duality that of man. . . . Only in this dialectical unity can knowledge remain knowledge, and faith remain faith, and yet both, related to one another but each free to carry out its own task, are an apprehension of the One Truth.'[38]

The secular interpretation of biblical concepts

If the process of secularisation in the modern age has its origin, directly or indirectly, in the Christian faith, then it is meaningless to appeal to the 'pure gospel' as a defence against its consequences. For this would be to appeal to the very force which brought this process into operation, and so would be to sink deeper into the alleged evil. As a matter of fact, such an appeal is not to the gospel but to the law; it seeks as far as possible to restore a religious constitution to the world, and therefore, albeit unconsciously, to bring back the world of ancient mythology in a Christian form. Anyone who honestly appeals to the gospel does not go back prior to the autonomy of man, but advances into the heart of the concept. It is here that Gogarten sees the decisive task of theology and the Church in the present age: 'It has become necessary to pose the question of Christian faith in a completely new way.'[39]

Carl Friedrich von Weizsäcker has come to the same conclusion. He too regards the 'ambivalence' of the modern world as inevitable. The clearest description of it he finds in Jesus' parable of the tares among the wheat, both of which grow together and are only separated at the end of time. Consequently, he too sees the decisive task of theology and the Church today not as in bringing the process of secularisation to an end, but rather in recognising it for what it is and, in honest confrontation, to continue the reinterpretation of Christian faith which has long been in progress.[40]

But the question is not how to reverse, with the aid of the gospel, the process of secularisation which is our historical destiny. Rather it is how we can preach the gospel so as to take into account the process of secularisation which is our historical destiny, and make it relevant to men in their secular condition. It is from precisely this position that the impulse for Bonhoeffer's theological endeavours arose.

Not only did Bonhoeffer reflect in terms of academic theology upon the familiar theme of 'modern' or 'secular' man, he also came into daily contact with him in prison, and even more, lived in fraternal solidarity with him. In his letters he writes of the experiences and insights which he gained through this: 'Don't be alarmed; I shall not come out of here a *homo religiosus*! On the contrary, my fear of and distrust for "religiosity" have become greater than ever here. . . . I often ask myself why a "Christian instinct" often draws me more to the religionless people than to the religious, by which I do not in the least mean with any evangelising intention, but, I might almost say "in brotherhood". While I am often reluctant to mention God by name to religious people – because that name somehow seems to me here not to ring true, and I feel myself to be slightly dishonest (it is particularly bad when others start to talk in religious jargon; I then dry up almost completely and feel awkward and uncomfortable) – to people with no religion I can on occasion mention him by name quite calmly and as a matter of course.'[41]

What Bonhoeffer here gives as his personal experience in contact with those who are without religion is in entire accord with the situation in which the Church today finds itself in its preaching. Gerhard Ebeling says: 'The criterion of intelligibility of our preaching is not the believer but the unbeliever', and Werner Jetter adds: 'The burning problem of preaching is the man who does not hear it.'[42] But the attitude of the contemporary Church is the very reverse. It still largely regards the believing congregation as the yardstick and audience of its preaching. As a result the Church's preaching has come to be uttered in what is virtually a foreign language, which no longer has anything to do with the true scandal of the gospel, because the latter, being concealed in a foreign and incomprehensible tongue, is not even perceived. But there is a risk that true faith may be forced into silence by shame and love. Or else it may begin to speak in a new and hesitant manner, not merely by looking for new words and a contemporary form of expression, but by asking what Christian faith really means, and by beginning once again to understand the word of God anew. Symptomatic of this is the remarkable and instinctive feeling of affinity which believing Christians have for those without religion, a feeling which we can observe not only in Bonhoeffer, but in an increasing number of other Christians in our time.

This affinity to modern man, and the question which derives from it, how is the gospel to be preached to them, if they are really to understand it, was always of crucial importance to Dietrich Bonhoeffer, in contrast to his master Karl Barth. As early as 1937 he wrote in the preface to his book *Nachfolge* (Imitation) a commentary on the Sermon on the Mount: 'It is not the fault of our critics that they find our preaching so hard to understand, so overburdened with ideas and expressions which are hopelessly out of touch with the mental climate in which they live. It is simply not true that every word of criticism directed against contemporary preaching is a deliberate rejection of Christianity and proceeds from the spirit of anti-Christ. So many people come to church with a genuine desire to hear what we have to say, yet they are always going back home with the uncomfortable feeling that we are making it too difficult for them to come to Jesus. Are we determined to have nothing to do with all of these people?'[43] If what Bonhoeffer writes here is a programme, then in the book of which these words are the preface he follows it through. By the standard of Bonhoeffer's later radical thought during his imprisonment it seems notably conservative. But also Bonhoeffer's preaching, in so far as its texts are preserved, is not nearly as radical as the fundamental reflection and writing concerning the task of the Church's preaching which he carried out at the same time. But this only shows that the theological ideas which came to him in prison were overwhelmingly new even to him, and that, in spite of their many links with his earlier life, they are a new departure, representing the final and ultimate stage in his life and thought. Bonhoeffer's whole reflection on the situation of the Church and on Christianity is now concentrated upon the question of how the gospel should be reinterpreted for mature men of the modern age which is now approaching its consummation. His undivided theological attention is concentrated upon this.

In a letter to his friend Eberhard Bethge, the first in which Bonhoeffer sets out at some length his ideas on the present situation of theology and the Church, almost all his decisive propositions are summed up in epigrammatic briefness. In drawing the relevant sentences together we obtain something like an outline of his theological reflection, or more precisely the tabulation of the complex of problems upon which his thought is henceforth unceasingly centred: 'What is bothering me incessantly is the question what Christianity really is, or indeed who Christ really is, for us today. . . . We are moving towards a completely religionless time . . . what does that mean for "Christianity"? . . . How can Christ become the Lord of the religionless as well? Are there religionless Christians? . . . What is a religionless Christianity? . . . The questions to be answered would surely be: What do a church, a community, a sermon, a liturgy, a Christian life mean in a religionless world? How do we speak of God – without religion? . . . How do we speak in a "secular" way about God? In what way are we "religionless-secular" Christians, in what way are we the ἐκκλησία, those who are called forth, not regarding ourselves from a religious point of view as specially favoured, but rather as belonging wholly to the world? In that case Christ is no longer an object of religion, but something quite different, really the Lord of the world. But what does that mean? . . . How this religionless Christianity looks, what form it takes, is something that I am thinking about a great deal. . . . It may be that on us in particular, midway between East and West, there will fall a heavy responsibility.'[44]

The direction in which according to Bonhoeffer the solution of all these questions is to be sought is described by him in the phrase the *non-religious interpretation* of biblical concepts. This solution is in complete accordance with Bonhoeffer's analysis of the present historical situation: if the age of religion has come to an end, and if men as they are now can no longer be religious, then the answer of theology to this religionlessness must consist not merely of the abandonment of traditional biblical concepts, but of an attempt to give them a non-religious interpretation.

What is the meaning of the 'non-religious interpretation of biblical concepts', 'to speak in a secular way about God', 'the religionless preaching of the gospel', 'religionless Christianity'? Bonhoeffer tackles the problem time and time again, endeavouring to elucidate it and penetrate it. Time and again he confesses that he is still at the beginning, and appreciates the size of the problem, without knowing how to solve it: 'It is all very much in the early stages; and as usual, I am being led on more by an instinctive feeling for questions that will arise later than by any conclusions that I have already reached about them.'[45] Moreover, in prison Bonhoeffer lacked any direct contact with those with whom he could have exchanged ideas in open dialogue. He had to rely on expressing himself in letters, and every time he began to set out at length what he really meant, his writing was interrupted: 'What is the place of worship and prayer in a religionless situation . . . I must break off for today.' (30. 4. 44.) 'I am thinking about how we can reinterpret in a "worldly" sense – in the sense of the Old Testament and of John 1:14 – the concepts of repentance, faith, justification, rebirth, and sanctification. I shall be writing to you about it again.' (5. 5. 44.) 'It is now possible to find, even for these questions, human answers that take no account whatever of God. . . . Enough of this; I have just been disturbed again.' (25. 5. 44.) 'The world's coming of age is no longer an occasion for polemics and apologetics . . . I am breaking off here, and will write more tomorrow.' (8. 6. 44.) 'You see how my thoughts are constantly revolving round the same theme. Now I must substantiate them in detail from the New Testament; that will follow later.' (27. 6. 44.) 'Jesus claims for himself and the Kingdom of God the whole of human life in all its manifestations. Of course I must be interrupted just now! Let me just summarise briefly what I am concerned about – how to claim for Jesus Christ a world that has come of age. I can't write any more today . . . So: To be continued.' (30. 6. 44.) 'Well, it's time to say something concrete about the secular interpretation of biblical concepts; but it's too hot!' (8. 7. 44.) Perhaps the reason why Bonhoeffer never brought to a conclusion his reflections upon the secular interpretation of biblical concepts, may not only lie in the unfavourable circumstances, but in the nature of the matter itself: the secular interpretation of the Bible is not something that one either gets hold of or not, but it is something which needs constantly renewed endeavour. And the very fact that Bonhoeffer's thought did not reach a conclusion only urged him on further. Bonhoeffer did not bequeath to theology any interpretative formula ready for use, but showed the direction such an interpretation of the Bible must follow. This direction is clearly recognisable.

The non-religious interpretation of the Bible tries to give its full weight to the incarnation of God in Jesus Christ. Bonhoeffer considered John 1:14 as the key to the secular interpretation of biblical terminology: 'The Word became flesh and dwelt among us.' Here Bonhoeffer puts the stress on the humiliation of God in his revelation, on his passion. From this starting-point he succeeded in elaborating a 'paradoxical conformity' between the understanding of God in Christian faith and the religionlessness of modern man. Bonhoeffer discovered a surprising parallel between the banishing of God from the world brought about by the movement towards autonomy, and the revelation in Christ. The essence of modern autonomy is that God is increasingly excluded from the world and that man finally lives 'without God'. But it is this living 'without God' which is confirmed by the message of the Bible! The same process takes place in the revelation in Christ: Christ must suffer in the world and finally be forced completely out of it, on to the cross. The watchword of the autonomy of the modern age, *etsi deus non daretur*, 'As if God did not exist', is paradoxically confirmed by one of Christ's words on the cross, 'My God, my God, why hast thou forsaken me?' Thus for Bonhoeffer there is a strange parallel between the knowledge of reality which the intellectual honesty of autonomous man requires, and the knowledge of God which Christian faith derives from the event of Christ. Christian faith understands the world that has come of age more and more thoroughly and clearly than it understands itself; on the other hand, however, the development of the world to maturity has done away with the false concept of God held by 'religion', and has opened the view on the God of the Bible, who gains potency and position in the world by his very impotence. Here the decisive difference between Christian faith and all forms of religion becomes manifest. Religion directs man in his distress towards the omnipotence of God, who intervenes in the world from above like a *deus ex machina*. But Christian faith proclaims the presence of a lowly God in the world, and directs man towards the impotence and the suffering of God: 'Only the suffering God can help.'[46]

Bonhoeffer's demand for a non-religious or secular interpretation of biblical concepts, therefore, is far from representing an anxious assimilation of Christianity to a secularised and religionless world. Rather, it derives from the very foundation and heart of the Christian gospel. For Bonhoeffer, a non-religious interpretation is a christological interpretation. Its basic theme is the *theologia crucis*, the theology of the cross. God himself has undergone man's abandonment by God in the world, and taken it upon himself. From this Christian life derives its binding force. The secular interpretation of the Bible is more clearly understood in existential life than in speculative theology. Basically, it cannot be defined, only practised.

The life of a Christian does not take place in a special religious province, but in the secular world. Because God entered the world and suffered in it, so Christians ought also to enter the world and live and suffer in it in a 'worldly' way. In so doing, they share in the suffering of God and the world. The experience of transcendence is realised not 'religiously' in a relationship to God as to the supreme and best being imaginable, but is realised in a 'worldly' way in living for others – in exactly the same way in which 'God [appeared] in human form', and in which Jesus was 'the man for others'. Since God became man, man is required to become man also. Christian faith does not make supermen – this is what religion does – but brings man as he is to the fulfilment of his earthly and human destiny, and therefore of the destiny given him by God. Christianity does not add something to being human, but brings it into effect: 'To be a Christian does not mean to be religious in a particular way . . . but to be a man – not a type of man, but the man that Christ creates in us. It is not the religious act that makes the Christian, but participation in the sufferings of God in the secular life. . . . Jesus calls men, not to a new religion, but to life.'[47] Gerhard Ebeling, in summing up Bonhoeffer's concept of the relationship between being a man and being a Christian, does it in this form: 'The Christian is man properly identified.'[48]

In Bonhoeffer's theological statements concerning the identity between being a Christian and being a man, a part is also played by his personal experience in the course of his 'activity in the worldly sector', as he called his participation in a political conspiracy. Thus in June 1941 he wrote concerning a journey through Italy which he made with Hans von Dohnanyi: 'I feel a resistance to everything "religious" growing in me. Often this is an instinctive revulsion – which is certainly not a good thing either. I am not a religious type. But I am constantly thinking of God and of Christ, and genuineness, life, freedom, and mercy mean a lot to me. Only the religious trappings they wear I find so uncomfortable. None of these are new ideas and insights, but since I think I'm beginning to hit on something important, I let things take their course and don't resist. I also understand my present activity in the worldly sector in the same sense.'[49] And Bonhoeffer seems to sum up all these experiences when he writes two years later from prison: 'During the last year or so I have come to know and understand more and more the profound this-worldliness of Christianity. The Christian is not a *homo religiosus*, but simply a man, as Jesus was a man – in contrast, shall we say, to John the Baptist.'[50]

Bonhoeffer's identification of the being of man and Christian becomes overwhelmingly clear in a personal experience which he describes in a letter – the day after the abortive uprising of 20th July. In it he recalls a conversation which he had thirteen years previously with a French pastor. The two young men were discussing the question of 'what we wanted to do with our lives'. The pastor wanted 'to become a saint'. At that time Bonhoeffer was deeply impressed. But he still disagreed, saying that 'I should like to learn to have faith'. But even by 'having faith' he meant at that time 'trying to live a holy life, or something like it'. He later discovered 'that it is only by living completely in this world that one learns to have faith. One must completely abandon any attempt to make something of oneself, whether it be a saint, or a converted sinner, or a churchman ... a righteous man or an unrighteous one, a sick man or a healthy one. By this-worldliness I mean living unreservedly in life's duties, problems, successes and failures, experiences and perplexities.' And Bonhoeffer concludes, 'That, I think, is faith . . . that is how one becomes a man and a Christian.'[51]

As Bonhoeffer proceeds with his non-religious interpretation of biblical concepts he gradually builds up an exact anti-type to what he has described as the nature of 'religion'. The chief distinguishing mark of religion is the acceptance of two worlds, one here below and another above and beyond, which brings with it an individualistic concern for the salvation of one's own soul, and a longing for redemption in a better world to come. The non-religious interpretation of the Bible emphasises instead that in a profound sense Christianity is *of this world*. Here Bonhoeffer explicitly states that he does not mean 'the shallow and banal this-worldliness of the enlightened, the busy, the comfortable or the lascivious, but the profound this-worldliness, characterised by discipline and the constant knowledge of death and resurrection'. This this-worldliness is not any kind of naturalism, pantheism or other philosophical belief in immanence, but again nothing but the revelation of God in Jesus Christ, his incarnation. Because God himself did not remain in the world above, but came into this world, man must encounter him not on the boundary between this world and the next, but in the midst of this world. That is why Bonhoeffer so sharply opposes 'this world' to the 'beyond', the 'centre' to the 'boundary', and 'life' to 'religion'. This does not mean that the transcendence of God is replaced by his immanence, but that the transcendence of God is only experienced in the immanence of the world. The transcendent, which surpasses our life, is not to be sought above or beyond the world, but only within this world: 'God is beyond in the midst of our life. The church stands, not at the boundaries where human powers give out, but in the middle of the village.'[52]

Consequently, for Bonhoeffer Christianity is not a 'religion of redemption' in the conventional sense of the word, having its main emphasis beyond the boundary of death. Rather, the Christian hope of resurrection is distinguished from all non-Christian redemption myths by the fact that it does not hold out to man yet another last line of escape into the eternal, but sends him back to his life on earth even more brusquely than the Old Testament. It is true that the Christian hope of resurrection also solves the problem of death, but only in order to set man free for fullness of life, a life, of course, which does not come to an end with death. Thus it does not devalue the here and now, but assigns it its true 'penultimate' significance on the basis of the 'ultimate'.[53]

By so extending the Christian gospel to the world – to this world, not to the world to come – Bonhoeffer believes not only that he is doing justice to the claim of the Bible but also that he is giving an appropriate response to the needs of our present secular situation. His view is that the individualistic question of the personal salvation of the soul has almost entirely disappeared today, and that we are now pre-occupied with far more important questions. He knows that this 'sounds pretty monstrous' but he considers it as basically a biblical view. In the Old Testament the question of the salvation of the soul is never raised, while in the New Testament the central issue is that of the kingdom of God upon earth: 'It is not with the beyond that we are concerned, but with this world as created and preserved, subjected to laws, reconciled and restored. What is above this world is, in the gospel, intended to exist *for* this world.'[54]

Naturally a Christian must long for and rejoice in eternity, beyond all the struggle and sufferings of the world – Bonhoeffer did this with all his heart, and he had good cause. Above all, one must avoid wrongly emphasising this world at the expense of the next, as many interpreters of Bonhoeffer have done, ultimately reducing Christianity to mere moral achievement and fellowship. This is to exaggerate the tendency of Bonhoeffer's polemics. What he is attacking is the 'pie in the sky' of a false Christian piety which has allowed this world to be almost entirely overshadowed by the world to come, and has therefore so corrupted the relationship of Christianity to the world that it needs to be renewed from scratch. Another thing that Bonhoeffer has no use for is the tasteless lumping together of this world and the next, the attempt to have both at once, the enjoyment of earthly happiness and a longing for eternal salvation: 'For a man in his wife's arms to be hankering after the other world is, in mild terms, a piece of bad taste and not God's will. If it pleases him to allow us to enjoy some overwhelming earthly happiness, we must try not to be more pious than God himself and allow our happiness to be corrupted by . . . unbridled religious fantasy.' As is frequently the case with Bonhoeffer, his sense of order, his feeling for style, and his pastoral sensitivity revolt against this tasteless lumping together of this world and the next, earthly good and eternal salvation: 'I believe that we ought so to love and trust God in our *lives*, and in all the good things he sends us, that when the time comes (but not before!) we may go to him with love, trust and joy. . . . It is presumptuous to want to have everything at once – matrimonial bliss, the cross, and the heavenly Jerusalem, where they neither marry nor are given in marriage.'[55]

All that Bonhoeffer says about the secular, non-religious interpretation of the Bible – that to be a Christian is to be human and that Christianity is of the world – amounts to a fundamental new understanding. The traditional Christian ways of *thinking in terms of two spheres* are being overcome. Bonhoeffer has already taken the decisive step in this direction in his *Ethics*, his last theological work, on which he worked until his arrest, and which remained unfinished.

Like a 'Colossus' a false mode of theological thinking in terms of two spheres faced and hindered for centuries anyone who inquired into the content and form of Christian life in the world.[56] Its underlying basis, conscious or unconscious, was the conception that in the universe there are two competing spheres which exist side by side: a divine, sacred, supernatural, revealed and Christian sphere, and another secular, profane, natural, rational and non-Christian sphere. This division of the whole of reality into a sacred and a profane sphere led to a corresponding dichotomy in human life between spiritual and secular existence. Either man seeks Christ without the world, like the monks of the Middle Ages, or he seeks the world without Christ, like the enlightened and civilised Protestant of the nineteenth century. Or else he attempts to remain in both spheres at once, and so becomes 'man in eternal conflict'.

In opposition to this traditional Christian division of human existence and secular reality into two spheres, Bonhoeffer chose a decisively new point of departure for his theology. It is the realisation that for Christian faith there are not two realities, but only a *single* reality. Bonhoeffer achieves this not by assimilating Christian faith to a world which has become secular, but impelled by his fundamental christological principle, that in Jesus Christ the reality of God has entered the reality of the world, so that in him both realities, that of God and that of the world, form *a single reality*: the reality of God in the reality of the world. Henceforth there are no longer two separate spheres of reality, but only 'one sphere of the realisation of Christ', in which the reality of God and the reality of the world are united with each other. Here Bonhoeffer reveals himself to be a faithful pupil of Karl Barth. Like Barth, he can proclaim the history of salvation triumphantly in the past tense of perfected being, announcing that by the reality of God the reality of the world has already been 'embraced', 'supported', 'accepted', 'possessed', 'held', 'reconciled', 'loved', 'drawn into itself', and 'comprehended in itself' – 'this is the mystery of the revelation of God in the man Jesus Christ': 'the process of history proceeds from and leads towards this central point alone'. Thus Bonhoeffer shows the same dominating 'christological concentration' as Barth. But the conclusion which he draws from it proceeds in a different direction, and Barth has always found Bonhoeffer's progress in this direction somewhat difficult to understand and regrettable. Whereas Barth is fascinated by heaven, Bonhoeffer is engaged in the world. Bonhoeffer of course firmly maintains the unity of the reality of God and the reality of the world which is founded in Jesus Christ, but his main emphasis is upon the experience of the reality of the world through faith. The reality of God is revealed only to one who involves himself wholly in the reality of the world. What is Christian exists only in the secular, the supernatural only in the natural, the sacred only in the profane, the revealed only in the rational. However, both aspects are not invariably identical; both aspects are in conflict with one another, but the very conflict shows that they belong together. The sacred opposes the profane, and keeps it from becoming autonomous, while the profane opposes the sacred and likewise keeps it from becoming independent. In this conflict, therefore, the emphasis has to shift from one aspect to the other. Bonhoeffer's conviction and purpose is that at the present day the polemical opposition between what is Christian and what is secular should be exercised as in the time of Luther, 'in the name of a better worldliness'. There is no secular reality outside the reality of Jesus Christ – but it is also not possible really to be a Christian outside the reality of the world! Anyone who testifies to the reality of Jesus Christ as the revelation of God is testifying 'in the same breath' to the reality of the world.

The overcoming of this false thinking in two spheres has manifest consequences for what can be called the 'sphere of the Church' in the world. The Church's primary mission is not to be something which exists for its own sake, that is, to form a religious organisation which makes a devout life possible for man; its primary mission is to exist for the world. But the Church does not fulfil its mandate to the world by disputing for part of its territory, and carving out of the world a space or 'sector' for itself, but by helping the world to be and remain the world. Otherwise the Church becomes a 'religious society fighting for itself', and ceases to be the Church of God and of the world, in analogy to the incarnation of Christ.

Dietrich Bonhoeffer was convinced that a transformed Church would once again succeed in so proclaiming God in a world which has become secular that the reality of the world would be affected and renewed by it. There was scarcely anyone more aware of the profound transition which Christianity is undergoing at the present day. But there was also scarcely anyone as hopeful for the renewal of Christian teaching. Bonhoeffer nowhere expresses this understanding and this hope so clearly as in the words which he wrote in prison in May 1944, on the day on which his godchild was baptised.[57] His words have almost prophetic power.

Bonhoeffer first summarises once again the situation in which the Church finds itself in its preaching. 'We are once again being driven right back to the beginning of our understanding. Reconciliation and redemption, regeneration and the Holy Ghost, love of our enemies, cross and resurrection, life in Christ and Christian discipleship – all these things are so difficult and so remote that we hardly venture any more to speak of them. In the traditional words and acts we suspect that there may be something quite new and revolutionary, though we cannot as yet grasp or express it.' Bonhoeffer considers the Church as guilty because in recent years it has fought only for its own existence, as though it were an end in itself, and was therefore incapable of bringing the new message of atonement and redemption to man and to the world. Here Bonhoeffer is making a tacit criticism of the Confessing Church, nourished by Barth's theology, of which he once stated that he who knowingly separated himself from it was cutting himself off from eternal salvation. During the period of transition, being a Christian can consist of two things alone, 'prayer and righteous action among men'. By this prayer and righteous action Christianity will be renewed. Bonhoeffer prophesies to his godchild that by the time he has grown up, the Church's form will have changed greatly, and he warns the Church against trying to hasten the process of transformation by prematurely setting up a new system of organisational authority. This would only have the contrary effect of unnecessarily delaying the repentance and purification of the Church. In his conclusion Bonhoeffer presents an almost eschatological vision of the future: 'It is not for us to prophesy the day (though the day will come) when men will once more be called so to utter the word of God that the world will be changed and renewed by it. It will be a new language, perhaps quite non-religious, but liberating and redeeming – as was Jesus' language; it will shock people and yet overcome them by its power.' The form of Christian preaching Bonhoeffer describes here is the realisation of the secular interpretation of the Bible. But since he fears his hope for the renewal of the Church's preaching will be misunderstood and regarded as Utopian, at the very end he turns from the future back to the present: 'Till then the Christian cause will be a silent and hidden affair; but there will be those who pray and do right and wait for God's own time. May you be one of them . . .'

Bonhoeffer did not see the renewal of Christian preaching which he hoped for. Nor have we seen it to this day. Bonhoeffer's godchild has long ago been confirmed and grown up, but the form of the Church has not yet been changed and renewed. To a large extent it is still fighting as before to maintain itself in being, as though it were an end in itself. What happened after the war was exactly what Bonhoeffer had warned the Church against: by setting up a new system of organisational authority the Church has delayed its repentance and purification.

Bonhoeffer's life-work remained a fragment. In a letter to his father he himself once spoke of this. Here he compares the life of his father with his own life. In his father's generation it was still possible for a person in his professional and personal life to achieve balance and fulfilment, whereas his own life and that of his contemporaries remained incomplete and fragmentary. But then he continues: 'But this very fragmentariness may, in fact, point towards a fulfilment beyond the limits of human achievement. I have to keep that in mind, particularly in view of the death of so many of the best of my former pupils. Even though the pressure of outward events may split our lives into fragments, like bombs falling on houses, we must do our best to keep in view how the whole was planned and thought out; and we shall still be able to see 'what material was used, or was to be used, here for building.'⁵⁸

This statement of Bonhoeffer's was fulfilled in himself. Although his work remained a fragment, it shows how the whole was conceived and of what material it was to be built. It was brought to completion in a higher way, a way which cannot be achieved by human effort alone. Bonhoeffer did not think out to the end what he desired – the renewal of Christian preaching by the non-religious, secular interpretation of biblical concepts – but he *lived* it to the end, and as it were died it. A human being can do no more.

Bonhoeffer became a martyr, though a martyr of a new kind, a non-religious martyr. He did not suffer directly for the Christian faith, but because he had acted on behalf of justice and humanity against an unjust and inhuman state. When he was once asked during exercise in the prison yard in Tegel by a fellow prisoner how he could take it on himself as a Christian and a theologian to participate in active resistance to Hitler, he answered, as far as he could in so short a time, and with the guards watching him, in a story: 'If he, as a pastor, saw a drunken driver racing at high speed down the Kurfürstendamm, he did not consider it his only or his main duty to bury the victims of the madman, or to comfort their relatives; it was more important to wrench the wheel out of the hands of the drunkard.'⁵⁹ Or again, 'The Church has only a right to sing plain chant if it is crying out at the same time for the Jews and the Communists.' Consequently Bonhoeffer became a political conspirator. But by so doing he was 'a witness to Jesus Christ among his brethren', as the memorial tablet in the church at Flossenbürg reads. Bonhoeffer fulfilled in his own person what, according to his own words, is all that there is left for man to do until God's time comes: he did right by men and prayed. The former camp doctor of the concentration camp at Flossenbürg gives this account of Bonhoeffer's death: 'On the morning of that day between five and six o'clock the prisoners, among them Admiral Canaris, General Oster, General Thomas and *Reichsgerichtsrat* Sack were taken from their cells, and the verdicts of the court martial read out to them. Through the half-open door in one room of the huts I saw Pastor Bonhoeffer, before taking off his prison garb, kneeling on the floor praying fervently to his God. I was most deeply moved by the way this lovable man prayed, so devout and so certain that God heard his prayer. At the place of execution, he again said a short prayer, and then climbed the steps to the gallows, brave and composed. His death ensued after a few seconds. In the almost fifty years that I worked as a doctor, I have hardly ever seen a man die so entirely submissive to the will of God.'[60]

The rediscovery of the worldliness of the world

Friedrich Gogarten and Dietrich Bonhoeffer raised questions and established positions from which theology can no longer retreat if it is not to fail in the task of preaching in our time. But they are only two voices, albeit two leading voices among a great chorus of theologians and non-theologians in many Churches and countries. However much they may differ individually, they all proceed from the same point and work in the same direction. They all face the question of total secularisation, as the decisive challenge to Christianity in our time. They see the sole adequate answer to this challenge not in reversing the process of secularisation, but in bearing witness to Christian faith in a secularised world, in such a way that the reality of God and the reality of the world are brought together in faith as a *single* reality.

Here we come to the decisive transformation which was initiated in Christianity after the Second World War. Whereas after the First World War theology rediscovered the deity of God, after the Second World War it discovered the worldliness of the world. What is new in this, and so surprising and unusual for many devout Christians, is that we are beginning to overcome the unhealthy and schizophrenic mode of thinking in two spheres, the division of a single reality into this world and the world beyond, the history of the world and the history of salvation, above and below, the profane and the sacred, the Sunday world of faith and the week-day world of knowledge and understanding. We are gradually beginning to learn that there is only *one* reality, even for Christians. This does not mean that God is simply a part of the reality of the world. It means that we cannot speak of the reality of God and the reality of the world as though they could be juxtaposed but not related. We can only speak of them by speaking of the reality of God in relation to the reality of the world. Either what Christian faith asserts affects this reality of ours, or else Christian faith has nothing at all to say to us.

The overcoming of the traditional Platonic and Christian pattern of thought in two separate spheres, and the associated rediscovery of the original worldliness of Christian faith, are not the result of adapting Christianity to secularisation, but are the fruit of a more profound understanding of the revelation in Christ, although secularisation no doubt provided the impulse. As a result of the encounter in our time of total secularisation with a deepened understanding of the revelation in Christ, theology has found a new opening towards the world. Just as a house becomes larger and more spacious when the walls inside it are taken out, so today God is becoming greater and more spacious, as theology is beginning to tear down the walls which it had set up between God and the world. At this point the retreat of theology, which had gone on for several decades, has now come to a halt, at least as far as its front ranks are concerned.

This profound change in theology is not limited to Protestantism, but can be seen in all denominations. It is a process taking place on an ecumenical scale. Consequently the significant theological divisions today lie not between individual Churches and denominations, but within them all. The question which divides minds is this: Do we take the secularisation of the world seriously, and are we prepared to find a new way to vindicate God before a world which has become secularised, by speaking of him in a language which even our contemporaries can once again understand as speaking of God? Or do we disregard the secularisation of the world, and speak of God in such a way that our contemporaries no longer perceive it as speaking about God, and hence are abandoned to their own unbelief? It is crucial that theology should succeed in finding a new way to speak of God, in order to express anew the reality of the world. In other words, theology should bear witness to the reality of God in such a way that it clarifies, illuminates and perfects the reality of the world.

But in what form is 'Christianity' to be realised in a world that has become secular? What is the answer of theology and the Church to the challenge posed by total secularisation? It is not that theology should acquiesce to the reality of the world without God; this (according to Gogarten) is the false way of 'secularism'. But neither is it the complementing of the reality of the world by God; this (according to Bonhoeffer) is the false way of 'religion'. The answer is to endure the whole reality of the world in the sight of God – this (according to Gogarten and Bonhoeffer) is the way of faith.[61] In this consists the demonstration of the Spirit and of the power – the only proof of the existence of God which is acceptable in a world that has become secular, or in any other world for that matter.

If Christians were to succeed in this 'proof of God', they would at the same time satisfy a longing on the part of many opponents of Christianity in modern times, of which they themselves have been unconscious.

Their attacks upon God of course contain a large measure of unbelief, arrogance, pride and hatred. But they also conceal a longing, a longing for a greater God – a God who is not merely comprehended in transitory ideas, images and concepts, who does not dwell in the gaps and deficiencies in our human knowledge, who does not encounter us merely at the margins and boundaries of life, ruling over a Christian enclave, a few acres marked off as belonging to the Church, but a God who is greater, vaster, more free, more sovereign, more universal, more awesome and more fruitful, who constantly creates for himself new forms of expression and symbols, whom we encounter in the midst of life, who also dwells outside the walls of the Churches and permeates the whole world.

In the face of total secularisation, the battle between faith and unbelief is in the last analysis not about God but about the world. The substance of the dispute is, which of the two realises the reality of the world in the right way. This 'realisation' is not only to be understood in the cognitive sense as an act of knowing, but also in the sense of making real. Gerhard Ebeling demonstrates this in a simile. Whoever takes on an office or seizes an opportunity, does not merely realise the possibilities that lie in this office or opportunity, but makes them real, makes use of them, by his personal efforts.[62] In this way, Christian faith is concerned with the 'realisation' of reality.

This does not by any means solve in a trice all the problems posed by total secularisation – the problems are only just beginning. We are now faced with the essential questions which have preoccupied Protestant theology since the Second World War. The first of these is: 'What are we to do now?'

CHAPTER SIX

THE TWO KINGDOMS

The Church and politics

On 18th–19th October, 1945, the newly formed Council of the Protestant
Church in Germany assembled in Stuttgart for its first sessions. At this
meeting an official delegation of the World Council of Churches
appeared, in order to restore, for the first time after the long years of
separation, its connection with Protestant Christianity in Germany. It
was a great and almost dramatic moment. The war brought about by
the Nazis had only been over six months, and the Churches already
sought to restore communion with one another. There was a moving
discussion. Impressed by this fraternal gesture the Council put forward
the declaration which has gone down in history as the *Stuttgart Confession of Guilt*: 'With great sorrow we declare that endless suffering has
been brought by us upon many nations and countries. What we have
often testified before our congregations, we now pronounce in the name
of the whole Church. For many long years we have fought in the name
of Jesus Christ against the spirit which found a fearful expression in the
rule of violence exercised by the National Socialists; but we reproach
ourselves that we did not bear witness more courageously, did not pray
more faithfully, did not believe more joyfully and did not love more
ardently.'

But the Stuttgart declaration did not speak only of the failures and
guilt of the past, but even more of the hope of a new future: 'Now a
new beginning must be made in our Churches. . . . We hope before the
God of grace and mercy that he will use our Churches as his instrument,
and give them authority to preach his word and bring about obedience
to his will on our part, and on the part of our whole nation. We hope
before God that by the common service of the Churches the spirit of
violence and revenge which is threatening to grow again at the present
day, will be restrained throughout the world, and that the spirit of
peace and love, in which alone a tortured humanity can find healing,
may come to prevail.'

The Stuttgart Confession of Guilt has been much criticised down to
the present day. It has been called politically imprudent and undignified.

But in truth it was a wise and worthy act, one of the wisest and most worthy in the post-war history of Germany, which has not been particularly rich in wise and worthy acts. Thus it must unquestionably be included in any attempt to give a balanced account of Protestant theology in the present century.

But if the declaration made by the Council of the Protestant Church at Stuttgart was to be more than a momentary upsurge of feeling and an emotional proclamation, then a promise which it contained had to be kept. This promise was concerned with the responsibility which the Church shares for the sustaining and ordering of the world, its concern not only for the eternal salvation but also for the earthly well-being of man. Here more than anywhere else lay the guilt of the Church and theology in the past, the guilt admitted at Stuttgart. And this was the point at which a new beginning had to be made.

For a long time the Church's preaching had been aimed principally towards man's interior life. It was concerned with his soul, and sought to prepare it for eternal salvation by consolation, exhortation and edification. The fact that man also has a body, and always exists in a concrete historical setting, and in particular social and political circumstances, and the fact that the world contains not merely persons but also things and institutions, was almost completely ignored. Care for man's bodily well-being was largely left to the State. The Church's theological conscience was appeased by appealing to Luther's doctrine of the two kingdoms, with its strict distinction between the kingdom of God and the kingdom of the world, and therefore between Church and State, between Christian private morality and secular public morality. But what in fact resulted from this almost complete separation between the two kingdoms was that a firm understanding prevailed between Church and State, a kind of harmony, which found its visible expression in the link between 'throne and altar', the throne quite evidently taking precedence. When the Court chaplain came out of the sacristy at the beginning of the service, he first bowed in the direction of the royal pew, and then went to the altar. And the Court news would report: 'The All-Highest Majesties attended the Cathedral to worship the Most High.' The Church served the authoritarian State as a moral institution; priest and policeman were good neighbours. And while it is a rationalist cliché that the Church blessed guns, it is true that in general governments could rely on the Churches in case of war. From the point of view of a citizen, this close link between Church and State corresponded to the passive attitude of submission to God and to the prince which has rightly been caricatured as blind, servile obedience. It was the same in Catholic Bavaria as in Protestant Prussia. For this reason one may doubt whether it was right after the First World War to indict Luther as the 'principal culprit'.

This theological and political tradition explains why the Churches at first welcomed the 'national awakening' of 1933. And undergoing a rapid change of heart, even the Confessing Church fought in the first instance for the purity of doctrine and the independence of the Church, and only in the second, or even in the third or fourth place, resisted the general injustice which the totalitarian State imposed upon men. Many Christians considered this a failure. They had the feeling that under the Third Reich the Church fought for its self-preservation, largely abandoning men to their misfortune. This pricked the Church's conscience.

At the beginning of the 1950's a conference was taking place in a Protestant academy on the theme 'Rearmament and Reunion'. In the course of his address to the conference the President of the Academy said: 'We are not for rearmament, but we are not against it either, and consequently we do not address ourselves to the State on this subject.' But then a pastor leapt to his feet and cried passionately to the assembly: 'Once before we kept quiet when we should have spoken. This must not happen again!' Thus one of the fruits of the Church struggle under the Third Reich was that the Church came once again to recognise that it is also responsible for the things of this world, and must take them under its care and guardianship.

This development, however, put a considerable new burden upon theology. The emphasis in its work, if such a distinction is at all permissible, moved away for a while from dogmatics, which asks, 'What shall we believe?' towards ethics, which asks, 'What shall we do?' Theologians came to be concerned with what has been called the 'political preaching' or even the 'political worship' of the Church. The guiding theme of this new political and ethical inquiry on the part of theology was the recognition of the totality of God's rule and the universality of his love. If God is really the creator, upholder and redeemer of the world, then there can be no area of life which is outside his dominion. This means that the almost total separation between God and the world, Church and State, Christian private morality and secular public morality is at an end. This means taking seriously the fact that God is Lord even in politics, that the commandments and promises of the Bible are also valid for political action, and that Christian love is a political fact of the first order.

We can see from the parable of the Good Samaritan how great a transformation had been initiated within Protestant theology, and the nature of the problems which arose as a result. The Church has always understood the significance of the Samaritan's actions in bandaging the wounds of the man who fell among thieves, taking him to the inn, and there placing him in the care of the landlord, and for centuries the Church sought to imitate him – from the Knights of St John to the modern sisterhoods, from the mill-owner's wife taking a kettle of soup to the sick wife of a worker to the institutions founded by the Home Mission in Germany. But if we were to suppose that the Samaritan had some official position, that he was, if there were such a thing, a city councillor in Jericho or a provincial deputy in Jerusalem, his 'Christian duty' would not have been satisfied by what he had done so far. He would have had to get the police to comb the whole district, perhaps weapons would have had to be used, arrests, trials and even executions would have taken place, and all this would have been carried out in obedience to the same commandment of love which the Samaritan sought to fulfil initially by giving his private and personal assistance to the victim. The new realisation which became so important to theology after the war was that the Christian commandment of love applies not only to private life, but also to public life. But here we come to the problems with which theology is faced: How can the Christian commandment of love be exercised in public life? How can a Christian basis be provided for political action? How can one conduct politics through Christian faith? These are the questions which have so seriously preoccupied Protestant theology and the Protestant Church since the end of the Second World War, if not before.

There is widespread agreement that Christian faith must be manifested in an I-Thou relationship, in a personal relationship to one's individual neighbour. It is easier to understand this than to act upon it. But difficulties arise, and theologians begin to disagree, when they turn to *suprapersonal* spheres of life such as politics, economics, technology, science, law, art, etc. No theologian of any weight nowadays tries to exclude the suprapersonal sphere of life from God's rule on the lines of traditional separation of God and the world, Church and State, and private and public morality. But where opinions differ, and theologians and politicians become heated, is over the question of the *form* in which the rule of God is to be exercised in these suprapersonal spheres of life, and of the connection which should exist between the commandments and promises of the Bible and human and historical reality, and consequently of the shape to be given to the 'Christian decision' in a concrete political situation.

The following example shows how in spite of all fundamental agreement theological debate leads to a wide variety of political proposals and decisions. At the aforementioned conference on the theme of 'Rearmament and Reunion', both those who were against and those who were in favour of rearmament tried to give their point of view a theological foundation by quoting the parable of the Good Samaritan. Both compared the man who fell among thieves with the eighteen million inhabitants of East Germany who needed help. But both drew quite opposite conclusions from it. Some said: 'There is no point in going to Jerusalem first to fetch police assistance', to which the others replied: 'But what else can we do, the thieves are still hiding behind the hedge?' The distinction is clear. There was perfect agreement concerning the motivation of political action: we are compelled by love. But there was disagreement about the form in which the practice of Christian love is to be realised in a concrete political situation. Or we may say that there was agreement with regard to the 'matter of principle' but disagreement about the 'evaluation of circumstances'. For the evaluation of circumstances brings political calculation into play; here earthly and human reality has to be interpreted, and the conditions under which the commandments and promises of God are to be applied to a concrete political situation must be included in the calculation.

This explains why the answers and advice given after the war by theologians and churchmen in the field of politics and ethics have been so conflicting. If one examines the theological core of these various answers and counsels, they can all be traced to two basic forms. In the end one always encounters the fundamental division of theological opinion represented by the two watchwords, 'the kingly rule of Christ' and 'the two kingdoms'. That of the kingdom of Christ derives from the Reformed tradition, while the doctrine of the two kingdoms belongs to Lutheran tradition. It is at this point, and not, as in the past, in the Eucharist, that the dividing line between the two Protestant confessions has to be sought. The point at issue is the degree to which a Christian, in his political decisions, has to take into account the structure of the fallen world, or more precisely, to what degree God himself takes that structure into account in the way in which he imposes his will, and whether, therefore, there may be only one or two ways in which God exercises his rule: the kingly rule of Christ or the doctrine of the two kingdoms.

The kingly rule of Christ

The kingly rule of Christ – this means that just as there is only a single will of God so there is only a single way in which God imposes his will in the world. This is his kingdom founded in Jesus Christ, in which from eternity everything in heaven and on earth is summed up, comprehended and restored, and which therefore also includes the State. Thus here from the very first there is a real link between the kingdom of God and the earthly State.

The most unequivocal, radical, brilliant and intellectually powerful representative of the christocentric approach to political ethics has been Karl Barth. He first put forward the political and ethical consequences of the christocentric point of departure in his theology, in the very midst of the Church struggle, in his study *Rechtfertigung und Recht* (tr. *Church and State*) in 1938. Then, immediately after the Second World War, his work *Christengemeinde und Bürgergemeinde* (tr. *The Christian Community and the Civil Community*) attracted wide attention, and in particular provoked disagreement from German Lutherans, who like their forefathers four hundred years previously were not eager to listen to the 'Swiss voice' in theology. In addition to this, there are the relevant sections in the *Church Dogmatics*, and of course above all Barth's numerous statements on everyday political matters, which because of their startling mixture of a lack of theological partiality and a lack of political caution have always been a violent irritant to the minds of the citizens of West Germany.

Barth traces the theological origin of the political misfortune which came upon Germany to the reformers, and in particular to Martin Luther. He sees a dangerous 'deficiency' in the theology of the Reformation. This lies in the fact that Luther does not provide any adequate christological foundation for human law and political authority. The doctrine of the justification of the sinner through faith alone of course dominates Luther's thought, but he does not derive from it any consequences for political ethics. Instead of establishing an intimate relationship between the justification of the sinner accomplished by God in Jesus Christ, and human justice, in this way making God's justification the sole source and norm of human justice as well, Luther set up a dangerous distinction between the two, considering the kingdom of Christ and the kingdom of the world, Church and State, as two separate entities, in such a manner that the life of Christians takes place in two distinct spheres, the 'spiritual' sphere governed by the gospel alone, and the 'secular' sphere governed by the law alone.[1]

In Barth's view, this distinction which Luther made between the gospel and the law, between the kingdom of God and the kingdom of the world, had damaging historic consequences for the German people. Their political development, already endangered, was given an even more powerful inclination towards evil and darkness. It led to the exclusion of the State from the sphere of God's rule, while at the same time the Church abstained from politics, with the final result that natural paganism went unrestrained. National Socialism formed the climax of this development. Karl Barth is quite serious in deriving the 'National Socialist form of nihilist revolution' and the rise of 'German paganism' from the Reformation doctrine of the two kingdoms, and so tracing an historical line from Martin Luther to Adolf Hitler. In December 1939 he wrote in a letter to France: 'The German people are suffering from the heritage of the greatest German Christian, from the error of Martin Luther concerning the relationship between the law and the gospel, the secular and the spiritual order and authority: as a result of which natural paganism has not been so much limited and restricted as transfigured, confirmed and strengthened.' Two months later, in February 1940, he spoke even more clearly in a letter to Holland: 'Lutheranism has in a way prepared room for German paganism, and with its separation of the creation and the law from the gospel, has as it were set aside a sanctuary for it. The German pagan can use the Lutheran doctrine of the authority of the State as a Christian justification for National Socialism, and a German Christian can feel himself encouraged by the same doctrine to accept National Socialism.'[2]

It remains to be shown whether Barth's severe criticism of Luther is correct or not, and whether he has properly understood at all the true intention of Luther's doctrine of the two kingdoms. What we are concerned with here is to understand Barth's own position. As everywhere in his theology, Barth is seeking a unity, the unity of the whole world, the basis of which is christological. He also includes the State in this christological unity: 'When the New Testament speaks of the State we are . . . in the *christological* sphere.'[3]

For Barth, the encounter between *Jesus and Pilate* is a parable which exemplifies the theological relationship between the Church and the State. In it he sees 'in a nutshell', as 'in a concave mirror', everything the gospel allows us to say about the sphere of the State. This seems surprising, since Pilate shows himself to be an extremely unjust human judge. In him the State rejects justice and becomes a 'den of robbers', a 'gangster state', an 'irresponsible clique'. And yet by delivering Jesus to crucifixion instead of Barabbas, Pilate becomes the 'middleman', the 'executor of the New Testament', the 'involuntary agent and herald of divine justification', the 'founder of the Church of Jews and Gentiles'. Consequently, in this 'most critical instance' in the history of the world of the relationship between the order of justice in the earthly State and the order of redemption in the kingdom of God, the close link between the two is made manifest. 'Pontius Pilate now belongs not only to the Creed, but to its second article in particular.'[4]

Thus Barth, in considering the State, does not place himself at the back, with the creation or the fall, but up in front, with Christ, the redemption and the kingdom of God: the State is not a 'product of sin', but an 'order of divine grace'; within its sphere, we do not encounter 'God the universal creator and ruler', but the 'Father of Jesus Christ'. Thus, on the part of the Christian congregation, what takes place is a 'singular opening of windows' in the direction of the State. Not that the State might be considered an anticipation of the kingdom of God or a repetition of the Church. The State is entirely a separate human order with its 'comparatively independent substance, its dignity, its function and its purpose'. But because of the relativity of this independence, the State belongs to the side of Jesus Christ, and is under his rule. It is not autonomous, but has a place and a function in God's plan of salvation. It is intended to protect men from the irruption of chaos and to bring a relative and anticipatory order into being among them, so that they may have time – 'time for the preaching of the Gospel, time for repentance, time for faith'. Thus the State is indeed 'outside the Church, but not outside the range of Christ's dominion – it is an exponent of his kingdom'.[5]

Concordantly, Barth describes the 'community of Christians' and the 'community of citizens' as two concentric circles, the Christians forming the inner and smaller one and the citizens of the civil community the outer and larger one. The common centre of both circles is the kingdom of God proclaimed by the Christian community. Barth's whole concern is to work out the relationship of these two circles to their common centre, and so to each other. The light shines down from the kingdom of God on to the earthly Church, and is transmitted by it to the earthly State, where it is reflected. Here we come to the central point of Barth's political ethics, at which its inner structure stands revealed. The principle of analogy dominates Barth's ethics, as it does his dogmatics. The same theological stage direction applies to both: 'On earth as it is in heaven.'

The State is a separate, human and transitory entity, and consequently the simple and absolute *equation* of the State and the Church with respect to the kingdom of God is out of the question. On the other hand, however, the State has no autonomy or independent substance of its own, so that a simple and absolute heterogeneity between it and the Church with respect to the kingdom of God is equally out of the question. Here again, what remains is an *allegory*, an analogy: the righteousness of the State from the Christian point of view is 'the existence of the State as an allegory, as a correspondence, and an analogue to the kingdom of God which the Church preaches and believes in'.

Because the State shares a common centre with the Church, it is *capable* of analogy, capable of reflecting a mirror image of Christian truth and reality. But because this mirror image does not come about naturally, but is always being distorted, the State at the same time *needs* analogy, that is, it needs to be constantly reminded of the Christian truth and reality. It is here that the Christian community has a political responsibility. Its duty is 'to remind the State of the kingdom of God' by its preaching and life, so that the State may become a reflection and analogy of the kingdom of God, and so fulfil its destiny. This does not provide the Christian community with a ready-made political system or programme, but determines the 'impulse and direction' of its political discrimination, judgement, will and choice. The decisions the community makes in the political sphere should always be such that they illuminate and do not obscure the connection between the State and the divine ordinance of salvation and grace. It should always choose among the political possibilities that are offered at any time those which display an analogy and reflection of the content of its creed. In short, the Church's constant concern must be 'that the shape and reality of the State in this fleeting world should point towards the kingdom of God, not away from it . . . , not that human politics should cross the politics of God, but that they should proceed, however distantly, on parallel lines'.[6]

In order to show the detailed form that this Christian political discrimination, judgement, will and choice may take, Barth gives a series of concrete examples which carry to extremes the principle of analogy. Because God became *man* and man's fellow, the Christian community concerns itself in the political sphere in the first instance with man, and not with any causes. Because in Jesus Christ God gave a human basis to his fundamental *justice*, the Christian community always stands for the rule of law, as opposed to any kind of anarchy and tyranny. Because the Son of Man came to seek and to save what was *lost*, the Christian community takes the side of the weak, the oppressed and the poor, and fights for social justice. Because Christians are called to the *liberty* of the kingdom of God, they affirm the *liberty* and emancipation of the citizen as the basic law of every state. Because the life of Christians is based upon *one* baptism, under *one* Lord in *one* Spirit, they are always in favour of the *equality* of all citizens who lack their full rights. But because the Holy Spirit gives *different* gifts, the Christian community is always vigilant in politics to preserve the *separation* of the legislative, executive and judicial powers. Because God *unveiled* himself in his revelation and his light *shone* in Jesus Christ, the Christian community always determinedly opposes all *secret* politics and *secret* diplomacy. Because the Christian community is based upon and nourished by the free word of God, it also has confidence in the political sphere in the freedom of the human word, and is therefore opposed to the control and censorship of the public expression of opinion. Barth goes on in this way at great length.[7]

Humanity, justice, freedom, equality, responsibility, the separation of powers, social justice – when one considers the analogies which Barth draws between the kingdom of God and the earthly State, they betray at first sight a notable inclination towards *democracy*. Nor does Barth deny this inclination. The view that all possible forms of state are equally close to or equally far from the gospel he regards as 'claptrap'. Of course it is possible for someone to be damned in a democracy and be saved under mob rule or dictatorship, 'but it is not true that as a Christian one can affirm, desire or strive for mob rule or dictatorship as resolutely as one can for democracy'. Barth considers it no accident that the democratic form of state has developed precisely within the sphere of influence of the Christian Church. He relates this development to a fundamental and central article of Christian faith, one which one would have thought the least likely to lead to democracy, the admonition to pray for those in authority. Prayer for those in authority does not imply pious submission and blind obedience, but in fact breaks down the structure of purely passive subjection, and demands active co-operation and shared responsibility. For one can only pray for the maintenance of the State if one is also ready to take personal action to achieve it, with all the consequences of such action, even including the necessity of replacing the State if it ceases to exercise the rule of law.

Thus from his strictly christocentric starting-point, Barth comes to the conclusion that Christian political judgement and action have a special tendency towards the democratic form of state: 'There certainly is an affinity between the Christian community and the civil communities of the free peoples.' In a discussion after the war, Barth answered the objection that he was far too incautious in providing a theological basis for democracy, 'I do not understand why people are afraid and grow angry when I occasionally say something in my "Swiss voice" about democracy. Perhaps people would not have been angry if I had said that the place of the gospel was in a truly authoritarian state, with strict order and everything that goes with it, or if I had perhaps developed a conservative point of view, instead of speaking clearly for freedom. There is a particular polemic being exercised against me which revolves round the word "democracy". I don't insist on the word; but I would regard what it signifies as a form of law that I could take pleasure in ... it could perhaps even signify the gospel.'[8]

One may perhaps wonder whether in deriving democracy from the gospel in this way, Karl Barth the theologian may not be beholden to Karl Barth the citizen of Switzerland, and whether he may not be drawing too close an analogy between the three original Swiss cantons and the three persons of the Christian Trinity. But it is not sufficient to point out that Barth's thought may possibly derive from and be coloured by the circumstances of his life. It also derives from a premise in Barth's dogmatic theology, that the gospel is anterior to the law, a principle which is a determining factor not only in his pleasure in democracy, but in the whole of his political ethics. Barth's famous definition of the law of God is that it is nothing other than 'the necessary form of the gospel, the content of which is grace'. In these terms it is no longer possible to make the distinction that the law rules in the 'secular' sphere of the State, while the gospel prevails in the 'spiritual' sphere of the Church; for the gospel is now the basis and determining factor of existence in both spheres. In this way Barth achieves the mutual co-ordination of Church and State, the kingdom of God and the kingdom of the world. He thereby corrects the wrong course which theology and politics have followed for centuries. He guards against the State becoming 'an ordinance of creation', constantly further exalted by different ideologies, existing alongside God's ordinance of grace, and following its own laws – as though there had been no Christian revelation and redemption, and therefore no unified direction and purpose for the world, provided by the history of salvation and including the State.

The great danger here, as elsewhere in Barth's theology, is that the unity he so fervently desires should turn into uniformity. By giving the gospel precedence over the law he prevents the State from lapsing into autonomy and falling back into natural paganism. This, however, brings with it the danger of using the gospel as it were as a constitution for the kingdom of the world and as a direct prescription for a particular form of political order. The analogies which Barth draws between the kingdom of God and the earthly State suggest this danger.

The fact that from any particular christological assumptions one can draw quite different or even opposed political conclusions should make us sceptical of these analogies. Helmut Thielicke gives two amusing and almost mischievous examples of this. Barth draws from the christological premise that God revealed himself in Jesus Christ the political conclusion that the Christian community should oppose all secret politics and secret diplomacy. But one could equally well draw from the 'Messianic secret', that is, the fact that Jesus wanted his messianic dignity kept secret, the opposite political conclusion that the Christian community should be in favour of the preservation of strict secrecy in politics and diplomacy. Again, Barth draws from the fact that the life of the Christian community is based upon one baptism and one Lord in one Spirit, political conclusions in favour of a democratic form of state. But one could equally well derive from the same christological premise the slogan of Nazism: *Ein Volk, ein Reich, ein Führer*.[9]

But the lengths to which certain analogies are carried, and their formalism and artificiality, are no more than symptoms of an even more profound and fundamental error, that of the unhistorical nature of the whole of Barth's theology, which we recognised as its principal weakness. This can be seen in Barth's political ethics, in the fact that in describing the nature of Christian political choice and action, Barth pays almost no attention to the structure of the world, for his arguments lead straight from heaven to earth. He crosses the threshold from the kingdom of God to the earthly State in a single step. Consequently the question of the shape and form in which the commandment of love of the 'wholly other' kingdom of God is to be realised in this world plays virtually no part in his thinking. But it is precisely with this that the Lutheran doctrine of the two kingdoms is chiefly concerned.

Luther has no intention to separate the kingdom of the world from the kingdom of God, or to release the State from the sphere of God's authority. The State is only the kingdom 'at the left hand of God'; even at the left hand of God the State is still under his rule.

In order to maintain an association between the two kingdoms, the kingdom of God and the kingdom of the world, Luther connects them by a twofold link. First objectively by assigning the State its place in God's plan of salvation as a divine ordinance for preserving and maintaining human life. Luther too regards the State from the point of view of the kingdom of God, and determines its nature and purpose from thence. He uses almost the same words as Barth when he says that the task of the State is to resist the evil in the world and so provide physical time and place for the preaching of the gospel, so that men may attain their goal, which is salvation. Subjectively Luther links the two kingdoms by postulating that the office holders who maintain order in the kingdom of the world are subject to the law of love originating in the kingdom of God, a law of unlimited validity, determining not only the motivation but also the content of political action.

To this extent Barth might have followed Luther without qualification, in so far as the idea of the unity between the kingdom of God and the kingdom of the world is also prominent in Luther. But Luther's principal theological concern is not the unity of the two kingdoms, but the distinction between them. For him, it is necessary to distinguish in which sphere of our existence the concrete exercise of love is to take place. It is at this point that for Luther the structure of the world comes to have a decisive influence upon the shape and form of Christian action. In the personal sphere, love exhibits a form different from that it takes on in the sphere of official duty and professional calling. In the former it must prevail in a 'pure' form, while in the latter it can do so only in a compound with power. But it should be noted that in both cases it is the same love, differing only in its expression.

The question is whether Luther's theological interest is not so strongly affected by the problem of the structure of the world and therefore of the distinction between the two kingdoms, that it threatens to destroy their unity, in spite of the double bracketing. This is the reason for the violent criticism levelled today, under the leadership of Karl Barth, against Luther's doctrine of the two kingdoms, a criticism all the more legitimate since the historical situation has changed since Luther's day. At the end of the Middle Ages there was a constant danger of the *clerical confusion* of the two kingdoms, and therefore the main concern of theology was bound to be for the *distinction* between them. But after all we have experienced, and continue to experience, the danger that faces us is the *secularist drawing apart* of the two kingdoms, so that the main concern of today's theology is for their *unity*. Still, we cannot even today abandon Luther's doctrine of the two kingdoms, because it recognises the permanent laws governing the structure of this world, laws that are valid not for a particular time, but for all time. Of course we have to rethink them and revise them, which is precisely what was done by Helmut Thielicke.

Thielicke's political ethics represent the most comprehensive attempt to bring Luther's doctrine of the two kingdoms up to date in such a way that 'in revising those elements in Reformation theology which were the product of its own time, we do not affect its basic structure, but constantly manifest anew its power to enlighten'.[10] Thus after the Second World War Thielicke became in theory and in practice the most outstanding advocate of a modified form of the doctrine of the two kingdoms.

The Christian interpretation of reality

After Barth's *Church Dogmatics*, Thielicke's *Theological Ethics* forms the most extensive work of systematic theology in the present century. The Hamburg dogmatic theologian, who prefers to call himself a 'teacher of ethics', worked on it for twenty years, from the end of the war to 1964, and although he did not attain to 8,000 pages like Barth, he nevertheless managed more than 3,000. The work is as extensive in content as it is in size. Although its material is occasionally over-abundant, and the author's delight in provocative images and epigrams sometimes leads him to excessive profusion, the extent of the material is due to the theological purpose that lies behind it. Thielicke seeks to answer the question constantly posed by both Christians and non-Christians today: 'What are we to do?' But he links this particular question to a much wider one: 'How are we to understand the reality within which we have to act?' Reality being infinitely rich and various, it was scarcely possible for him to make do with less than 3,000 pages, if he were to carry out his theological intention.

The guiding line for Thielicke's understanding of reality with regard to Christian action is the doctrine of the justification of man before God through faith alone. Consequently, Thielicke's ethics can be seen from their very starting-point to be consciously Lutheran: the love of God which man encounters in the act of justification compels him to exercise love in his turn. Here attention is focussed on the 'motivation' of Christian action, which sounds alarmingly like a return to mere inwardness and good intention. 'Motivation', however, must not be understood simply as a subjective 'attitude', but here signifies a 'new way of living'. The Christian is taken up into a new *motus*, into a movement of love which God himself has kindled, and only through this does he become capable of a new attitude. This is the implication of Augustine's famous dictum *Dilige et fac quod vis*, 'Love and do what you want'. Thus strictly speaking Christian ethics teaches not what we ought to do, but what we *may* do. Its theme is the 'freedom of a Christian man', and its principle is the 'dialectic between freedom and obligation'. 'It shows us how the Prodigal Son lives after he has left bondage in a foreign land and has outgrown the legalistic virtue of the brother who remained at home.'[11]

Thus the justification of man before God through faith alone forms the 'heart' of all theological ethics. But it is not Thielicke's intention merely to observe the 'heart' and carry out a kind of 'theological cardiology'. He goes on at once to ask: 'What is the meaning of "justification through faith alone" for existence, especially within the ordinances of human life: within a marriage, in politics, in society, in economic competition, in the conflict between employers and trade unions, etc.?' Here it is Thielicke's intention to make up for what in his view Luther omitted. He is concerned that the heart should pump its blood back into the limbs of the *whole* body, so that the entire circulation becomes the subject of theology. To abandon or rather to change the metaphor, Thielicke seeks to 'decline the Reformation doctrine of justification through all the cases provided by the grammar of our existential life'.[12] Throughout, his ethics is the *applied doctrine of justification*.

Thielicke is dominated by a passionate desire to express the Christian faith in concrete terms. He sees the 'real problem of ethics' as lying in the fact that man never exists as a being in the abstract, but always finds himself 'in a situation': 'in a situation' implies that man stands *before God*, but he stands before God *in the world*. Our attitude to God is always actualised in our attitude to the world. The world is always present when God is spoken of, otherwise God is not spoken of at all.

Thus Thielicke sets out 'on the trail of the concrete'. He seeks man in his 'situation', as someone who has a profession, who is caught up in a complex web of reality, who is affected by an immense variety of circumstances, who is constantly brought into contact with people and things, who is entangled in innumerable supra-personal patterns of guilt, who is an actor in a thousand plays which he himself has not put on the stage, who is pushed into a system of different overlapping institutions, and who sees himself threatened by the autonomy of areas of life which are greater than the individual. His subject is man as husband, father, bachelor, politician, merchant, entrepreneur, judge, artist, officer, trade union leader, as someone living in a particular period, rooted in the milieu of a particular society, endowed with particular hereditary factors. We meet in this work personalities as different as Machiavelli and Bodelschwingh, Hegel and Kierkegaard, Bismarck and Hitler. Thielicke goes to the root of what the 'existentialist theology' of the present day is so ready to emphasise: that man is an 'historical' being, who 'exists in the world', and that his life proceeds in the form of an 'encounter'. But whereas these concepts elsewhere remain empty and abstract, Thielicke fills them with an intense, concrete and living content. That is, Thielicke does not follow the deductive path from above to below, but the inductive path from below to above. He begins with the details of concrete reality and works back from them to basic principles, in order to throw light upon them anew by conducting his inquiry in this reverse direction.[13]

Thielicke rightly calls his *Theological Ethics* a *Christian interpretation of human and historical reality*. He claims that it fulfils the thesis of 'secular Christianity', so frequently quoted and so rarely taken to heart today. 'I would like to bring the Christian dogmas out of the world to come and out of the ghetto of the Church, and establish them upon earth, where man lives his secular existence.' Thielicke also hopes in this way to bring about a new dialogue with non-Christians. When one speaks to them of heaven and hell, they do not listen, but when the subjects are such secular matters as marriage, the State, society, economics, art and law, they pay attention, for it concerns them, it is part of their own lives.[14]

The method followed by Thielicke in his concern to give secular concrete expression to the Christian faith is that of the presentation of what he calls *model cases*. These model cases are not intended to be illustrative examples, but are meant, in accordance with his theological purpose, 'to make visible in concrete detail the complicated network of total reality'.[15] But the 'pressure of reality' upon man is never so strong as in the *boundary and conflict situation*. Thus in Thielicke the analysis of the boundary and conflict situation becomes the methodological 'axis on which everything turns'. He discusses conflict situations in the political underground movement, resistance against the tyranny of a totalitarian state, the conflict between one life and another in the concentration camp, theft as the only way to avoid death, illegal help to the Jews, the boundary situation and the artistry of the tightrope walker, the labour situation in mass production industry, the white lie, the diplomatic concealment of the truth from a political opponent, the doctor's dilemma in confronting a dying person, the problem of honesty with regard to taxes, the truth drug and the lie detector, economic competition, and the trade union as a model for the modern problem of group organisation.

In none of this is it a question of a generalised phenomenology of life. Thielicke takes the concept of the 'boundary situation' in strict theological terms. The expression itself of course was coined by Karl Jaspers, but Thielicke transfers it from the sphere of the existential life of the individual, where Jaspers uses it, to the totality of the world; this again is typical of him. Here he is guided by the Bible. The ultimate limits of the world lie in the fact that on the one hand it is created and determined by God, while on the other hand it has fallen from God and failed in its divine destiny; yet it is nevertheless not God's will to abandon it, but to restore it, and bring it back to its original destiny. Thus the two extreme limits of the world are its beginning and its end, the creation and the last judgement. Thielicke sees this universal boundary situation of the world reflected in every individual boundary situation.

But this means that the 'pressure of reality' which can be perceived in the boundary and conflict situation is *eschatologically* determined. It does not derive merely from unfavourable contemporary circumstances, but from the fact that in the redeeming act of Jesus Christ, in his life, death and resurrection, the eschatological crisis of history has already taken place and the 'new aeon' has already come 'in the midst of us', while at the same time the 'old aeon' continues to run parallel with it. The second coming of Christ, and therefore the final redemption of the world, are still to come. This places us in a relationship of both continuity and discontinuity with the 'old aeon'. The continuity consists in the fact that with the coming of the kingdom of God in Jesus Christ, the secular world order was not put out of action in a single stroke, but continued to possess a relative autonomy, so that we still stand in a certain relationship to it. But the discontinuity is shown by the fact that the new world to come is keeping this ancient and transitory world under a constant harassing fire, so that we no longer live in the night, where everything is still dark and obscure, but are in the dawn of the day of God which is breaking, and see the outline of things becoming clear. Thus the sphere in which the Christian actually lives his life is neither the old aeon by itself, nor the new aeon by itself, but the field of tension between the two aeons. Paradise lies behind us and the last judgement before us. We cannot return to Paradise, for outside stands the angel with the flaming sword. But the day of the last judgement has not yet come; it is not yet apparent what we are to be. Thus we live in an interim period, in a transition which comprehends the whole world. This is the sphere in which Christian ethics must be exercised. Their task is to find a *modus vivendi* in the field of tension between the two aeons, between what is already present in the kingdom of God and what is yet to come. Its theme is that of the 'pilgrimage between the two worlds'.

The eschatological character of ethics and the method of choosing model cases which results from it, determine what can and what cannot be achieved by theological ethics. One cannot set up a doctrine of morality or virtue which is guided by certain fixed principles and in any given case can provide easily applicable guidance for Christian action. Such a legalistic and casuistic view of ethics not only overlooks the overwhelming fullness of any given historical moment, but also creates an illegitimate balance in the tension between the two aeons. Just as the tension between godhead and manhood in the person of Jesus Christ cannot be resolved in a dogmatic formula, so no ethical formula can be found to express the unity of Christian existential life in the kingdom of God and in the kingdom of the world. Such a formula would only give rise to the illusion that in the field of tension between the two aeons there was a 'right' form of action which could be determined unambiguously. Theological ethics can only show 'what is at issue, what is *ultimately* at issue'. It can help to clarify the situation, by identifying the issues present in it; it can bring a decision to a head, by analysing its content, and can even propose solutions. But it can never make decisions and provide solutions itself, or provide a formula for Christian action.[16]

The most that Christian ethics can achieve is to mark out an approximate channel. But even this it is only able to do indirectly, by pointing out the shallows which threaten to the right and to the left. Here God's commandments have something of the function of a compass needle, to show the right direction. But Thielicke also uses the metaphor of the compass to make clear how it is impossible to draw from the Bible fixed and directly applicable laws. Even if one possesses a compass, and observes its needle, this is no substitute for the exact knowledge of the area to be traversed, by the aid of charts or a pilot. Finally, even when the channel is marked in this way, there is room for some variations of course within it.[17]

The doctrine of the two kingdoms

If we apply Thielicke's fundamental principles concerning the task and methods of theological ethics to the special field of *political ethics*, they imply that theological ethics, also, are unable to devise a systematic doctrine of political virtue which could lay down in advance the correct solutions and the permissible means of obtaining them. Here again, all theological ethics can do is to mark out an approximate channel by pointing to the dangerous shallows.

On this basis Thielicke excludes two kinds of political attitude, as being outside the 'scheme' of the salvation of the world: enthusiastic radicalism and *laissez-faire* conservatism.

It is in the nature of political *radicalism* that in its enthusiasm it overleaps the present condition of the world. It is anticipated eschatology. It attempts to apply the radical laws of life which the Sermon on the Mount lays down for the kingdom of God directly to this present aeon, and so denies our situation in the history of salvation, the fact that we live in an interim period, in the field of tension between the two aeons. By its longing for revolutionary action which destroys the structure of the world, radicalism seeks to escape from the pressure of reality and to anticipate the redemption of the world by God through its own power. The consequence is that instead of helping to maintain the stability which God wills for the world, it casts it into even greater disorder and so brings about chaos. As Thielicke constantly and explicitly emphasises, the reason for this is not that the Sermon on the Mount is too alien to the world to be realised within the world, but that the world is too 'alien to the kingdom of God' for the Sermon on the Mount to be taken over to the letter as its political constitution.

False *conservatism* is the exact opposite of the radicalism just described. Whereas radicalism disregards the present situation of the world, conservatism acts to prolong it beyond reason. Its attention is riveted with such single-mindedness on the autonomy of the world as it exists, that it completely loses sight of its purpose in the history of salvation. False conservatism as it were wallows in the fallen creation. It accepts the conditions of the world exactly as they are, by interpreting them, in a hasty over-simplification which ignores the intermediate causes of human sin and guilt, as a product of divine providence, seeing profit as God's 'blessing' and poverty as God's 'trial'. The consequence is the reduction of love of one's neighbour to a purely private matter, with apathy in the political sphere.

Thielicke regards *compromise* as the form of political and ethical action which is best suited to the secular structure. Compromise adapts itself to the situation of the world in the history of salvation: it takes account of what is 'no longer' in the kingdom of this world, and what is 'not yet' in the coming kingdom of God. It is already orientated towards vital processes in the new aeon, yet still gives its due to the old aeon. Compromise too aims at fulfilling the commandment of love of the kingdom of God, but it is also aware that the commandment of love of the kingdom of God is distorted in the structural laws of this world. Thus it constantly seeks to strike a balance between the absolute demands of God and what the structure of the fallen world, with its autonomous institutions, its overlapping and conflicting duties, and the rules of its technology, can permit. This means that every political and ethical decision has the nature of an insoluble *mixtum compositum* of decisions of principle and matters of practical judgement. It is this that obliges political action to take the form of compromise.

The form of compromise, which is that of human political action, corresponds to the compromise which God himself has made with the world by 'accommodating' himself to its nature, in order to maintain it until the judgement day within the framework of the possibilities remaining to it since the fall. The example which Thielicke constantly quotes of God's patient 'accommodation' to the fallen world is that of the *Noachic ordinance*. The term 'Noachic ordinance' refers to the covenant which God concluded with Noah after the flood. The significance of this covenant is that God promises to preserve his creation in the future, but that in order to carry out this purpose, he builds on the foundation of facts created by man and appoints the means available in the fallen creation, such as killing and force, for the purpose of preserving it. This does not mean that God approves the laws of conflict by which this world is governed, but that he tolerates them and builds them into his ordinance: God makes use of force to restrain force; he uses killing to control killing; he uses the egoism of the State in order to keep check on the egoism of individuals and groups. From henceforth all political rule in the world is linked to the principle of force, and is therefore associated with fear, coercion, punishment, battle, inequality, self-assertion and self-interest. The peace of this world is always an 'armed peace' and therefore a 'peace based on fear'. But by adapting the law of God in this manner to the fallen world, God saves it from the destruction to which it is liable of itself. Thus he exercises a kind of 'higher homoeopathy'. God conceals his 'true' will under the 'alien' work of accommodation. In spite of the world's sin, he sustains it with the aid of its sin, and in this way grants it further time. But this implies that all political institutions in this world are only 'emergency institutions'. They do not derive directly from God's creation, but neither do they derive directly from the fall of the world. They are brought about by both. Their origin and form are those of the fallen world, but at the same time they act against the destructive force inherent in them, and so serve to preserve the creation.[18]

The 'Noachic covenant' plays a dominant role in Thielicke's political ethics. He sees it as the clearest example of the way in which all political action in the world takes the form of a compromise, by analogy to the way in which God sustains the world. In Thielicke the idea of compromise occupies almost the same place as the principle of analogy in Barth.[19] But however much Thielicke may emphasise that in our political action we never avoid compromise either in practice or in principle, he nevertheless utters a warning against what he calls the 'spirit of compromise'. The spirit of compromise defies the laws of conflict by which this world is governed, and makes a virtue of necessity. It says: 'Because the world is a forest full of wolves, let us cry with the wolves.' Consequently it dwells thoughtlessly and unconcernedly in the realm of compromise. Or else it interprets compromise in a tragic sense as a necessary law of existence, or even as a law which obliges us to sin, and to which we are subjected of necessity. But compromise is never merely our destiny, but is always our fault as well. It points back to the suprapersonal guilt of this aeon, in which we are enmeshed. We share in the responsibility for the world's being as it is. Consequently the politician must never use compromise to quiet his conscience, but must always bear in mind the problematic nature of all the worldly means he uses, and the doubtfulness of all compromise. He must never reduce the tension between the two aeons to a timeless state of balance by regarding compromise as the resultant of a parallelogram of forces, as the ultimate product of two extremes, and setting up universally valid and timeless rules and maxims by which he can live and act with his mind at rest. This would be to forget that the law of compromise has a 'limited place within the history of salvation', and that it does not correspond to the 'real' will of God, but is only the expression of his patience with us during the interim period for which this world endures. A glimmer of understanding that the world, and compromise with it, is at the deepest level not 'in order' must be present in all our actions. This knowledge is the 'salt' which purifies all our political passions. It is like the 'gauze in the wound' which keeps the wound open and prevents it from closing. Because compromise is not an excuse for our guilt, but an expression of it, it requires forgiveness. But in the certainty of forgiveness the Christian can also live in reality and carry out political action. Here Luther's saying to Melanchthon applies: '*Pecca fortiter sed fortius fide*', 'Sin boldly, but believe more boldly!'

The knowledge that compromise is open to question is realised in the quantitative evaluation of the means that are available. Whoever knows that compromise bears the mark not of tragedy but of guilt, and is only an expression of God's patience with the fallen world, cannot use the secular means at his disposal unrestrained by his political action, but in every case will make a careful distinction between the greater and the lesser evil, between unacceptable and less unacceptable means, between better and worse possibilities. In so doing he is conscious that even what is quantitatively the best solution is never equivalent to the redemption of the kingdom of God, but always retains the anticipatory character of this present world, and is therefore in need of forgiveness. Perhaps the only difference between a Christian politician and a non-Christian politician is that the former knows his guilt and lives under forgiveness.

Thielicke's exposition of his own political ethics is permeated by the critical view he adopts of Luther's doctrine of the two kingdoms.[20] This is why we called him 'the outstanding advocate of a *modified* form of the doctrine of the two kingdoms'. What does this modification consist of? Thielicke himself considers that his 'critical questioning' of Luther's doctrine of the two kingdoms applies less to the principle of the doctrine than to the form in which it occurs in Luther. But he is not content with revising its historical expression, but also revises the conception itself.

Luther stresses the distinction between the kingdom of God and the political institutions of this world. He fixes his theological attention on the fact that the manner in which the Christian commandment of love must be fulfilled is determined in part by the sphere in which this happens. Otherwise, it might come about that Christian love works in the world like poison, and serves to destroy its institutions instead of maintaining them. Therefore Luther emphasises the *difference* between the two kingdoms, and the resultant *distortion* of the Christian commandment of love in the structural laws of this world. Thielicke agrees with this theological theme and point of departure in Luther. To this extent he is in agreement with Luther rather than with Barth.

But the critical question which Thielicke asks concerning Luther is whether Luther built into his own doctrine of the two kingdoms guarantees against a complete break between the two kingdoms sufficient to turn the distinction between them into a separation which he did not desire. Because Luther's main concern is for the distinction between the two kingdoms, he can on occasion speak of them so incautiously that they sometimes appear to be two different spheres which lie apart in space and time. For Christian existence this means that it may appear to be conducted at one and the same time in two different spheres which are subject to two different sets of laws, with the consequence that it bears on the one hand all the marks of a Christian existence, and on the other hand all the marks of secular existence. Furthermore the boundary between the two kingdoms seems to cut the Christian right down the middle and to divide him into two persons completely isolated from one another, a Christian with regard to his private personality and a man of the world with regard to his official personality.

Luther may have been able to risk such an objective distinction because in his time the two kingdoms were subjectively linked, since the bearers of secular authority were understood to be Christians, and were willing to listen to the Church when an appeal was made to their faith, even in the political sphere. But as this firm Christian basis disappeared, the distinction between the two kingdoms was bound to lead to separation, with the ominous consequence that the State regarded itself as a taboo area within the world, basing its right to autonomy on Luther's doctrine of the two kingdoms. But that it should have been so easy for the State to achieve emancipation with the assistance of theology, makes it clear that the way in which Luther in practice linked together the two kingdoms was inadequate. Consequently, we cannot avoid the conclusion that the causes of the deficiencies in Luther's doctrine of the two kingdoms which came to light in the course of history were not merely historical but also theological.

According to Thielicke, the principal deficiency of Luther's doctrine of the two kingdoms is that the eschatological factor is not sufficiently objective in it. What it lacks is the consciousness that we live in the field of tension between the two aeons, and that the new aeon is already penetrating the old and calling it into question, or – to use one of the military metaphors of which Thielicke is so fond – that the world to come is already keeping this world under harassing fire. In spite of the well-known critical judgements which Luther levelled against the world, one may admit that he did not call the world sufficiently into question. That is, his criticism of the world does not have an adequate eschatological basis. The fact of the challenging of the old aeon by the new, though already in process, takes second place to the recognition of the continuing autonomy of the old aeon. That is why the same Luther, whose judgement upon the world was so critical, and who longed so fervently for the 'blessed last day', could arrive with such surprising ease at the conclusion that the two kingdoms are separate and parallel, and that the same divine commandment of love must be carried out differently in the two different kingdoms. Luther does not point out with sufficient clarity that the distortion of the divine commandment of love taking place in the institutions of this world is also a symptom of the disease from which this world is suffering, and a sign of God's patience with it. He is too hasty in identifying existing political and social institutions with the will of God. What he fails to do is to look at them objectively and question them critically. In Luther Christian love has principally a corroborative force; that is, it guarantees to those who bear office that even in secular institutions they are fulfilling the commandment of God and can have a good conscience. But it has too little critical and dynamic power; that is, it does not sufficiently impel those who bear office to recognise, in the light of the coming kingdom of God, that the institutions which they control are called into question and that the conditions of the present time must even now be altered.

All this leads to the familiar criticisms which have been made, if not of Luther himself, at least of the political attitude of Lutheranism, and which in our own time have been kindled once again by the experiences of the Church conflict under the Third Reich in recent years, those of a 'double standard', 'conservatism', 'quietist indifference', 'slavish obedience', and 'political naïveté'.

But does Thielicke sufficiently modify Luther's doctrine of the two kingdoms? Do not his criticisms of it to some extent, even if to a lesser degree, apply to himself? According to Thielicke the weakness of Luther's doctrine of the two kingdoms is that the eschatological theme of all Christian theology is not a sufficiently operative factor within it. This is certainly not true of Thielicke. From beginning to end his political ethics are based upon our situation within the history of salvation, where we live in a field of tension between the two aeons, so that the overlap between them cuts right through our own existence. For Thielicke the fact that according to Luther's doctrine of justification man is 'righteous and a sinner at one and the same time' is not merely true of him as an individual, but reflects this 'aeonic' situation. Thus, by emphasising the eschatological factor in ethics, Thielicke is saved from Luther's error of co-ordinating the two kingdoms as existing in a deceptive harmony, of too easily compromising with the distortion of the Christian commandment of love in the structural laws of this world, and of accepting with too little criticism its existing secular institutions.

Thielicke has done in fact what in his view Luther failed to do: he has pumped the life-blood of the doctrine of justification from the heart through the whole body, and so has succeeded in bringing to life the limbs which still remained lifeless and cold in Luther. It is this, together with his use of 'model cases', which brings his theological ethics so close to reality. He gives Christian faith a concrete secular expression, as secular and concrete as anything we can imagine. His ethics exemplify a true 'secular Christianity'. He really penetrates to the fullness of human life, and nothing human is alien to him. He brings dogma down to earth, out of the world to come and out of the ghetto of the Church. He exemplifies Christian faith in the concrete detail of reality. He does what Gogarten and Bonhoeffer demanded, and tries to endure the total reality of the world in faith before God.

But does Thielicke here not perhaps give way too much to the 'pressure of reality'? The dominant position occupied by the 'Noachic ordinance' in his political ethics gives him away. He regards it as the outstanding model case of the patient accommodation of God to the fallen world, which is the guide for all political action. But besides this 'patient' accommodation of God, there is another 'gracious' accommodation of God to the world, which Thielicke himself also discusses: the revelation of God in Jesus Christ. Why did Thielicke not go further and make this the dominant model case for his political ethics? The choice here is between Noah and Christ. In Thielicke's ethics the basic image of Noah sometimes seems to play a more decisive role than the basic image of Christ. But this means that although Thielicke lays powerful emphasis on the eschatological character of Christian ethics, he too focusses more on the fallen world than on the coming kingdom of God. We must consequently ask Thielicke, albeit less urgently, the same questions which he asks of Luther: Does he not accommodate political action too much to the present situation of the world, does he make Christian love sufficiently 'critical', does he not strive too much merely to maintain existing institutions and conditions, rather than to improve them, and is it sufficient only to interpret human and historical reality instead of changing it – in short, does Thielicke's *Theological Ethics* give sufficient emphasis to Christian *hope*, and to the necessary redirection of Christian consciousness towards the *future*?

How strongly this lack is generally felt in present-day theology is shown by the response, otherwise scarcely explicable, which was provoked by Jürgen Moltmann's book *The Theology of Hope*. Though this book does not deal explicitly with political ethics, Moltmann's discussion of Christian hope directly affects the central problem of all Christian political ethics.

The theology of hope

Promise, comfort, expectation, hope, mission, unrest, openness, readiness, elasticity, driving force, revival, exodus, pilgrimage, change, transformation – all these terms have one feature in common – they all refer to a movement, and this movement is a forward movement, towards the future. Thus the very vocabulary which Moltmann chooses reveals the permanent basis of his thought, or more properly, not its permanent basis, but rather the movement which drives it on. For Moltmann, the decisive dimension of all Christian faith is the *future*. As though no other form of time existed for him, not the past and just barely the present, he lifts everything that exists out of the repose of being into the movement of becoming. In the opening pages of his book we find the sentence which sets out his programme: 'There is only one real problem in Christian theology: the problem of the future.'[21]

For Moltmann the precedence granted to the future over all other forms of time does not derive from the general nature of history, from the fact that man as an historical being is always journeying towards the future, and that history conceals within itself an infinite abundance of future possibilities. Instead, it is based on the uniqueness of the history of Jesus Christ. More precisely, what matters is the future of Jesus Christ himself, or even more so the future which is implied in his resurrection. The resurrection of Jesus is not a completed event belonging to the past, but has set in motion a developing process which points towards the future. This future prospect, however, is not unlimited, but finds its fulfilment in the event to which the Bible refers as the 'coming' of Christ. Thus history extends from the resurrection to the second coming of Christ, and it is this which irreversibly directs everything that takes place within it towards the future. Consequently, a Christian does not travel through history 'with his back to the future', looking backward to the unalterable source which determines all future events. Instead, he faces his future, looking forward to the promised fulfilment which is still to come.

Because of this direction of history towards the future, Moltmann comes to accord to *eschatology* a completely dominant position within theology. The rediscovery of the central significance of eschatology for the preaching of Jesus and for primitive Christianity was, as we have seen, one of the most important theological events at the end of the nineteenth century. Admittedly theology did not immediately draw the theological consequences from this discovery in the historical field: 'The so-called "consistent eschatology" was never really consistent.' Now Moltmann is certainly not the first to make up for this deficiency; others have already done the same. But no one hitherto has brought eschatology forward in such a consistent fashion from the end of dogmatic theology, where it was 'like a loosely attached appendix that wandered off into obscure irrelevancies', to the beginning. In Moltmann eschatology ceases to be the 'doctrine of the last things', which comes at the end of all history and dogmatics, and becomes as it were the 'doctrine of the first things', with which everything begins and which determine everything: 'The eschatological is not one element of Christianity, but it is the medium of Christian faith as such.' Christianity is a 'religion of expectation', which does not 'flee the world' but 'strains after the future'. For Moltmann it is of decisive importance that not merely the existential life of an individual man, or even only his own understanding of himself, is determined by God's future, but that the whole of history, or indeed the whole cosmos, is drawn into the eschatological process which began with the resurrection of Jesus and extends to his second coming. He sees in this the decisive significance of late Jewish apocalyptic with its expectation of the imminent end of the world, which was shared by Jesus. Through apocalyptic, eschatology becomes 'the universal horizon of all theology as such'.[22]

Moltmann's book, therefore, is characterised by its title, *The Theology of Hope*. The title does not imply that the author was intending to write merely a theological monograph upon the Christian virtue of hope, but that he proposes to evolve his whole theology out of this theme. For Moltmann eschatology is the be-all and the end-all of theology; it forms the 'foundation' and 'mainspring' of all theological thought. Moltmann changes Anselm's definition of theology as *'fides quaerens intellectum'*, 'faith seeking understanding', into *'spes quaerens intellectum'*, 'hope seeking understanding', and the corresponding saying of Anselm, '*credo, ut intelligam*', 'I believe in order to know', into '*spero, ut intelligam*', 'I hope in order to know'. It is hope which 'mobilises' the intellectual activity of faith, both its consideration of what it is to be human, and also its reflection upon history and society. It becomes 'the ferment in our thinking, its mainspring, the source of its restlessness and torment'. All theological statements are 'statements of hope' and all theological concepts are 'anticipations'. 'They do not limp after reality and gaze on it with the night eyes of Minerva's owl, but they illuminate reality by displaying its future.' And hope is the mainspring not only of intellectual thought but also of love, so that 'with creative, inventive imagination', it is always in advance of the present condition of the world. 'It constantly provokes and produces thinking of an anticipatory kind in love to man and the world', it arouses 'inventiveness and elasticity in self-transformation, in breaking with the old and coming to terms with the new'. It is in this context that a decisive statement, reminiscent of Karl Marx, occurs in Moltmann, a statement which does not explicitly mention Thielicke, but is in fact a critical comment upon his ethics: 'The theologian is not concerned merely to supply a different *interpretation* of the world, of history and of human nature, but to *transform* them in expectation of a divine transformation.'[23]

Here Moltmann associates with the 'future' and 'hope' as a third related concept that of *mission*. Moltmann calls for 'a hermeneutics of the Christian mission', that is, 'a missionary exposition of the biblical witness'. Christianity has also to vindicate its future hope 'publicly', by taking stock of the new possibilities, prospects and goals which the resurrection of Jesus reveals to man and to the world, and by transforming the political and social situation in accordance with them. There must be a 'transforming mission in practice', which is in accordance with the principle of hope. From this point of view Moltmann works out a 'general ethical field-theory of Christian hope'.[24]

The guiding theme of his ethics of hope is formed by the idea of the *Exodus Church*. In order to explain this expression, Moltmann refers to the Epistle to the Hebrews: 'Let us go forth therefore unto him without the camp, bearing his reproach. For here we have no continuing city, but we seek one to come' (13:13 f.). These two verses of the Bible sum up the whole structure of Moltmann's ethics. Christians are warned against behaving in society as 'a group which is wholly adaptable' and of accepting without criticism the situation which they find there. Thus they should not serve mankind in order that the world may remain what it is, but 'in order that it may transform itself and become what it is promised to be'. 'Church for the world' means 'Church for the kingdom of God' and so for the renewal of the world. That is why the Church must undergo an exodus and go outside the 'camp'. Christianity has no right to keep its future hope for itself, but must mediate it to the whole of society. By 'transforming in opposition and creative expectation the face of the world' it must call what now exists into question in the light of the purpose of the world within the history of salvation, and work for what is to come. As a result, it comes into a 'conflict-laden but fruitful partnership' with society. It instils 'a constant unrest' in it, and is 'like an arrow sent out into the world to point to the future'. 'With its face towards the expected new situation, it leaves the existing situation behind and seeks for opportunities of bringing history into ever better correspondence to the promised future.' Consequently, Christianity is not concerned merely with individuals and therefore with individual salvation, but is always concerned as well with their circumstances and therefore with the renewal of society: it 'is in search of other institutions'. In this way Christianity concerns itself with the 'other side' of reconciliation with God, which has always been played down in the history of the Church: 'the realisation . . . of justice, the humanising of man, the socialising of humanity, peace for all creation'. Thus from the 'open foreland of its hopes for the world', Christianity gains new impulses for the shaping of man's public, social and political life.[25]

Like the ancient apocalyptic writers, Moltmann takes us up on to a high mountain, and shows us from there the whole of the future, as far as the highest peaks which stand on the farthest horizon; and he then summons us to scale these peaks. But in order to do this, we must first descend into the valley, where it is raining, and the roads are bad. Furthermore, we need maps, a compass, a guide, ropes and crampons; but even when we have all these, the ascent remains arduous and uncertain, and we advance only with difficulty. Moltmann relates all Christian political action to the ultimate eschatological horizon; in this way, he sets its goal in the future and fills it with the power of hope and the consciousness of mission. He is right to do this. If Christians really believe in the resurrection of Jesus Christ from the dead, they cannot simply be content to maintain this world just as it is at the moment, but must also set out at once to change and renew it, not only the persons who live in it, but its circumstances as well. This is the genuine and passionate concern which is revealed in Moltmann's stirring language. But Moltmann is only setting out a programme, if the term 'programme' can be applied at all to the mere impulse he gives. He gives no consideration to the question of the manner in which Christian political action is to be carried out. But if Moltmann were obliged to state what is to be done in the concrete historical situation, he would at once find himself subject to the same pressure of reality as Helmut Thielicke. He would have to come down from his mountain into the valley and analyse the situation, interpret reality, use his discretion and make compromises.

Here we come to the decisive point at issue in the violent theological and political disputes which have strained the unity of the Protestant Church and Protestant theology since the Second World War, to the point of destroying it. The question is how far the political action of Christians is already determined by the laws of life in the kingdom of God, and how far it is still bound by the structural laws of this world. There is *agreement* that we stand in a relationship both of continuity and also of discontinuity to the old aeon, and that the commandment of love of the kingdom of God is consequently always refracted and distorted when it comes into contact with the existing institutions of this world. Even someone who would like the police to be armed only with rubber truncheons is assuming that the Christian commandment of love is refracted and distorted in this way. There is *disagreement*, however, concerning the proportion between continuity and discontinuity, and therefore concerning the size of the angle of refraction, the degree of distortion. Here theological and political differences of opinion begin to manifest themselves. Some direct their gaze ever more firmly towards the laws of life in the kingdom of God, and therefore towards the discontinuity between the old aeon and the new, thereby running the risk of eluding the pressure of reality and soaring above the concrete political situation in their enthusiasm. If they are theologians, they must take care that politicians do not suspect them of being doctrinaire preachers of Utopia, remote from reality, who without any political mandate are offering outside advice to those who are engaged in politics. Others, however, direct their attention ever more firmly to the structural order of this world, and therefore to the continuity between the old aeon and the new, and thus run the risk of succumbing to the pressure of reality and becoming engrossed in a purely pragmatic approach to the concrete political situation. If they are politicians, they must take care that theologians do not suspect them of being unprincipled tacticians and opportunists, who in their political activities are denying their faith. But all, both theologians and politicians, must take heed of the reminder given by the philosopher Karl Jaspers that today's political situation demands more than the 'rebirth of man', and that it is the task of theologians to repeat with a new seriousness the eternal challenge to mankind: 'To be changed in its foundations.' And Jaspers also says: 'Every chance of the churches lies in the Bible, provided they can, in awareness of the turning point, make its original voice ring again today.'[26]

This leads us directly to the other reservation concerning Moltmann, and not him alone, but every rash and uncritical repetition of primitive Christian eschatology. There is no question that eschatology, associated in fact with strongly apocalyptic conceptions, was of central importance for the primitive Church. But for the first Christians eschatology was more than just an important article of theological doctrine; it was a living conviction of their faith, directly rooted in their religious experience. They really awoke every morning with the thought: '*Today* may be the day when he comes!' Which of us can still do this? Which of us still seriously takes account in his life of the imminent end of the world? Apart from a few borderline sects, no Church and no Christian does this any longer. Otherwise, the outward form of their life would be completely different. Consequently, the great emphasis placed on eschatology by present-day theologians seems to us to be likewise abstract and theoretical – mere 'academic eschatology', like the earlier 'academic socialism'.

Certainly, the rediscovery of primitive Christian eschatology has led to the rediscovery of the *future* as the decisive dimension of the Christian faith. But the emphasis laid on the future by many theologians at present is so exaggerated that it becomes suspicious. It almost gives the impression that the future has today taken the place formerly occupied by the Beyond. The vertical has become horizontal: the flight 'upwards' from the pressure of reality has now been replaced by a flight 'forward'. But whether the flight is upwards or forward, the demonstration of the truth of God, whether in space or in time, retreats into an indeterminate distance. Consequently, the question posed by modern man, where God is here and now, remains unanswered as it did in the past.

This leads to the second question which has preoccupied and almost split Protestant theology since the war. It touches on the very heart of the Christian message, the revelation of God in Jesus Christ. Whereas we formulated our first question by quoting the Bible, 'What are we to do?', we can now quote the Bible again and ask, 'What do you think of Christ?'

CHAPTER SEVEN

REVELATION AND HISTORY

The 'dreadful gulf' of history

Christian faith is faith in Jesus Christ – what else could it be? This is immediately evident from the expression 'Christian faith', which makes it clear that Christian faith is not something that could have come about at any time or anywhere in the world, and is not merely a particular species of a universal and timelessly valid concept of faith, but has its unique origin and enduring foundation in a particular event of history, the revelation of God in the appearance of Jesus Christ. For this reason Schleiermacher calls Christianity a 'positive historical religion'; that is, it assumes as its basis a concrete person and a concrete book: Jesus Christ and the Bible.

Other religions also appeal to divine revelation given to specially chosen persons, and to sacred books, but Christianity does this in a special and unique way. The Christian revelation does not regard itself as the unveiling and imparting of eternal ideas and universally valid and timeless truths of being, such as for example a new concept of God, or the idea of love, nor does it see itself as the imparting of a religious experience or the proclamation of an ecclesiastical dogma. Instead, it sees itself as closely related to a concrete historical event, or more precisely, to what happened to a concrete historical person. One cannot separate Christian truth from this person, by bringing its message forward into the present, but leaving the person himself in the past, as though one were cracking a nut, taking out the kernel and throwing away the shell. The message itself consists of what happened to this person, his birth, life, teaching, death and resurrection. The certainty of Christian faith is based upon concrete events of history. The truth it proclaims consists of the 'foolishness' that God spoke and acted in the man Jesus of Nazareth.

The validity of the revelation of God in Jesus Christ is final, conclusive, unsurpassable and universal. Although God may also have revealed himself, and may still reveal himself, in many other ways, in different places and at different times – through sibyls, prophets, priests, teachers of wisdom, artists or poets – he has revealed himself decisively through Jesus Christ. Consequently, theology treats the event of Christ as an 'eschatological event'. This word signifies that what took place through and in Christ was something 'ultimate' in the history of the world, beyond which there can be nothing 'more ultimate' or greater. In him God 'spoke' finally and once for all to the world: Jesus is the 'Word of God' to the whole of mankind.

But the consequence is that we are dealing not with a past event complete in itself, and limited to the years A.D. 1–30 in Palestine, but with a 'continuing' event, which extends into the present and also determines the future. Although the revelation in Christ is a single past historical event, it nevertheless possesses a significance which is absolute and which affects the present, and this significance for the present endures. What happened once happened once for all, and therefore happens again and again.

The fact that God revealed himself in Jesus makes faith and theology dependent on the *Bible*, which contains the still extant testimonies to this revelation. Consequently the Bible is called 'holy scripture', and all theology, or all Protestant theology at least, is essentially the interpretation of holy scripture. The Bible is the source and canon of faith and of the life of the Church. Luther adds: *sola scriptura*, scripture alone! It must be noted that Jesus Christ is not important to us because he is mentioned in the *Bible*. The reverse is true: the Bible is important for us because *Jesus Christ* is mentioned in it. The New Testament derives its authority from Christ, while the Old Testament in its turn receives its authority from the New.

The Bible as the testimony of the revelation of God is an historical entity. But we live and believe at the present day. How can something which took place and was written two thousand and more years ago be of significance for us today, not only in the sense of its continuing historical effect, but in its existential relevance to our lives? How can an historical tradition, even one which is also a word of God, be heard anew by us at the present day as addressed to us by God? How can what happened then happen again today? How can the *factum esse* of the past become the *fieri* of the present?

Here we come to the problem of the repetition of revelation, or more precisely, the *realisation of it in the present*. This is the problem of bringing revelation out of the past into the present, of making the truth proclaimed long ago into a present reality. Every preacher faces this problem when he goes into the pulpit on a Sunday morning. His task there is to make an event of the past, the revelation to which the Bible bears witness, a present reality in such a way that his congregation can feel that it is addressed to them. On every occasion he must bridge the historical gap of almost two thousand years, which Lessing called the 'dreadful gulf' of history. This aim is satisfied when what took place long ago in the synagogue at Nazareth takes place once again on Sunday morning in a village or city church, and one can say again: 'Today this scripture has been fulfilled in your hearing.' But how is this possible? How can a revelation which has already taken place, to which historical testimony exists, and which is therefore indirect, become a direct revelation effective in the present?

It is this which gives theology the task of *translation*; the biblical testimony of the revelation of God must be translated from the past into the present. This task of translation is a twofold one. First of all, theology must make sure that the biblical message is brought forward the whole distance from the past to the present day. Secondly, theology must make sure that in so bringing up to date the biblical message, it has translated the whole message and not left any of it behind in the process.

Thus the work of theology is like an arch spanning the distance from the biblical texts to their interpretation in any particular age. This arch is comparable to the arch of a bridge resting upon two piers. One pier stands in the past, and it is vital that the arch of the bridge rest firmly upon it; that is, that it should be made perfectly clear what the testimony of biblical revelation is, and that it should be shown to be reliable. The obligation and the difficulties of historical verification apply to the biblical statements concerning Jesus Christ as they do to every other historical event. The other pier of the arch is in the present, and everything depends once again upon the arch being firmly secured to this pier also. That is, the biblical revelation must be made a present reality in such a way that it 'concerns' me in my existential life, and that in the light of it I can understand my life anew. The understanding of the revelation of God attains its purpose when our interpretation of the biblical text is transformed into the interpretation of our existence and the world we live in by the text, and we experience once again what was formerly experienced by the first witnesses, an encounter with the reality of God in the reality of their lives and of the world they lived in.

The question of the realisation of revelation in the present leads on to that of the *reality* of the revelation. What kind of reality does faith believe in, when it believes in the revelation of God in Jesus Christ?

The divine and the human are intimately linked in it. Christian faith believes *at the same time* in a specific event of history and act of God. Jesus Christ, as the heavenly Lord whom we worship, is *at the same time* an earthly human person. The Son of God from heaven is the carpenter's son from Nazareth. And we encounter the Bible, the testimony written and handed down by men of the revelation of God, as the word of man and the word of God *at the same time*. What do we mean here by 'at the same time'? How can we conceive of the unity which prevails here between a divine and a human reality? This is the question which is at the heart of the problem of bringing revelation to realisation today. Whether or not Christian revelation will be understood and brought to realisation in our time depends upon the right or wrong answer to this question.

Since the days of the early Church, theology has tried to understand, or rather to describe, the reality of the Christian revelation and the tradition concerning it with the conceptual instrument of metaphysical thought, borrowed from classical antiquity. The event on which Christian faith was based was treated as qualitatively different from every other event in the world. The revelation of God was set apart as a special province, distinct from all the rest of history, and isolated from it. The specific characteristic of the history of revelation, so sharply distinguished from the secular history of the world, was that it was miraculous, and that at every step it infringed the laws which otherwise prevail in nature and history.

A particular world view underlay this *supranaturalism*. This was the cosmic dualism taken over from Greek philosophy, which endured throughout the Middle Ages into modern times, and according to which real existence was ascribed to two different and separate worlds, one higher, supernatural, spiritual, and divine, and the other lower, natural, physical, earthly and human. Based on this metaphysical dualism the early Church formed its christological dogma, and sought to describe the mystery of the person of Jesus Christ in the form of the doctrine of the two natures, as 'true God' and 'true man'. And based on this same metaphysical dualism, early Protestant orthodoxy later developed the doctrine of verbal inspiration in a similar way to the dogma of the two natures, and isolated the Bible from the general history of literature on the grounds of its miraculous origin by divinely inspired dictation.

But the philosophical foundations of theological supranaturalism were challenged as early as the beginning of the modern period, if not before. The powerful force which brought about this upheaval was that of *historical understanding*, which is the basis of *critical historical method*. It meant that the fate of theology was decided by history. The problems with which historical study is concerned are not merely individual questions about the tradition of Christian revelation, such as whether a saying was really uttered by Jesus, or an epistle really written by Paul, but affect the nature of Christian revelation itself. It is an inquiry into the nature of the reality on which Christian faith is based.

The radical and universal power of historical thought is a consequence of the process of secularisation which has taken place in the modern age. As we have seen, the essence of this modern process of secularisation is that the concept of another, divine and higher world which acts upon this world from above, creating it and providing its meaning, becomes empty and fades away. From henceforth man no longer exists on two levels, a lower and an upper one, between which he can alternate according to the situation. Instead, he exists upon one level alone, the firm ground of this world. The basic experience of historical understanding is the same. Thus secularisation and historicisation are basically alternative concepts to describe the same experience. The secularisation of the world means its total historicisation; man, the world, and man's thought about the world all become radically historical. The characteristic of historical thought is that it sees the whole world as history and makes man responsible for it, so that it becomes man's world.

Thus critical historical inquiry is not simply a new method of academic study, but a new total view of human life. Ernst Troeltsch says 'the words "purely historical" imply a complete world view', and he compares historical method to a 'leaven' which penetrates everything. All life is now drawn into the 'flow of an onward motion' (J. G. Droysen) and all reality now becomes historical reality. All that is now held to be real is that which can be understood historically. Either something is history, or it does not exist – there is no third choice.

The rise of historical thought brings to an end the era of metaphysical thought which goes back to classical antiquity, and with it, the attempt undertaken with the aid of this mode of thought to understand the event of the Christian revelation as something distinct and wholly other in its nature, and to isolate it as a quiet enclave outside the rest of nature and history. Historical thought represents the end of all supranaturalism. Once it has begun its task, it stops at nothing, but includes even those events and testimonies which according to Christian faith contain the revelation of God to mankind within universal history, and submits them to critical historical inquiry. It will no longer tolerate enclaves where historical laws are not followed and others, metaphysical or theological, prevail. It permits no 'supra-nature' and no 'supra-history', but draws everything into the broad stream of historical becoming and passing away. Even when faced with the Christian revelation and its tradition it holds firmly to its strict alternative: either something is history, or it does not exist – there is no third choice.

As a result, the basis of all Christian faith and life has been challenged in the modern age. The authority of Jesus Christ and the Bible which has hitherto prevailed seems likely to be destroyed from within. The Christian revelation is now no longer an 'absolute', 'eschatological' event separate from the rest of history and determining all history, but is one historical phenomenon among many in the wider context of the general history of religion. Jesus Christ now becomes one founder of a religion among others, and the Bible is no longer a book free from error and inspired by God, which one day appeared whole upon the altar at Jerusalem, but is a religious document written by men, which consequently must be read, understood and interpreted by the same methods as other human documents.

Of all the upheavals which Christian faith could undergo this was bound to be the most severe, for it seems to deprive faith of its very foundations. The affirmation, 'The Lord has spoken' is now followed by the critical question, 'But has he spoken?' The business of theology now consists not of the interpretation of holy scripture with authority, but to a considerable degree of the justification and defence of its authority to carry out such an interpretation.

Thus the question of the relationship between *revelation and history* is the central theological problem of the present day. Whereas the Middle Ages were principally concerned with the question of the relationship between faith and reason, the modern age is clearly preoccupied with the question of the relationship between faith and history. The great difficulties with which Christian preaching is struggling today are all connected in some way with this question. If preaching and faith have grown more difficult for Christians in our time, the reason is that the understanding of the Christian revelation has become more difficult as a consequence of radical historical thought. The replacement of a metaphysical understanding of reality by an historical understanding demands a transformation of Christian thought, and we are only beginning to understand where it will lead and how great it will be. In the light of this change, the question of the possibility of Christian faith must be posed in a completely new way.

It is not surprising that severe tensions and disputes on the subject of the problem of history have arisen between academic theologians and the 'believing' Church. By comparison with these tensions and disputes, the struggles which took place during the first five years after the war on the problems of political ethics seem to be almost incidental and already forgotten. It sometimes seems almost as though the different views of the authority of the Bible could lead to a new schism in the Church. But theology cannot escape this dispute, not only because the course of history cannot be reversed, and because it is no more possible to undo the rise of critical historical thought than to undo the discovery of atomic energy; but also because the problem here is one which is implicit in the very origin and nature of Christian faith. Since Christian faith in fact possesses its basis and foundation in a particular event of history, it cannot merely tolerate the critical historical examination of this event and its historical tradition, but must actually demand it – as a demonstration of the historicity of the revelation in which it believes. And if secularisation is in fact a legitimate consequence of Christian faith, so also is historical thought. Historical thought, then, is not something brought to Christian faith from outside, but something in which Christian faith itself is claiming its due, so that modern man can claim the support of Christian faith for his historical thinking. The obstinate and devout clinging to supranaturalist thought is not in truth as 'Christian' as it makes out. Rather, it betrays the persistence of the ancient religious structure of the pre-Christian world, with its distinction between the sacred and the profane, between cultically pure and cultically impure spheres. But it is this distinction which has been removed by the freedom of man and the worldliness of the world proclaimed in the revelation in Christ. And this proclamation of the freedom of man and the worldliness of the world, which once had the effect of removing distinctions of cult, nowadays demands the disappearance altogether of isolated enclaves in history, and that instead everything in history possesses the same historical nature and reality.

But how are we then to conceive of the reality of the Christian revelation? How are we to understand the unity which prevails within it between divine and human reality? How is it to be understood *anew*, now that the traditional metaphysical understanding of reality has

210 THE QUESTION OF GOD

been replaced by an historical understanding? How can the Christian message be understood historically, and yet be authoritative and certain? How is it possible for the account of an event which took place in the past to possess present reality and concern me directly? In short, how can what Christians say concerning the revelation of God still be vindicated, when only what is historical is real?

Faith and understanding

No other theologian of our time has undertaken the task of understanding the Christian message anew in the framework of historical thought with such inexorable tenacity, resolute honesty, and at the same time with such a vast and rich knowledge of theology, history, philology, philosophy and comparative religion, as Rudolf Bultmann of Marburg. A New Testament scholar by profession, Bultmann is both a profound exegete and an outstanding systematic theologian. The tension which is so painfully experienced today between exegetical and dogmatic theology seems to be concentrated in his person, and overcome there. With Karl Barth and Paul Tillich, Rudolf Bultmann is one of the three truly great Protestant theologians of the twentieth century, who have each brought about a decisive advance in theology and who, each in his own way, have been epoch-making.

Bultmann stands at the crossroads between the two decisive theological developments of the nineteenth and twentieth centuries: liberal theology and dialectical theology meet in him. Like Karl Barth, Bultmann's origins are in liberal theology; they are both pupils of the 'Marburg school'. But whereas Barth believed that he could set aside his theological past like a garment and simply disassociate himself from the critical historical inquiry of liberal theology, Bultmann has felt an obligation to it throughout his life: 'We whose origin is in liberal theology could not have become or remained theologians if we had not encountered in liberal theology a serious and radical honesty; we felt the work of orthodox theology at the universities, of whatever complexion, to be an attempt at compromise, within which we could only have sustained an existence which was inwardly fragmented. . . . Here – so we felt – was the atmosphere of truthfulness in which we could all breathe.'[1]

But at the same time, Bultmann has a place with Barth, Gogarten, Brunner, Thurneysen and the rest in the great transformation of Protestant theology after the First World War. What he has in com-

mon with other representatives of dialectic theology is the rediscovery
of the deity of God which they so passionately advocated: that God is
God and that theology deals in consequence with God and his revelation,
and not with man and his religion; that the revelation of God contains
its basis within itself alone, and that no effort of man of any kind can
attain to it. There is no direct knowledge of God: no human emotion,
inquiry or experience, no philosophical speculation and no historical
knowledge can apprehend the revelation of God and provide the foundation of faith. Man's faith can never come from himself, but can only
be his answer to the word of God previously given to him, in which
God's judgement and grace are proclaimed to him. And there is no
guarantee of this word apart from faith.

   This shows what is so frequently forgotten in today's polemic against
Bultmann: that, like Barth, his origins are in liberal theology, but that
he too left liberal theology behind after the First World War and
together with the others underwent the great theological transformation. This theological transformation became more decisive for his
thought than his origins in liberal theology. It is possible that Bultmann
has in fact preserved the original intention of dialectical theology in a
purer form than Barth himself.

   On the basis of the fresh starting-point provided by dialectical
theology, Bultmann sought to develop the critical historical inquiry
which is the legacy of liberal theology for the theology and the Church
of our own time. Of great theological importance to him in this was
the rediscovery at the same time of Reformation theology, while
Heidegger's philosophical analysis of existence was of importance for
his method. Here we have the most important elements of Bultmann's
theology: the historical criticism of liberal theology, the close relationship between revelation, word and faith in dialectical theology, the
doctrine of justification in Reformation theology and Heidegger's
existentialist philosophy. But Bultmann did not merely accept these
different historical, theological and philosophical elements and combine them, he drew them together, with the utmost systematic power
and logic, into a new coherence of his own. The theological purpose
which guided him is summed up in the title of the four volumes of his
collected essays: *Glauben und Verstehen*, 'Faith and Understanding'.

   The same title, *faith and understanding*, could be used as a heading for
the whole of his theological work. He would see his theology as 'a
task parallel to that performed by Paul and Luther in their doctrine of
justification by faith alone without the works of Law. Or rather, it

carries this doctrine to its logical conclusion in the field of epistemology'. Just as man cannot rely on any ethical action in the sight of God, so also he cannot rely on any objective knowledge, thought, and perception: 'There is no difference between security based on good works and security built on objectifying knowledge.' And just as there are no sacred enclaves, consecrated persons and houses of God isolated from the world, so also there are no miraculous and visibly divine events separate from history, on which faith can be based. Rather, the whole structure of nature and history is secular, and only in the light of the biblical word which is preached do the happenings within it take on for the believer the character of divine operation. Like Luther, Bultmann seeks to destroy all man's false longing for security: anyone who believes steps into the 'darkness' and stands in the 'vacuum'. He can rely on nothing other than the word of the Bible which is preached, and this word cannot be proved to be the word of God: 'The word enters our world entirely fortuitously, entirely contingently, entirely as an event. . . . No one's summons has a claim [Platz] in the faith of others, whether it be Paul or Luther. Indeed faith can never be for us a standpoint toward which we take a position but always and ever a new act, new obedience. Always uncertain, as soon as we look about ourselves as men and question; ever uncertain, as soon as we reflect on it, as soon as we talk about it. . . . Only certain as faith in the grace of God unto the forgiveness of sins which justifies me – when it pleases him.'[2] If there is any theologian today who clings to the *sola fide* of the Reformation doctrine of justification it is Rudolf Bultmann: he is concerned with faith, with faith alone, and with faith through the word alone.

But this does not mean that faith implies blind submission to a dogma or the acceptance of absurdities. Whoever listens to a sermon should not simply swallow the truths of the New Testament on the 'like it or lump it' principle, like pills that either bring about death or are at once eliminated (the best thing to do!). Rather, these truths must be believed and *understood*: 'Faith and unbelief are never arbitrary decisions. They offer us the alternative between accepting or rejecting that which alone can illuminate our understanding of ourselves.' The gospel demands of man that he make a decision in faith; but man can achieve a true decision in faith only when he has understood that for or against which he is to make his decision. 'If this were not the case, and if faith were faith in an unintelligible object, it would be a movement based upon one's own resolution, a purely arbitrary and chance procedure; it would be the beginning of the righteousness of works.'[3] Anyone who believes that he must sacrifice his understanding and his reason, surrender his intellect unconditionally to the divine revelation, and accept it as an absurd and incomprehensible event offends not only against the commandment of intellectual honesty, but also against the nature of faith; he reduces faith to a meritorious work of the intellect and thereby perverts it into its very opposite. It is because Bultmann is concerned with faith alone that he is also concerned with the understanding. Faith is faith in the word, and the word is addressed to someone; consequently it must be offered to man in a form in which he can understand it.

But this requirement that the word of God must be understandable does not mean that Bultmann wishes to give a rational explanation of the gospel and so make it acceptable to modern man. Rather, what he seeks to do is to remove from it false and unreal causes of offence, and to bring to light and draw to the attention the genuine and real scandal it contains. The true and real scandal of the gospel consists of the paradox that God has acted in an event of history, that he forgives sin in Jesus Christ. There is nothing offensive or paradoxical to the reason in this as such. Anyone can understand what forgiveness is if he wishes. But that God has truly given forgiveness and that he has done it in Jesus Christ, in an event of history, is not evident, and demands that man make a decision of faith. But this decision of faith is only possible if man has truly understood the Christian message. Only then does he become aware of its real scandal.[4]

The two terms 'faith and understanding' accurately sum up Bultmann's theological purpose, the principal theme which governs the whole of his theology. He seeks, in the changed conditions of modern historical thought, to interpret the Christian message in such a manner that a proper and undiminished role is accorded to its relationship to history and equally to its relationship to God. It is astonishing, but also somewhat alarming, that Bultmann has maintained the same views virtually unchanged throughout his life. This parallels the outward course of his life: he was born in Oldenburg in 1884, but from 1921 up to his retirement he was Professor of New Testament Studies in Marburg. All this gives Bultmann's work an imposing unity, but at the same time imparts to it something of a rigid and monolithic quality – Karl Jaspers was not entirely wrong in speaking of Bultmann's 'shut-in obstinacy'.[5] Whereas it took the development of many years for Barth to become what he finally is, we find Bultmann's thought almost complete in his earliest writings. All he has really done in his later works is to expand and increasingly clarify the views which he held from the outset, and which were already implicit in his point of departure.

Bultmann's achievement has become widely known outside the circle of his academic colleagues only since the Second World War. But from then on his reputation has rapidly become world-wide. What brought him so prominently into the public eye was in fact a single lecture entitled 'The New Testament and Mythology'. Bultmann gave it on 4th June, 1941, at the conference of the *Gesellschaft für Evangelische Theologie* (Society for Protestant Theology) in Alpirsbach; it was printed later in the same year, scarcely fifty pages in length. At first this work made little stir. The Church had other concerns at that time; it was fighting for the purity of its doctrine and for its very existence. It was certainly interested in the message of the New Testament, but not in its mythology. Moreover, most pastors and theologians were at the front. But after the war Bultmann's essay on the demythologising of the New Testament provoked a public discussion wider than that aroused by any theological work since Harnack's *Nature of Christianity* and Barth's *Epistle to the Romans*. Bultmann's influence on German theology after the Second World War was as great as that of Karl Barth after the First World War, and in fact in the judgement of the American theologian J. M. Robinson his suggestions and ideas as they spread through the world have constituted Germany's greatest contribution to theology since the war.[6] What is astonishing is that it should have been of all things this essay on demythologisation which had such an effect, and indeed provoked such a shock, for it contained scarcely anything which Bultmann had not said before. Theologians at least were in a position to be acquainted with all it contained.

Certainly the easily comprehensible but unfortunate slogan 'the demythologisation of the New Testament' contributed to the stir caused by Bultmann's essay. Gogarten too regarded the word 'demythologisation' as scarcely a happy choice, but thought it of immense value because of the alarm it provoked – for 'the Church's sleep is profound'.[7] But the real reason for the repercussions of Bultmann's essay went deeper than its title. The essay delineates a programme for the future, and is almost in the nature of a 'manifesto'. Bultmann had taken up once again a forgotten but unresolved line of inquiry and brought it back into public discussion.

The powerful stream of dialectical theology had swept past the problem of history, as though two hundred years of critical historical study of the Bible and the sources of Christianity had never taken place, and as though Gotthold Ephraim Lessing, Johann Salomo Semler, Ferdinand Christian Baur, David Friedrich Strauss, Julius Wellhausen, Johannes Weiss, Albert Schweitzer, Adolf von Harnack, and all the others had never lived or thought. But the attempt of dialectical and orthodox denominational theologians as it were to run amok in dogmatics and pass by the problem of history was a failure. In spite of all radical dogmatic solutions and reactions against historicism, the problem raised itself again. Since Bultmann's essay on demythologising, if not before, we are once again caught up in the problems posed to theology by the modern concept of history.

Bultmann gave expression to a feeling of unease which pervades us all, in so far as we genuinely belong to the twentieth century, something that at least the more serious and more honest of his critics admit without reservation. Bonhoeffer, in a letter of summer 1942, reacted to Bultmann's essay with the following words: 'Bultmann has let the cat out of the bag, not only on his own account, but with regard to many others (the liberal cat out of the bag of doctrinal belief), and I am pleased. He has dared to say what many have suppressed within themselves (I include myself in this), without having succeeded in overcoming it. He has thereby rendered a service to intellectual decency and honesty. The doctrinal Phariseeism with which he is now being opposed by many of the brethren is intolerable to me. Now he has spoken and must be answered.' Admittedly Bonhoeffer continues: 'But the window must of course be closed again. Otherwise the company will grow cold too quickly.'[8] Julius Schniewind likewise begins his 'A Reply to Bultmann' with the affirmation: 'Bultmann's essay deals with a question the importance of which no preacher can overlook. . . . Bultmann's desire to emancipate the gospel message from mythology is something which he shares with every preacher who is worth his salt.' And Helmut Thielicke says in his reply to Bultmann: 'This is the most serious challenge theologians have had to face for many a day.'[9]

But a number of Church leaders, not a few theologians and many ordinary worshippers felt Bultmann's essay to be not an appeal to their conscience, but the work of one who was destroying the faith of the Church. 'This worthy, devout and learned man has brought down much opprobrium upon his old age by this essay,' commented the well-known Stuttgart lawyer Otto Küster, who was no mean theologian.[10] Pietist pamphleteers spoke in handouts and circulars of 'neo-rationalism', 'the dismantling of the Christian gospel' and 'blood-poisoning'. Of much greater importance is the fact that the General Synod of the United Lutheran Protestant Church of Germany came very close in 1952 to a public condemnation of Bultmann's theology. The Bishop of Hamburg, Volkmar Herntrich, late at night from the pulpit of St Mary's Church in Flensburg, persuaded the Synod to abandon such a course, an action deserving our grateful remembrance. Those who allow themselves to be horrified at Bultmann and his theology only reveal that consciously or unconsciously they are closing their eyes to a reality which is also their own, and which they simply have been suppressing with more or less success.

Bultmann, however, is not concerned merely with the much quoted 'modern man', nor with intellectual honesty only, nor is his principal interest a pastoral and missionary one. He is not concerned merely with his audience. It is Christian faith itself which he seeks to vindicate. Friedrich Gogarten, who skilfully helped and defended Bultmann in the conflict over demythologisation, was right when he wrote: 'But one would be taking a totally inadequate view of the object of the controversy if one were to suppose that its sole purpose was to enable modern thought to assume its rightful place. It is concerned with very much more than that. It is the Christian faith itself which demands its due, and it is for its sake that the controversy must be pursued.'[11] It is in this spirit that Rudolf Bultmann conducted the theological controversy: for faith alone and for faith in the word alone.

The programme of demythologisation

In his essay on demythologisation Bultmann summed up with the utmost precision and clarity, and concentrated upon a single issue, what has been the theme of his whole life's work: faith and the understanding of the Christian message in the framework of modern historical thought. Bultmann seeks to make the word of the Bible intelligible to modern man in such a way that he can receive it as God's word addressed to him. What at the present time conceals the nature of the biblical word as direct address, and so obscures its intelligibility and impedes or even perverts faith, if it does not make it impossible, is the profound difference between the conceptual world of the New Testament and our own. Our own world view is irrevocably determined by science and technology, whereas that of the New Testament is a mythical world view.

The New Testament conceives of the world as made up of three storeys, heaven above, hell beneath and, between the two, earth as the field of conflict between the heavenly and demonic powers, between God and Satan. The New Testament speaks even of its real content, the event that brings salvation, in mythological language. It proclaims Christ as a pre-existent divine being who appears upon earth as a man, who works miracles, drives out demons, dies on the cross in atonement for the sins of men, rises on the third day, returns to the heavenly world, and who in a short time will return on the clouds of heaven, in order to bring into being, through cosmic catastrophes, the resurrection of the dead and the judgement, a new heaven and a new earth. All this is mythological language, formed of elements derived from the contemporary mythology of late Jewish apocalyptic and the gnostic redemption myth.

All these mythological conceptions of the New Testament are no longer credible to us. To use an image of Otto Küster's, they are like a currency which is no longer in circulation, and which at best is accepted by a handful of collectors and connoisseurs.[12] But anyone who demands that it should be accepted in faith, perverts faith into the mere believing of miraculous things, and so reduces it to a meritorious work. For us the mythical world view has vanished once for all, and it is not possible to repolish a vanished mythical world view and bring it back by a simple act of will into the world in which we live and think, which has been formed irrevocably by science.

Firmly, and relentlessly, and almost monotonously, Bultmann hammers out the word 'abolished': the stories of Christ's descent into hell and ascension into heaven are *abolished*; the concept of a final age, the onset of which is accompanied by cosmic catastrophes, is *abolished*; the expectation of a Son of Man who comes on the clouds of heaven is *abolished*; miracles as mere miracles are *abolished*; belief in spirits and demons is abolished ('The Blumhardt legends are to my mind preposterous'). 'It is impossible to use electric light and the wireless and to avail ourselves of modern medical and surgical discoveries, and at the same time believe in the New Testament world of daemons and spirits. We may think we can manage it in our own lives, but to expect others to do it is to make the Christian faith unintelligible and unacceptable to the modern world.'[13] The fact that the world view held by natural science is itself in the midst of a radical transformation does not make any difference to this. The attempt undertaken by many of today's theologians to rescue the New Testament belief in miracles by relating it to the radicalisation of the laws of causality that result from the discoveries of modern atomic physics are rightly rejected by Bultmann as 'naïve': 'As though this relativisation opened the door to the intervention of forces from another world!'[14]

But an impetus even more powerful than the scientific world view was provided for Bultmann's criticism of the mythological conceptions of the New Testament by the *way in which modern man understands himself*. Modern man no longer understands himself as a dualist being, always open to the intervention of supernatural forces, but regards himself as a unified being complete in himself, with his thinking, will and emotion originating within himself. As a result, he no longer understands what the New Testament states concerning the nature and destiny of man. The word which Bultmann now repeats is not 'abolished', but 'unintelligible': for modern man the conception of the divine Spirit as a supernatural 'something' penetrating the structure of natural forces is *unintelligible*; the interpretation of death as a punishment for sin brought about by an ancestor is *unintelligible* to him; the doctrine of vicarious satisfaction by means of the death of Christ on the cross is *unintelligible* to him; the resurrection of Christ as an event releasing a life-giving force which one appropriates to oneself through the sacraments is *unintelligible*; the hope of being taken up into a heavenly world of light and there clad with a new spiritual body is *unintelligible* to him. Indeed, all this is not merely unintelligible to modern man, it is completely meaningless. No one nowadays takes into account the possibility of the course of nature and history being interrupted by the direct intervention of transcendental forces, and still less is it possible for anyone to understand that the meaning of his life may be determined by this in any way.

Thus the world view held by modern man, and his understanding of himself, contradict the mythological conceptual world of the New Testament. How can this contradiction be resolved? The decisive question is whether the truth which the New Testament contains is essentially bound up with these mythological conceptions to the extent that it has vanished with them, or whether this truth is still valid today, even though the mythological terms in which it is expressed have been shown to be valid only for their own time. And if the truth of the New Testament is still valid, what is the relationship between the gospel and the myth? How are we to interpret and understand the witness of the New Testament?

One way which Bultmann excludes, because he is convinced that it does not do justice to the essence of the New Testament message, is the process of reduction carried out by the critique of liberal theology. This reduced the New Testament message to certain religious and ethical principles, either to an idealistic ethic with a religious motivation, or to a religious emotion and piety with a mystical flavour. In this Jesus possesses either a purely pedagogical significance as a teacher and example, or else a religious and sociological significance as the unifying centre and symbol in the cult. Against this process of reduction as practised by the critique of liberal theology, Bultmann makes it perfectly clear that the New Testament speaks of an event, through which God has brought about the salvation of the world. Salvation is linked to the historical person of Jesus, and this person himself is the decisive event of salvation. Consequently, anyone who eliminates this person also eliminates his message.

Thus the New Testament proclamation cannot be rescued by the critical selection or deletion of certain elements. The choice is between the acceptance of the mythical world view as a whole or its rejection as a whole. For the reasons given, its acceptance is no longer in question today, so that only the second possibility remains: 'If the truth of the New Testament proclamation is to be preserved, the only way is to demythologise it.'[15] The question whether it is possible to follow this course and in so doing preserve the validity of the New Testament proclamation depends upon whether one succeeds in presenting without a myth the saving event and the person of Jesus Christ, conceived of in the New Testament as a mythical event and a mythical person; and whether one succeeds thereby in so presenting the truth of the New Testament message that it becomes intelligible and credible even for the contemporary mind, which does not think in mythological terms.

Bultmann derives the necessity of demythologising the New Testament not in the first instance from the world view of modern man, or from the way in which he understands himself, but rather from the nature of myth and from the New Testament itself. He describes the nature of *myth* as follows: In myth man becomes aware that the world in which he lives is full of riddles and mysteries, and that he is not lord of the world and of his own life but dependent upon forces which are at work beyond what he can know, dispose of and control, and which provide the basis, limits, and goal of his existence. But myth speaks of these forces in an inadequate and unsatisfactory way. It objectivises in this world what lies beyond it; it speaks of what is unworldly in a worldly way and of what is divine in a human way; the gods appear as human beings and their actions as human actions, but on a super-human scale. By so doing myth impedes and obscures its own real purpose. For the real purpose of myth is not to provide an objective picture of the world by means of which it can be controlled, but rather to express the way in which man in the world understands himself as dependent upon forces which he cannot control. Thus the impulse for the criticism of myth lies in myth itself. In accordance with the intention of myth, it should not be interpreted cosmologically, but anthropologically or rather 'existentially'; that is, its purpose is to propound not its objectivising conceptual content, but the understanding of human existence expressed in it.

Secondly, Bultmann derives the necessity of demythologising from the *New Testament* itself. A strange contradiction runs through all the New Testament writings: on the one hand sin is regarded as a doom come to man from outside, whereas on the other hand it is regarded as personal guilt. On the one hand man is understood as a cosmic being whose faith is determined by objective forces and events, while on the other hand he is addressed as an independent self, who must make his own decisions. On the one hand, eternal life lies in the future as a miraculous blessing, while on the other hand it has already been obtained by faith in the present. Consequently, the New Testament itself demands that myth be subject to criticism, and justifies the process of demythologisation.

The point of departure for the criticism of myth which is contained in myth and in the New Testament themselves, indicates how this task should be tackled. Bultmann reduces the process of demythologisation to a simple formula: myth must not be critically eliminated, but interpreted existentially. That is, Bultmann does not seek to eliminate the mythological conceptions of the New Testament out of hand, in order to retain a 'Christian residue', as it were the *evangelium purum*, the pure substance of faith. Instead, he seeks in these conceptions the understanding of existence which is expressed within them. Thus it is not his intention to reject the Bible in part or as a whole, but only to set it free from the obsolete world view which it contains. This he does not by eliminating mythological conceptions, but by illuminating the more profound significance present in them and underlying them, thus bringing out the true intention of the myth itself. Demythologisation, therefore, is not 'a process of subtraction, but a hermeneutic method', a 'method of interpretation'. Demythologisation means 'an existentialist interpretation': 'I call such an interpretation . . . an existentialist interpretation, since under the impulse of the interpreter's own inquiry into the meaning of his own existence, it inquires into the existential understanding always present in any historical work.'[16]

This positive purpose of demythologisation needs to be constantly maintained and stressed since it is easily obscured by the negative connotation of the word itself. For this reason it might be preferable to speak of 'existentialist interpretation' instead of 'demythologisation'. The principal intention is not the negative one of criticising the mythological statements of the New Testament, but the positive one of demonstrating the understanding of existence which it contains. This is what the criticism of myth consists of. The existentialist interpretation achieves its aim when it succeeds in demonstrating that the New Testament opens up to man an understanding of himself which faces him with a genuine decision.

Bultmann has no intention to provide theologians with a formula that can be learned and applied in a moment. He knows that demythologisation or existentialist interpretation is a task 'much more formidable than that. It cannot be done single-handed. It will tax the time and strength of a whole theological generation.'[17] Here, as in other academic fields today, a particular task has become the central issue of theology and the dominating concept in it: the task of hermeneutics, the art of understanding. Bultmann's pupil Ernst Fuchs refers to it as the 'linguistics of the Christian faith'.

Hermeneutic method

In every field of knowledge, the method of understanding is determined by its object. This is also true of theology: 'The interpretation of biblical writings is not subject to conditions different from those applying to all other kinds of literature.'[18] The biblical testimonies to the revelation of God form the object of theology. Since the Christian revelation explicitly claims to have taken place in an historical event, the testimonies to this event cannot be interpreted in a way different from other historical testimonies. There is no special sacred method for the exegesis of the New Testament. It is never appropriate to speak of a special 'theological' or 'spiritual' exegesis: 'There is nothing "theological" here to begin with. The work of the exegete becomes theological not through his premises and his methods, but by virtue of its object, the New Testament . . . the attention he pays to it as a scholar is profane and the only thing that is sacred is the word that is written.'[19]

Anyone who wishes to interpret the Bible requires like any exegete the appropriate intellectual tool, that is, a conceptual framework appropriate to his text. Since the Bible makes statements about God, and therefore about human existence, in this case the conceptual framework must be one which speaks in appropriate terms and methodically about human existence. It is not the task of theology but of philosophy to provide the conceptual framework on which the process of interpretation is based. Here the question of the 'right' philosophy arises. Bultmann's theological purpose requires the question to be posed as follows: 'Which philosophy today offers the most adequate perspective and conceptions for understanding human existence?' For Bultmann 'the "right" philosophy is simply one which has worked out an appropriate terminology for the understanding of existence, an understanding involved in human existence itself'.[20]

Bultmann considers that he has in fact found this 'right' philosophy in the works of Martin Heidegger. Although he was already a professor himself, he followed Heidegger's lectures when Heidegger received a chair at Marburg two years after his own arrival there. In the course of his work as a New Testament exegete, Bultmann became a pupil of Heidegger. He chose Heidegger's philosophy not because it provided the likeliest possibility of a point of contact for theology, or because it seemed to be particularly close to Christian faith, but because in his view it interpreted human existence in the most appropriate practical and conceptual terms – and it is human existence of which the New Testament speaks. With regard to Heidegger, Bultmann followed as it were the advice of St Paul: 'Whatever is true, whatever is honourable, whatever is just . . . think about these things' (Phil. 4:8).

But Bultmann makes use of Heidegger only for the clarification of his concepts, and does not adopt the content of his philosophy. Existentialist philosophy plays for him the role only of a *formal* discipline; it serves only to reveal the structures of human existence, with complete neutrality regarding the material and the content which is under consideration; it is neither believing nor unbelieving, neither Christian nor atheist. It describes in purely phenomenological terms what the *structures* of existence are, but does not proclaim any material *ideal* of existence. It does not tell us '*how* we ought to exist', but only says to us, 'You ought *to exist*' – 'or, if even this is going too far, it shows us what existence means.' Thus it no more takes into account the concrete encounters and events of personal life than it does the relationship between man and God. But precisely because of this complete neutrality,

Bultmann considers existentialist philosophy to provide the most appropriate conceptual structure for the interpretation of the scripture: 'Existentialist philosophy, while it gives no answer to the question of my personal existence, makes personal existence my own personal responsibility, and by doing so it helps to make me open to the word of the Bible.'[21]

Existentialist philosophy shows that the being of man, by contrast to all other being, does not have the character of mere presence but, in so far as it is a truly human mode of being, consists in the carrying out of the act of existing. It calls man from his 'inessentiality', in which he seeks to give himself security by the aid of outside means and forces, running the risk of losing himself, and demands of him that he take responsibility for his own existence, so attaining by the act of existing to his 'essentiality', by constantly realising himself in the concrete situation in which he finds himself here and now. This brought Heidegger to a more profound understanding of history, and it is this more profound understanding of history which was of great value to Bultmann in his interpretation of the Bible.

In order to understand what is new and distinctive in Heidegger's understanding of history, we must distinguish it from the positivist understanding of history which is known as 'historicism'. The characteristic of positivist historicism is that it uses the texts and monuments of history as 'sources' and seeks to reconstruct from them a picture of the past. It 'finds out' and 'establishes'; it is concerned with facts and dates – that an historical event has objectively happened, and that it should be recorded as accurately as possible. One might almost say that it is taking a photograph of history. But the event described remains remote in history, and its importance for our present existence is not brought to light. One could apply to history of this kind Hegel's famous saying about philosophy: 'When history paints its grey in grey, then it has a shape of life grown old. By its grey in grey it cannot be rejuvenated, but only understood.'[22] The Göttingen historian Reinhard Wittram made an acute comment on this statement when he wrote: 'The great historical occurrences of the past always appear to me like frozen waterfalls: images from which the life has fled, cold, rigid, and remote from us. . . . We grow chilly when we contemplate the greatness of fallen empires, vanished civilisations, burnt-out passions, dead intelligences. . . . If we take this seriously, we are seized by the thought that as historians we are practising a strange business: we dwell in cities of the dead, we embrace shadows, and pass judgement on the departed.'[23]

The same is true of the study of the biblical testimonies, if they are studied only by the methods of 'historicism'.

Underlying historicism is a particular attitude of man towards the world: it is a special case of the universal prevalence of the *subject-object pattern* in the modern age. Since the Renaissance, and since Descartes at the latest, which means for about three hundred years, our thought, and in particular our study of history, has been conducted within this pattern. The essence of the modern age and its thought is that it has come to look at the world as at a picture. Heidegger has summed this up in a single sentence: 'The basic procedure of the modern age is the conquest of the world as a picture.'[24] This prepared the way for a profound change in the relationship of man to the world: man becomes the subject and the world his object. Instead of being apprehended by reality, man attempts to comprehend it. He 'lays hands' upon the world, and accordingly the world becomes an 'object' in his eyes. Here man has isolated himself from his existence. Whether he describes the world as an object in one way or another, and whether the resultant 'picture of the world' is idealist or materialist, is largely a matter of indifference – in any case he has constructed it without reference to his own existence.[25]

Heidegger's decisive contribution to historical understanding is that he has liberated it from the traditional subject-object scheme of thought. If the being of man is distinguished from all other being by the fact that it has more than the character of mere presence, and consists in carrying out the act of existing, this means that an historical source does not just mediate what is simply present, the so called 'facts', but is always the expression of a possibility of human existence: 'the theme of historiology is . . . the *possibility* which has been factually existent'.[26] Consequently, 'historical understanding' is not merely the establishment of bare facts, 'as they actually happened'. It means becoming aware of the possibilities of past human existence and becoming aware of them as possibilities for one's own existence. The ultimate reason for studying history is not to reconstruct past events, but to become conscious of the possibilities of human existence. But this means that man is no longer a subject standing back from history and comprehending it as the object of his thought, but allows himself to be apprehended by it and drawn into it as part of it. His understanding of history takes place in an encounter with history, in which his own existence is at stake. He experiences history as his own destiny. Thus existentialist philosophy shows man that history is the *historicity* of his own existence. By achieving a relationship of understanding to history, man at the same time understands himself. The degree to which an historical fact or source is understood is therefore dependent upon the degree to which man is open and receptive with regard to his own existential life. Thus the interpretation of history and the interpretation of one's own self must be co-ordinated.

Bultmann's essay on demythologisation was not his first attempt to apply this understanding of history to the interpretation of the Bible. The first comprehensive discussion of the way in which he thinks history should be understood is to be found in the introductory chapter of his book *Jesus*, published in 1926, where he speaks of the 'mode of observation'. Here the most important basic principles of his whole hermeneutic method are already present: if man is to grasp what is essential in history, he cannot observe it as something which is simply there, like his environment or nature. He himself is part of history; consequently, when he focusses his attention on history, he is inquiring into a complex of circumstances in which he and his own being are involved. With every word he utters about history, he is in some way saying something about himself. Thus the right way to deal with history is that of a *dialogue* with history. Man pursues this dialogue not as a neutral observer, but as one who knows that he himself is moved by historical forces, and is therefore ready to listen to the 'demand' which history makes: by his 'interrogation' of history he seeks to learn about how he should conceive of his own existence. Such a concern with history does not lead to 'the enrichment of timeless wisdom' but to 'an encounter with history', which in itself is an historical process. What he gains from this is not the knowledge of hitherto unknown facts, but an understanding which demands a personal decision.[27]

Bultmann's comments, on the 'mode of observation' of the history and message of Jesus, in the introduction to his book *Jesus* are strikingly reminiscent of what Barth, in the preface to the second edition of his *Epistle to the Romans*, has to say on the dealing with the texts of the Bible: he sets out to rethink the text of the Bible and to wrestle with it 'till the walls . . . become transparent. Paul *speaks* and man . . . hears. The conversation between the original record and the reader moves round the *subject matter*.'[28] Barth expressed similar ideas in the introduction to his *Protestantische Theologie im 19. Jahrhundert* (Protestant Theology in the Nineteenth Century). Here he warns explicitly against the attitude of the mere spectator, who looks upon history with the eye of a scientist, and is content to observe and establish objective facts, by merely looking at them: he sees nothing of history as such. The true understanding of history takes place in 'an action which is an encounter', in which 'we ourselves are taken up into a positive movement': 'we never apprehend history except as the result of something which happens to us and for us, or perhaps even against us, and except as a result of an event which so concerns us that we are involved in it, that we take part in it. . . . We apprehend history when some alien action begins to raise a question in us to which our own action has somehow to provide an answer.'[29] There could be no better description of the meaning of the existentialist interpretation of history. It is regrettable, however, that Barth seems to have forgotten all this when he grappled with Bultmann's existentialist interpretation of the New Testament and airily dismissed the serious problem of historical understanding as a *cura posterior*, reducing it to the trivial question: 'How do I make the child see reason?'

That historical understanding is not merely a matter of technique and method, but that human existential life is involved in it, and indeed is at stake in it, is made clear by Bultmann in a number of examples based on personal relationships: 'I might be told that my mother has secretly made a sacrifice in order to procure me some pleasure or to make my studies possible. I would not have understood this if I had merely established it as a fact, but only if, on the basis of this information, I understood anew my relationship to my mother and therefore to myself.' Or again, 'A young man who tried to find out about his (future) bride through information supplied by a detective agency would not get to know her at all in her personal being, because this is something which is revealed not to objective inquiry but only in an existential encounter.'[30]

Of course an encounter with history involves texts and sources, and also facts and events of the past.[31] But I cannot understand the texts and sources, facts and events of the past by observing them within a subject-object scheme of thought, while keeping my own existential life out of the encounter, but only by surrendering my own existential life and laying myself open to them, accepting them as my own possibilities. Thus the encounter with history and with historical texts always involves personal life and personal decision.

This also applies to the study of the texts of the Bible, and of the events, persons and things of which they tell: 'One cannot tell someone what death, life, sin and grace are, in the same way as one can tell him that there are carnivorous plants or species of fish who give birth to living young. For if we are speaking to somebody about death, life, sin and grace, then we are speaking to him about his own life, to which all these things belong, just as light and darkness, love and friendship belong to it. . . . The text does not make known to me things which exist, but which were hitherto unknown; it reveals to me potentialities in myself which I can understand only in so far as I am open to and willingly disposed to my own potentialities. I cannot receive what the text says simply as information, but understand it only if I affirm or deny it. . . . Thus understanding is always resolution and decision as well.'[32] There is nothing either irrational or unscientific in all this.

But the person who encounters history in a text is not a *tabula rasa*, an unexposed photographic plate on which no impression has yet been formed. Rather, he approaches any text with certain questions already formed in his mind. But in order to ask them, he must already be guided by a 'line of inquiry', a particular concern. His interpretation assumes a 'living relationship' to the content which is expressed – directly or indirectly – in the text. For example, anyone who seeks to interpret philosophical texts must himself be exercised by the question of truth: 'Only those understand Plato who philosophise with him.' Thus the subjectivity of the historian is not something to be suppressed, but is a necessary factor in objective historical knowledge. This can be expressed in the paradox that 'the most subjective interpretation of history is at the same time the most objective'.[33]

This preliminary living relationship to the matter which is expressed – directly or indirectly – in the text always has inherent in it a certain prior knowledge, and this prior knowledge is never neutral, but always exists in a particular form which is 'already interpreted'. Bultmann describes this as a *prior understanding*.[34] Without such a prior understanding there is no communication between the text and the interpreter, the texts remain dumb. Thus for example I must have a prior understanding of thankfulness and duty, hatred and love, sin and forgiveness, and indeed I must understand these as possibilities which are truly my own, if I am to understand what is said to me. The same is true of death: 'I do not really know what death and life are; for these are things which can only be known when life comes to an end. . . . And yet we have a strange foreknowledge that death is not merely a process of nature, a simple ceasing to be, but that it is the test to which our life is put. . . . We know that it is possible to know about love and friendship, even when one has not found love or encountered any friends; we know about these, just as the blind man knows about light and the deaf man knows about sound. We know – and yet we do not really know until we are given love, and meet a friend. But in order really to know this, it is necessary to know first that it is a possibility of life.'[35]

But is this also true of God and the Bible? Can man also have in advance a living relationship to the *Bible*? Is it already possible for him to have a prior understanding of *God*? Can he already know, *before* God's revelation, who God is? Bultmann's answer to this is: 'Man may very well be aware who God is, namely, in the enquiry about him.' Man's asking and seeking for God is already a conscious or unconscious expression of the relationship of man to God. In this context, Bultmann recalls the famous statement of St Augustine: *Tu nos fecisti ad te, et cor nostrum inquietum est, donec requiescat in te*, 'Thou hast made us for Thyself, and our heart is restless, until it rests in Thee'. For Bultmann, this statement of Augustine's is the 'classical expression' of the fact that even before the revelation of God man stands in a relationship to God: If this were not the case, and if man were not already thus pre-occupied with the question of God, then he would not recognise God as God, in any revelation by God.[36]

The relationship of man to God which exists in advance of the revelation of God can be expressed in various forms. It does not need to consist of a direct verbal inquiry about God on the part of man, but may also appear in the form of a search for 'fortune', 'salvation', or the 'meaning' of the world and history. But at any rate, it is always the question which man asks about himself, about the *essentiality* of his existence. Man knows that in everything that belongs to the here and now he is not yet essentially himself, and does not yet exist as or possess what he would like to be and possess. Consequently, he constantly focusses on the future, he is constantly moving towards an essentiality which lies before him. Because the life of man is, consciously or unconsciously, kept moving by the question of his own existence, it is also, consciously or unconsciously, moved by the question of God: 'The question of God and the question of myself are identical.'[37]

In this way Bultmann has also answered the question of the 'point of contact' of God's revelation. This does not consist of any 'religious' faculty or any other special ability or receptiveness on the part of man for the word of God: 'Rather is man in his existence, taken as a whole, the point of contact.' But the existential life of man as a whole is concentrated in the question of his essentiality. Thus the question concerning the essentiality of man forms for Bultmann the point of contact for the divine revelation.[38]

The question of the essentiality of man, however, is never present in a pure form, but always takes a particular concrete shape, and appears in a particular 'interpreted form': in a concept of God, in a religion, in a world view, a system of ethics or philosophy. But the result of this is that man is already provided with ready-made answers to the question of himself and so of God, while for the very same reason all his answers to the question of God and himself are 'illusions'. Through them, he places himself in rebellion against God. Therefore Bultmann can also say that the point of contact for the revelation of God is man's rebellion against God. But the very fact that man is in rebellion against God shows that he already has a relationship to God; for even a perverted relationship is a relationship.

The concept of the 'prior understanding' makes it possible for Bultmann to maintain the totally transcendental character of the revelation of God, its radical other-worldliness, and at the same time to avoid breaking the continuity of man's historical existence by the divine revelation, as though by a natural event. The continuous element is formed by man's self, or more precisely, by his inherent impulse to be himself, which is expressed in the search for his essentiality, and which is operative even when he has gone astray or is altogether lost. In the encounter with the revelation in Jesus Christ, man's prior understanding of God is brought to the conscious level and subjected to a fundamental criticism. In the negative sense its perversion is confirmed, while in a positive sense it is brought to fulfilment.

This is the conceptual framework which Bultmann finds appropriate for the interpretation of the Bible as an historical document. We can now turn to his way of realising the demythologisation, or rather the existentialist interpretation of the New Testament.

The existentialist interpretation

Concordant with his understanding of history Bultmann, in unfolding the message of the New Testament, does not take his starting-point from the event of Christ, describing it as an objectively verifiable part of the story of redemption, and going on to draw from it specific consequences for the destiny of man and of the world. Instead, he takes as his point of departure the *understanding of existence* in the New Testament. Since the Bible is an historical document, he approaches it, as he would any historical text, with the question: 'How is man's existence understood in the Bible?'[39]

The New Testament recognises two modes of human existence: unbelieving and unredeemed existence, and believing and redeemed existence. Both modes of existence are determined by the fact that man is focussed upon the future, and that he seeks to attain to what he really is. Not only does he desire to attain to his essentiality, he *ought* to attain to it! It is in this that his historical nature consists. The only question is the manner in which man proceeds to attain to his essential nature, and whether the way he chooses succeeds or fails.

The life of *unbelieving, unredeemed* man is based on what is immediately at hand, visible and tangible. He seeks to attain to the future and to his essentiality by his own means and therefore having it under his own control. He is not prepared to understand himself as God's creation; he would like to secure his life himself, either by acquisition of this world's goods or through great moral achievements. But this brings him into a fatal error. For in truth man is not secure, which is why he loses his life by seeking to secure it. By clinging to the visible, tangible sphere, he clings to what is transitory, and so his life is subject to transitoriness and to death. Anyone who lives by what is tangible, places himself in dependence upon it. He becomes enslaved to fear; he is afraid that his life is slipping away from him. But the more he is seized by this fear, the more strongly he clings to himself and to what he possesses. Underlying this endeavour on the part of man is his justifiable desire to attain to his essential nature; his mistake is that he strives to attain to it through his own power, and therefore shuts himself off from his true future. It is this attempt at self-sufficiency on the part of man which the Bible calls sin. Bultmann follows Paul in characterising it as the 'glorying' of man. It is man seeking to assert himself as man, and thereby making himself God.[40]

Believing, redeemed man abandons all security created by himself, and bases his life on what is invisible and intangible. He understands himself as God's creature, and receives his life as a gift. In this 'radical self-commitment to God, which looks for everything from God, and nothing from oneself', man is set free from himself. A genuine life in freedom only becomes possible through faith in God's grace, that is, by trusting that what is invisible, unknown and intangible will encounter man as love and open up to him a future which is not one of death, but of life. Thus to exist means 'eschatological existence', it means being 'a new creature'. By 'eschatology' Bultmann intends not the catastrophic destruction of the world at the end of time, but the end of the world which in faith is an event taking place even now. The

believer stands back from the world and looks at it critically. Having
committed himself to God, he is free and liberated from all that is
tangible in the world. Bultmann describes this attitude as *desecularisation*.
By which he does not imply a totally inward asceticism, nor a pietistic
withdrawal from the world, but that paradoxical freedom from the
world by means of which man remains in the world, but while in the
world understands himself as one who is given all he has, and therefore possesses the things of the world as though he did not possess
them.[41]

But how does the transition from one kind of existence to the other
take place? The New Testament states that faith in God's grace is
faith in Christ, and that the new understanding of existence is only
possible as the consequence of a particular event in history, the event of
Christ. But this raises the question whether this New Testament statement is not also a 'mythological relic' which must be eliminated.
Cannot the Christian understanding of existence also be achieved without Christ? Has not the New Testament merely discovered for the
first time, albeit still obscurely and veiled in the garment of mythology,
that understanding of being which is in fact man's universal and natural
understanding of being; and has not philosophy simply worked out
this understanding of being more clearly and logically by taking away
its mythological shell and so superseded theology once for all? Does
Martin Heidegger in particular not say the same about man, only
in a secular philosophical mode, as the New Testament says about him
in a theological mode? Bultmann replies, undismayed: 'Some critics
have suggested that I am borrowing Heidegger's categories and forcing
them upon the New Testament. I am afraid this only shows that they
are blinding their eyes to the real problem, which is that the philosophers are saying the same thing as the New Testament and saying it
quite independently.'[42]

Bultmann answers 'Yes and no!' to the question whether theology
and philosophy are not saying basically the same thing about human
existence.[43] Theology and philosophy both agree and disagree. They
agree that they are both concerned with the true 'nature' of man, that
is, that man neither can nor ought ever to be anything but what he
already is. Even Christian faith is not a 'mysterious supernatural quality'
but 'the disposition of genuine humanity', and Christian love is not a
'mysterious supernatural power', but 'the "natural" disposition of man'.
When the New Testament understands the existence of man in faith
and love as a 'new creation', it does not mean by this a supernatural

existence, but only the authentic existence of man brought back to his own proper creaturely condition: 'There is no other light shining in Jesus than has always already shone in the creation. Man learns to understand himself in the light of the revelation of redemption not a bit differently than he always already should understand himself in face of the revelation in creation and the law – namely, as God's creature.'[44] But the question now is how this natural and authentic existence of man is to be realised. And it is at this point that philosophy and theology part company.

Philosophy believes that no divine revelation, but only human reflection, is necessary to bring to light the 'natural' attitude of man. Philosophy also presumes that man has to some extent lost himself and gone astray, but it holds the view that the awareness of his own essentiality is sufficient to bring it into man's power, on the principle 'You can, therefore you ought'. It regards a possibility 'in principle' as a possibility 'in fact', and consequently does not regard the human situation with despair. It does not consider that man's fallen condition extends to his essential self, and so it regards man as still able to understand his situation and escape from it by reflection and resolution.

The *New Testament*, on the other hand, asserts that man's true nature is no longer at his own disposal, even if he is aware of it. Every movement on the part of man is a movement made within his fallen condition, because it is determined by his attempt at self-sufficiency. Not only is man attempting to be self-sufficient when he lives by attempting to control what is within his grasp instead of by committing himself to something beyond himself; he is also attempting to be self-sufficient when he recognises that this self-commitment is a possibility of his existence, and imagines that he can bring it about as a goal which is within his own attainment. In such an endeavour, and even in his knowledge that he is fallen, he still remains the old man, whose destiny is determined by his own past, that is, by himself and his will. The very knowledge that he is an historical being, and therefore the knowledge that he is responsible for the future, arouses in him the delusion that he is the master of the future, and so results in a self-contradiction. By demonstrating this self-enmeshment of man, the New Testament pronouncements on sin go to the heart of the matter. Anyone who regards the New Testament's pronouncements on sin as mere mythology only reveals his blindness towards sin, and therefore his own radically fallen nature.[45]

Thus the understanding of the true situation of man leads directly to the question how man can be set free from himself. There is no other practicable way for him to come to true life. Such a liberation cannot take place through man's own power, but only from outside himself. Only the love of God is able to free man from himself and to bring him to a life in faith and love. But the love of God must not be a human ideal, a product of his own wishful thinking, for that again would only mean that it derived from his own self, from his desire to be in control. Instead it must be revealed as an *act of God*. 'Only those who are loved are capable of loving. Only those who have received the gift of trust can show trust in others. Only those who have encountered self-commitment become capable of self-commitment.' It is in this that the meaning of the event of Christ in the New Testament is contained: 'It means that at the very point where man can do nothing, God steps in and acts – indeed he has acted already – on man's behalf.' The event which takes place in Christ is the revelation of the love of God, which makes possible for man a life of self-commitment in faith and in love, and so sets him free from himself, to be himself.

This is the decisive point which distinguishes the New Testament from philosophy, and Christian faith from the 'natural' understanding of being: 'The New Testament speaks and faith knows of an act of God through which man becomes capable of self-commitment, capable of faith and love, of his authentic life.'[46] What Bultmann sets forth as the message of the New Testament, with the help of his existentialist interpretation, is the pure Pauline and Lutheran doctrine of justification, interpreted for present-day man. If ever a theologian of our own time has held firm to the doctrine of justification as professed by the Reformation, it is Rudolf Bultmann.

But the liberating act of God, the revelation of his love in Jesus Christ, is represented in the New Testament as a mythical event. Yet here again, it is the New Testament which provides the possibility of demythologisation. By contrast to contemporary Hellenistic cults, in the New Testament 'we have here a unique combination of history and myth': the mythical figure of the Son of God from heaven is at the same time a particular historical person, whose father and mother are known, the man Jesus of Nazareth. This combination of myth and history provides Bultmann with the key to his demythologising interpretation. The significance of the mythological language of the New Testament for him is that it expresses the 'meaning' of the historical figure of Jesus and the events of his life as a saving figure, and a saving event.[47]

For Bultmann, the saving event is wholly and completely concentrated upon the *cross and resurrection of Christ*.[48] By showing how history and myth are entwined in them, Bultmann brings to light their significance as salvation. The *cross* of Christ is a past historical event which can be dated like any other. But even this past historical event which took place at a particular date 'acquires cosmic dimensions' through the use of mythological language, and so its significance as a saving event is revealed: it becomes an 'eschatological' event, which brings the old world to an end, and transforms its destiny once for all. But as an eschatological event it is no longer a past historical event, but is constantly present for us: 'To believe in the Cross of Christ does not mean to concern ourselves with a mythical process wrought outside of us and our world, or with an objective event turned by God to our advantage, but rather to make the Cross of Christ our own, to undergo crucifixion with him.' Anyone who does this, no longer lives by what is tangible, but is free from himself and his imprisonment in the world.

The *resurrection* of Christ is inextricably bound up with the cross. What the New Testament says about the resurrection of Christ is simply 'an attempt to convey the meaning of the cross'. It signifies that the death of Jesus on the cross is to be regarded as 'not just an ordinary human death', but as 'the judgement and salvation of the world', through which he has brought the world salvation and created the possibility of true life. But in this case the resurrection of Jesus is 'not a miraculous proof', which in retrospect – through the return of someone dead to the life of this world – provides an assurance for faith in the cross. Rather the resurrection of Jesus is itself an object of faith. The cross and the resurrection form a unity, and are the origin and object of one and the same faith: 'Faith in the resurrection is really the same thing as faith in the saving efficacy of the cross, in the cross as the cross of Christ.' For Bultmann Good Friday and Easter fall on the same day.

But how can I come to see the death of Jesus as not just a human death, how can I come to believe in it as the saving event which has also transformed my own destiny, so that I accept the cross of Christ as my own? This question, how one comes to apprehend the 'significance' of the event of Christ, is identical with the second question, how it is 'made present'. Bultmann's constantly repeated answer is: 'Christ meets us in the preaching as one crucified and risen. He meets us in the word of preaching and nowhere else . . . through the word of preaching the cross and the resurrection are made present . . . in the word of preaching and there alone we meet the risen Lord.' Thus to believe in the resurrection of Christ means for Bultmann to believe in the word which is preached to me here and now: 'The real Easter faith is faith in the word of preaching which brings illumination.'[49]

Bultmann's critics have interpreted his exposition of the resurrection to mean that he considers Christ to be risen in the faith and preaching of his disciples, that is in the kerygma. Bultmann, moreover, is prepared to accept this interpretation, provided that it is rightly understood, that is, 'that Jesus is really present in the kerygma, that it is *his* word which comes to the hearer in the kerygma'. Here all speculation concerning the mode of being of the risen Christ is pointless: Christ is present in the kerygma – this is sufficient answer to the question of the manner, place and purpose of his resurrection. 'The meaning of the Easter faith is to believe in Christ present in the kerygma.'[50]

The concept 'kerygma', already a familiar one in the New Testament and in theology, becomes for Bultmann the essence of his theological thought. The word kerygma means 'the cry of a herald', 'the message', 'proclamation', 'testimony', 'preaching' – the word expresses the idea that through the preaching taking place today the New Testament proclamation becomes a personal word of God addressed to me, striking my conscience here and now as a call to decision. Consequently, the content and the carrying out of the kerygma are identical: the content of the kerygma is the event of Christ, and it is this event of Christ which takes place here and now in preaching. Wherever the word of Christ is preached, the event of Christ is present, not as a timeless truth, but as something which takes place here and now. Consequently, preaching itself becomes an eschatological event: 'Preaching is itself revelation and does not merely speak about it.'[51]

For Bultmann the whole event of revelation is concentrated upon the kerygma. What in the Bible forms a chain of events, a long line stretching through the past, present and future, from the creation of the world, through the election of Israel to the birth, life, death and resurrection of Christ and on through his ascension and Pentecost to the day of judgement, Bultmann sees as being all compressed into a single point of present time, that is, into the word which is uttered at this moment in preaching. Bultmann sees not only Good Friday and Easter, but also Advent, Christmas, Ascension Day, Pentecost, All Saints' Day and All Souls' Day as falling on one and the same day. This day is the Today of preaching. The whole character of an event contained in revelation is summed up for Bultmann in the event of preaching. Preaching belongs to the saving event, and is itself the saving event.

There is no return to a saving fact which can be isolated from it, either to the 'historical Jesus' or to a cosmic apocalyptic drama. Bultmann's theology is wholly and entirely a theology of the word. It has rightly been described as 'kerygma-theology'.

The concept of *self-understanding* forms a parallel in Bultmann to the concept of the 'kerygma'. God's act of revelation which we en-counter in the kerygma bestows upon us a new understanding of ourselves. This does not mean that preaching effects a magical trans-formation of our life, or that our relationship to God is added on to our existence in other spheres of life, as an extension. It means that preaching opens our eyes to ourselves, and that we understand ourselves anew in the concrete existential circumstances of our lives, in the light of the divine act of revelation. Consequently, Bultmann speaks of faith as a new 'understanding of existence' or 'understanding of oneself'.

It is here that we begin to see what the existentialist interpretation can achieve. It is one way, the only possible way, in which the truth of the statements of Christian faith can be demonstrated. Even theology cannot put forth any statements it pleases, but must show that their truth would be meaningful. But it cannot do this like the natural sciences, by subjecting its truths to objective experiment, but only by demonstrating their relevance to reality and their significance for existential life. Theology must show how far man in reality obtains through faith a new understanding of his own self in the world.

This, however, has important consequences for theological lan-guage. The object of theology is God. But one cannot speak 'directly' of God, that is, in general propositions and verities, which do not take into account the concrete existential situation of the speaker or the person addressed. One can only speak of him 'indirectly', that is, in propositions and verities which have a relevance to the concrete existen-tial situation of the person addressed. All theological propositions are true and valid only as existential statements; all pronouncements concerning God and his revelation require to be 'expressed in terms of existential life'. The point of intersection of divine truth is always man. Consequently, Bultmann never tires of emphasising that one can only speak of God and his action if one speaks at the same time of man and his existential life: 'If one wishes to speak of God, one must obviously speak of oneself.' In this sense, Bultmann is ready to accept the assertion of the critics that he is transforming theology into anthropology: 'I *am* trying to substitute anthropology for theology, for I am interpreting theological affirmations as assertions about human life.'[52]

But is this not to deprive the action of God of all objective reality and reduce it to subjective experience? Are God and faith in him not made simply an inward experience, a psychological process? This is the usual theological objection raised against Bultmann's existentialist interpretation. Helmut Thielicke is expressing the views of many others when he writes: 'The event in the process of revelation is not an objective reality, it is simply a change in the subjective consciousness of man.'[53] This sentence conjures up the ghosts of Schleiermacher and of Feuerbach.

But they are not Bultmann's theological and philosophical ancestors. The assertion that with his existentialist interpretation he is destroying the transcendence of God and the objectivity of his revelation misses the mark. It is Bultmann's intention to be a theologian of revelation in the strictest sense of the word. Even as an existentialist interpreter of the New Testament he unreservedly maintains the transcendence of God: faith in God 'sees the world and life in the light of a reality lying beyond them'.[54] Even in the existentialist interpretation, the act of God is the indispensable prerequisite for human existence: Jesus Christ is not a timeless ideal or an eternal cultic symbol, but an event, a fact, a person, a happening, the event in which the decisive saving act of God has taken place once for all. Bultmann can of course write: 'Christ meets man nowhere other than in the kerygma', but he continues, 'The kerygma does not proclaim general truths, a timeless idea, neither the idea of God nor the idea of a redeemer, but an historical fact.' Clearly and unambiguously he declares: 'Revelation consists in nothing other than the fact of Jesus Christ.'[55] Bultmann clings so firmly to the character of the revelation as an event, as an 'act of God', that he even arouses the suspicion that he is allowing 'traces of mythology' to persist.

The conception of revelation as a unique and prior act of God is in accordance with Bultmann's view of human faith. He obstinately insists that faith is not based upon a human attitude or faculty, but is directed towards an object lying outside man; only in this can man find a foundation and foothold: 'Faith *is* not faith at all as a human attitude, an intellectual function, a pious state of mind, a numinous emotion or the like. It is *faith* only as faith *in* something, that is in an object, in God in his revelation.' Faith does not come into being by a kind of self-incitement, but through an encounter, through an encounter with an historical event, the event of Christ. Consequently, it is 'nothing but a simple hearing', 'my response to a call', 'the answer to the question put to man through a particular revelation of God', and therefore it is 'not a

result of development in the field of the history of religion, nor something blossoming forth in the garden of the human mind, but an exotic
plant brought into the world of men from beyond; and only in that way
and for that reason an attitude which forges a link with the transcendent
world of God'.[56] All this is a clear sign of Bultmann's life-long connection with dialectical theology. He is not conjuring up the ghost of
Schleiermacher, but joining battle with him. And Bultmann is no more
suspect with reference to Feuerbach than any other theologian.

Bultmann does not assert that God is not *real* outside faith, but that he
is not *knowable* outside faith. Admittedly, he devotes his whole attention
to this issue. He emphatically asserts that faith alone is capable of recognising God's action, and that therefore it is possible to speak of the action
of God only in relation to human existence. The aim of Bultmann's
demythologisation, or existentialist interpretation, is to give expression
to this relationship between God's action and human existence, and so to
bring the revelation of God forward from the past into the present. His
intention is to follow Melanchthon's principle: 'To know Christ is to
know his benefits, not to contemplate his natures and the mode of his
incarnation.' Or again, in the words of Wilhelm Herrmann: 'We
cannot say what God is like in himself, but only what he does for us.'[57]
But Bultmann can appeal to an even higher authority. The Christ of St
John says: 'If any man's will is to do his will, he shall know whether the
teaching is from God or whether I am speaking on my own authority'
(John 7:17). Luther constantly found new ways of expressing the same
idea: 'If you believe, you possess; if you do not believe, you do not
possess – everyone always has as much of God as he believes!' This does
not mean that for Bultmann, or indeed for the Bible and the Reformers,
God and his revelation do not also really exist outside the act of faith,
but that they only become real and effective for me through preaching
and faith.

There is a saying that to know God is to suffer God. To suffer means
to be changed, to be transformed. And it is this that Bultmann means
when he calls faith a 'new self-understanding': not a change of opinion,
nor an act of the consciousness, but 'a movement in man's existence',[58]
brought about through the encounter with the act of God in the preaching of the Church.

But this new self-understanding is not, once it has been revealed and
appropriated, an enduring possession of man. It must be constantly
brought about anew into the constant new encounter with the word of
God: '"The kindness of God is new every morning"; yes, provided

I perceive it anew every morning, For this is not a timeless truth, like a mathematical statement. I can speak of the kindness of God, which is new every morning only if I myself am renewed every morning.'[59]

The existentialist interpretation throws the whole weight of the revelation of God into the actual preaching. The word of preaching is the basis of faith, and it is its only basis. The hearer of the word may not cast about for any other foundation for the truth of the divine revelation, either in the historical Jesus, in a cosmic process, or in any authenticating miracles or spiritual experiences. Faith depends upon the word and preaching alone. But there is no other authority and no other basis for the word than the word itself.

Therefore, Bultmann constantly repeats that faith may not go behind the kerygma in order to verify its historical reliability and the authority of its claim. It is as though he could never find words enough to castigate the perversity of this attempt: 'It would be wrong at this point to raise again the problem of how this preaching arose historically, as though that could vindicate its truth. That would be to tie our faith in the word of God to the results of historical research. The word of preaching confronts us as the word of God. It is not for us to question its credentials.' Or again, 'An inquiry into the legitimacy of the claim of preaching is virtually a rejection of it; this must be transformed into the question which the questioner must ask of himself, whether he will acknowledge the lordship of Christ, which faces his self-understanding with a decision.'[60]

Consequently, for Bultmann the question of the historical basis of the kerygma of the person and message of Jesus is also without significance. He sees no reason to ask it. Or rather, he has only a polemic interest in it, to exclude it: 'One must not go behind the kerygma, using it as a "source" in order to reconstruct an "historical Jesus" with his "messianic consciousness", his "inwardness", or his "heroism". This would be the "Christ according to the flesh", who has passed away. It is not the historical Jesus, but Jesus Christ who is preached, who is Lord.'[61] Faith is concerned only with the kerygma, and is shown to be faith by the fact that it is not historically demonstrable. There is only a single criterion for the truth of the kerygma, that is, that the word which encounters us with the claim to be God's revelation faces us with a decision as to how we are to understand ourselves: whether we wish to gain our life through our own reason and power, or through God's grace.

This is Bultmann's programme for demythologisation; this is his
existentialist interpretation. The question that finally arises is whether
there are still 'traces of mythology' present. Bultmann asks this question
himself, and the answer he gives is that 'there certainly are for those who
regard all language about an act of God . . . as mythological'.[62] But this
is no longer mythology in the old sense. The distinguishing mark of the
old mythology was that it conceived of the divine and the transcendent
as an objective world, which lay above or beyond this world, and
intervened from thence in this world of ours, constantly breaking into
the continuity of nature and history. Even the New Testament largely
describes the coming about of God's revelation in such concepts. But
the process of secularisation within the modern age has destroyed this
'world view', and therefore the question arises whether the message of
the New Testament is not also 'abolished'. This is the question and
problem with which Bultmann is faced. By the demythologisation of
the New Testament, in the sense of an existentialist interpretation of it,
Bultmann responded to the challenge offered to Christian faith by the
historical thought of the modern age. With the aid of this principle, he
interprets anew the relationship between the transcendent and this
world, the history of salvation and the history of the world. He
attempts to take historical thought seriously, and yet not abandon the
revelation of God. The method of existentialist interpretation provides
him with the means to maintain at one and the same time the relationship of faith to history, and its relationship to God.

The revelation of God is not a miraculous supernatural event, which
is isolated from all the rest of history as something totally different,
wholly alien in its nature. It is an historical event in space and time. But
this historical act, objectively verifiable in space and time, is the act of
God's revelation, through which he brings about the salvation of the
world. Jesus Christ, who was an historical person of flesh and blood, and
who underwent everything that happens to a man in this world, is the
eschatological event which is constantly made present here and now in
the preaching of the Church. Consequently Bultmann asserts 'the
paradoxical identity of God's action with worldly events'. The act of
God does not take place 'between' the events of the world, but 'in'
them. We look upon the course of the world with its natural and
historical occurrences; there is nothing in them which our eyes and ears
perceive as divine. But the believer recognises in them the mysterious
action of God, albeit only when he allows himself to be drawn into this
action, and understands his own existence anew through it.[63]

The divine and the transcendent is here no longer superimposed upon this visible world as a 'higher' sphere, into which the devout believer can soar up in a 'religious' act, but lies concealed in this same visible world of ours; and the believer attains to it not by leaving this world, but by remaining in it. But this world becomes transparent to him, and in the existential circumstances of his life, he becomes aware of his relationship to God. It is no longer possible for modern man, who thinks in historical terms, to accept the idea of God in any other way. Taking even further the ideas of his essay on demythologisation, Bultmann has emphasised in recent years: 'The only possible idea of God for modern man is that which can seek and find the absolute in the conditional, the beyond in the here and now, the transcendent in the immediately present, as something which it is possible to encounter there.'[64]

In this, Bultmann has not adapted himself to the thought of modern man, but has put forward the true intention of the New Testament, as it were the Christian element in Christianity. The New Testament asserts that the transcendent God is present in history, or as the prologue of St John's Gospel expresses it, 'The Word became flesh'! Bultmann's essay on the demythologisation of the New Testament closes with this quotation.

But can 'traces of mythology' still be found in Bultmann? What remains are not traces of mythology, but the paradox of divine revelation as the New Testament expounds it. And it is this paradox of divine revelation which Bultmann sought to express through the demythologisation of the New Testament. This at least was his theological purpose. The question is whether he has carried it out to the full.

Kerygma and history

No one can dispute that Bultmann's hermeneutic theory is relevant to the present day. No exegesis has ever been more contemporary and more existential than his. One looks with admiration and astonishment at the logical way in which he attempts to relate the operations of God to human existence, and thus to bring revelation forward from the past into the future. The question which remains is whether Bultmann has really succeeded in bringing forward the *whole* message of the Bible, or whether he may not have lost some of it in the process.

The first impression is that in Bultmann's theology all biblical statements without exception are brought to bear on human existence, and

that this concentrated focussing leads to a radical reduction of the
biblical message to abstractions. The suspicion arises that both the
positive and the negative aspects of this process betray the influence of
the existentialism of Heidegger's early period.

On the basis of principle there cannot be any exception to Bultmann's
making use of the concepts of existentialist philosophy in his New
Testament exegesis. No theology can do without the assistance of
philosophical categories and concepts in its mission of expressing the
Christian truth. Concerning the dependence of all theologians upon
philosophy Karl Barth once said: 'We all wear spectacles of one kind or
another. . . . We use some key, some pattern of thought as an instrument
to "make sense" of our theology'; with regard to Bultmann in particular he admits that 'there is an element of philosophy in all theological
language'.[65] Augustine spoke in Platonic language, and Thomas
Aquinas in Aristotelian language. Luther was more of a neo-Platonist,
Calvin more of a classical Platonist. The theology of the nineteenth
century was largely worked out in Hegelian categories, while Gogarten,
Bonhoeffer and others used the I-Thou philosophy of Ferdinand Ebner.
Why should Bultmann not have the right to speak in the language of
Heidegger?

A danger only arises when theology surrenders its freedom to
philosophy and allows philosophy to lay down how it shall think and
speak. The concepts and categories borrowed from philosophy can then
become masters instead of servants, and can draw the Christian kerygma
into their embrace and empty it of its content. This is the critical
question which must be asked with regard to Bultmann's existentialist
interpretation of the New Testament: Is the embrace of philosophy so
overwhelming that Christian faith is crushed by it? Or in other words,
has Bultmann maintained the purely *formal* link with Heidegger's
philosophical analysis of existence, which is all that he intended, or has
he inadvertently allowed this formal link to become one of principle?
And has the prior understanding which Bultmann derives from existentialist philosophy led him to diminish the Christian message in a way
which is inadmissible?

We have already seen what Bultmann has gained by taking existentialist philosophy as his point of departure. No other theologian has
succeeded as he has in relating the event of Christ, which took place two
thousand years ago, to human existence, and in carrying it over the
'dreadful gulf' of history into the present day. But has he not brought
the Christian message up to date in this radical manner at the expense of

its content? At least one must concede that in Bultmann's case an 'anthropological concentration' has taken place, the precise opposite of the 'christological concentration' which we found in the case of Barth. And there is no doubt that this anthropological limiting of the Christian message in Bultmann's theology is due to a prior understanding which he derives from existentialist philosophy.

One of Heidegger's theses in particular had this kind of narrowing effect on Bultmann's theology: his assertion that possibility takes onto-logical precedence over reality, so that all history is localised in the historicity of human existence. Heidegger, like Dilthey before him, places the origin of all history in the historicity of man, and thereby transforms into its opposite the relationship which has hitherto pre-vailed between the two. The historicity of man is no longer based on the experience of reality as history; but instead the possibility that there should be history at all is derived from the historicity of human exis-tence.

But a simple alternative is not sufficient here. One cannot say that there is a straight choice between history as an already present reality, or history as a possibility of human existence. These are not simple altern-atives, but the two elements of a dialectic. Man would not experience history as reality if he did not encounter it as his own possibility; on the other hand, he would not encounter history as his own possibility, if he did not experience it as an already present reality. Jürgen Moltmann has summed up this double relationship of man to history, and of history to man, in the following brief formula: Man 'is historic and he has history'; he encounters history 'in the modus of being and in the modus of having'.[66] History already exists for man as something which is real and has happened; the limits of his existence are always already laid down. It is this aspect of the experience of history to which Heidegger fails to do justice by giving to possibility ontological pre-cedence over reality.

By adopting this inversion of possibility and reality from Heidegger, Bultmann necessarily restricts the Christian message to anthropological terms. The existentialist interpretation includes everything within human existence, the reality of God and the reality of the world. We have seen that this does not mean that the revelation of God is reduced to a subjective human experience. Bultmann is proof against this general objection put forward by his theological critics. He does not deny the character of the revelation in Christ as an act of God lying out-side and beyond man. But Bultmann fails to do justice to the cosmic scope of this revelation, its relationship not only to the existential life of the individual, but also to the destiny of the whole world.

The Bible is as it were writing the history of the universe. In it, the revelation of God is described as a universal event, which has a beginning and a goal, which comprehends the creation, the atonement and the redemption, which extends from the creation of the world to its consummation at the end of time, and which therefore contains a past, a present and a future. Nothing, or virtually nothing, of this remains in Bultmann. All that is left of the whole long process is a single point, that actual moment in time in which an individual man apprehends life in faith as a gift of divine grace, and experiences within it the meaning and the aim of history. Bultmann's *History and Eschatology*, in which he inquires into the meaning of history, concludes with the significant words: 'The meaning in history lies always in the present. . . . Man who complains: "I cannot see meaning in history, and therefore my life, interwoven in history, is meaningless", is to be admonished: do not look around yourself into universal history, you must look into your own personal history. Always in your present lies the meaning in history, and you cannot see it as a spectator, but only in your responsible decisions. In every moment slumbers the possibility of being the eschatological moment. You must awaken it.'[67]

All this indeed is true, but it is inadequate as an interpretation of biblical eschatology. Its cosmic universalism is in this way reduced to something wholly *private*, present in an individual existence understood as an isolated entity. Bultmann himself says: 'Eschatology has entirely lost its meaning as the goal of history, and is understood basically as the goal of the individual being.'[68] Thus God's great drama has become an 'existentialist private performance'.[69] Everything in it is concerned wholly with man's understanding of himself. The kerygma which bears witness to the act which God carries out upon the whole world is reduced to a call to decision which comes to man within his existentialist life, to lead him from his inessentiality to his true nature. God's future is reduced to the future of man, and the past is seen only as a pattern or model against which the decision to be taken by us in the present moment is understood.[70]

Bultmann's reduction of eschatology to the level of the private individual is accompanied by his *spiritualisation* of Christian existential life. It is hardly by chance that the last of his *Marburg Sermons* concludes with a quotation from Tersteegen: '*Ins Heiligtum, ins Dunkel, kehr' ich ein. Herr, rede du, lass mich ganz stille sein*' ('Into the sanctuary, the darkness, I enter. Lord, speak, and let me be quite still').[71] There is much elsewhere in these sermons concerning the silence, the peace, and the coming to rest of the soul. This is all in the familiar tradition of pietist spiritualisation, which is part of the mystical tradition of the West, and extends from Augustine to Adolf von Harnack. Attention is focussed on one's own self; what is lacking is the consideration of the whole world as God's world. Once again, Moltmann is right to ask, 'Is any self-understanding of man conceivable at all which is not determined by his relation to the world, to history, to society?'[72] One's self-understanding and one's understanding of the world must correspond and be correlated to each other. Man can never understand himself except as one who lives in a particular situation, and is therefore involved, in a way too vast and complex to comprehend, in the world, the family, the State, society, the Church and the twentieth century.

The consequence of Bultmann's excessive concentration on the individual is that human existential life in his theology is wholly abstracted from its situation in the world. We have compared Barth's thought in his early days with the expressionist art of the same period. Bultmann could be compared with the abstract painters.[73] Bultmann's theology does not do justice to the fact that God does not speak only from person to person, but acts upon the world as a whole; that the human person is also a man who possesses not merely a mind, but also a heart and a body; and that the world contains not only persons, but also things, animals and plants, the sun and the stars, the mountains and the seas. These facts exist, but are excluded from faith, and therefore abandoned to their own devices. Theology does not take them into account. Just as in Bultmann's work faith apprehends historicity, but not history, so also it apprehends creatureliness, but not creation.

There is a risk here of a new dualism, no longer between this world and the world above, but between two elements here below; man on the one hand, who understands himself as God's creature, and on the other hand the world, which forms a closed system of cause and effect and which is abandoned to a purely objective mode of observation. But neither side can tolerate such a division. Carl Friedrich von Weizsäcker comments on this: 'A division between existential life and nature of such a sort that existential life becomes the sphere of Christian faith, and nature the sphere of exact science, would relegate both faith and science to a realm too narrow for either, and one moreover which does not really exist.'[74]

Yet it cannot be denied that the Bible speaks of God's action in the

world as a whole, of its creation, atonement, and redemption, in mythological terms. But how else could it speak of such things? Even Bultmann does not wholly avoid mythological language. For example, what
is the expression he uses so frequently, 'the act of God', if not a mythological mode of speech? Otto Küster rightly says: 'These two words set
up a whole mythical universe.'[75] The danger only arises when mythological concepts are given an objective existence of their own, and when
the myth is not seen as a code, but is identified with the substance which
it expresses. This happens, for instance, if the divine sonship of Jesus is
understood in physical terms, and thus the situation of an earthly and
human family is transferred to the inner life of the Godhead. This would
make of God a phenomenon within the world, and at the same time
demand the impossible of human belief. Such an identification of the
mythological code with the substance it expresses is already forbidden
by the second commandment: 'You shall not make for yourself any
image or likeness of God.' Thus Bultmann is right to demythologise,
and also right not to eliminate myth in his criticism, but to interpret it
existentially.

But this does not allow us to reject mythological language as such.
Without myth faith would be speechless, or else the grey mist of an
insipid intellectualism would descend upon its language about God. It
may well be that the sometimes grotesque anthropomorphisms in
which the Bible speaks of God do more justice to the reality of God
than subtle philosophical speculations or an existentialist interpretation
free of all mythological images and conceptions. This is not to deny
that we ought to remain aware that all mythological concepts are
inadequate to their subject, that myth must therefore be critically interpreted and the meaning concealed within it brought to life, and that this
is only possible with the aid of philosophical and theological reflection.

We are walking a tightrope here. But an infallible practical test
exists. Whether or not the mythological way in which the Bible speaks
of God's action upon the world is seen for what it is, a kind of code,
while at the same time it retains its significance, can be seen from the
manner in which Christians conceive of their mission in the world –
whether they concern themselves with the fate of the whole world as
God's world and are ready to assume responsibility for it. The existentialist interpretation of myth is necessary, but not merely, as in Bultmann's case, with regard to the private existential life of the individual,
but also with regard to the public future of the whole world. Thus
man's self-understanding and his understanding of the world must be

related. The statements of the Bible which concern the whole universe must also pass through the eye of the needle; that is, they too must be judged by the standard of the Christian belief in justification, and it is essential that they should pass this test. Where there is an understanding of the world without a new self-understanding, the biblical text applies which asks, 'What will it profit a man, if he gains the whole world and forfeits his soul?' But where there is only self-understanding, without a new understanding of the world, man lives as it were within a glass cube, and sees only himself reflected in the walls.

Let us affirm once again that the arch formed by Bultmann's interpretation of the Bible has one pier firmly rooted in the present. He has been successful in bringing the Christian message up to date. But there is the danger that Bultmann may be overloading the pier grounded in the present day, while keeping its foundation in the world too narrow. There is a danger of its giving way, and uprooting the other pier which is grounded in the past. To put it unmetaphorically, the locating of the whole substance of the Christian revelation without exception within human existential life threatens to deprive revelation of its foundation in history.

We have seen again and again that Bultmann firmly insists that God has revealed himself in an event of history, and that the event of Christ is therefore not an idea or a symbol, but an event, a fact, something that has actually happened. But if we ask more closely what it is which has actually happened, Bultmann's answers remain remarkably unforthcoming, reserved, and even polemically brusque. He regards as a sufficient historical basis for God's revelation the bare and formless fact that Jesus has come: 'To understand Jesus as the eschatological phenomenon . . . all that is necessary is to proclaim that he has come.' 'As far as content is concerned, nothing needs to be taught about Jesus than this one fact which began in his historical life and takes place once again in the preaching of the Church.'[76] This limiting of revelation to the bare fact that it has taken place is linked to Bultmann's predilection for Paul and the Gospel of John – for Paul, who writes that he no longer knows 'Christ according to the flesh' (2 Cor. 5:16), and for the Gospel of John, because in it revelation – at least in Bultmann's interpretation – is wholly concentrated upon the bare and formless fact that Jesus has come as the 'revealer': as the revealer of God, Jesus reveals nothing more than that he is the revealer.[77] Thus Bultmann prefers the Gospel of John not in spite of the fact that it is so unhistorical, but because of that fact.

What is the reason for this unhistorical and indeed anti-historical attitude on Bultmann's part, his inflexible refusal to attempt any close description of the event of Christ, and his consequent total lack of interest in the historical Jesus?

In the first place, it is an effect of his historical criticism: 'I do indeed think that we can now know almost nothing concerning the life and personality of Jesus.'[78] This scepticism on Bultmann's part is entirely in accordance with the results of the historical and critical study of the New Testament, especially as carried out by the methods of form-criticism. The whole tradition we possess of Jesus consists only of the testimonies of the primitive Church contained in the New Testament. But from the very first moment they came into being, these testimonies owed their form to the faith, life and preaching of the primitive Church. Consequently, no reliable picture of the historical Jesus can be obtained from them. It is no longer possible for us to see in them the character of Jesus, or a clear picture of his personality and his life. The reconstruction of such a picture can only be the product of fantasy.[79]

But this historical scepticism is only part of the reason why Bultmann is content with the bare fact that Jesus has come. This flimsy *historical* conclusion provides a welcome support to Bultmann's *theological* purpose; Bultmann makes a theological virtue out of historical necessity. His historical criticism of the New Testament is determined by the point of departure of his thought in Reformation theology. Faith must not be based upon any 'work', or in this case upon any result of historical study, but must rely solely upon the word that is preached. This gives Bultmann's historical criticism from the outset a purely negative significance. Its task is not to establish what actually happened, but what did not happen, in order to knock away all the historical props by which faith is supported. Because historical study *ought* not to find anything relevant to faith in the whole of history it *does* not find anything there: 'Historical study comes to an end here with a great question still unanswered – and so it ought to come to an end.'[80] It is in line with this that Bultmann's own book, *Jesus*, is basically 'a book about Jesus without Jesus'[81] and that in his *Theology of the New Testament* the preaching of Jesus is relegated to a kind of preliminary Jewish chapter, appearing not as the actual content, but only as a prior assumption of the New Testament message.

In this critical radicalism on Bultmann's part, the passionate assertion of dialectical theology that in the whole world there is nothing from which faith can derive a direct knowledge of God joins with the results of form-criticism, which demonstrates that the gospels are not historical accounts, but testimonies of faith. In Bultmann, revelation, the word, preaching and faith have a close mutual relationship and form a closed circle into which no historical consideration can penetrate or make a breach. Because Bultmann makes faith dependent solely upon the word that is preached, he can be indifferent to history as it actually took place, and because he transfers the whole weight of revelation to the present, he can be content, as far as the past is concerned, with the mere fact that revelation has taken place, adding, with a complete lack of concern: 'However it may have happened.'[82] Bultmann asserts almost triumphantly: 'I have never felt ill at ease in my critical radicalism, but have always been completely at ease. But I often have the impression that my conservative colleagues feel very ill at ease in the New Testament; for I always see them hard at work trying to rescue it. I let it blaze away, for I can see that all that is being consumed in this fire is the pictures imagined by the theology of the historical Jesus, and that this is "Christ according to the flesh". But we are not concerned with "Christ according to the flesh"; what went on in the heart and mind of Jesus I do not know and do not want to know.'[83] This is a triumphal hymn of historical criticism and of faith in one.

But this combination of historical criticism and faith in Bultmann's work leads to a dangerous *methodological dualism*. On the one hand, the event of Christ is emptied of its historical content until it becomes a formless relic, the bare fact that Jesus existed as an historical person. On the other hand, in the kerygma the same event of Christ is filled with significance as the eschatological event through which God has brought about the salvation of the world. On the one hand Bultmann has carried out a more thorough-going historical criticism of the New Testament than anyone else, scarcely leaving one stone upon another. But on the other hand Bultmann asserts that when a preacher goes into the pulpit, the Bible should lie before him as though it were nothing less than 'the printed book that has fallen from heaven', and that everything which he knows about its origins as a matter of historical criticism should cease to be of any concern to him at that moment.[84]

While this *methodological dualism* does not lead to a double standard of truth, it does lead to a dangerous duplication of the person of Jesus into an 'historical Jesus' and a 'kergymatic Christ', and here Bultmann explicitly adds that the one is not to be found in the other. As far as the Christian is concerned this duplication of the person of Jesus corresponds to a similar double existence on the part of the Christian. He has no sooner applied historical criticism to the kerygmatic Christ and watered him down to the mere fact that he exists as an historical person, than he finds that he has suddenly made a mighty leap into faith in the kerygmatic Christ. Or to use another image: 'At one moment he was in the Arctic, where the past is frozen to ice, and now he suddenly finds himself under the tropical sun, which melts and makes significant all the ice of the past . . . first he buries the text by means of historical criticism, and then he has to resurrect it again by means of existentialism.'[85]

The danger concealed in this methodological dualism is that the arch of Bultmann's interpretation of the Bible is in danger of collapsing at the very point at which it builds up, the transition from the historical Jesus to the kerygmatic Christ. Where there is so little interest in the question of the historical basis of the preaching of Jesus Christ and in the preaching and person of Jesus himself, and where the event of Christ forms only a 'flimsy bridgehead in the no-man's-land of the historical'[86] and when 'it does not matter how it happened', the link between the earthly Jesus and the Christ who is preached threatens to break down, and in spite of all protestations to the contrary, there is a danger that the identity of the two may become incredible. Why, one may ask, is it not possible for the assumption on which the Christian kerygma is based to be an idea or a myth? If the kerygma is so strictly isolated from the historical life of Jesus, and historical knowledge of his life is declared to be of so little significance for theology, as with Bultmann, there is a danger of the kerygma becoming a universal and timeless truth, and the appeal to history a mere formality. It seems that Barth is right to suggest that Bultmann's 'demythologised New Testament looks suspiciously like docetism'.[87]

This threat that the kerygma may be made completely unhistorical leads to a further consequence. Because all the historical and concrete, living and bodily, visible and tangible elements are taken away from the event of Christ in Bultmann's theology, there is a danger of its losing its character as a gift and as the gospel. All that remains is a single and naked saving fact, characterised only by its mere existence as a fact. It is the 'empty paradox',[88] that God acted in this man Jesus. What he actually did, and how he did it, is not stated. With regard to Bultmann's assertion of the mere fact, and nothing more, of the revelation of Christ, Barth writes: 'Although much of this remains obscure and is not susceptible to proof, I can, I think, see certain contours and colours. I can see a person and his work. I can, I think, hear a word which is self-explanatory, where all Bultmann can see is darkness and silence, where all he can see is that the cross is God's saving act.'[89]

There is something of the late medieval 'nominalist' in Bultmann: it has pleased God, in his unbounded omnipotence, to choose a tiny fragment of event from the universal history of the world and to label it 'revelation', and man must believe for better or for worse in the event put forward in this way as divine revelation. It is strange how Bultmann, who in other respects goes to such great lengths to interpret and understand the Christian message, can leave the event of salvation itself standing on its own, like an erratic boulder, virtually without interpretation or understanding. Is Bultmann here not dominated by the same positivistic view of revelation as orthodox theology, except that such 'miraculous' things as the virgin birth, miracles, the empty tomb and the ascension are replaced by the bare fact that Jesus has come? Is he not demanding the same faith in an 'unintelligible X' which it is in fact his intention to avoid? Is Bultmann not saying exactly the same as Barth, 'Like it or lump it!'? Otto Küster says of Bultmann's nominalist view of the revelation of God in Jesus Christ: 'We are not prepared to believe Bultmann when he tells us that we must content ourselves with the bare fact that Jesus lived. We cannot postulate that God accepts as a sacrifice a person of any kind of composition, or that ultimately Paul also might have become Christ, or for that matter that the suffering of the thief on his right hand, or indeed even the one on his left, might have redeemed us, that mere meaningless contingency was at work, so that we would be faced with any kind of individual, a person arbitrarily chosen, the role of being the incarnate Word given to him as a separate adjunct.'[90]

How can a 'mere saving fact', an 'empty paradox', not only call me *to* faith, but call *forth* faith in me? And it is this that matters, if the event of Christ is not merely to be a demand and a law, but gift and gospel; and if faith in its turn is not to be performance and work, but abandonment and trust. It is not by chance that Bultmann so strongly emphasises the element of decision and obedience in the New Testament concept of faith. Here he echoes not so much Jesus' call to follow him as Heidegger's call to essentiality. It is this which gives Bultmann's whole theology its profound seriousness, but it also imbues it with a note of sadness and melancholy. On this point the philosopher Karl Jaspers and the theologian Karl Barth, as a rule at opposite poles, are in accord. Jaspers writes: 'His style is neither ponderous nor light, but conveys an atmosphere of sullen rigidity.'[91] And Karl Barth: 'I don't know how many of our

contemporaries have been helped by Bultmann and his disciples to
know the real joy of believing. I shall not ask, but just hope for the
best. Speaking for myself, I must say I find it hard to imagine how
Bultmann could inspire me to study theology, to preach, or even to
believe.'[92]

Theology always arrives at a point where it must 'tell a story'. And
it is the same story which it repeats: the story of Jesus of Nazareth, of the
road he followed from the Jordan to Gethsemane and Golgotha. Of
course this story must be told in several variations, always in such a way
that it responds to the questions of a specific age, and that the story
which is narrated helps men to bear their own history. This corresponds
to the nature of the New Testament gospels. They not only proclaim, but simultaneously are telling a story; they do the one through
the other. And it is this 'story-telling' aspect of the gospel to which
Bultmann's 'demythologisation' fails to do justice. It is upon this point
that his critics have seized. And their criticism has not come from outside, but has originated among Bultmann's own pupils. It has led to the
rediscovery of the 'historic Jesus'. It is from here that the latest stage of
twentieth-century Protestant theology sets out.

CHAPTER EIGHT

THE REDISCOVERY OF THE
HISTORICAL JESUS

The 'post-Bultmann era'

When Ernst Käsemann, at the time Professor for New Testament Studies in Göttingen, in 1952 wrote a paper on the 'Problems of New Testament Study in Germany', he made, among other things, the following point: 'The whole New Testament asserts that at Easter the disciples did not recognise some heavenly being, far less some abstract entity such as a series of dogmatic articles, but Jesus himself. Thus Christ who has been believed in and proclaimed ever since the first Easter day stands in a continuity with the "historical Jesus", and without this continuity faith and preaching would have been meaningless in the view of primitive Christianity. To become aware and certain of this continuity is an indispensable theological necessity. A theology which seeks to abandon it either from historical scepticism or for its own peculiar dogmatic reasons is not worthy of the name.'[1]

Käsemann immediately set to work himself upon the theological task which he had described. Within a year, in October 1953, he read a paper on the theme of the 'Problem of the Historical Jesus' at a gathering of 'old Marburg students', the annual reunion of friends and pupils of Bultmann with their master. The following year this paper was published. Though it was not obvious at first, this was the opening of the 'post-Bultmann era'. Its point of departure and central issue was the problem of the historical Jesus, still argued against the background of the recurrent question of the relationship between revelation and history, although the emphasis was now placed much more firmly upon history.

Looking back upon the first stages of the new line of inquiry which he initiated, Käsemann wrote ten years later: 'The purpose of my paper on the historical Jesus was to revive debate within the circle of Bultmann's pupils, and if possible to bring about a certain self-correction on the part of our master himself, for I considered his historical scepticism on this issue exaggerated, and the theological consequences of this scepticism dangerous.'[2] Käsemann succeeded in his first purpose, but not in his second. He did in fact arouse considerable debate among his fellow pupils, but he was unable to bring about any self-correction on the part of Bultmann himself.

In the last few years, provoked by Käsemann's paper, a wide-ranging discussion concerned with the 'new inquiry' about the historical Jesus has been going on, while the problem of demythologisation has receded into the background. Bultmann's pupils have turned against their master, the master has turned against his pupils, and some of the pupils have turned against one another, while all of them in their turn have been violently attacked from outside. Käsemann speaks of a 'world-wide guerrilla war' into which theological discussion has degenerated, and he adds a question which is tragic and pessimistic in tone: 'Can we pursue our trade without being aware that those who will be our pall-bearers are standing anxiously waiting outside our door?'[3] In the meantime, a new theological generation has grown up, the pupils of Bultmann's pupils, and some of these in their turn have turned against their masters, though not all of them have set out in new directions.

It is not possible to give a final judgement on the outcome of this most recent stage in Protestant theology. At the present moment the debate is still completely open, and in fact seems almost confused. Furthermore, in the last few years the issues have become so many and so complex, and the problems so sophisticated, that they seem scarcely comprehensible to anyone who is not an expert. When Käsemann suggests that theological problems in our time have reached a complexity which puts them above the level of comprehension of a third of the theological students, who therefore have no place in the university,[4] what can the non-theologians say, for whose good all this thought and discussion is supposed to be taking place?

In seeking to understand the rediscovery of the historical Jesus it is important to realise that it originated among Bultmann's own pupils. Besides Ernst Käsemann, we have only to mention Günther Bornkamm, Gerhard Ebeling, Ernst Fuchs, Hans Conzelmann and Herbert Braun. Not that, as has been suggested, there has been a 'revolt' of the pupils against their master: they remain conscious of being guided by the questions he has posed, and by the results and methods of his studies. That is why this section is entitled 'The post-Bultmann era': this is intended to make it clear that the most recent stage in Protestant theology, like that which preceded it, is still dominated by the name of this great scholar. What has taken place is not a 'revolt' but a 'change of course'. Although the pupils are still in basic agreement with their master's point of departure, they have thought critically beyond it, and are going further in a new direction – which according to Käsemann is proof 'that the master has succeeded in performing the Socratic function of a midwife, leading to truth and freedom'.[5]

What started this 'change of course' on the part of Bultmann's pupils was the realisation that his reduction of the coming of Jesus to a bare fact is insufficient to describe the content of the kerygma and the basis of faith, and to identify the gospel as 'Christian'. 'We must go beyond the bare fact' – this is the slogan of the new line of inquiry.[6] But the necessity of attaining to something beyond the bare fact was bound to lead to a new inquiry concerning the 'historical Jesus'. The motive for this inquiry was not, as Bultmann had earlier suspected of his 'conservative New Testament colleagues', and later of his disciples, a desire to provide an historical legitimation for the kerygma and for faith. Such an historical legitimation was explicitly rejected by all Bultmann's disciples; Käsemann dismisses it out of hand as 'blasphemous' and 'absurd'.[7] Nor does the question of the historical Jesus simply come, as Bultmann had constantly suggested, from the need of the human heart for security. Rather, what is at issue is a problem inherent in the essence and the nature of Christian faith itself – that Christian faith derives from a particular event of history, the event of Christ. This event of Christ is handed down to us in the New Testament alone. But the grounding in life of the New Testament tradition, the situation in which it came into being, is that of the primitive Church; it is determined in its entirety by the faith of the first Christians in Jesus as the Christ. Every record of the words and deeds of Jesus is conditioned by his resurrection and from first to last is illuminated by the Easter faith. This light is so bright, and indeed so dazzling, that the outlines of the earthly figure of Jesus tend to grow hazy in it. The question then inevitably arises, whether faith in Christ has its roots in the person and preaching of Jesus himself, or whether it derives only from the faith and preaching of the first Christians.

The problem comes down to that of the transition from the preaching of Jesus to the preaching about Jesus. There is no question that there is a profound difference between the two, which is caused by the abrupt discontinuity represented by his death and resurrection. Anyone who does not take this break seriously does not take his death seriously as a true end, nor his resurrection as a genuine new beginning. But the question is how continuity has been maintained within this discontinuity and what kind of historical link exists between Jesus of Nazareth and the preaching of the primitive Church. What matters now is a new and better understanding of the relationship between the preaching of Jesus and the gospel of the crucified and risen Christ. The statement that the Christian message depends upon the Easter faith of the disciples must not be made so absolute that every link is broken with the earthly Jesus, thus making his person and preaching completely irrelevant as historical realities. It is for this reason that Bultmann's disciples do what was explicitly forbidden by their master, and look beyond the kerygma of the early Church, or more precisely through it, to seek the historical Jesus. They are here posing an historical question which is of outstanding theological significance. Their interest is both historical and theological: they are concerned with the *historical* aim of maintaining the identity between the earthly Jesus and the exalted Christ; but this theological aim can only be achieved by an *historical* demonstration that the kerygma of Christ is already contained in essence in the words and deeds of Jesus. Both belong together; the historical element is theologically relevant. It is true that faith is not based upon historical study, but neither is it unaffected by it.

The kerygma itself permits an inquiry concerning the historical Jesus. Indeed, not only does it permit such an inquiry, it demands it as an obligation. The kerygma explicitly states that its criterion is Jesus himself, and speaks of this criterion as of an historical phenomenon. This requires that the name of Jesus of which the kerygma speaks should not remain a mere word, a fortuitous and meaningless symbol, but should appear as that of an historical person. Günther Bornkamm asks: 'How could faith of all things be content with mere tradition, even though it be contained in the gospels? It must break through it and seek behind it to see the thing itself, and perhaps in this way to understand the tradition afresh and to regain it.' Gerhard Ebeling asks: 'A strange dogma has become widespread, that one should not inquire beyond the testimonies of the New Testament concerning the historical Jesus. Who would forbid this?' Bornkamm's answer is: 'But it cannot be seriously maintained that the gospels and their tradition do not allow inquiry after the historical Jesus. Not only do they allow, they demand this effort.' And Ebeling answers: 'Any attempt to lay down prohibitions at this point, or to insist that the kerygma cannot be affected by such questions, would be to insinuate that the kerygma does not take the name of Jesus seriously, and that it flees the light of intelligible speech by taking refuge in the obscurity of his name.'[8]

The inquiry concerning the historical Jesus does not derive from the curiosity which underlies all science, but from a vital concern of Christian faith. It is of the utmost importance to Christian faith that the kerygma should not be a religious product of the primitive Church, but should be based upon a concrete historical person, that is, that there should be a continuity between the historical Jesus and the Christ proclaimed by the primitive Church, that in consequence the foundation of faith in Christ should lie in Jesus himself, and that the profession of faith, that Jesus is Christ, should be justified. If this link were missing, there would be a dangerous tendency towards docetism, and at the very origin of Christianity there would not be an historical fact but a myth, not the earthly and human Nazarene but a gnostic heavenly being. This shows that the quest of the historical Jesus is not one inquiry which may be pursued among others, but touches the basis and content of Christian faith. Ebeling does not hesitate to point out the consequences with which faith is threatened here: 'If the historical study of Jesus were in fact to show that faith in Jesus had no support in Jesus himself, that would be the end of Christianity.' And: 'If Jesus had never lived, or if faith in him were shown to be a misunderstanding of the significance of the historical Jesus, then clearly the ground would be taken from under Christian faith. If it lost its support in the historical Jesus, it would perhaps not be simply devoid of an object, but it would lose the object which has always been proclaimed by Christianity as the central object of faith.'[9] In the face of this imminent danger it is not sufficient simply to fall back on the bare statement that Jesus has come; it has to be elaborated to a statement on who he was, how he came and what he said and did. This can only be done by historical means.

The reason for elaborating in historical terms on the bare fact of Jesus' coming lies in the simple fact that the New Testament contains *gospels*, an argument which Käsemann constantly reiterates.[10] This fact is all the more remarkable in that all other New Testament writings, notably the epistles of Paul, which are earlier than the gospels, concentrate the whole event so exclusively on the significance of the death and resurrection of Christ, that by comparison the historical life of Jesus shrinks down to virtually nothing, and remains a mere 'shadow'. Nevertheless, the gospels are there in the New Testament, and contain not merely proclamation, but narrative: they present the kerygma of Christ in the framework of the earthly life of Jesus. Although of course they recount and interpret the past in the light of Easter, they nevertheless show an interest in the events of Jesus' life before Easter, and give expression to them. Even John, to whom Bultmann appealed as his

principal witness, and in whose gospel history is so emptied of verifiable
fact that it appears to be virtually nothing more than a 'projection of the
present into the past', nevertheless seems to regard the gospel as the
literary form appropriate to his theological purpose, and accordingly
describes the history of the exalted Lord as the history of the earthly
Jesus. The literary form of the gospel has a theological significance in
itself: it signifies 'the rejection of myth'.[11] Since the gospels contain a
narrative, they testify that faith is not dependent upon itself, but upon
something that exists prior to it, and that this prior entity is a history,
the history of Jesus of Nazareth. This expresses the conviction that 'God
acted, before we believed'. The literary form of the 'gospels' makes it
clear that the events which they record are the 'good news of the
gospel'.

Thus everywhere we see the rediscovery of the historical Jesus! This
does not mean, however, that the impossibilities of the earlier quest of
the historical Jesus by liberal theology have all of a sudden been declared possible, and that an attempt is being made to reconstruct a 'life
of Jesus' from the gospel, with the naïve intention of making such an
historical reconstruction the direct basis of faith for our time. In
spite of the reconsideration of the question of the historical Jesus, which
began with Käsemann's essay, the view is still held that we encounter
Jesus in the kerygma alone, and therefore in faith alone. What distinguishes the new line of inquiry both from the earlier quest for the
historical Jesus, and also from Bultmann's one-sided existentialist interpretation, can clearly be seen in a New Testament verse: 'But when the
time had fully come, God sent forth his Son, born of woman, born
under the law, to redeem those who were under the law, so that we
might receive adoption as sons' (Gal. 4:4 f.). The liberal quest of the
historical Jesus focussed its attention on the first half of the statement, on
the 'history': it was satisfied to demonstrate with historical certainty that
the events recounted had actually taken place. Bultmann, on the other
hand, concentrated his whole attention on the second half of the statement, on the 'kerygma': for him all that mattered was the existential
interpretation of what had happened, the proclamation of the 'benefits of
Christ'. The reconsideration of the quest of the historical Jesus which is
taking place today puts both halves of this statement together: it sees its
task in the seeking of the history in the kerygma and the kerygma in the
history.[12] Willi Marxsen established as an important rule for accom-
plishing this task: 'We cannot inquire into the historical by ignoring
the christological, but only by going through the christological.'[13]

This is the way we must follow. We must begin with the kerygma of the primitive Church, as it is handed down to us in the New Testament, and above all in the gospels, as the ultimate historical datum which is directly accessible to us. But we must not stop there, we must attempt by means of precise and detailed critical study, to trace the way back to Jesus himself, in order to demonstrate within the discontinuity implied by the cross and resurrection of Jesus the continuity between the historical Jesus and the Christ of the kerygma. Thus our way leads from the maximum uncritically asserted by the theology of the primitive Christian Church to the minimum critically established by the quest of the historical Jesus. But in following this way, we never leave the kerygma for a moment. Thus the new quest of the historical Jesus is carried out not 'by seeking to get behind the Word of proclamation, but on the contrary, by penetrating further into the Word'.[14]

This theological concern with the question of the historical Jesus is in accord with the objects of recent historical research. In particular, the work of form-criticism has advanced since its early stages after the First World War, and has attained to new and better established insights. We can distinguish more clearly nowadays that part of the substance of the New Testament tradition of Jesus which is historically certain. The historicising tendencies of that tradition stand out more clearly along-side its kerygmatic tendencies. The well-known argument that in the light of the purpose and extent of the New Testament tradition it is impossible to write a biography of Jesus is as true as it ever was. But it is qualified by the recognition that it is evidently in accordance with historical fact if the gospel narrative tells principally of the final events of Jesus' life and reduces his earlier life to an account of the sermons he preached in his wanderings, and of his miracles. Thus what is essential in the story of Jesus' life seems in fact to have been handed down to us.[15]

Consequently scepticism and resignation over the question whether we can ever learn anything reliable about the historical Jesus from the gospels has decreased. In his book *Jesus* Bultmann wrote: 'I do indeed think that we can know almost nothing concerning the life and per-sonality of Jesus', whereas today we read in Günther Bornkamm's *Jesus of Nazareth*: 'Nevertheless, the gospels justify neither resignation nor scepticism. Rather they bring before our eyes, in very different fashion from what is customary in chronicles and presentations of history, the historical person of Jesus with the utmost vividness. Quite clearly what the gospels report concerning the message, the deeds and the history of Jesus is still distinguished by an authenticity, a freshness, and a distinctiveness not in any way effaced by the Church's Easter faith. These features point us directly to the earthly figure of Jesus.' And Ernst Käsemann, after describing undismayed the whole problem and difficulty of the quest of the historical Jesus, continues: 'On the other hand, I cannot concede that in view of this situation the last word should be one of resignation and scepticism, and that we should cease to be interested in the earthly Jesus. . . . What I am concerned with is to show that in the obscurity of the history of Jesus, characteristic features of his preaching become discernible with relative clarity, and that the message of primitive Christianity was based on them.'[16]

From the kerygmatic Christ to the historical Jesus

In recent years, many theologians have attempted to trace a new way through the kerygma to the historical Jesus, and this has been done in particular by pupils of Bultmann. Although each of them has set out in his own direction, nevertheless a spirit of agreement astonishing in theological study has prevailed among them, in spite of many differences and variations in detail. We shall not attempt to describe the whole scope of this new quest of the historical Jesus, and to set out all the different courses it follows, with their sometimes highly complex historical reasonings. A number of model cases will serve to demonstrate in concrete terms what has already been stated in principle about the point of departure of the new quest of the historical Jesus, and the method by which it seeks to answer its questions.

Let us begin with Ernst Käsemann.[17] As a criterion for testing whether any tradition concerning Jesus in the New Testament is genuine, he posits a strict methodological principle: We can only consider that we have a firm historical basis when the tradition cannot be derived either from the Jewish environment or from the body of ideas held by primitive Christianity. Guided by this basic principle, Käsemann sets out to elaborate 'the distinctive characteristics of the mission of Jesus'.

He begins with the well-known antitheses of the Sermon on the Mount: 'You have heard that it was said to the men of old . . . But *I* say to you . . .' (Mt. 5:21). These words are among the 'most astonishing in all the gospels': their utter novelty bears witness to their authenticity. In the words, 'But I say to you', Jesus claims an authority which is greater than that of Moses. There is no parallel to this in Judaism, and none is possible. For a Jew who claimed such authority had broken the bounds of Judaism. Whether Jesus presented himself as a rabbi or a prophet, in this claim he exceeded the authority of every rabbi and prophet, for according to Jewish belief both were subject to the authority of Moses. Consequently, Käsemann concludes that the only category which does justice to his claim is that of the Messiah, even though Jesus did not use or demand this title himself.

The same is true of the way Jesus treats the Jewish law. Jesus opposes to the many commandments concerning the cultic purity of objects the requirement of the inner purity of the human heart: 'Not what goes into the mouth defiles man, . . . what comes out of the mouth proceeds from the heart, and this defiles a man.' (Mt. 15:1 ff.) Here again Jesus goes beyond the letter of the Jewish law and the authority of Moses with an unparalleled sovereign authority, while at the same time he unhinges the whole structure of ancient cultic practice, with its distinction between pure and impure, and sacred and profane.

The teaching activity of the Jewish rabbis took the form of theological reflection upon the scripture, and was closely tied to it. The preaching of Jesus, however, especially in his parables, reveals a use of direct visual imagery which is characteristic not of a rabbi but of a teacher of wisdom. But the full significance of this observation comes to light only against the background of a second and more important circumstance. Jesus undoubtedly understood himself to be 'inspired'. This is shown among other things by his characteristic use of the word 'Amen'. The word 'Amen' was also used in contemporary Judaism, but then, as now, it was used at the end of a prayer or scripture reading as a response to it, and someone other than the speaker had to say, 'Amen'. In Jesus' case, however, the word comes at the beginning and he himself utters it: 'Amen, I say to you.' This expressed 'an ultimate and direct certainty, such as is imparted by inspiration'. And Käsemann says again of Jesus: 'Regardless of whether he said so expressly, he must have understood himself as an instrument of the living Spirit of God, which Judaism expected at the end of time.'

The examples given show that Käsemann finds the distinctive characteristic of the earthly Jesus in his preaching; but he sees Jesus' preaching in its turn as determined by his eschatological understanding of himself: With the words of Jesus the kingdom of God is making its way upon earth, and faces men with the decision whether they will accept it or not. It is the parables of Jesus in particular which point to this eschatological orientation in his message. They do not proclaim general religious or moral truths, but announce in concrete terms the onset of the kingdom of God: 'that God has come close to man in his grace and with his demand.' Jesus did not merely *teach* the fatherhood of God and the sonship of man, but as Käsemann explicitly states, 'He *brought* and *lived* the freedom of the children of God'; in the message of Jesus God *came close* to man in his grace and in his demand. Here Käsemann takes a decisive step beyond the conclusions of the liberal quest of the historical Jesus. He sees the message of Jesus as containing not merely ethical and religious teaching, but as being an eschatological event, involving on the part of Jesus himself not merely the proclamation of a message, but the adoption of a particular attitude.

This leads to our second model case, Ernst Fuchs.[18] Fuchs places even greater importance upon the 'attitude' adopted by Jesus than Käsemann does. He sees in the attitude of Jesus 'the real framework of his preaching', the key to his message. In his view, one cannot speak in the strict sense of the preaching of Jesus; all that has been handed down to us consists of individual sayings and parables. All these sayings of Jesus are basically a 'testimony to himself': they reflect a decision which he has made. This decision concerns man's situation with regard to God, and consists of Jesus' resolution to accept 'the consequences of his own eschatological experiences and to begin here, on earth, the work of God which is revealed only in heaven'. The attitude adopted by Jesus is concordant with this. It involves 'a truly bold undertaking': Jesus dares, as a 'person without any accepted office', to set himself in the place of God and to make directly effective in the attitude he adopts himself the will of God as a gracious will. 'This attitude is neither that of a prophet nor that of a sage; it is rather that of a man who dares to act in God's place by drawing to himself sinners who without him would have to flee before God.'

In making this connection between the attitude adopted by Jesus and his preaching Fuchs refers, as an example, to the parable of the Prodigal Son (Luke 15). The reason for which Jesus tells the parable is of decisive importance in understanding it. He tells it as an answer to the reproach of the Pharisees and the scribes that he eats with tax collectors and sinners. Thus Jesus has 'already provided the interpretation of the parable by an act of kindness': it is not the parable which explains Jesus' attitude, but Jesus' attitude which explains the parable. He dares to make the word of God known as a gracious will, and it is this which can be seen in his behaviour towards the tax collectors and sinners, in his table fellowship with them. His words are only the echo of the decision he has already taken.

Thus Fuchs sees the attitude of Jesus as 'an approach of love', and his words as 'words of love'. Through his behaviour and through his words Jesus promises himself to his disciples as a 'pledge for the history of love'. Love does not come in answer to the demand of love, but love comes as it were gratuitously; that is, love comes from love. Jesus encourages his disciples to love, by making everything turn on the Word, which is the word of love. Because of this bold action, he was executed outside the gates of Jerusalem, which was anything but an irreligious city. One may say of the picture of the historical Jesus given by Fuchs, in the words of the Fourth Gospel: 'Having loved his own . . . he loved them to the end' (John 13:1).

The central role of love in Fuchs's picture of the historical Jesus is for Gerhard Ebeling vested in faith.[19] Behind Ebeling's quest of the historical Jesus lies a particular view of history and its reality. His understanding of history is not based on the positivist concept of fact, but on the 'word-event', and so on the 'nature of reality as speech'. Ebeling does not inquire into the bare facts: 'What happened, what events took place and how are they to be explained?' Instead, he asks, 'What came to be spoken of?' 'For if one has to do with Jesus, one has to do not with mere facts but with pure Word.' This does not mean that in Jesus' actual life he talked incessantly, but that in the events themselves something is uttered as speech, that the historical reality bears the character of statement and address, and that therefore we encounter it as 'word'. The problem posed by the term 'the historical Jesus' consists for Ebeling in 'bringing to utterance what came to utterance in Jesus'.

But what came to utterance in Jesus is faith. This forms the 'utterly decisive and determinative factor' in the attitude of Jesus: it is the 'point at which all lines converge with astonishing unanimity'. Everything which Jesus said and did is reduced to this common denominator: Jesus is the 'witness of faith'. Ebeling also regards this unity of the tradition as a testimony to its historical authenticity. He answers the criticism that Jesus may perhaps in reality have been a quite different person from the one in whom the primitive Church later believed, and in whom we believe today, with the following argument: Whereas in other historical phenomena a complex diversity and discrepancy reigns between a person and his work, Jesus forms a 'remarkable exception'. In him everything, his preaching and his attitude, his person and his work, is concentrated upon a single point: the coming to speech of faith. This concentration of every element in the tradition of Jesus in the coming to

speech of faith seems to Ebeling 'simply compelling': it must have
occurred in the existential life of Jesus and not in the imagination of the
primitive Church. This very concentration made all biographical and
psychological details superfluous. In the one-sided limitation of the
tradition of Jesus to that of the bringer of faith the authentic picture of
Jesus has been preserved.

Faith comes to speech in Jesus not through his speaking of his own
faith, for example by describing his own awareness of God, but through
his arousing and calling for faith in others by exercising his own faith.
This faith is not faith in his person, yet it cannot be separated from his
person. It comes about by the fact that Jesus is there. Where Jesus
appears, he arouses faith. Nothing shows this as clearly as the stories of
healings in the gospels. Something emanates from Jesus which causes
the sick to come to him with the request to be healed, and he heals them
by encouraging them to faith and by telling them: 'Your faith has
saved you.' Because this faith is faith aroused by Jesus, it is faith which is
related to him. But this leads us back to the authority of Jesus. For only
someone who possesses authority can demand and arouse faith. It is in
this sense that Jesus shows himself to be the 'witness of faith'. Faith is not
merely a demand which he makes, but the decisive gift which he gives.
It is the 'attainment' of what came to speech in Jesus. Consequently,
'Anyone who believes has attained the historical Jesus' – 'The historical
Jesus is the Jesus of faith'!

Ebeling lays particular weight on the affirmation that the resurrection
added nothing new to Jesus. Easter is not a matter of the communication
of new, additional revelations, but solely of the revelation of Jesus himself. The belief that arose after Easter is nothing more than the 'right
understanding of Jesus as he was before Easter'. Jesus now appears as
who he really is, the witness of faith. But one can only acknowledge the
witness of faith by accepting his testimony and becoming a believer
oneself. Thus to believe in Jesus and to believe in the Risen One is the
same thing. Through the resurrection Jesus does not become the 'object'
of faith, but as the 'witness of faith' he becomes the 'basis of faith'. To
believe in Jesus means to believe in God with respect to him.

According to Ebeling, it is this which shows the continuity between
the historical Jesus and Christ. It is based on the faith of Jesus, which
arouses faith. Ebeling expresses this in a statement taken from the
Epistle to the Hebrews: Jesus is the 'pioneer and perfecter of faith'
(Heb. 12:2).

A number of other examples could be added to those we have given, but they would not provide us with any new point of view. For all those who at the present day are inquiring once again into the historical Jesus are in essential agreement in their point of departure and in their method and results. They all start with the primitive Christian kerygma, and study it in order to find out how far the figure and preaching of Jesus himself can be clearly recognised in the primitive Church's proclamation of Christ. The results they obtain are the same.[20]

No one nowadays would think of regarding Jesus merely as an example and teacher, as a proclaimer of the message of the kingdom of God, in the sense that the person bringing the message can be isolated from the message itself, in such a way that the message is effective and valid as a universal and timeless truth. However, all see the person and message of Jesus, his preaching and his activity, as a unity. The preaching of Jesus is inextricably linked with his person and with the events of his life. What joins the two into such a unity is the eschatological orientation of Jesus' mission. Jesus is not himself the kingdom of God, but the imminence of the kingdom of God is intimately related to his own appearance. For it is he who announces the imminence of the kingdom of God, and through this announcement, he himself, his person, is the decisive factor in the process which is now set in motion. Consequently, the eschatological statements must not be isolated from Jesus' self-consciousness. It is the announcement of the imminent kingdom of God which gives Jesus' preaching and attitude the directness and authority which distinguishes him from all prophets and rabbis.

On the other hand, no one now attempts to derive the preaching and attitude of Jesus, his message and his person, from his 'Messiahship' or 'divine sonship' as a ready-made pattern of faith and concepts. This can be seen, for example, from the structure of Günther Bornkamm's *Jesus of Nazareth*, the first monograph on Jesus by one of Bultmann's pupils, which came out thirty years after Bultmann's own book *Jesus*. In this book the question of the Messianic consciousness of Jesus, which played a central role in the quest of the historical Jesus conducted by liberal theology, and was usually dealt with in the opening chapters, is not discussed until the last chapter but one.[21] This ordering of the material is in exact accordance with the specific nature of Jesus' own preaching and activity. It makes clear that Jesus did not make his messianic dignity a separate basic theme of his preaching, and did not seek to legitimise his mission on the basis of a pretended office. Jesus used none of the many honorific titles which later tradition puts in his mouth, neither that of Messiah, nor of the Son of Man, nor of the Son of God. Even his journey to Jerusalem does not show that he understood himself as a *Messias designatus*.

But for the new quest of the historical Jesus this is not a negative conclusion, it is positive in the extreme. For the mere fact that Jesus never claimed to be the Messiah, or applied any other title to himself, is extraordinarily characteristic of him, and confirms the authenticity of the historical picture of his life and ministry. This distinguishes Jesus both from the expectations of his Jewish environment, and also from the preaching of the primitive Christian Church. Jesus did not speak of his own consciousness of himself, but simply did 'what was necessary at the present moment'.[22] He did not make his person the central issue of his preaching: he proclaimed what he knew God had called him to, and acted accordingly. What is 'Messianic' about him is 'his words and deeds and the unmediatedness of his historic appearance'.[23]

In the light of this picture of the historical Jesus, the question of the Messianic consciousness of Jesus, and the titles which he claimed for himself, a question which was regarded as crucial by the liberal quest of the historical Jesus, has become both historically and theologically irrelevant. Today two theologians as different as the conservative Lutheran Paul Althaus and the critical pupil of Bultmann, Ernst Käsemann, can come to almost the same conclusions. Paul Althaus writes: 'What does it matter whether we answer yes or no to this question, if those who give different replies to it are nevertheless agreed that Jesus was certain that "a man's attitude towards him was decisive for his fate"' (Bultmann). '. . . The content of Jesus' claim is not dependent on any claim he may have made to a title.' And Ernst Käsemann says: 'The only category which accords with his claim is entirely independent of the question whether he himself did or did not use or claim it and which was therefore accorded to him by his disciples themselves, the appellation "Messiah".' Bultmann too is in fundamental agreement with them, when he writes: 'Whether or not he was conscious of himself as the Messiah remains a matter of indifference. All it would signify is that he used a contemporary Jewish conception to bring to awareness the call to decision in his work among men. But his call to decision does imply a christology, though not in the form of metaphysical speculation about a heavenly being, or as a character portrayal in terms of a presumed Messianic consciousness, but a christology consisting of proclamation and address. If the primitive Church called him the Messiah, it was expressing in its own way the fact that it understood him.'[24]

Here we can draw up an interim balance sheet: The 'bare fact' that

Jesus has come, asserted by Bultmann, can be so extended in historical terms that the characteristic features of his teaching and person will become clearly recognisable against the obscurity of history. The Christ-kerygma of the New Testament is contained 'in a nutshell' in the words and the actions of Jesus. This means that the kerygma of the early Church is not left hanging in the air, but has its foundation in the historical events of Jesus' life. There is a continuity between the historical Jesus and the Christ of the kerygma; the earthly Jesus and the exalted Christ are identical. But this means that faith in Christ has a basis in Jesus himself. At the beginning of Christianity there stands not a myth or an idea, the leader of a cult or a symbol, but a person and what happened to him. *The kerygma begins with Jesus of Nazareth.*

Conzelmann characterises the continuity between the historical Jesus and the kerygmatic Christ as an 'indirect christology'; Ebeling speaks of an 'implicit christology'; others again of a 'christology *in nuce*'; the present author in his turn has proposed the expression 'christology in the making'. It is at this very point that the most recent disagreements among Bultmann's pupils themselves have broken out. They have arisen over the question of the precise definition of the relationship between indirect and direct, or implicit and explicit christology. This question is equivalent to that which asks what place must be accorded in the formation of the primitive Christian kerygma to the event of Easter, through which indirect christology becomes direct christology, and implicit christology explicit.

When, in his essay of 1954, Käsemann opened the recent discussion concerning the problem of the historical Jesus, he intended only to put forward the view that the event of Easter did not form the exclusive basis of the New Testament kerygma. For him the earthly Jesus was a very important, but not the sole, criterion of the primitive Christian kerygma. Thus ten years later he wrote: 'The reduction of the gospel to the historical Jesus was not part of my intention when I argued against my master. I would regard that as a relapse into the Ebionite form of Judaeo-Christianity.'[25] For Käsemann the earthly Jesus is only one of the factors on which the primitive Christian kerygma was based. After Easter other elements were added to it which were not present in the same way in the historical Jesus. Consequently, the primitive Christian kerygma is not to be interpreted on the basis of the historical Jesus, but the historical Jesus on the basis of the primitive Christian kerygma – which is what takes place in the New Testament itself.

On the other hand, in the case of Fuchs and Ebeling the pendulum has swung in the other direction. Admittedly, Ernst Fuchs writes in the preface to his collected essays *On the Question of the Historical Jesus*: 'Whereas we previously interpreted the historical Jesus with the aid of the primitive Christian kerygma, we nowadays interpret this kerygma with the aid of the historical Jesus – both directions taken by our interpretation are complementary.'[26] But one cannot overlook the fact that in both Fuchs and Ebeling the direction taken by the interpretation is almost exclusively from the historical Jesus to the primitive Christian kerygma. For Fuchs and Ebeling agree that the question of the historical Jesus provides the 'hermeneutic key' to christology. The historical Jesus is the 'criterion of christology': the kerygma must only bring to utterance what came to utterance in Jesus himself. This means that the task of christology can only consist of the interpretative reproduction of what is contained in the historical Jesus himself, in his message and in the events of his life: 'From the christological point of view, nothing should be stated concerning Jesus which is not founded in the historical Jesus, and which is not limited to the statement of who the historical Jesus is.'[27] Anything which is not related to the historical Jesus can no longer have any place in christology. This strict reduction of the kerygma to the historical Jesus is of considerable consequence for the interpretation of christological dogma, and Ebeling is in no way afraid to accept these consequences: either we must reduce dogmatic statements about Christ to statements about Jesus which we can historically vindicate, or else we must interpret dogmatic statements concerning Christ in such a way that they are not contradictory to what can be historically vindicated: 'The *vere homo* (true man) must be so understood that it remains within the bounds of what is historical – which also means, of what is historically possible. And the *vere Deus* (true God) must be so understood, that it does not do away with the understanding of the *vere homo* as we have defined it.'[28] Here there is no longer any room for the introduction, following the event of Easter, of new facts on which the kerygma can be based. The primitive Christian kerygma is constituted exclusively by the historical Jesus.

It has become increasingly evident in recent years that different points of view as to the significance of the historical Jesus for the primitive Christian kerygma have considerable theological consequences. By giving a place to the events of Easter, as well as to the historical Jesus, in the formation of the primitive Christian kerygma, Käsemann makes room once again for the cosmic scope of divine redemption. That God is seeking again to be vindicated in his creation, that his action is effective not only for individual men but for the whole world, that its goal is not merely a new self-understanding on the part of man, but the rule of Christ over the cosmos, and that the Church consequently understands itself as the new people of God and becomes aware of its mission within the world – all these are elements which have been restored to prominence in the work of Bultmann's pupil Ernst Käsemann. At the same time, he accords to 'apocalyptic', hitherto generally despised as a late Jewish doctrine of rewards and punishments, a new theological significance as the cosmic framework of the gospel; he describes it as the 'mother of all Christian theology'.[29] This is the issue in today's theological dispute: apocalyptic or anthropology.

In Fuchs the danger of an 'anthropological constriction', which we noted in their master Bultmann, is not overcome. If the historical Jesus is the exclusive criterion of the primitive Christian kerygma, if the principal aim of the preaching of the historical Jesus is a new self-understanding on the part of man, and if believing *in* Jesus is in consequence scarcely different from believing *like* Jesus, then there is a risk that the cosmic dimension of the Christian message, which is based on the resurrection of Jesus, may disappear, and that Jesus may only play the part of the 'pioneer and perfector of our faith' in the sense that he has brought into the world a new understanding of faith and existential life.

But the position maintained by Ebeling and Fuchs seems to be a moderate one compared with the critical existentialist interpretation of the primitive Christian kerygma taken by the Mainz New Testament scholar Herbert Braun. Braun's interpretation has stirred up the greatest theological storm of recent years.

The self-understanding of faith

Herbert Braun is likewise dissatisfied with the mere fact that Jesus has come, and inquires into the content of the preaching of Jesus. He regards its content as twofold:[30] Jesus intensified the *torah*, the Jewish law, to the point at which it became impossible to carry out; and at the same time he abolished the striving for reward associated in Judaism with the fulfilment of God's commands, and promised divine salvation to those who had no religious and moral achievements to point to: God rejoices in the repentance of those who are lost. The paradox of Jesus' preaching is that the demand of God is made more radically urgent, while the grace of God is radically intensified. This paradox of a radical demand and radical grace, a radical 'I ought' and a radical 'I may', is seen by

Braun as characteristic of the preaching of the historical Jesus. This is what was new and without parallel in it, and which was so offensive to Jewish ears. It did not come about by the chance coinciding of two traditions which were originally unrelated, but 'belongs to and is typical of the life of the historical Jesus'.

But in the preaching of Jesus the radicalisation of God's demand does not appear as a system of ordinances, and the radicalisation of the grace of God does not appear as a systematically developed doctrine of grace. Characteristic of the activity and teaching of Jesus is that it is 'unsystematic'. From the very first Braun regards this lack of system as of great importance. For it shows that neither the command enunciated by Jesus nor the grace of God proclaimed by him are general truths of moral judgement, but 'admonitions' which are applied to individuals through his preaching: the teaching and actions of Jesus form 'an event applied in each case to the individual'. Braun concludes from this that 'the earthly Jesus already belongs in the gospel'.

Thus the unity of the radical demand and the radical grace of God, paradoxical in its nature and taking the form of an event, is regarded by Braun as the essential characteristic of Jesus, which goes back to the historical Jesus himself, and he considers that in this he has discovered the 'canon within the canon' of the New Testament. Using this canon as his criterion, he studies the christological content of the three main bodies of tradition in the New Testament – the first three gospels (the Synoptics), Paul and John.[31]

In all three bodies of tradition we find a great number of titles ascribed to Jesus. But what do they signify? They are 'post-resurrection honorific titles'. The earliest congregations used them to signify that Jesus did not remain subject to death, which for Braun means that what is essential and new in Jesus' preaching is still, and indeed more than ever, valid in spite of the catastrophe of Good Friday. The titles express the '*novum* contained in the life of Jesus', the significance of what Jesus of Nazareth set forth: the paradoxical unity of a radical demand and radical grace, of utter seriousness and limitless acceptance. At the same time they show that this paradox is a matter not of general timeless truths, but of an event 'analogous to that which once happened in Jesus of Nazareth'. It is this which it is the purpose of the different post-resurrection titles to affirm.

But these titles are very different in their detailed significance. The vast difference between them is due to the fact that in them the first Christian congregations were not creating something completely new, but were making use of a terminology which already existed. They adopted the religious and political honorific titles in use in their various environments and referred them to Jesus of Nazareth. Thus the earliest congregation expressed the significance of Jesus in Jewish terminology, and made use chiefly of the titles 'Messiah' and 'Son of Man'. In the Hellenistic sphere this process then continued – with an 'appreciable increase of dignity': here Jesus is venerated as 'Son of God', 'Lord', 'Saviour', 'Logos', 'God'. These titles are 'interchangeable' and the appellations are drawn from widely different sources. This shows that the christological titles in the New Testament are only 'ciphers' and 'outline descriptions', a 'christological code' for the 'basic phenomenon' which underlies them all. This basic underlying phenomenon is the self-understanding of faith, a universally valid evaluation of the situation of man in the sight of God: man is lost, and yet he has God's acceptance. At this point Herbert Braun arrives at the statement which has become famous, or rather notorious: 'Anthropology is the constant; christology is the variable.'[32] That is, man's self-understanding in faith remains constant throughout the whole New Testament, while the christological code in which this is expressed is different in each case.

The constant – the self-understanding of faith – derives from the 'experience' which men have undergone in the encounter with Jesus of Nazareth. In the encounter with him they have become aware of the paradoxical unity of radical demand and radical grace, the 'I ought' and 'I may' has come upon them, and with it 'God's acceptance, which Jesus of Nazareth lives out among men'. In the further stage of the development, of course, this acceptance on the part of God is to an increasing extent 'encoded' in christological and metaphysical terms, but when these further stages speak of faith in Jesus in various christological ciphers, they are always referring to this acceptance. Yet Braun considers it important that the continuity of this constant of the self-understanding of faith exists only 'in fact', and has not been transmitted historically. In Braun's view, the existence of a continuous historical tradition of the earthly Jesus, through the primitive Palestinian Church to Paul and the Johannine circles, cannot be demonstrated. The various nomenclatures differ too much from each other to provide the unifying factor which would make it possible to accept such an historically transmitted tradition. All that historical study can establish is that 'the historical Jesus, Paul and the Johannine writings *teach* – in very different forms – the same concerning the situation of man in the sight of God'.[33]

It is different for the believer who understands himself in this way, and who derives his self-understanding from Jesus, and therefore calls

him 'Christ', 'the Son of Man', 'the Son of God', 'Lord', etc. What he
is making is not an historical judgement but a confession of faith. As a
confessor of faith, who refers these various christological titles and concepts to Jesus of Nazareth, he acts from a double knowledge. First, he is
aware that he does not derive his self-understanding in faith from himself, but that it comes to him from outside; secondly, he knows that
what comes to him in this way from outside himself is identical with
what once happened around Jesus of Nazareth. But again, Braun sees the
continuity expressed in this relation of christological titles to Jesus of
Nazareth not as an historically mediated continuity, but as an actual one,
experienced and professed in faith.

Braun never ceases to emphasise that 'God's acceptance, which Jesus
lives out among men', is 'not to be expected', and is 'something which
only comes about through what is beyond man', 'an event which takes
hold of man'. In accordance with the self-understanding of faith, it is 'a
happening', 'an event', 'an adventure'. But the question inevitably
arises whether the New Testament kerygma does not turn into a mere
idea, if the constant element in it is the self-understanding of man in
faith. Braun himself poses this question: 'Is the essential element in
Christianity, the New Testament constant of the self-understanding of
faith, simply an *idea*? . . . Does the New Testament constant of the self-
understanding of faith amount to the *idea* that man is lost, the *idea* that
he is taken hold of by a miracle from beyond?' Braun denies this. He
does not intend that the self-understanding of faith of the New Testament should be seen as an eternal truth, which, once it has been known,
is ever after theoretically evident and therefore valid for all time. He
constantly repeats that the New Testament self-understanding of faith
happens to man, that it comes to him from outside himself, and that
therefore it must be preached again and again in order to elicit it. It
belongs to 'that third category of phenomena, which, like my relationship to my father, to my wife or to my friend, falls neither into the
category of ideas nor into the category of tradition: this category consists of phenomena which come about, and only become valid and
binding in the process of coming about'. This is what Braun means
when he writes: 'The New Testament self-understanding of faith is a
happening, an event, which constantly renews itself.'[34]

This coming about, this event, remains associated with the name of
Jesus. It takes place wherever 'I ought' and 'I may' are preached and
come about anew through preaching. But wherever 'I ought' and 'I
may' come about anew through preaching, 'Jesus is present', because

there we have 'an event analogous to that which once happened in history around Jesus of Nazareth'. 'Jesus comes about on each occasion in my "I ought" and "I may",' and it is Jesus' will to 'come about time and again'.[35]

Braun does not stop at the question of the historical Jesus, but quite logically extends the question of the historical Jesus to that of God: who God is, where and how we experience him today, where and how God 'happens', today. He poses this question at the end of his essay *Die Problematik einer Theologie des Neuen Testaments* (Problems of a Theology of the New Testament). The answer he gives there covers a single page. It is this single page above all which has elicited a sharp verdict of condemnation upon Braun and his theology. But anyone wanting to understand correctly and to judge fairly what Braun wrote there, ought to read it in its context. He will not then be able to deny that Braun has boldly uncovered a complex of problems which is unquestionably present in the New Testament, and which no one can sidestep who is genuinely concerned to interpret the New Testament for our time.

Braun establishes that the statements made by the authors of the New Testament concerning the salvation of man and his position with regard to God vary so much that they cannot be reconciled with one another.[36] The *christology* of the New Testament 'cannot be reduced to a common denominator'; its *soteriology*, that is, the question of man's salvation, is not given 'a unanimous answer'; its position with regard to the *law* of God 'oscillates through the whole spectrum'; its *eschatology* is 'full of severe tensions'; and its *sacramental doctrine* is 'not unanimous'. Braun warns against hasty conclusions meant to reduce this 'disparity' within the New Testament to a higher unity. The contradictions are too great for this, and the difficulties facing our understanding are too severe.

In order to demonstrate this, Braun goes through the five afore-mentioned central theological themes of the New Testament.[37] The assumption of its *christology* is that there is a Messiah or Kyrios – and our present world-view makes it impossible to accept the odds in this 'handicap'. In *soteriology* the time of salvation is conceived of either in terms of this world as 'a life free from sorrow on a renewed earth' or transcendentally as 'a non-terrestrial condition localised in the presence of God' – this conception of eternal life as an 'extension and variation' of earthly life is for us 'too naïve either to believe or to strive for'. The view of the *law* of God is dominated by the general assumption that God has laid down binding ordinances which are binding simply because God has laid them down – 'this naïve heteronomy is alien to us and is beyond our capacity to accept'. New Testament *eschatology* assumes an 'existent deity' who guides the course of history, and lays down its beginning and its end – this 'naïve acceptance' of God as a 'datum' is no longer acceptable to us with our present world-view. Finally, the New Testament *doctrine of the sacraments* conceives of salvation 'in terms of things' and speaks of the coming of the deity 'in time and as an object' – we can no longer maintain this 'naïve idea of God'.

In all five groups of conceptions which have been mentioned, the difficulties which face our understanding converge upon a single point – that of 'objectivising thought', which disregards man in its statements about God: 'The world of God is considered here as an entity existing in itself, present or becoming present at a particular place or at a particular point in time.' But this idea of God as 'an entity existing in and for itself' implies a 'handicap' the odds of which man has to concede and which we are no longer able to concede. Braun closes his exposition of the 'disparity' in the New Testament testimonies with the statement: 'To be aware of all this is at the same time to recognise that this outlook and this concept of God is impossible for us.'

But at the same time the New Testament contains statements which explode the conception described above, overcoming objectivising and material thinking about God and his world. Braun demonstrates this again by reference to the same central theological themes.[38] In *christology* Jesus is not merely thought of in terms of a naïve objectivity, but also 'happens' in my awareness that 'I ought' and 'I may', which in fact occurs 'within the framework of his common humanity with us'. For *soteriology* this means that final salvation is brought down 'from the lofty heights of the metaphysical world of God' and established 'on the profane ground of true common humanity': salvation is to be found in this common humanity and not in a realm lying above and outside man. In the doctrine of the *law* there are important tentative statements which begin to break down the structure of heteronomy: here God is not merely the external authority or the content of an ordinance, but is 'the expression of the phenomenon of an ability to act conscientiously, with assurance and with conviction' – for to act in accordance with God's ordinances means to act conscientiously, with assurance and with conviction. In *eschatology* the imminent expectation of primitive Christianity, the hope of the onset of the kingdom of God in the immediate future, contains within itself an element which completely breaks down all objective thinking about God. This imminent expectation implies that each proclamation of man's call to God and God's seizure of man is irrecoverably unique and ultimately valid: God is present wherever 'the actual moment is accepted and lived in its fullness'. Again, in what the New Testament has to say about the *sacraments*, the mode of thought which thinks in terms of things and objects is 'frequently transcended'. This, however, does not occur as unambiguously as in the case of the four other themes, so that 'a bold interpretation' has to state that the sacramentalism evident in the New Testament is opposed to the personal 'I ought' and 'I may', and therefore to the non-objective idea of God.

According to Braun the 'disparity' of the statements in the New Testament points to the problem at a deeper level. It exhibits the effect of the contradictory language of the New Testament about God. On the one hand God is presented in the New Testament as a material, given entity, while on the other hand he is presented as non-objective, not 'given'. The objectivising of God does not accord with the 'true trend' of the New Testament, but it cannot be disputed that in the New Testament God and his world are also conceived of as an object and a thing.

But what is God ultimately, in the New Testament sense? What is God understood to be in the New Testament? Braun first answers this question negatively:[39] 'He is certainly not considered as an Existent existing in himself, as a species definable by that term.' But then he goes on to the positive statement that 'God is the goal towards which I am being driven'. But lest anyone should get the idea that what is implied here is the 'restless heart' (*cor inquietum*) of Augustine, or the 'restless compeller' (*inquietus actor*) of Luther, Braun explicitly adds that this compulsion comes to me only from my fellow man. For Braun, New Testament theology can be summed up as the determination of human existence by an unconditional 'I may' and 'I ought', by a sense of security and of obligation. But security and obligation do not come to me 'from the universe', but only from others, through my fellow men, just as the word of preaching and the act of love reach me only from my fellow men. Thus Braun arrives at this more precise definition: 'God is where the security and the obligation which I derive from my fellow man comes from.' It follows that for Braun God is 'a particular kind of common humanity': 'God is there where I have an obligation, where I am committed; where I am committed in an unconditional "I may" and "I ought".' But this means 'man as man, man in his common humanity implies God'. It is therefore only logical for Braun to go on to ask whether there can be such a thing as an atheist. Basically, for

Braun there is no such thing, and there cannot be: 'For,' he asks, 'does not every kind of common humanity already contain something of the link, so vital for the New Testament, between "I may" and "I ought"?'

The existence of God

Braun believes that his 'theology' is supported by the New Testament, not as a whole, but at least in its decisive statements, in those which are valid for us. He believes that in his radical existentialist interpretation of the New Testament he is simply bringing out the significance for our time of the 'true trend' of what the New Testament itself says about God and man. But this view is not shared by many other theologians, nor, in particular, by non-theologians. Whereas, in spite of his demythologisation, one might still recognise in Bultmann's work the indestructible core of the gospel, Braun's existentialism seems to have dissolved even this. That is why, in recent years, something like a united front of churchmen and theologians has formed against him, in which Lutherans and Calvinists, High Churchmen and Barthians, sacramentalists and pietists, Church Consistory members and professors, disregarding their other differences over theology, Church politics and pastoral matters, have banded together in a strange alliance – a manifestation rare in the history of theology, not only in recent years but at any time.

The school of Barth in particular, believed by many to have come to an end, seems to have revived and found itself once again in the reaction to existentialist theology. For a long time the pupils of Barth had been chiefly occupied with the political and ethical problems of the post-war years, which involved them with the quarrels of Church politics; also, they had never formed so independent a group as Bultmann's pupils, but now they are forming ranks once again.

The most comprehensive argument with existentialist theology has been conducted by Helmut Gollwitzer. His criticism is by no means restricted to Herbert Braun, but since the latter takes existentialist theology to its furthest extreme, the main burden of Gollwitzer's criticism is aimed at him.

Gollwitzer makes his judgement upon Braun's theology abundantly clear. He states without qualification: 'This is the disintegration of theology into humanism, and it is distinguished from other forms of humanism only by its different philosophical basis and terminology.'[40] According to Gollwitzer, Braun has 'overcome' the subject-object pattern of thought by falling back upon one pole of the encounter between God and man, human existence, and subsuming within it everything which the Bible says about the relationship of man to God. The other pole of the encounter, the existence of God, evaporates. The biblical concepts, which taken together describe the relationship between man and God, are reinterpreted as 'descriptions of an attitude which in reality is only exercised between man and his fellow man, but not (or only verbally) between man and God'. Consequently the content of Christian preaching, the history of Jesus Christ, is lost. Christian faith becomes 'a faith in existence', a 'believing attitude'. For this believing attitude 'God' is nothing more than 'the point of reference which itself remains in the dark', the 'unknown quantity which is implicit as a point of reference in the basic experiences of being human, the experience of being subject to a demand, and the experience of being allowed to have life in spite of guilt'.[41]

According to Gollwitzer, nothing of the Christian message remains in Braun except an 'idea of man', which is realised whenever it is preached and accepted. Both the New Testament authors and the historical Jesus are only the 'initiators' or 'discoverers' of a particular possibility of human experience. Everything that the New Testament teaches about God and Christ serves only as a 'vehicle and aid' in bringing man to the point at which he can experience in his life the paradoxical unity of radical demand and radical grace, of 'I ought' and 'I may'. Who Jesus was, and whether he lived at all, at bottom is a matter of indifference to Braun. Even the word 'God' is used by him only in an 'improper' sense; he could manage perfectly well without it. 'God and Jesus disintegrate into humanism, and at best can have for the New Testament and for preaching only the function of recalling their basic points of reference.'[42]

Gollwitzer makes his negative criticism of Braun's theology against the background of his own positive view that theology may speak not merely 'indirectly' about God, by talking about human existence, but that it must also do so 'directly', by speaking about God himself, about God in his separate and independent reality, in his own initiatives and activity. In his dispute with Herbert Braun, Gollwitzer is ultimately concerned for the meaning of theology as language about God. Here the decisive question is whether and to what extent theology can say 'that God is'. Consequently he entitles the book in which he discusses existential theology, The Existence of God in the Confession of Faith.

Gollwitzer concedes to Braun that one cannot speak of the existence of

God in the same way as in other statements that something 'is'. All statements which speak of God as an existent alongside other existents, and which therefore treat him as an object about which one can make completely neutral affirmations, are theologically illegitimate. The only statements about God which are theologically legitimate are those in which man also professes something concerning himself, that is, which are statements of judgement and in this sense statements of faith. Consequently, the demand for a non-objective language about God cannot simply be rejected. Gollwitzer shares the repudiation by modern atheism of 'a God who exists in himself'. Here he appeals to the well-known statement in Bonhoeffer's inaugural lecture: 'There is no God of whom one can say "there is a God"', and to Rosenstock-Huessy's often repeated admonition that one can really only speak of God in the vocative.

But all the rejections of false language about the existence of God take for granted the view that God 'is'. They merely pose the question how this 'is' is to be understood. Here Gollwitzer answers Braun by working out his own conception of the specific nature of biblical language about God. Braun attempts to distinguish two separate threads in the way in which the Bible speaks of God, and to exclude one of them. Gollwitzer opposes this view by his own assertion that everything the Bible says about God has a 'common horizon', and that this horizon is 'theist': 'The whole Bible is theist, and if words still have any meaning at all, it is theist to the highest degree imaginable . . . here theism is taken seriously; here the word "God" becomes irreplaceable, indispensable.'[43] The basis of the seriousness of biblical theism is that God reveals himself and in a living concrete history makes himself man's partner. Consequently, the biblical texts are testimonies to an *encounter* between God and man; but this encounter assumes that God is the opposite partner in it, who speaks, acts, and wills, who is identical with nothing which is earthly and human, and who, as Barth says, is 'wholly other'. God's part in this encounter is a command and a promise, and this requires of man in his turn appropriate attitudes. Gollwitzer describes them as 'trust, obedience, the acceptance of judgement, the confession of guilt, prayer, petition, thanks and praise'. It is prayer which is the test case: wherever God no longer remains outside man and opposite him, the boundary between prayer and meditation becomes fluid, and the theological significance of prayer becomes confused with the philosophical significance of self-contemplation.

The Bible speaks with the 'most solid', 'most massive' objectivity of

God, but this it does not in order to reduce God to the status of an object; in fact the real purpose of its apparently objectivising language about God is to place him outside the range of all human conceptualisation and categorisation. The biblical authors 'do not conceive of God, but hear him'. But even if one of them at some point genuinely slips into the error of objectivising language about God, in Gollwitzer's opinion one cannot speak as Braun does of the struggle between two different tendencies in the Bible, one towards objectivising and material language about God, and another towards non-objectivising, non-material language about him: 'The authors of the Old and New Testaments do not fit into this pattern; it has been imposed upon them.'[44] The way the biblical authors speak about God has a 'common horizon'.

According to Gollwitzer this common horizon of the biblical proclamation of God requires that theology also affirm that God 'is'. The importance which Gollwitzer attaches to this statement concerning the existence of God is not speculative but soteriological in nature: his ultimate concern is for the salvation of man. 'Grace must not be a hypothesis'[45] – consequently, statements concerning the existence of God are of the utmost importance for faith. Consequently, a theologian must say not merely 'that God is', but also 'who God is as such' and 'what he is in the first instance in himself'. Theological statements of this kind containing the word 'is' – concerning the Trinity, the persons, and the attributes of God – should not be immediately mistrusted as metaphysical speculations. Rather, they indicate the '*terminus a quo* of the divine mercy', that is, that the basis of man's salvation is to be found outside himself in God. Without such 'statements' all propositions concerning the relationship of man to God lose their ontological substance. 'What is evangelical in the gospel' is for Gollwitzer intimately related to the fact that one can and must say that *God is*.

One cannot better characterise the theological disagreement between Gollwitzer and Braun than by the concluding words of their two papers. Whereas Herbert Braun's article 'The Problems of a Theology of the New Testament' closes with the words 'I may' and 'I ought', Gollwitzer's book *The Existence of God in the Confession of Faith* concludes with the cry 'He is!'

Braun was not deterred from his radical existentialist interpretation of the New Testament by Gollwitzer's fierce criticism. In the *Festschrift* for Rudolf Bultmann's eightieth birthday he replied to Gollwitzer, and set out his own theological view even more clearly.[46] As before, he is concerned with where and how we 'observe' God at the present time, where and how God 'happens' today. Challenged by Gollwitzer's emphasis on the existence of God before and outside our own existence, Braun now seeks in his turn to show more clearly how we can experience the existence of God only within our own existential life, and therefore cannot speak of the existence of God in isolation from our own existence. To reduce this to a simplified formula, one might say that Gollwitzer is interested in the *person* of God, that it should exist before and outside the world, whereas Braun is interested in the *place* of God, that it should be in the world. When he speaks of God he remains resolutely 'within the framework of this world', and he regards this framework as 'a closed sphere governed by natural law and history'. He does not look for God as an objective person existing above and outside the world, but in seeking God he begins below with the text of the New Testament; and these texts are human words, and only become the word of God for us when we understand them.

What takes place when he reads the New Testament as an 'understanding pupil', and perceives the 'I ought' and 'I may' in his own existence, and God 'happens' for him in this process, Braun describes in very personal terms, both concisely and convincingly: 'When I read and listen in this way, what may happen is that my conscience registers: I "ought" to do this or that, and I "ought" not to do that or this. I can then say that here I am faced with an "ought" which concerns me absolutely; it is the will of God. If I continue my study of the New Testament texts and remain vigilant, I notice that I cannot respond appropriately to this "ought". And it may then happen, through the text, and of course never entirely without some relation to what my fellow men are doing and saying to me, that to my shame and joy it becomes clear that this "ought" applies to me nevertheless, although I am what I am. And this life of mine succeeds in a way which I cannot comprehend, and which makes me very humble and very thankful. Then I say, God has given me his strength. "I ought" and "I may" happens, and thereby God happens, in my hearing and doing the word.' Braun is not intimidated by Gollwitzer's charge that such an interpretation of the New Testament turns theology into humanism. He replies: 'If, instead of "humanism", we say "love", which draws its life from the "I may", then we are sitting on the very lap of the New Testament.'[47]

Braun is anxious that there should be no anticipatory certainty of the existence of God, of such a kind that I first acknowledge in an act of anticipation that God is, and that he breaks through the closed horizon of nature and history, intervenes in the world and speaks in the Bible.

This means that faith would be dependent upon a 'handicap' in which it had to concede the odds itself. But the certainty of faith is not strengthened by the concession of such a handicap: 'Does an obligation upon me become pressing because I hear that a transcendent God wills it? Does a consolation sustain me because I am assured that it comes from a transcendent God?' Rather, I can only become certain of the existence of God by coming to grips with the biblical text, which I encounter as human words uttered by my fellow men, and experience in them the fact that I am commanded and sustained in the world, so that God manifests himself in my existence. Braun seeks to substantiate this with regard to two of the test questions posed by Gollwitzer: the prayer of petition, and the absolute claim of Jesus.

Braun does not object to the *prayer of petition*,[48] but draws attention to the fact that it is to be found over the whole range of religion outside the Bible, and that there is no specific difference in this respect between the New Testament and non-Christian antiquity. An event like the healing of the sick was expected from the direct intervention of the divinity in this world, whether worked by Christ or Asclepius. But nowadays we think differently about prayer: 'It does not replace the doctor, but accompanies his skill.' There is no need here for the doctor to understand himself as the instrument of God, and if he does, this has no influence on the measures he takes, which are guided by a science which is looked upon as entirely immanent. With regard to the world view it implies our prayer is no longer in accordance with the statements of the New Testament; the God who from the beyond intervenes directly in this world has been replaced by the God who works indirectly in the world through men and things. Moreover, Braun draws attention to the fact that the New Testament teaches that the highest prayer is that in which man submits himself obediently to the will of God. Thus the transition from prayer to meditation has already taken place in the New Testament.

As far as the *absolute claim* of Jesus is concerned,[49] Braun refuses to concede such a claim in advance. For him, the verification once again follows the very opposite course: 'I must listen and let myself be carried along by what I have heard. And then I will see.' As far as he is concerned himself, Braun can only confess: 'The whole extent of the religious world of Judaism and Hellenism has hitherto offered me nothing which binds my conscience more powerfully than the word of the New Testament.' In Braun's opinion, the New Testament witnesses arrived at their certainty in exactly the same way: 'Men heard Jesus, they heard

Paul, and they were called to make a decision in their conscience. If they understood and accepted willingly the substance of what they had heard, they received comfort and exhortation, and said that God was present. Then, in the words of Jesus and of the apostles, they hear the binding decree of "I may" and "I ought", and hear the word of God in the word of man.' If this were not so, faith in Jesus would not come about by hearing the gospel, but by a preliminary recognition of his claim, and the hearer would be asked for a contribution which can only be furnished by an encounter with the word.

One can understand that Braun's radical existentialist interpretation of the New Testament provoked much opposition and indeed indignation, especially in the 'believing Church'. But no one has any right to oppose Braun or even to be indignant at him unless he is prepared to approach with an open mind the whole difficult complex of problems posed at the present time by New Testament exegesis. As an interpreter of the New Testament, Braun faces the problem of total secularisation; he is trying to interpret the New Testament honestly and courageously in the face of this situation, which Dietrich Bonhoeffer characterised as 'the end of religion'.

In the nineteenth century, and even at the beginning of the twentieth century, the foreground of theological debate was occupied not by the question of God, but by the question of Jesus. The existence of God was generally taken for granted; the question was always how this universally accepted God revealed himself, and how far this revelation was associated with a particular event of history, and the particular person of Jesus Christ. A 'universal theism' prevailed, determining human life and thought, especially the attitude to history. All christology was also rooted in this generally accepted world view. Since then a fundamental change has taken place. This universal theism, which in any case was a relic of the world view of the Christian West, has in our own time lost every last trace of its influence. This has deprived Christianity at the same time of the world view which was hitherto automatically assumed as its basis. But how is it then possible to understand the New Testament and think of Jesus as the Christ? This is the question with which the interpretation of the New Testament and of christology is concerned today. It is this question which Herbert Braun asks. But it is more exact to say that he is not really trying to interpret the New Testament, but to rescue it for his unbelieving contemporaries. He would like to show how far the New Testament can still be a meaningful book for them, although its religious presuppositions and world view have disappeared. Consequently he prescribed a radical existentialist cure for christology. Just as the captain of a ship which is in danger at sea throws all the ballast overboard, so that, even if its cargo is lost, it remains floating, Herbert Braun also throws overboard all the ballast of traditional ideas and an outdated world view, so that at least men's faith may be saved.

Braun carries Bultmann's existentialist interpretation of the New Testament to its logical conclusion. Bultmann once defended himself adequately against the critical objection that in his demythologisation he stopped short before God. Braun no longer does this. One may say that in his writings God too is demythologised. Braun's motive here is completely legitimate: he is seeking to show his contemporaries how God 'happens' here and now. In doing so, he looks simultaneously, as a theologian should, towards God and towards man. For the sake of *God*, he tries to avoid everything which will make God a remote and alien thing, an objectivised person, an objective entity. For the sake of *man*, he tries to avoid everything which might prevent man from hearing the gospel as personally addressed to him, and as a call to make a decision in his own life. Both these purposes are related.

But Braun in his turn runs the risk of making God a being dependent upon his own existential actions. For Braun, the rediscovery of the historical Jesus leads not to the correction but to the radicalisation of Rudolf Bultmann's position. For him the significance of Jesus is limited to the assertion that the paradoxical unity of radical demand and radical grace was first understood and proclaimed by Jesus. Expressed in various christological codes, this new understanding of existence forms the basic anthropological phenomenon which runs through the whole New Testament, and accordingly Braun describes anthropology as the constant and christology as the variable in the New Testament. There is a risk here that the Christian message may be reduced to an idea: Jesus remains only as the 'initiating factor' and Christ only as the 'mythological cipher' of a new understanding of existence and the world – and one must ask whether this understanding of existence and the world is in fact as unique and as new as Braun asserts. That the constant of anthropology and the variable of christology have a common constant in the relationship of believers to Christ is overlooked. Ernst Käsemann is right when he says: 'I am not content simply to be informed who initiated faith as the *prima causa* . . . the attribute "Christian" would then simply become a name-plate supplied by tradition which was basically only historical, "historical" referring here to the starting-point in time of the historical development of an idea, even though the preaching of this idea has been carried on unremittingly throughout its historical development.'[50] Braun of course defends himself energetically, as we have seen many times, against the suggestion that the self-understanding in faith found in the New Testament is only an idea; he constantly protests that the paradox of the radical 'I may' and 'I ought' 'takes place', and that wherever it takes place, 'Jesus happens'. But it is simply not clear why the self-understanding found in the New Testament, even if it does 'take place', should take place in a different way from any other self-understanding on the part of man, and why Jesus should be indispensable, once he has given the initial impulse to this self-understanding or has been transformed into it. In the passage just quoted, Käsemann continues: 'I can also hear the call and the challenge to decision in the history of other ideas,' and he goes on, 'and for the great majority of men today, the greatest attraction of preaching is found not in Christianity but in Marxism.'

Braun has nothing further to say about the fact that the New Testament is not anonymous, but appeals to a particular name, and has a concrete history as its content. His sole concern is that the self-understanding found in the New Testament is a right one, and convincing to present-day man. It is ultimately a matter of indifference who originated it and set it in motion. But at this point the existence of God becomes identical with the self-understanding of man in faith, and theology is transformed into anthropology. 'I may' and 'I ought' could in themselves form a sound Pauline and Lutheran doctrine of justification, but by verifying them solely in other men, Braun falsifies the gospel by regarding it from a one-sided ethical point of view.

Braun's attempt to rescue the New Testament is a desperate enterprise, and at the same time a highly interesting experiment. He shows what would be left of the gospel if God were dead and Jesus had not lived, or had been someone completely different from the person in whom we have hitherto believed, along with the biblical witnesses. Braun rescues the gospel at the cost of the gospel. But why does he rescue it at all? Because he himself is a believer!

God's history within history

At the same time as Braun was trying to rescue the New Testament by an ultimate radicalisation of Bultmann's existentialist interpretation, Wolfhart Pannenberg was trying to do so in the very opposite way, by completely reversing Bultmann's position. He seems to have taken it on himself to stand Bultmann on his head and at every point to assert the opposite of what Bultmann says. Instead of the demonstration of God from existence, he puts forward the demonstration of God from history. If Bultmann's intellectual ancestor was Sören Kierkegaard, Pannenberg's was Hegel.

Pannenberg's first article attacking existentialist theology is entitled 'Heilsgeschehen und Geschichte' (1959: 'The Saving Event and History'), and begins with the following sentences: 'History is the furthest horizon of Christian theology. All theological questions and answers have meaning only within the framework of the history which God has in association with mankind, and through mankind, with the whole creation, and which is directed towards a future that is still hidden to the world, but has already been revealed in Jesus Christ.'[51] These sentences contain Pannenberg's theological programme in a nutshell. Pannenberg seeks to present an outline of universal history, in which he describes the self-revelation of God from the creation of the world to its consummation, and displays history in its unity as the history of God. Just as the early Church once called upon Greek philosophy to support its witness to the universality of the Father of Jesus Christ, Pannenberg seeks to demonstrate the universality of the God of the Bible through the unlimited extension of historical study, and in this way to provide an intellectual vindication of Christian faith for our time.

With Pannenberg and his friends, who were of the same age, and who studied at virtually the same time, the 'third generation' has entered the debate. They alleged their ability to master the theological problems over which their fathers and forefathers had apparently reached a deadlock, within a comprehensive theology of history. Theologians and non-theologians pricked up their ears, and a few of them thought that faith and the Church were already saved. For while others were lamenting the 'death of God' and the 'loss of the Centre', withdrawing fearfully into a residual Christian life, here was a group of theologians which was asserting that the whole of history was the history of God, and not only asserting this, but believing they could demonstrate it historically. If this demonstration were to succeed, then it seemed that God would be safe, for Marxist atheism would have been defeated with its own weapons.

Since then, silence has descended once again upon Pannenberg and his circle. Their outline of universal history seems to have shared the fate of all similar conceptions. These appear at the end of every historical

period and organically contain the seeds of the end. The words of
Hegel come to mind: 'When philosophy paints its grey in grey, then it
has a shape of life grown old. By its grey in grey it cannot be rejuvenated, but only understood. The owl of Minerva spreads its wings only
with the dusk.'[52] On the other hand, now that the first uproar over
Pannenberg and his friends has died down and their outline of universal
history has been reduced to its proper proportions, it is possible to make
a more balanced judgement on what was right and good in it.

Pannenberg fights on two fronts: in the first place he attacks the
existentialist theology of Bultmann and Gogarten and their pupils,
while on the other hand he attacks the theology of salvation-history in
its various shadings. He charged both with side-stepping the threat to
Christian faith implied in historical criticism by means of a retreat. The
theology of salvation-history retreats from the advancing tide of
historical criticism into what it hopes is the safe harbour of a 'supra-
history'. But since Christian faith is by its very origin and nature
related to history it is impossible for it to find safety in 'a region free
from storms' – 'on pain of losing its historical basis'.

By contrast, existentialist theology retreats from the threat to faith
posed by the objective and scientific study of history, and falls back
upon the 'significance' of history and the 'historicity' of the individual.
It is this above all that comes under Pannenberg's critical attack. In the
existentialist interpretation of the New Testament he sees a consequence
of the presently prevailing danger of dissolving history in the historicity
of the individual human existence, a danger which to him is part of the
general intellectual background of the modern age. As man, consistent
with the general movement towards an anthropocentric view which
began with the Enlightenment, comes to take the place of God, he
becomes the active agent in history and draws it into his subjectivity.
From henceforth everything that happens in history is considered as
nothing more than an expression of human life. The 'final culmination'
of this radical humanism is the 'emancipation of historicity from
history', which we find in Dilthey, Heidegger, Bultmann, Gogarten
and others. By locating the origin of history in the historicity of man,
they turn the relationship prevailing between the two into its very
opposite. This has the double consequence that history is deprived of
reality and that its unity is broken up into a multitude of individual
human aspects. Pannenberg fears that the next step in this direction will
be the 'atrophy of the historical consciousness' altogether, or at least of
any interest in universal history.

But how can theology escape this dilemma between a 'historicity' understood in purely existential terms, and a 'salvation-history' understood as supra-historical? It cannot for ever be satisfied with the distinction drawn by both between the study of history and Christian faith, between historical method and biblical history. Pannenberg's real theological concern is with this issue: if the revelation of God is contained in an historical event of the past, then there can be no other reliable access to it than that of historical study, and therefore the truth which the historian seeks must also be 'in some way related to divine history'.[53] And therefore while some speak of a 'supra-history', 'archetypal-history' or 'salvation-history', and others of mere 'historicity' and 'historical existence', Pannenberg seeks to proceed from history as it happened in fact and to turn attention back to the priority of historical reality over all human faith and understanding. He wishes to let the 'language of fact' be heard, in order to show history in its unity as God's history.

According to Pannenberg the conception of a unity of history requires two assumptions. The first is that the unity of history has a *transcendent* basis. History consists of purely contingent and temporal events, and one must never detract from this 'contingency' of history, that is, what it is like as a result of being composed of temporal events; but at the same time a universal significance links together the individual contingent events. But if history possesses both contingency and a universal significance, it can only be because of its transcendent basis; it is God who is at work in the contingency of events, and thereby establishes their continuity. Therefore, without the idea of God there is no unity of history, and the historian who tries to think in terms of the unity of history cannot do without the idea of God. Pannenberg boldly draws from this the scandalous conclusion: 'Since only the idea of God makes it possible to think of the unity of history while preserving the distinctive nature of the historical, it is in fact indispensable to the historian.'[54]

The second assumption of the conception of the unity of history is that history has *reached its conclusion*. Only by looking back from the end of history can we see it as a whole in its meaningful unity. Otherwise, the future would still lie before us, and we cannot work out what it will be. But how can we have access to the end of history while we are still in the middle of it? Pannenberg's answer is that in Jesus Christ the consummation of history has already taken place. 'According to the witness of the New Testament, in the life and death of Jesus Christ, the end is not merely beheld in advance, but has taken place in advance. For in him has already occurred, in the resurrection from the dead, what all other men have still to undergo.'[55] This interpretation of the 'life and death' and the 'raising' of Jesus from the dead is based upon the prophetic understanding of history of Israel, and above all upon late Jewish apocalyptic. Late Jewish apocalyptic, which is for the most part ignored by theologians as a conglomeration of muddled and fantastic visions of the future, plays a central role in Pannenberg's outline of universal history. It conceives of a universal history in which God reveals himself progressively in his historical acts, but is only finally manifested at the end as the one and only God, so that the nature of God, although it is the same from eternity to eternity, has a history in time. Only in the light of this prophetic and apocalyptic expectation of the end is the resurrection of Jesus discernible in its significance as the 'anticipated event of the end'. The very fact that the disciples interpreted the event which they experienced at Easter as the 'resurrection from the dead' was possible only within the framework of the apocalyptic expectation of a resurrection of the dead at the end of time.

Only now, in the 'anticipated end' which has taken place in Christ, is history recognisable as a whole. By a kind of process of induction Pannenberg seeks to know the self-revelation of God 'indirectly', 'reflected in his historical acts', and thereby to show the unity of history as God's history. Only now has the connection between the Old Testament and the New become clear. In Pannenberg, the basis of this is the familiar pattern of prophecy and fulfilment. The usual objection to this pattern is that the connections made between prophecy and its fulfilment in the Bible are in many respects artificial and are mostly historically incorrect. Pannenberg gets round this objection of historical criticism by the theological argument that the Old Testament promises were simply fulfilled by God in a different way from that understood by those who first received them. The life and death of Jesus is comprehensible to us only within the framework of the promise contained in the history of God's dealings with Israel; only in this light can Jesus be seen to be the revelation of God. In the life and death of Jesus of Nazareth the God of Israel has made the final demonstration of his deity, and is revealed as the one God for all men. For the interpretation of the Bible this means that what we must look for in the biblical texts is not the possibilities which they contain for existential life, but their historical location in the context of God's history. The link between 'then' and 'now' is to be made in such a way that they are 'included as factors in the unity of an historical structure which comprehends them both'.[56]

The difference between Pannenberg's universal theology of history and the traditional theology of salvation-history is that 'in principle it claims to be historically verifiable'. The historical revelation of God is 'open to everyone who has eyes to see'; the events in which God manifests his deity are 'self-evident' within their historical structure. One can listen to the 'language of facts' in which God has made manifest his deity, without any further prerequisites: no special work of interpretation is needed, no 'additional perfection in man' which 'goes beyond his normal faculty of knowledge', and above all no inspiration by the Holy Spirit. 'One need not have faith in order to find the revelation of God in the history of Israel and of Jesus Christ.' Of course faith is not superfluous, but faith is built on a prerequisite; this prerequisite is the historical knowledge of the facts in which God has revealed his deity, and the historical knowledge of these facts is a matter of reason. The objection that many men, and indeed most men, clearly do not perceive the 'evident and visible truth', is regarded by Pannenberg as invalid. He replies: 'That there are those who are strangely blinded, . . . does not release theology and preaching from the obligation of affirming and demonstrating the simple and in no sense supernatural truth of the revelation of God in the life and death of Jesus Christ. Theology has no cause to accord to the point of view of blindness the attribute and the dignity of a general truth of reason.'[57]

Thus according to Pannenberg, not only the theologian, but also the historian has a duty to recognise God's revelation. If the saving event possesses the nature of revelation by virtue of the event itself as the historian sees it, and not by virtue of what is read into the events by faith, then 'one cannot rule out *on principle* that an historical investigation of this event can and must discover its nature as revelation'. In fact Pannenberg expects the historian to take on the 'burden of proof' that God revealed himself in Jesus of Nazareth. He is perfectly well aware of what he is doing, and adds: 'Although a few decades ago, in the age of the positivist theory of knowledge, to expect this would have been a scandal, in fact it is almost inevitable.'[58]

The resurrection of Jesus itself must also be recognised by the historian as an historical fact, if he possesses reason and has eyes to see. The postulate that all historical events are fundamentally of the same nature, which is usually advanced as the main argument against the historicity of the resurrection of Jesus, is in Pannenberg's view 'remarkably ill-founded'. For, he concludes, if only equivalences are regarded as historically possible, then nothing new can ever happen in history.[59] But here Pannenberg is in conflict not only with historical science but also with the Bible. For everything new that takes place within history, however new it may be, remains inside the boundary of death; but the resurrection of Jesus breaks through the boundary of death. Consequently, its 'novelty' is something completely different, and is not comparable at all with the 'novelties' of history. Thus we must note that Pannenberg takes seriously neither death as the true end of life nor the resurrection as the true beginning of a new life in the biblical sense. Here we enter the criticism of Pannenberg's outline of the universal theology of history.

Pannenberg, as it were, adopts a middle position between Karl Barth on the one hand and Rudolf Bultmann on the other. Whereas Barth begins above, in eternity, in heaven, and Bultmann begins below, in the kerygma and in human existential life, Pannenberg takes his stand on history as it happened. His motive for this is both clear and justified. He is trying to do justice to *revelation as history* – which is the title of the work in which he sets out his view in greatest detail. Consequently, he opposes the theology of salvation-history of the old school, which by retreating into 'supra-history' breaks the link between the revelation of God and true history; and he attacks even more strongly the new kerygmatic theology, which reduces the unique concrete event of the revelation of God to the preaching of the Church and the self-understanding of man. As a corrective against these two dangers, on the right and on the left, there is a relative justification for Pannenberg's theology of history. But he has allowed the pendulum to swing too far to one side for it to play the role of a genuine 'mediating theology'.

What happens in Pannenberg's theology of history is precisely that against which Bultmann gave so stern a warning: he goes behind the kerygma and studies history, in order to find a basis for faith in knowledge. Almost unwillingly, Conzelmann concludes his brief criticism of Pannenberg: 'Whichever way you look at it, what he is trying to do amounts simply to a new attempt to find a basis for faith in historical fact. I just don't understand why people will not admit this. Is it because of a lingering respect for Lessing – or a lingering fear of Bultmann?'[60]

By his 'hypostatisation of historical knowledge' Pannenberg damages both faith and preaching. Preaching becomes a 'vehicle of publication',[61] information about something that *has been*, but about which I have no clear idea what it ought to *be* for me. Faith accordingly becomes 'something on the side', a mere appendage of historical knowledge.

And what does Pannenberg gain by restricting preaching and faith in this way? If only he had at least set out what might have been a great, powerful, or even overpowering vision of history, originating far back in eternity, and extending not to Hegel's professorial chair in Berlin, but to Pannenberg's chair in Mainz! But after all, Pannenberg's outline of universal history only extends as far as the resurrection of Jesus. From that point on he has nothing to say about history except a few sporadic observations. Consequently, what he has to say about the 'taking place in advance' of the end of history remains markedly abstract. Pannenberg makes one think of an architect who draws the blueprint of a house, and hands over the keys and assures you that the building is finished, while the builder has not yet even begun to dig out the foundations. A remark by Gottfried Benn applies to Pannenberg's theology of history: 'Anyone who says history, has nothing to say to the present.' God's 'being' remains hidden in the 'has-beens' of history.[62]

History and existence

The theological question which still remains open today is that of the proper relationship between *history and existence*. This question is implicit in the Christian revelation, which claims that it took place in a particular event of the past, and yet concerns' the present existence of man. Within the school of Bultmann strong disagreements have arisen in recent years, so that one is almost tempted to speak of a 'right-wing' and 'left-wing' Bultmann School. On the right wing, which may not be in liaison with Pannenberg, but does relate to Moltmann, stands Ernst Käsemann, while to the left, in liaison with Camus, stands Herbert Braun. Between them circulate, some more inclined to the right and some more to the left, such theologians as Günther Bornkamm, Gerhard Ebeling, Ernst Fuchs and Hans Conzelmann. Thus at present theology displays a wide spectrum. Walter Künneth is no doubt right to state in his book *Glauben an Jesus?* (Faith in Jesus?): 'The encounter between christology and modern existential life has not yet been concluded'[63] – though one must add at once that Künneth himself has not advanced this encounter.

'The theology of history', or 'the theology of existence' – in simple terms,[64] this is the basic question which dominates the debate in present-day Protestant theology, and which will certainly continue to do so in the immediate future. Thus theology today is once again pre-occupied with its most fundamental issue; the dispute between theologians is not about any subsidiary problem, but is in fact about God; not whether there is a God – this question long ago ceased to be interesting – but where God is, how he happens, in what way we can experience him, and in what way we have to speak of him. Manfred Mezger, in his sermon at the opening of the synod of Hessen-Nassau on 11th November, 1963, went to the heart of the matter: 'Where is God? Where can I see, hear, observe and learn that God happens? That is, what action will make it clear to me what is meant by the word "God"?'[65]

Faced with the problematic nature of all previous language about God, existentialist theology has side-stepped the problem to talk about human existence. Not that it confuses God and man, or actually denies the existence of God, but it seeks to prove the existence of God in the existence of man, before making any attempt to describe what he has done or to define what he is. This has perhaps been done most unambiguously by Braun's colleague in the theological faculty at Mainz, Manfred Mezger: 'Anyone speaking of God, in this world of ours, without a happening, without an exchange between one man and another, says nothing at all, at best a mere word. This word can no longer be buoyed up by the accent of pathos or by an appeal to sacred emotions . . . "You keep saying 'God'. But where can I meet him, so that I can understand what you mean?"' For Mezger it is only possible to speak of God 'in the movement of human behaviour'. What this signifies, he has explained in a kind of 'children's catechism' for theologians: 'If someone asks, "Why do you behave in this way?", the answer is, "Because of him who compels me to do so." "How does he do this?" "He tells me by word and preaching what I ought to do and may do." "But what does he say?" "He tells me who I am and where my way leads to." "Where does it lead?" "To my neighbour." He, my neighbour, provides the evidence for my attitude; he is the witness to the fact that I do not understand myself on the basis of my own self, but on the basis of the call which comes to me through this person, which commands me, gives to me and, as the case may be, delights, angers or denies me. But it either happens in this way or nothing happens at all – only words.'[66]

The verification of God is in no way different from that of any other kind of truth in the world: it has to convince me with overwhelming force, so that I have literally no choice left. First of all the truth is demonstrated in my existential life, and only then, as it were as an automatic consequence, is it defined or described in words. In his great plea on behalf of existentialist theology before the Lutheran faculty in Erlangen, Mezger says: 'No title confirms the truth, but truth always confirms its title. That is, the "name" which truth bears is a matter of complete indifference to me, so long as it is really true. Why I believe and what I believe is not dependent on the why and what written in the book of truth. What does "the book of truth" mean? First of all I want to hear, and after that we will see whether it is true. I call the book a "book of truth", when the word has already brought about faith and trust in me. Thus what I believe or why I believe is not that, or because, someone is called "Christ". In the first instance, Christ is nothing more than a word . . . but if his word is manifested to me as an overwhelming truth, which I simply cannot ignore, then I call him "my Lord".' Mezger's plea on behalf of existentialist theology culminates in the statement: 'Never and nowhere does salvation come from the historical, but only from the concrete.'[67]

But the question arises whether there is not in fact a considerable risk of 'the concrete' virtually disappearing in existentialist theology, both with regard to the historical process and also in existential life. Existentialist theology is concerned with 'unobjectivity' and 'personality'; it seeks to be wholly a 'theology of the word'. But the word presupposes events and things. Existentialist theology speaks of the significance of the cross, but forgets that someone had first to hang on the wood of the cross before it was possible to speak of its significance. And existentialist theology speaks of the historicity of human existence, but forgets that man must first have had a history before one can speak of his historicity. The consequence is that the very theology which arose in the name of the reality of the modern world has largely lost sight of the reality of the world and abandoned it to its own devices.

This leads to the question whether 'existentialism' in theology is not itself the expression and culmination of a development, which, beginning with the modern age and constantly growing, has today achieved the reverse of what it intended, or, in Hegelian terms, 'cancelled itself out'. Driven on as he is by the anxiety that nothingness may fall upon being and swallow it up, man's questions in the modern age have been concentrated ever more radically upon his own existential life: What is man? Who am I myself? In this way he draws everything into his subjectivity. This has unquestionably led to the concentration of all the phenomena of life upon the mathematical point of human existence, and the complex living relations between them as it were condense and are separated out; the 'quintessence' of human existence is distilled

from it. But at the same time this concentration upon human existence
has brought a loss of 'reality', by drawing us away from what has bodily
form, a concrete place in history and a living reality – for 'abstract'
signifies 'drawn away'. A process 'of abstraction', 'a movement "from
corporeality towards the cipher"', has taken place.[68] Names, images
and melodies have disappeared, and have been replaced by signs,
ciphers, and rhythms. It is as though the historical destiny of Protestantism is being fulfilled in our own time – especially with regard to the
displacement of the image by the word. Here again we may recall the
words of Gottfried Benn:

> Ob Rosen, ob Schnee, ob Meere,
> was alles erblühte, verblich,
> es gibt nur zwei Dinge: die Leere
> und das gezeichnete Ich.

> Though roses, the snow, the seas
> and all that blooms, should fade,
> there are only two things: the emptiness
> and the 'I' that is marked out.

'The emptiness and the "I" that is marked out' – in its own way,
Protestant theology also takes part in this 'taking away of reality' and
'solipsism'. This is common ground to a surprising extent for three
entities as apparently different as pietism, liberal theology and existentialist theology. Pietism is concerned with the conversion of the
individual; liberal theology, such as that of Harnack, with God and the
soul, the soul and its God; and existentialist theology, for instance in
Bultmann, with the essentiality of existential life, or, in the case of
Herbert Braun, with the paradox of 'I may' and 'I ought'. What all
three share is the danger of being entangled in subjectivity, with the
consequent risk of a loss of reality. This danger is of course mitigated by
the fact that each has its 'objective' aspect: in pietism, the 'mighty acts of
God', in liberal theology, the results of critical historical study, and in
existentialist theology the kerygma, or alternatively the persons with
whose existential life it is concerned. But this objective aspect is in no
case sufficiently powerful to banish effectively the danger of becoming
entangled in subjectivity and the risk of a loss of reality.

The concern of Protestant theology in the future must be to bring
the reality of the world back into the reality of faith. In this respect Paul
Tillich has already taken a considerable step forward into the future.

CHAPTER NINE

THE REALITY OF GOD
IN THE REALITY OF THE WORLD

The third way

Every consideration of the present task of theology, of the ineffective-
ness of Christian preaching and the necessity of renewing it, is faced
ultimately, in our times, with the same question: How is the reality
manifested by revelation related to the reality which we know and
experience? How is faith related to thought, prayer to work, religion to
culture, in short, how is God related to the world? How can we experience and bear witness to the reality of God in the reality of the
world in such a way that it has the appearance, not of an alien law imposed upon us from outside or from above, but rather of something
which concerns us directly and unconditionally and happens in the
midst of us? The decisive question for theology and the Church today
is how faith becomes *real* and how the message of faith can be *credibly*
conveyed to men. Both questions are identical: the question of the
credibility of Christian faith is that of its reality. And this is the very
question which Paul Tillich has asked, and to which his whole life's
work was devoted.

When Paul Tillich, as the first non-semitic German university teacher
to be dismissed, emigrated to America in 1933, German Protestantism
lost sight of him for a long time. As a result, he largely remained unknown to the younger generation. It is significant of Tillich's isolation
from Protestant theology in Germany that his works and writings
since the war have had to be translated from English into German. But
it did not take long for Tillich's influence to take hold again. And at
present it appears as if the rediscovery of Tillich, particularly by the
younger generation, is likely to be one of the most important theological
events of the post-war period in Germany.

Paul Johannes Tillich was born in 1886. In the same year Leopold von
Ranke died, and Karl Barth, Oskar Kokoschka and Gottfried Benn were
born. Niels Bohr was born the year before, Karl Jaspers and Walter
Gropius were born three years earlier, and Béla Bartók five years

earlier. All these names stand as symbols – each of them signifying an end and a beginning. Together they represent the transition, or rather the breach, between two eras which is the hallmark of our age. And it is this feeling of belonging 'to a generation between two periods of history', and therefore of living in a breach or transition of world-wide proportions, which has determined Tillich's thought and writings throughout his life: 'We are in the midst of a world revolution affecting every section of human existence, forcing upon us a new interpretation of life and the world' – 'The only thing we can hope to be is a bridge between the ages.'[1]

This sense of coming at the end of the old and the beginning of the new links Paul Tillich with Karl Barth, Emil Brunner, Karl Jaspers and many others of his generation. They share the consciousness of the beginning of the 'twentieth century'. As far as Europe is concerned, Tillich dates the beginning of the twentieth century from August 1914, the outbreak of the First World War, while for America he places it half a generation later in November 1929, at the outset of the great economic crisis; but for the whole of humanity he sees the two world wars as forming 'the radical transformation of one historical era into another'. Thus the twentieth century is presented in the first instance as the *period of the world wars*. The world wars are a part of the 'world revolution' which involves every sphere of human life in every part of the earth. These 'storms of our times' are not fortuitous events caused by a handful of evil men, but are a 'structural necessity', brought about by the structures and tendencies of the bourgeois society of the nineteenth and twentieth centuries.[2]

What Tillich experienced during the First World War (he was, for four years, an army chaplain on the Western front) was the collapse of the bourgeois civilisation and way of life of the nineteenth century, and with it that of idealist philosophy and liberal theology: 'The experience of those four years of war revealed to me and to my entire generation an abyss in human existence that could not be ignored.' Tillich even believes he can affix an exact date to this experience. He recalls a night before the battle of Verdun when he wandered about during the bombardment among the dying and finally fell asleep exhausted among the dead. 'When I awoke, I said to myself, "This is the end of the idealistic side of my thought!" In that hour I realised that idealism had been destroyed.'[3]

The idealist endeavour of the nineteenth century was replaced in the twentieth century by existential despair and anxiety, and the consciousness of constant progress by a feeling of a permanent crisis. This is the picture which Tillich gives of 'twentieth-century man': 'Not only has he a series of immense catastrophes behind him, but he continues to live in a situation pregnant with possible catastrophes. He speaks not of progress but of crisis . . . he has experienced the nothingness which rages around all being like a threatening ocean. He has experienced the destiny which brings sudden incalculable assaults on everything which seems secure, upon his life and the life of nations. He has experienced death in the dying of countless millions for whom nature had promised a fuller life, and he has experienced death as an hourly threat to his own being. He has experienced guilt of a proportion which the human imagination cannot conceive and he has experienced the fact that he himself cannot escape guilt, even if he is only guilty through his silence. . . . He has learned to doubt, not only the judgement of others, but even what was most certain in his own eyes. No fortress of belief has remained into which elements of doubt have not penetrated. And if it occurs to him to ask what the meaning of his being is, then an abyss opens to him into which only the most courageous dares to gaze: the abyss of meaninglessness.'[4]

This has provided Tillich with the theme which has occupied his thought throughout his life. As the result of a personal and intensive encounter with history during two world wars, history became the 'central problem' of his theology and philosophy, not merely in the narrow sense of critical historical research, but in the wider sense of an *inquiry into the meaning and nature of all historical reality*: 'The situation demanded interpretation as well as action.'[5]

In spite of the dominant role played in his work by ontology, the doctrine of being, Tillich's world view, his outlook upon human nature and life, is wholly and entirely historical. His ontology is not static, as is usually the case, but is *existential and dynamic*. Everything that is seeks to attain to existence, to take its place in time and destiny. Thus Tillich consciously remains within the tradition of biblical religion. Truth is not to be found, as in Plato, as an eternal and immutable pattern of ideas above us, but is involved in time. Idea and existence cannot be separated. Like existence, truth is also subject to destiny; for the truth can only be recognised by someone who is himself subject to destiny. 'The logos is to be taken up into the kairos . . . truth into the fate of existence. . . . There is no point at which either logos or kairos alone is to be found.' Consequently, all knowledge of the truth has the character of history and decision; every act of knowledge is an historical act. Since the truth

comes about in history, it never exists once and for all, it is never ultimate, never final, never universal, but always remains open, always
reaches beyond itself towards a new concrete realisation, always
demands a new venture under the commandment and the promise of the
present historical moment. This is the only way in which any truth is
revealed to man, who is a finite, historically conditioned and earth-
bound being.[6]

This is true not only of philosophy, but also of theology. The truth of
theology is also bound up with destiny, and even Christian truth is
always valid only as historical truth. Thus from the very first there is a
decisive difference between Tillich and Barth in the foundation of their
concept of truth. Whereas Karl Barth looks up into the heights of
heaven and contemplates the eternal interplay of the Trinity, Paul
Tillich looks down into the depths of reality and is captivated by the
constant flux of history. Whereas Barth has always endeavoured
throughout his life to preserve the identity, the purity and the immut-
ability of the Christian gospel, Tillich's efforts have from the first been
aimed at its flexibility, not in order to alter this gospel, but in order to
reinterpret it and translate it into the changed situation of our time and
the world.

Tillich is impelled to ceaseless, penetrating thought in the first place
by *eros*, the love for truth which is striving to realise itself in a new form
in our own age, and secondly by *agape*, love for man, especially for
those to whom Christian preaching no longer has anything to say;
those who are indeed autonomous, but who have become insecure in
their world; who have lost the dimension of death and therefore of the
absolute and the religious; who go on producing simply because production is possible, and no longer ask the meaning of it; who possess
mere traces of a world view or even none at all; who no longer have
any courage to be and who are at the point of despair, unless they subject themselves once again to an alien authority or alternatively become
completely indifferent to the question of truth. Tillich has a special love
for 'modern' man in this sense, and seeks to reach him with what he has
to say. He would like to restore to him the courage to believe, by
convincing him of the power of faith that lies hidden within himself, in
order to reconcile him with God, with himself and the world. Consequently, for Tillich 'healing' is the word which expresses for our own
time the most important aspect of Christian redemption.

The reproach which constantly recurs in Tillich's books, articles and
lectures is that in its day-to-day preaching the Church does not do this

with sufficient selflessness, courage and truthfulness, but merely recites old concepts and formulas in the self-satisfied possession of its inherited truth, and so forces present-day men to transport themselves back into the sixteenth century or the years A.D. 1–30: 'The ecclesiastical, and to a great extent the biblical, terminology is removed from the reality of our historical situation. If it is used, nevertheless, with that attitude of priestly arrogance which repeats the biblical word and leaves it to the listeners to be grasped by it or not, it certainly ceases to be "the Word of God" and is rightly ignored by Protestant people. And the minister who feels himself to be a martyr of "divine frustration" – and even becomes ecstatic about this frustration – is guilty of a lack of contemporaneity.'[7]

The consequence is that the average sermon no longer reaches the men of today. Because the word which the Church has received is distorted in the mouths of the preachers, it meets a stubborn resistance in the ears of those who hear it. It is listened to – 'but it has lost its voice'. Men no longer understood the words which used once to be spoken in such a way that they spoke to them in their own situation and from the depths of their own situation. Even the very central themes of the Bible and the Church's tradition – God, Christ, the Church and revelation – have been called into question among both theologians and non-theologians. Consequently, one cannot preach them directly to present-day men. Where the Church nevertheless seeks to do this, it fails to take seriously the situation of contemporary men, and must be prepared to be rejected by those among them who are most serious and honest. This rejection of the Church's preaching can become so passionate that it calls for a word of God *against* what the Church, basing itself on the Bible, puts forward as the word of God. As long as the official representatives of the Church's preaching refuse to take cognizance of this situation, Tillich regards their work as 'entirely hopeless'.[8]

Tillich sees the value of every theology as determined by what it can do for preaching. Consequently, the problem of *language* has been very important for him throughout his life. In a lecture he once proposed as a motto: 'You must first save concepts before you can save souls.'[9] In every case the decisive question must be whether a traditional religious concept still has anything to communicate to us or not: in the case of every word and concept, God and Christ, the Spirit and the Church, sin and forgiveness, faith, love and hope, eternal life and the kingdom of God, we must ask ourselves whether this touches the very depths of our being, and whether it still has anything to say to us which concerns us absolutely, and then we can decide whether we wish to abandon it or restore it to life. Faced with the fact that traditional Christian words and concepts have been virtually emptied of meaning, Tillich once put forward the suggestion that the Church might impose a thirty-year silence on all its archetypal words. But as he says himself, this suggestion was meant symbolically rather than literally. In practice, theology can do nothing but interpret the traditional biblical words and concepts in every case as intelligibly as possible, and where this is no longer possible, to replace them by others. To this end it must develop a new terminology and create for itself a new conceptual tool, not in order to replace the archetypal language of the Bible and liturgy by a contemporary language – such attempts have always been lamentable failures – but in order to recapture it and make its ancient words and symbols intelligible once again for the contemporary situation.[10]

In his sermons (*The Shaking of the Foundations, The New Being, The Eternal Now*) Paul Tillich has put this thought to the test, pointing towards a future form of Christian expression.

With regard to Tillich's efforts to find a new theological language and conceptual instrument, one may consider his forced emigration to the United States in 1933 almost as a sign of divine providence. For it obliged one who was firmly rooted in the tradition of Western thought and language, and in particular that of Germany, to cast what he had originally thought and said in a highly complex manner into a completely different shape, the mould of a foreign language, and so to think and utter it again in a new, clearer and simpler form. Tillich himself considered his emigration in this way. Looking back upon it, he writes: 'The change of country and continent, the catastrophe of a world in which I had worked and thought for forty-seven years, the loss of the fairly mastered tool of my own language, the new experiences in a civilisation previously unknown to me, resulted in changes, first, of the expression and then, to a certain degree, of the content of my thinking. . . . The spirit of the English language has demanded the clarification of many ambiguities of my thought which were covered by the mystical vagueness of the classic philosophical German; the interdependence of theory and practice in Anglo-Saxon culture, religious as well as secular, has freed me from the fascination of that kind of abstract idealism which enjoys the system for the system's sake.'[11]

In a conversation with his friend Fedor Stepun, Tillich once expressed beguilingly what was behind his constant endeavour to find a new theological language and conceptual structure. 'It has been said of the

English,' said Stepun, 'that when they say "God" they mean "cotton".
One might assert of you, Mr. Tillich, that when you say "cotton" you
mean "God". Can you not simply say God instead?' Tillich replied, 'As
long as men no longer understand the word God I will say "cotton",
always assuming that they understand that I am intending to say something to them about God.'[12]

Tillich is concerned 'to understand and to formulate anew the overwhelming power of the word "God"' – in the first place with regard to
men, who no longer are able to associate anything with the name
'God', and in the second place with regard to God, so that his name
should not be misused. One might say that Tillich's whole theology is
concentrated upon the first and the second commandments. It contends
for the deity of God and against the misuse of his name. Consequently,
when Tillich speaks of God, he prefers to speak of 'being-itself', of the
'power of being', of the 'ground and meaning of being', or of the
'depth', of the 'absolute', and of the 'unconditional': 'Not that these
concepts are substitutes, but they form a key with which to open to
oneself and to others the closed door which leads to the sanctissimum of
the name "God", whereafter one can throw the key away.'[13]

Of course there are many who no longer recognise that Tillich
intends to speak to them of God. They consider that the way in which
he expresses himself so obscures and defaces the Christian message that
they no longer hear it as such. Tillich defends himself energetically
against insinuations and criticisms of this kind: 'I cannot accept criticism as valuable which merely insinuates that I have surrendered the
substance of the Christian message because I have used a terminology
which consciously deviates from the biblical or ecclesiastical language.
Without such deviation, I would not have deemed it worthwhile to
develop a theological system for our period.'[14]

Tillich does not intend, for misconceived missionary purposes, to
make the Christian message more comfortable for contemporary
secularised man by replacing a handful of concepts and words, and
selling the gospel at a cut price. Rather, he considers that it is the nature
of truth which is at issue, more so even than the salvation of men. Since
truth always comes about within time, and the logos is never to be
found without a corresponding kairos, theology is constantly in tension
between two extremes: between the eternal truth of its object on the
one hand, and on the other the contemporary situation at any given
time. A true theology must always fulfil two basic conditions: it must
give expression to the truth of the Christian message, and this expression

must be appropriate to its contemporary situation. Tillich includes in the 'situation' the whole creative interpretation of human existence in a particular period, the sum of the scientific, artistic, economic, political, social, and moral forms in which the self-understanding of the generation is expressed.[15]

Thus Tillich describes the task of theology as a *work of mediation*: 'Mediation between the eternal criterion of truth as it is manifest in the picture of Jesus as the Christ, and the changing experiences of individuals and groups, their varying questions and their categories of perceiving reality. If the mediating task of theology is rejected, theology itself is rejected; for the term "theo-logy" implies, as such, a mediation, namely, between the mystery, which is *theos*, and the understanding, which is *logos*.'[16]

Thus Tillich makes respectable once again the term 'theology of mediation', which since Barth's firm 'No!' against any mediating 'and' has become almost a term of opprobrium; and he consciously applies it to himself.[17] All his thinking, writing and speaking are directed first and foremost towards mediation, reconciliation, reunion and healing – and therefore its purpose is not analysis but synthesis, not tearing down but building up, not polemic but apologetic, not reaching the individual but the whole, and always to fit the isolated phenomenon, with the aid of conceptual thought, into a systematic and ordered structure. Thus Tillich is one of the great speculative minds who by this very fact are the great reconcilers, the system builders, for whom all things must be made to serve their intellectual construction and for whom even what is negative lives only from the positive which it denies.

Whereas the two other great figures of twentieth-century Protestant theology, Karl Barth and Rudolf Bultmann, set out to draw a precise boundary, Tillich seeks to bring back what theological fashion has strictly separated for several decades. Schleiermacher once asked the anxious question: 'Are the knots of history to be untied in such a way that Christianity walks with barbarism and science with unbelief?'[18] Unfortunately, the knots of history have been untied in the very way which Schleiermacher feared: science has very largely walked with unbelief, while Christianity has been associated with barbarism.

Dialectic theology forced God and the world so far apart, in an unbridgeable separation, that it was scarcely possible to find a single point of contact between them; liberal theology on the other hand sought an impermissible synthesis between God and the world, and threatened to efface completely the boundary between the two. Tillich's position lies midway between these two solutions: 'My theology can be understood as an attempt to overcome the conflict between these two types of theology. It intends to show that the alternative expressed in those names is not valid.'[19] Rejecting what is false in them and accepting what is right, Tillich follows a new way, or as he calls it himself, a 'third way'.

Synthesis is the aim of this philosophical theology: 'My own way has been the way of synthesis. In it I have followed classical German theology from Kant to Hegel, and it has remained the driving force of all my theological works.' As far as its content is concerned, the way of synthesis for Tillich is that of constantly relating Christianity and civilisation to one another: 'In spite of the fact that during most of my adult life I have been a teacher of Systematic Theology, the problem of religion and culture has always been in the centre of my interest. Most of my writings – including the two volumes of *Systematic Theology* – try to define the way in which Christianity is related to secular culture.'[20] In fact Tillich makes the whole of reality the theme of his theological inquiry. There is nothing which he cannot make the object of theology. Philosophy, psychology, psychotherapy and educational theory, politics, economics, sociology and technology, liturgy, law, art and town planning are all drawn upon by him; he binds the whole fullness of reality into the ordered structure of a comprehensive system. But he is not interested merely in making a general survey of reality as it has always been and always will be, but in interpreting a changed reality through a new confrontation between it and Christian faith.

Here Tillich makes clear the position from which he speaks – his thought takes place *on the boundary*: 'The boundary is the best place for acquiring knowledge.' Thus it was appropriate for Tillich to give the short autobiographical sketch with which he introduced himself to his new American readers and hearers in 1936 this same title: *On the Boundary* – though for Tillich the concept of the 'boundary' always implies more of a link than a separation. In the preface to this outline of his life he writes: 'When I was asked to give an account of the way my ideas have developed from my life, I thought that the concept of the boundary might be the fitting symbol for the whole of my personal and intellectual development. At almost every point, I have had to stand between alternative possibilities of existence, to be completely at home in neither and to take no definitive stand against either.'[21]

Tillich's professional career corresponds to his intellectual position on the borderline. His father was a pastor in the Neumark. He studied

304 THE QUESTION OF GOD

theology and philosophy in Berlin, Tübingen and Halle, completed his theological degree in 1909, took the degree of Doctor of Philosophy in 1910, and of Licentiate in Theology in 1912. He took part in the First World War as an army chaplain and after the end of the war was accepted by the university as a *Privatdozent* (unsalaried lecturer) in theology at Berlin. In 1924 he became professor extraordinary in systematic theology and the philosophy of religion in Marburg, in 1925 professor of religious studies at the Institute for Technology at Dresden, and at the same time honorary professor of theology in Leipzig. In 1929 he succeeded Max Scheler in the chair of philosophy and sociology at Frankfurt am Main. As early as 1933 he was suspended from his post because he belonged to the 'Religious Socialists', and because of his intervention on behalf of Jewish students against the terrorisation carried out by the Nazi Student Federation. Through the mediation of Reinhold Niebuhr, he became a professor at Union Theological Seminary in New York; in addition he lectured in philosophy at Columbia University. After his retirement in 1955, Harvard University bestowed upon him the highest academic honour in the United States, granted only to a very few: he was appointed 'University Professor of Harvard', with the function of lecturing whenever and on whatever he wished. During the final years of his life he taught at the University of Chicago and as a guest lecturer in Europe. He had planned the beginning of a new course at the New School of Social Research in New York for the end of February 1966; his first lecture was to have been on 'The Religious Dimension of Political Ideas'. His death on 22nd October, 1965, intervened.

Thus he constantly alternated between different faculties, different countries, the Old World and the New; but the essence of his teaching never varied. As a theologian Tillich tried to remain a philosopher and as a philosopher to remain a theologian: 'Philosophical theology is the unusual name of the chair I represent. It is a name that suits me better than any other, since the boundary line between philosophy and theology is the centre of my thought and world' – 'Against Pascal I say: The God of Abraham, Isaac and Jacob and the God of the philosophers is the same God.'[22]

Thus throughout his life Tillich walked on the boundary – not merely on the boundary between theology and philosophy, but also on the boundary between theology and all other spheres of life – but he was never a renegade, neither to one side nor to the other. In his own person he united the existential life of faith and that of thought, and sustained

the tension between the two. He was simply what is now such a rarity –
a *devout thinker*. Because his position always remained on the boundary,
he never formed a theological school, in contrast, for example, to
Karl Barth or Rudolf Bultmann. Tillich was not the leader of a
school, but a great teacher. He comforted many men with his ideas;
he was a pastor of souls through his thought. We find this union of
faith and thought, of theology and philosophy, of devoutness and
doctrine, in many respects astonishing, alien and almost suspicious. But
in essence Tillich was only returning to a great tradition of the West
which for centuries had been obsolete, forgotten or even consciously
rejected.

The method of correlation

Anyone who sets out to describe Tillich's theological thought finds
himself in an apparent dilemma: whether to begin 'outside', on the edge
of his thought, with the anxiety and questioning of man, with that
which concerns us unconditionally, with religion and philosophy; or
whether to begin 'within', in the centre, with the revelation of the
universal logos in the concrete person of Jesus as the Christ. But anyone
who sees here a dilemma has misunderstood Tillich's main theological
purpose. 'Mediation', 'reconciliation', 'synthesis', 'the third way' – all
point towards the 'connection' between different aspects. And this is
also true of the method of Tillich's philosophical theology. He explicitly describes it as the *method of correlation*. Regardless of whether it
began 'outside' or 'inside', both aspects would always have to be related
to each other.

Tillich's method of correlation rests upon the link between God and
man. The link between God and man is formed by the mutual dependence of 'God for us' and 'We for God'. God, of course, in his eternal
concealment is independent of man, but in his self-revelation he comes
to him in a free, living and mutual relationship between one person and
another. The divine-human encounter 'means something real for both
sides': God acts, man reacts, God in his turn reacts, and so forth. In this
way, God and man affect each other in a living relationship. This is true
both with regard to religious experience and also with regard to theological knowledge.[23]

The way in which God and man affect each other is found first of all
in *religious experience*.[24] By contrast to Barth, Tillich lays down no
absolute opposition between revelation and religion; for him the

history of religion is not a 'witches' sabbath of ghostly fantasies, idolatry, and superstition'. Instead, and to the great surprise of most German theologians, though less to that of American theologians, Tillich uses the word 'religion' in an entirely positive sense. Religion is 'the name for the reception of revelation'. The revelation of God always contains an objective and a subjective element, which are closely dependent on each other and ought not to be separated. The objective element consists in God's revealing of himself, and the subjective element in man's receiving this revelation. The one does not exist without the other. If nothing objective takes place, nothing is revealed; if no one receives what has taken place, nothing is revealed; revelation is given in a vacuum and ceases to be revelation. Only where the objective event and subjective reception are united can one speak of revelation.

Tillich calls the subjective side of revelation, the act of reception, 'religion'. Without religion there is no revelation. Wherever the divine is revealed, it is revealed 'in the flesh', that is, in a concrete physical and historical reality, in a particular intellectual and social situation. Whoever receives divine revelation receives it with particular assumptions and in particular circumstances, and this means 'in terms of his religion'; and anyone who gives an account of divine revelation is at the same time giving an account of his own religion. Thus there is no pure revelation, but revelation is always and from the very first coloured in a particular way by religion, which is its 'vessel'.

Although it is true that the Christian revelation is not identical with the general history of religion, it forms part of it. Tillich brings back the doctrine of the Greek Church Fathers concerning the logos, which had already sown its seed in every direction – before and apart from Christ – and had aroused questions and given answers. These questions are admittedly vague and the answers anticipatory – but the Christian revelation could not have been understood and accepted by men if there had not been a preparation for it in human religion and culture. It would otherwise not have spoken to men, but would have remained an alien entity in human history. Revelation would not have been possible even for God, if man had not been able to receive it. Consequently it is justifiable to speak of 'biblical religion'. The Bible is a document both of the self-revelation of God and also of the way in which men received his revelation. It is not a question of some of its words and statements belonging to 'revelation' and others to 'religion'; rather that revelation and the acceptance of revelation are inseparably linked in the same passage: 'Every passage in the Old Testament is both revelation and religion.' The same is true of the revelation of Christ in the narrower sense of the word. There are two aspects to the event on which Christianity is based: the fact of Jesus of Nazareth and the acceptance of this fact by those who acknowledged him as the Christ. Christianity was not born at the moment when the man Jesus of Nazareth was born, but when one of his disciples confessed with regard to him: 'You are the Christ' (Mt. 16:16), and it will last only as long as there are men who repeat this confession. Thus from the point of view of religious experience, the relationship between God and man is a correlation.

From the point of view of *knowledge*, the relationship between God and man is also one of correlation. It is realised in the mutual relationship between question and answer. Here we come to Tillich's real 'method of correlation'. He defines it as follows: 'Symbolically speaking, God answers man's questions and under the impact of God's answers man asks them. Theology formulates the questions implied in human existence, and theology formulates the answers implied in divine self-manifestation under the guidance of the questions implied in human existence . . . it makes an analysis of the human situation out of which the existential questions arise, and it demonstrates that the symbols used in the Christian message are the answers to these questions.'[25] Thus the work of theology is like an ellipse with two foci: one focus represents the existential question, and the other the theological answer.

The answers which Christian revelation gives are only meaningful when they are correlated with the questions which concern the whole of human existence: 'Only those who have experienced the shock of transitoriness . . . the threat of non-being, can understand what the notion of God means. Only those who have experienced the tragic ambiguities of our historical existence and have totally questioned the meaning of existence can understand what the symbol of the kingdom of God means.'[26] Only by asking questions in which *we ourselves* are at issue can we receive revelation as the answer.

To be human signifies a ceaseless process of question and answer: man poses his questions and receives the answers which are given to him, and under the influence of these answers he asks his questions once again. The basic questions of human existence are age-old. They were formulated very early in the history of mankind – this is shown by every analysis of mythological material. It is a very remarkable fact that they are the same questions which arise in the early childhood of every human being. I recall a conversation with Paul Tillich during his last session as a guest lecturer in Hamburg in the summer of 1961. We were sitting in the top storey of a block of flats on the edge of the city, and discussing how man was changing and how the preaching of the Church had to change in consequence, and whether the end of religion might not have come in our time. Then Paul Tillich, after a moment of silent thought, said: 'Just think of the people who are asleep beneath us in this building – what are the questions which preoccupy them? They are still the same questions which preoccupied men two thousand and more years ago: questions of guilt, suffering, love, justice in the world, the meaning of life, and death.'

The identification of the questions of existence is a philosophical task, even when it is undertaken by theologians, and in this analysis of human existence the theologian makes use of the whole of the material which man's self-interpretation has placed at his disposal in every branch of culture: philosophy, poetry, literature, psychotherapy, sociology, etc. Today, existentialism is of particular use to him.

Tillich regards *existentialism* as 'a natural ally of Christianity'.[27] Just as Kant once said that mathematics is the good luck of human reason, so Tillich would say that existentialism is the 'good luck of Christian theology'. It has brought to light the true situation of man both in the modern period and in history as a whole. Thus at the same time it has helped – in spite of its largely atheistic character – 'to rediscover the classical Christian interpretation of human existence'. It expresses in conceptual terms what myth once stated in religious form about the human situation, and so it can help religious myths and symbols, in which an answer is given to the question of the human situation, to be understood anew in our own time. Tillich believes that 'theological attempts to do this would not have had the same effect'.

The theologian must employ the aid not only of the philosophers who study existence from the theoretical point of view, but also of those who inquire into it in practice, the minister, the teacher, the psychoanalyst and the psychological counsellor. In the light of the material they place at his disposal, he has to reinterpret traditional religious symbols and theological concepts. For example, words like 'sin' and 'judgement' have lost none of their inner truth in our own time, but they are certainly not able to express for our own time the truth which is contained in them. Consequently, they must be filled with new meaning by the insights into human nature which existentialism, inclusive of psychology, provides. We must 'read the Bible with eyes opened by existentialist analysis'. Existentialism poses in a new and radical way the questions to which theology gives the answers for faith.

Existential questions and theological answers are at the same time both *dependent* on and *independent* of each other.[28] They are *independent* of each other: the question contained in human existence may not be derived from the answer of revelation, for then it would no longer be a genuine question. On the other hand, the theological answer cannot be derived from the existential question. The question does not contain the answer. The answer must come from the event of revelation, and must be given to the human situation from beyond human existence. Man is the question, but he is not the answer; God is only revealed by God.

But at the same time the existential question and the theological answer are *dependent* upon each other: the questions are already formed by the theological system within which they arise, and are therefore already directed towards the answer. The theologian stands within the 'theological circle'; when he approaches the questions of human existence, he has already heard the Christian gospel. But on the other hand, the existential questions also influence the theological answers. The form of the answers depends upon the structure of the questions which they are intended to answer. The theologian may not hurl Christian answers at man's head like foreign bodies from another world, but must adapt their form to the questions previously posed, if they are to be a true answer and not merely a meaningless combination of words. For we cannot understand any answer which is not an answer to a question already asked, and this is also true of the answer of divine revelation.

In concrete terms, the process of correlation, the mutual adaptation of question and answer, is seen by Tillich as follows: 'If the notion of God appears in systematic theology in correlation with the threat of non-being which is implied in existence, God must be called the infinite power of being which resists the threat of non-being. In classical theology this is being-itself. If anxiety is defined as the awareness of being finite, God must be called the infinite ground of courage. In classical theology this is universal providence. If the notion of the Kingdom of God appears in correlation with the riddle of our historical existence, it must be called the meaning, fulfilment, and unity of history.'[29]

Because of this mutual relationship between question and answer Tillich calls his theology *apologetic theology*. This is not meant in the feeble sense of a theology which is attempting to prove the existence of God by dishonest means, so that it is always panting breathless behind the times, without ever catching up with them. Apologetics is not a special section of theology, but 'an omnipresent element' in it: 'Apologetic theology is "answering theology". It answers the questions implied in the "situation" in the power of the eternal message and with the means provided by the situation whose questions it answers.'[30]

Paul Tillich followed this method in his *Systematic Theology*. The work consists of five parts, each of which is divided into two sections. Each first section analyses the human situation and identifies the existential questions, while in the second section the symbols of the Christian gospel are set forth as answers to them. Thus the correlation of question and answer falls into the following five parts: the question of *reason*, and the answer of *revelation*; the question of *being*, and the answer of *God*; the question of *existence* and the answer of *Christ*; the question of *life*, and the answer of the *Spirit*; the question of *history*, and the answer of the *kingdom of God*.

The question of being (man)

Tillich's method of correlation and the definition of theology that results from it as 'apologetic theology' express the special relationship between *theology and philosophy* in his work. He sees the question of the relationship between theology and philosophy as the question of the nature of theology as a whole. No theology which seeks to express the truth concerning God in a way intelligible to men can do without philosophy: 'It is infuriating to see how biblical theologians, when explaining the concepts of the Old or New Testament writers, use most of the terms created by the toil of philosophers and the ingenuity of the speculative mind and then dismiss, with cheap denunciations, the work from which their language has been immensely enriched. No theologian should be taken seriously as a theologian, even if he is a great Christian or a great scholar, if his work shows that he does not take philosophy seriously.' The attempt to avoid philosophical concepts in theology leads to 'self-deception' or 'primitiveness': 'The fundamentalist minister who said to me, "Why do we need philosophy when we possess all truth through revelation?" – did not realise that, in using the words "truth" and "revelation", he was determined by a long history of philosophical thought . . . We cannot avoid philosophy, because the ways we take to avoid it are carved out and paved by philosophy.'[31]

The close link between philosophy and theology is due in Tillich's view to the simple fact that both are concerned with being. For Tillich the central issue of philosophy is *ontology*. Philosophy asks what one means when one says that something 'is'. This is 'the simplest, most profound and absolutely inexhaustible question' which can ever be asked. 'This word "is" hides the riddle of all riddles.' It is the mystery with which all philosophy is concerned. Philosophy is trying to discover what is embodied in everything that exists, 'being-itself', and so to know the principles, structures and categories which underlie everything that exists.[32]

But theology is also concerned with being, and therefore with ontology. All these statements which theology makes concerning God, the world and man fall within the sphere of being and therefore necessarily contain ontological elements. Even the simplest theological statement, that God *is*, implies the ontological question and therefore calls for philosophy: 'Without philosophies in which the ontological question we have raised appears, Christian theology would have been unable to interpret the nature of the being of God to those who wanted to know in what sense one can say that God *is*.'[33]

So the two foci of the ellipse formed by theology, the existential question and the theological answer, are presented by Tillich with the aid of a comprehensive doctrine of being, first in the form of the question, and then in the form of the answer.

Nothing is as characteristic of man as the fact that he asks questions. This distinguishes him from all other beings we know: 'Man ... is that being which asks what being is.' The question of being which man asks is born out of the 'ontological shock' which he undergoes. The ocean of non-being rages around being and threatens it. It is this which drives man into anxiety and questioning. Seized by the shock of the possibility of non-being, by his 'basic anxiety' that non-being may triumph over being, man asks the question of being. His question leads through successive layers of reality and finally cuts through them all to the very foundation: Why is there being and not non-being instead? What is the ground and meaning of all being? What is the ground and meaning of my being? Why does something exist at all instead of not existing? Why do I exist? By asking the question of the ground and meaning of being in this way, man is asking about ultimate reality, about the 'really real', about what concerns him ultimately.[34]

The question of what concerns man ultimately, of the ground and meaning of all being, is not associated with any social class or any level of material or intellectual possessions. It is not a matter of intellectual agility. There are scholars who have absorbed the content of the hundred most important books in the world and yet have never asked the question of what concerns man ultimately; and there are uneducated working men who carry out monotonous tasks every day, and who one day ask themselves: What meaning is there in my doing this work? What does it mean for my life? What is the meaning of my life?[35]

Man asks the question of being because he is 'a mixture of being and non-being': he partakes in being and at the same time is separated from it. In this his *finitude* is revealed. Finitude is the 'fundamental attitude' of all human existence; it determines its content and its form.[36] Tillich illustrates this by an experience from his youth, which he recounts in a sermon in *The Shaking of the Foundations*: before his confirmation he had to choose a verse of the Bible to say, as the practice was, when he was actually confirmed. He chose the verse: 'Come to me, all ye who labour and are heavy laden.' He was asked with astonishment and some irony why he had chosen that particular passage as his confirmation verse, for his childhood was happy and had little apparent 'labour' and 'burden' in it. He could not answer at the time, and felt a little embarrassed, yet had a feeling that he was basically right: 'And I was right, indeed; every child is right in responding immediately to those words; every adult is right in responding to them in all periods of his life, and under all the conditions of his internal and external history. These words of Jesus are universal, and fit every human being and every human situation.'[37]

Man exists on the boundary between finitude and infinity; by comparison with all other living beings, he has 'finite freedom'. This is his 'labour and burden'. It is this which makes him a fragment, an enigma to himself, obscure, mysterious, confusing and painful. His misery and grandeur are reflected in this. His misery is that he is finite, imperfect, transitory and mortal; his grandeur is that he knows all this. Thus it is a pertinent question whether his grandeur is not merely the grandeur of his misery. He experiences that he is finite, but he would not experience it if he did not have some foreknowledge of infinity; he experiences that he is imperfect, but he would not experience it if he did not have some foreknowledge of perfection; he experiences that he is transitory, but he would not experience it if he did not have some foreknowledge of eternity.[38] Unconsciously, man always measures himself against the dignity of his origin and his true being. Admittedly this dignity is lost, but this loss points to the fact that he once possessed it.

The separation of man from being points to the *fall* of man.[39] Tillich interprets the fall as the transition of man from *essence* to *existence*. In Tillich's own words, the distinction between essence and existence, between the 'created' and the 'real' world, forms the 'backbone' of his whole theological system. But everything depends upon a right interpretation of the transition of man from essence to existence, namely that it be not an historical interpretation but an existential one. It is not an event in space and time, not the first fact in a temporal sense. 'The notion of a moment in time in which man and nature were changed from good to evil is absurd, and it has no foundation in experience or revelation.' Rather, the transition from essence to existence is 'the trans-historical quality of all events in space and time', 'that which lends reality to every fact'. 'It becomes real in every reality.'

The result of the transition of man from essence to existence is *estrangement*.[40] The nature of estrangement consists in man's being estranged from that to which he essentially belongs. He is separated from the ground of being and therefore from the origin and goal of his life. Man is not what he ought really to be. 'Existence' and 'estrangement' are synonyms: existence always signifies the estrangement of man from his true and real being, and therefore implies a threat from non-being, bringing with it anxiety and the question of being.

The state of estrangement in which man exists implies a three-fold separation: we are separated from the ground of being, the origin and goal of our life, and at the same time we are separated from ourselves and separated from our fellow men. Consequently, a disastrous rift runs through all being. It is this which the Bible calls *sin*. Tillich resists the conventional moral misunderstanding of the Christian concept of sin; for him, sin is a 'trans-moral', a religious concept. It signifies not merely an ethical defect, far less merely a subjective attitude on the part of man, and is not merely personal guilt, but is always a tragic destiny and misfortune as well, albeit a fate and misfortune in which we share by our actions, so that it is always also a guilt for which we are personally responsible. Tillich, in emphasising the trans-moral and tragic element in sin, does not intend to dissolve the biblical concept of sin into that of fatality, but only to make clear that there is no situation in which man is not guilty: to live under the circumstances of existence means to live in sin. Although Tillich is of the opinion that it is no longer possible for us to make use of the concept of 'original sin', he retains its content. *Before* all acts, sin is an ontological state: it is the 'state of the estrangement' of man from God. Consequently, Tillich insists that the word 'sin' should only be used in the singular and not in the plural; that is, not to refer to particular moral failings on the part of man, but to describe his state of separation from God. Consequently for him sin means simply 'unbelief'.

Tillich holds that it is not only Christian faith which is aware of the estrangement of human existence, for most other philosophies, world-views and religions have some conception of it, including Plato and Buddha, and also Karl Marx. Consequently all the more profound religions, world-views and philosophies have a tendency towards the tragic, and a tinge of sombre melancholy colours them all. The roots of their melancholy and tragic feeling lie in man's ability to see beyond this world.

Thus this is man's existence: he is separated from the ground of being, he is alienated from his true being. But only because he is alienated from his true being can he ask the question of being at all. Neither God nor the non-human creation asks it. For God is infinite, beyond the gap between essence and existence, and so has no need to ask this question; while non-human creation does not know that it is finite, and is there-fore not able to ask it; it merely waits, insensible, submissive, uncon-scious. Only man asks, for only he knows that he is finite, separated from the ground of being and yet not completely apart from it, however much he might like to be.[41]

The power of being (God)

When man asks the question of being, he is asking about the power which resists non-being, sin, guilt, meaninglessness, transitoriness, and death. It is this 'power of being' which Tillich calls God. Thus anyone whose questions penetrate the surface of reality into the depth, and who asks about ultimate reality, about the meaning and ground of all being, is asking, whether he knows it or not, about God: 'The name of this infinite and inexhaustible depth and ground of all being is *God*. That depth is what the word *God* means. And if that word has not much meaning for you, translate it, and speak of the depths of your life, of the source of your being, of your ultimate concern, of what you take seriously without any reservation. Perhaps, in order to do so, you must forget everything traditional that you have learned about God, perhaps even that word itself. For if you know that God means depth, you know much about Him. You cannot then call yourself an atheist or unbeliever.

For you cannot think or say: Life has no depth! Life itself is shallow. Being itself is surface only. If you could say this in complete seriousness, you would be an atheist; but otherwise you are not. He who knows about depth knows about God.'[42]

In order to express who God is and where man encounters him, Tillich replaces the familiar concept of 'height' by that of 'depth'. This signifies more than merely a change in a spatial conception. 'Depth' does not refer to a 'level' of reality, in such a way that God, instead of being understood, as before, as the 'highest being', is now regarded as the 'deepest being'. 'Depth' refers to a 'dimension' of reality. The changed image is intended to express the fact that the reality of God is not to be sought *above* all the reality of the world as its highest level, nor *beneath* all the reality of the world, but as the '"really real" among all the things and events that offer themselves as reality'.[43] Thus anyone who asks about God must not turn away from the world and look upwards into the heights, into an imaginary heaven, but must in fact turn towards the world, exploring more deeply the world, his own existence, and its relationship to the existence of other men. Then he will encounter in the depth the reality of God as the ground and meaning of all being.

The metaphor of 'depth' corresponds in Tillich to the concept of the *unconditional*. Whenever anything is manifested to me in its depth, it is manifested to me as something which concerns me unconditionally. Just as depth does not signify the existence of a particular place, so the unconditional does not signify the existence of a particular being; both concepts refer to a potential quality of all that exists. It can happen at any time and in any place that a part of finite being is revealed to me in its depth, and so becomes for me an 'ultimate', 'infinite concern', 'something which concerns me unconditionally'. Whenever and wherever this takes place, I encounter God. Thus Tillich can repeat in innumerable variations: Religion is what concerns us ultimately and unconditionally, and to be religious means to ask about the ultimate and unconditional meaning of life.

By conceiving of God as 'being-itself', Tillich succeeds in pointing to God in all that exists, but in such a way that at the same time God infinitely transcends all that exists. Tillich does not make any statement about God which is not at the same time a statement about reality. Through the same kind of argument, Tillich succeeds by means of his concept of the 'unconditional' in overcoming traditional thinking on the subject-object pattern. In the act of being apprehended unconditionally, man is not overpowered by the unconditional, but experiences the unconditional as what concerns him unconditionally – and in this way subject and object are united in the unconditional.[44]

But does Tillich not succeed in making this close link between the unconditional and the conditional only at the price of an immense abstraction? Does not his ontology necessarily make his language about God colourless and monotonous? God – 'being as being', 'being-itself', the 'power of being', the 'ground and meaning of all being': do all these expressions not sound empty and completely abstract? But for Tillich 'being' is in no sense an empty and abstract concept; it is the richest and fullest he can think of. It signifies for him 'living creativity'. Being contains non-being within itself, and is therefore constantly forced to affirm itself creatively, and so to overcome its own non-being. It is this which forces being out of its closed isolation, gives it its creative dynamism, and makes it a process of constant becoming. Applied to God, this means that God is the 'living being', who in himself and his creation constantly overcomes non-being, and is therefore the ground upon which all that exists rests, receiving from him the power of being over non-being.

Here, as elsewhere in his theology, Tillich follows the 'third way' between supranaturalism and naturalism, between heteronomy and autonomy.

The 'third way' lies in the first place between *supranaturalism and naturalism*.[45] 'Supranaturalism' is a 'relic of hierarchical thought'. It thinks of reality in 'levels' and identifies the highest level, which lies above all other levels, with 'God'. In this way God becomes the 'highest being'. The superlative shows that God is a being above all other beings, distinct from all beings beside, outside and above him, but nevertheless an existent being among other existent beings, a person among other persons, and therefore a being whose existence may be disputed. As the highest being God is the 'unconquerable tyrant' who brought the universe into existence at a particular point in time and rules it according to a fixed plan, who has imparted information concerning himself to a few men, and intervenes in the regular course of the world in order to break down the resistance of his disobedient creation and bring it to the goal which he has laid down for it – 'This is the God Nietzsche said had to be killed because nobody can tolerate being made into a mere object of absolute knowledge and absolute control.' But if one thinks of God as the 'highest being', then not only does man become the object of what God does, but God in his turn becomes the object of what man does. He is inextricably bound up with the subject-object structure of things on which rational doubt may be cast, so that atheism has an easy task. 'Naturalism', on the other hand, equates God with the universe, accepts him only as a name for the creative basis of nature, for the power and meaning of all reality, and in this way likewise draws God down into finitude.

Tillich follows neither supranaturalism in separating God and being, nor naturalism in equating them, but sets up a *relationship* between them. God would not be God for him if he were not the creative ground of all being, the infinite and unconditional power of being, being-itself; he is neither alongside nor above being, but he is closer to everything that exists than it is to itself. Once again, God is wholly and completely different from all that exists, and is infinitely remote from it; not, however, as a different form of being, the highest there is, over and above the world, but as the ground and meaning within all being. Tillich here rightly appeals to Luther, who constantly and forcefully emphasised the omnipresence of God in all processes of life, while at the same time he stressed his total transcendence: God is 'totally present in a grain of sand, and at the same time not being comprehended by the totality of all things'. Tillich expresses the same idea in his philosophical language: 'In symbolic terms, God is the dimension of the unconditional in being and meaning, present in everything that is, and remote from everything that is.'

Tillich's third way between supranaturalism and naturalism corresponds to his third way between *heteronomy* and *autonomy*,[46] although we must add at once that he has a much greater liking for autonomy. What he objects to is merely 'pure', 'empty' 'formal' autonomy, which has forgotten the question of the ultimate and unconditional meaning of life and culture, and has therefore become secularist and arrogant; in the course of his life he has become suspicious of the 'free-ranging intelligence'. His whole passion is directed against the 'Grand Inquisitor' in the Church, against the 'heteronomy' which is imposed upon God's world like an alien yoke, and does such violence to it from outside and above it that it defiles the visage of the truth and destroys the moral dignity of man. Its theological expression is supranaturalism, and its consequence religious or ecclesiastical terror. Tillich describes his own position between autonomy and heteronomy as *theonomy*. The expression signifies that while God is the law and the power of all life, he is so not from outside and above, but from within, ruling within being itself, as its ultimate ground and meaning. He does not subject man to an alien law, but encounters him as that which concerns him unconditionally, and leads him to self-fulfilment.

For Tillich, the connection between God and being determines the way in which one should speak of God: one can only speak of God in indirect, *symbolic* statements.[47] Basically, there is only one direct and non-symbolic statement which can be made about God, which is the statement that God is 'being-itself'. All other more concrete statements about God are based upon this. But all these other more concrete statements which we make about God – about his person, that he is the creator, that he is spirit, and wholly personal; or about his attributes, that he possesses love, mercy, omnipotence and omniscience; or about his actions, that he has created the world and sent his Son – are indirect, symbolic statements.

Religious symbols are drawn from the material of tangible reality; they use something finite to express our relationship to the infinite. Consequently, all religious symbols have a twofold aspect: a *negative* aspect, in that they point beyond themselves to something which is infinitely more than they are; and a *positive* aspect, in that they partake in the power and meaning of that to which they point. Thus in a symbol the finite is both denied and affirmed. For example, God is called 'Father'. But here our concept 'Father' is superseded: God is infinitely more than everything contained in our concept of 'father'. But at the same time our concept of 'father' is confirmed: all finite fatherhood has its basis in God; what exists in perfection in God is present in a fragmentary form in finite fatherhood.

Symbolic statements about God are no less true than non-symbolic statements. In Tillich's view this means that one is in fact never able to say 'only a symbol'; rather, one should say 'nothing less than a symbol'. Symbols have the task of protecting the mystery of God and preserving it from becoming something finite, directly present, and within the world. But at the same time, it is essential that symbols should not be understood literally and identified with the divine itself. Anyone who does this falsifies the symbol and distorts the reality which it represents. 'A faith which understands its symbols literally becomes idolatry. . . . But the faith which understands the symbolic character of its symbols gives God the honour due to him.' Thus the motive behind symbolic language about God is not the lessening of the reality of God, but a passionate defence of the mystery of God. The attempt to speak of God in non-symbolic language is godless. Even a single non-symbolic statement about God is a threat to his transcendence.

Symbols cannot be deliberately invented and then cast aside, but 'are born and die' like living beings. They arise in the collective unconsciousness of a group and disappear at the moment in which the inner link between the group and the symbol comes to an end; for then the symbol has nothing more to say. It is not for the theologian who has to interpret the symbol to judge whether it is still capable of life. Rather, this judgement takes place within the life of the Church: in the liturgical sphere, in preaching and instruction, in the actions of the Church towards the world, and in personal devotion.

Tillich's view of the value of religious symbols also determines his judgement upon Bultmann's programme of demythologisation. He is in agreement with it, in so far as it implies that 'a symbol must be understood as a symbol, and a myth as a myth'. If this is not the case, and the symbol or myth is understood literally, then the sanctity of God is profaned, and language about God appears to contemporary men as superstitious, unintelligible and absurd. But Tillich rejects demythologisation when it does away altogether with myths and symbols as forms of religious statement, and replaces them by substitutes such as science and morality: 'There is no substitute for symbols and myths; they are the language of faith.' The consequence of a demythologisation of this sort would be to deprive religion of its language and to reduce the experiences of the saints to silence.

The close connection which Tillich introduces between being and God undoubtedly leads him to a 'metaphysical exaggeration' of the concept of being. This precisely is the charge made against him by the philosopher Wilhelm Weischedel in his 'respectful disagreement' with Tillich.[48] Weischedel's objection is undoubtedly justified. Tillich superimposes upon the general philosophical concept of being a specifically theological concept. The reason for this theological exaggeration of the general concept of being by Tillich is clear: it originates in the biblical belief in creation. That God has created the world, that he has created it from nothing, and that this creation from nothing is a continuous process, forms the theological background to everything that Tillich says about the process of life, about being and non-being, and about being and God. The same is true of the concept of the 'unconditional'. Tillich himself says that it represents the 'abstract translation' of the great commandment of the Old Testament: 'The Lord our God is one Lord; and you shall love the Lord your God with all your heart, and with all your soul, and with all your might' (Deut. 6:4).[49]

This raises once again the question of the fundamental relationship between *theology and philosophy* in Tillich.[50] He describes their mutual relationship as follows: 'Philosophy and theology are not separated, and they are not identical, but they are correlated.' Tillich introduces the philosophical element into the structure of the theological system itself: in the first place, as the material from which the questions answered by theology have originated; secondly, as the material from which the answers given by theology are formed. Philosophy is unable to provide the *content* of these answers; indeed, it is not even able to identify and expound the question of God implied in human existence: how could it then be capable of answering it? That God is the answer, or indeed that he is the expounded question itself, cannot be derived from human existence, but must be spoken into it. The form in which this happens is laid down already by philosophy, for the form of the answer must correspond to the form of the question originally asked – this is the requirement of Tillich's theological method of correlation.

It is possible for Tillich to regard philosophy and theology as partly in opposition and partly in alliance in this way, because ontology plays a decisive role in both disciplines. Both philosophy and theology ask the ultimate question which can be posed, the question of being. Both ask it from different points of departure and with a different purpose in mind: philosophy asks it 'theoretically', as the question of the 'form of being in itself', while theology asks it 'existentially' as a question of the 'meaning of being for us', and therefore as the question of God. But when the philosopher asks the question of being, he asks it not only from a remote and theoretical point of view, as the question of the structure of being, but also with regard to its direct existentialist relevance, as the question of the meaning of being; and when he gives an answer to the question, then covertly or openly he becomes a theologian, even when he does not really wish this. On the other hand, the theologian cannot avoid standing back to make a critical examination and contemplating theoretically the structure of being, and when he does so his attitude is a philosophical one. Consequently, Tillich sees philosophy and theology as both 'divergent' and 'convergent'. They are divergent, in so far as philosophy is basically theoretical and theology basically existential, and they are convergent, in so far as both can be at the same time theoretical and also existential. As a result it is impossible for a fundamental conflict to take place between theology and philosophy in Tillich; at best, there can only be practical conflict between theologians and philosophers, and then only in the sense that the theologian and the philosopher are in conflict with each other either on the theological level or on the philosophical level.

Here again Tillich is setting out upon the 'third way', which means not the confusion of philosophy and theology, but the complementing of the one by the other: they are mutually dependent, and both are impoverished when they are separated. Tillich writes as follows against a philosophy which cuts itself off from theology: 'Philosophy becomes logical positivism . . . or mere epistemology, always sharpening the knife of thought, but never cutting . . . or it becomes history of philosophy, enumerating one philosophical opinion of the past after the other, keeping itself at a noble distance, faithlessly and cynically – a philosophy without existential basis, without theological ground and power.' Tillich writes against a theology which cuts itself off from philosophy: 'Such a theology speaks of God as of a being beside others, subject to the structure of being as all beings are . . . the highest being but not being itself, not the meaning of being and therefore a merciful tyrant limited in power, who may concern us very much, but not ultimately, or unconditionally; whose existence, doubtful as it is, must be argued for as the existence of a new chemical element or a disputable event in past history. Such a theology separates man from nature and nature from man, the self from its world and the world from the self to which it belongs.' The conclusion which Tillich draws from his definition of the relationship between philosophy and theology is: 'Thus theology and philosophy, religion and knowledge embrace each other, and it is precisely this which seems to be, as judged from the border, the true relation of both.'

Wilhelm Weischedel, as a philosopher, has protested against this mutual embrace between philosophy and theology. He considers that in Tillich's philosophical theology philosophy has 'clearly been brought into subjection to theology'.[51] There is some justice in this suspicion on the part of the philosopher. Admittedly, it is not Tillich's intention to subject philosophy to theology, but this takes place in his work as it were 'of itself', because he is a Christian, and has therefore already accepted the answer before he hears the question. Consequently, the philosopher's protest that Tillich is changing philosophy into theology is more justified than the complaint of theologians that he is perverting theology into philosophy. In Tillich's own words, philosophy and theology embrace each other – but the arms of theology are stronger.

The new being (the Christ)

If all theological language about God is determined by the situation in which man finds himself and the questions he asks, how then does Tillich see the situation of man today, and how does he see the question which man is asking?

The fear of non-being which drives man to ask the question of being can occur in various forms. Tillich distinguishes three types of fear, corresponding to the three ways in which non-being threatens being.[52]

Firstly, non-being threatens the *ontic* self-affirmation of man: fear appears in relative terms as fear of *destiny*, and in absolute terms as fear of *death*.

Secondly, non-being threatens the *moral* self-affirmation of man: fear appears in relative terms as fear of *guilt*, and in absolute terms as fear of eternal *damnation*.

Thirdly, non-being threatens the *intellectual* self-affirmation of man: fear appears in relative terms as fear of *emptiness*, and in absolute terms as fear of *meaninglessness*.

Tillich then ascribes to every period its own particular fear, peculiar to itself, and in such a way that in each age one particular type of fear predominates, though containing within it the other types of fear. In each case, fear in its absolute form is particularly evident at the end of an era, in its crisis, when the familiar structures of meaning, power, faith and order are crumbling. Thus Tillich believes that at the end of the civilisation of the ancient world the dominating threat was that of ontic non-being, bringing with it the fear of fate and death; at the end of the Middle Ages the dominating threat was that of moral non-being, bringing with it the fear of guilt and eternal damnation; while at the end of the modern age the dominating threat is that of intellectual non-being, bringing with it the fear of emptiness and meaninglessness. In Tillich's judgement contemporary man – in the third great era of fear, the end of the modern age – experiences his situation 'in terms of disruption, conflict, self-destruction, meaninglessness, and despair in all realms of life'. The decisive question arising for man from this experience is not the question of finitude and death, as in the ancient Greek Church, nor the question of the merciful God and the forgiveness of sins as at the Reformation, nor is it the question of personal religious life as in pietism, or of the christianisation of society and culture as in the modern age. 'It is the question of a reality in which the self-estrangement of our existence is overcome, a reality of reconciliation and reunion, of creativity, meaning and hope.'[53]

This is how Tillich sees the situation of modern man: he is not suffering from sin but from the meaninglessness of his existence; he is terrified not by the anger of God, but by his absence; he is longing not for forgiveness, but for healing and power; consequently, he does not ask for the gracious God, but the true God. 'This is not a picture of man without God. . . . But it is a picture of man who no longer knows that, and how, he is in the hand of God.' The two deities of late antiquity – Tyche and Heimarmene, Chance and Fate – seem to Tillich to have brought men once again under their spell, and to dominate them.[54]

Our age, like all periods, is also concerned with the reconciliation of man with God. This as always is the very heart of all true religion. But if this reconciliation is really to be an answer to the existential question of modern man, not only should it appear as an answer to the limited question of the eternal salvation of the individual soul, but it must also appear as an answer to the much wider, cosmic question of a new creation, a new reality, a new being.

New being – here again, for the third time, the concept of being occurs in Tillich at a decisive point. We met it for the first time in the doctrine of *man*: man is separated from the ground and meaning of being, and exists in a state of alienation – consequently, he asks the question of true being. We met it a second time in the doctrine of *God*: God is being-itself, the ground and meaning of being, the power of being, who resists his transition into non-being – consequently, he is the answer to man's question about being. Now the concept of being occurs for the third time in the doctrine of *Christ*: Jesus, as the Christ, is the manifestation of the New Being.

In Jesus the Christ, the New Being has appeared in a personal life. In him the universal logos, who is present in all that exists, became concrete reality in an individual self. This is the paradox, the sole, albeit all-embracing, paradox of Christianity. It consists of the fact that in Jesus Christ true and essential being appeared under the conditions of existence, without being overwhelmed by it. Tillich's whole christology can be summed up in a brief statement from the Epistle to the Hebrews: 'One who in every respect has been tempted as we are, yet without sinning' (Heb. 4:15). This means: 'Subjection to existence', and at the same time 'the conquest of existence'.[55]

'In every respect tempted as we are' means *subjection to existence*: Jesus Christ does not function like a 'divine-human automaton', but he is, as

far as flesh and blood are concerned, like one of us, a man, a real historical
man, and consequently his life is like that of any man, in a tension
between birth and death. He is 'thrown into existence', that is, he is
subject to the condition of the estrangement between God and man;
he has 'finite freedom'. He is uncertain in his judgement, not protected
from error, limited in his power, exposed to the vicissitudes of existence.
In his life there were temptation and fear, poverty and failure, law and
tragedy, conflict and death. Any picture of Jesus Christ which omits this
'complete finitude of Christ' is unbiblical.

   'Yet without sinning' means *the conquest of existence*: Jesus Christ,
living under the conditions of existence, of the estrangement between
God and man, remained linked with God, by contrast to all other men.
Although he shared in the ambiguity of life, he lived in unbroken unity
with God. There was no separation and estrangement in him, and his
life was determined by God at every moment. He was one with God,
the ground and meaning of being, and therefore he was one with himself and one with his fellow men – and he upheld this threefold unity
up to his death. Nothing could force him into separation; he had
conquered all the forces of estrangement which sought to separate him
from God. He did not seek to be an 'idol', a God alongside God: consequently, he sacrificed everything in himself which was only 'Jesus'
to that which he represented as 'Christ'. Therefore, he was wholly
transparent to the divine mystery which shone through him, bringing
this transparency to its perfection in his death. But it is not his moral
achievement which makes him the Christ, but his 'being', the presence
of God in him. Everything that took place in his life – his work, his
acts, his suffering, his inner life, were only effects of this divine presence
in him, and are therefore manifestations of the New Being. This is the
meaning of the symbol 'Son of God': 'It is not the picture of a divine-
human automaton without serious temptation, real struggle, or tragic
involvement in the ambiguities of life. Instead of that, it is the picture of
a personal life which is subjected to all the consequences of existential
estrangement but wherein estrangement is conquered in himself and a
permanent unity is kept with God.'[56]

   Under the conditions of existence, of the estrangement between God
and man, Jesus Christ maintained the unity of God as the meaning and
ground of all being. The cleavage between essence and existence,
between true and real being, was thereby overcome 'in principle'.
'Principle' means 'beginning' and 'power' – this signifies that from this
single point, at which the cleavage between essence and existence has

been overcome, a process of healing has begun which is taking effect as a redeeming power in all existence. The disastrous rift which runs through all being and separates one life from another, one man from another, one self from another, has been healed, and unity restored. And it is this old being healed which is the New Being.[57]

Here Tillich sees the answer of Christianity to the existential question of our time: 'If I were asked to sum up the Christian message for our time in two words, I would say with Paul: It is the message of a "New Creation" . . . the New Being, the New Reality which has appeared with the appearance of Jesus . . . we should not be too worried about the Christian religion, about the state of the Churches, about member-ship and doctrines, about institutions and ministers, about sermons and sacraments. . . . The New Creation – this is our ultimate concern; this should be our infinite passion – the infinite passion of every human being. This matters; this alone matters ultimately. In comparison with it everything else, even religion or non-religion, even Christianity or non-Christianity, matters very little – and ultimately nothing. . . . It is the maturest fruit of Christian understanding to understand that Christi-anity, as such, is of no avail. . . . The message of Christianity is not Christianity, but a New Reality.'[58]

Belief-ful realism

The universalist interpretation of the message of New Being makes Tillich a truly 'ecumenical' theologian, not in the geographical, organisational or even tourist sense of the word, but in the original meaning of the word. Tillich is trying to bring back the *oikumene*, that is the whole world, and every province of life within it, into the life of the New Being, and so to overcome its inherent tendency to separation and division: 'All these differences are transcended through the power of the New Being, which works in all of them.'[59] Consequently, theology is concerned not merely with 'religion in the narrower sense', with faith, Christianity and the Church, but equally with 'religion in the wider sense' – and so with society, politics, science, culture and art. In all the phenomena of human experience and activity it seeks the dimen-sion of depth, the ultimate and unconditional which is expressed in them, and therefore seeks their religious meaning. This leads to what Tillich has called 'belief-ful realism'.

The concept of *belief-ful realism* is Tillich's most telling answer to the question asked in our time concerning the relationship between the reality of God and the reality of the world: in it, God and the world are contemporaneous.[60] The word 'realism' implies that religion is concerned not with a special reality, or a supra-reality, but with the reality which surrounds us and in which we live. The word 'belief-ful' describes the proper attitude to this reality: that it is important not to remain on the surface of reality, but to penetrate to its depths and to apprehend in it the divine ground and meaning or, more precisely, to let oneself be apprehended thereby. Belief-ful realism does not identify the divine with reality, but shows how the divine appears in finite reality, as its transcendental ground and meaning: 'It is as in a thunderstorm at night, when the lightning throws a blinding clarity over all things, leaving them in complete darkness the next moment. When reality is seen in this way with the eye of a self-transcending realism, it has become something new. Its ground has become visible in an "ecstatic" experience, called "faith". It is no longer merely self-subsistent as it seemed to be before; it has become transparent or, as we would say, "theonomous". . . . We are grasped, in the experience of faith, by the unapproachably holy which is the ground of our being and breaks into our existence and which judges us and heals us. This is "crisis" and "grace" at the same time.'

Belief-ful realism criticises all forms of supernaturalism which drive God out into a supernatural sphere and thereby separate him from all that exists; it presses for 'contemporaneity': theology should not speak of a unique act of creation in the past, but of the creatureliness of all things and their relationship to the creative ground of their being; it should not continue to exercise itself with traditional christological problems, with the person and work of Christ, but should describe the New Being which in Jesus Christ has become visible with regard to nature and history; it should not defend the apocalyptic of Judaism and primitive Christianity, but ask what is the ultimate meaning inherent in all historical activity, and how we should interpret our life in the light of the eternal. 'The word of God' is not an act of divine utterance in the past; every reality through which the unconditional breaks into our present and speaks to us, whether a person, a thing, a spoken word or a written text, can become the 'word of God'.

Tillich came to see what belief-ful realism means through modern art. First of all, through expressionism: this broke down the outward form of things, in order to make their inner significance visible; secondly, through the so-called 'new realism': this kept closely, once again, to the outward form of things, not for their own sake, but only in so far as the outward form expresses the inner content of things. The new realism in art sought to point to the content of meaning in the real; and the same is true of belief-ful realism.

A particular epistemological attitude to reality is implied in belief-ful realism. In it, the subject-object dichotomy between man and reality is overcome. To know reality does not mean domination, but union; it is something which takes place not in the attitude of standing back from reality, but in participation in it; it requires not that one should analyse something into separate parts, but that one should allow oneself to be apprehended by the whole. Knowledge cannot be separated from experience. Only by intuition can one attain to that depth of reality, or rather, can one be apprehended by that depth of reality, in which its divine ground and meaning become visible.

Tillich tells the following story as an example: 'I was sitting under a tree with a great biologist. Suddenly he exclaimed, "I would like to know something about this tree!" He, of course, knew everything that science had to say about it. I asked him what he meant. And he answered, "I want to know what this tree means for itself. I want to understand the life of this tree. It is so strange, so unapproachable." . . . A Chinese emperor asked a famous painter to paint a picture of a rooster for him. The painter assented, but said that it would take a long time. After a year the emperor reminded him of his promise. The painter replied that after a year of studying the rooster he had just begun to perceive the surface of its nature. After another year the artist asserted that he had just begun to penetrate the essence of this kind of life. And so on, year after year. Finally, after ten years of concentration on the nature of the rooster, he painted the picture – a work described as an inexhaustible revelation of the divine ground of the universe in one small part of it, a rooster.'[61]

This is the attitude in which belief-ful realism knows reality. But in Tillich's own words, with this epistemological attitude he stands in the line which extends 'from Parmenides to Hegel'. More precisely, one must call it the neo-Platonic, Augustinian and mystical tradition of the West. It is characterised by names such as Augustine, Eckhart, Paracelsus, Böhme, Goethe, and Schelling. It is a tradition which has ceased to be fashionable.

By associating himself with it, Tillich takes a stand against the purely technical 'dominating knowledge' of the modern age, which seeks to subject things to itself, and so degrades the whole of reality to the level of an object, with the consequence that man thereby becomes an object himself. At the same time, Tillich attacks the one-sided intellectualising of the life of the spirit, which has suppressed 'the soul', the vital and emotional foundation from which man draws his life, with the consequence that man is now divided up into a 'bloodless intellect' and a 'vitality without mind or meaning'. Christian faith has also participated in this false development.

Against this, Tillich once again lays powerful emphasis on the ecstatic aspect of all faith: 'Jesus felt differently and so did the early Church. They knew that without the abundance of the heart nothing great can happen. They knew that religion within the limits of reasonableness is a mutilated religion.'[62] That faith is 'ecstasy' does not mean that what happens in faith is meaningless, but that in it man is seized hold of by the deepest meaning of reality. This can never take place on the basis of man himself, but is always possible only as an act of grace, and therefore signifies on man's side 'acceptance', 'reception', 'encounter', 'being apprehended', 'shock'. Faith is a 'central act', which takes hold of the whole of man, not merely his head, but also his heart, not merely the conscious levels of his being, but also the unconscious levels.[63]

Belief-ful realism leads Tillich to extend the *concept of religion* in a universalist sense. If the divine and the unconditional can appear at any moment in reality, as its transcendental ground and meaning, then everything in the world has a relationship to God, and there is no sphere *in addition to* the divine, and no sphere of life can exist without being related to something unconditional, to something which concerns us unconditionally. Religion is not a special sphere of life nor a special function of the human spirit, but is 'the experience of the element of the unconditional' *in* all other functions of the human spirit and all other spheres of life. Religion is 'the most human of all experiences', it is 'at home everywhere', it is 'the ground and the depth of man's spiritual life'. Every function of the human mind without exception, and every sphere of life, however profane it may appear to be, is related to the unconditional and therefore possesses a hidden religious dimension. Political ideas, secular poetry, philosophical arguments, scientific investigations, 'if they point to something infinite and ultimate in meaning and being . . . point to the same reality for which religion in the narrower sense uses the symbol "God"'. And therefore, while Christians and non-Christians today are proclaiming the 'end of religion', Tillich can assert with optimistic confidence: 'Religion, like God, is omnipresent; its presence, like that of God, can be forgotten, neglected, denied. But it is always effective, giving inexhaustible depth to life and inexhaustible meaning to every cultural creation.' Or again, 'Religion cannot imagine any past or future in which man has lived or will live without an ultimate concern, i.e., without religion. . . . He may avoid "religious symbols" in the narrower, traditional sense of the word. But he cannot avoid religion in the larger, more profound and more universal sense. Religion lasts as long as man lasts. It cannot disappear in human history, because a history without religion is not *human* history.'[64]

As a result of this broad understanding of the concept of religion Tillich sees a close connection between *religion and culture* which is particularly characteristic of his theology.[65] As early as 1920 he wrote a book on 'The Idea of a Theology of Culture', and ever since then he has been preoccupied with the problem of the connection between religion and culture, even as a professor of systematic theology. He has summed up the result of his consideration of this matter in a brief formula which he has often repeated: 'Religion is the substance of culture, culture is the expression of religion.' This formula means that religion deals with the unconditional meaning itself, the substance, and the forms only serve as symbols for it; while culture deals with the form, the conditional meaning, and the unconditional meaning, the substance, takes effect only indirectly and in a hidden way through the form.

Tillich adduces numerous examples of this mutual and indissoluble connection between religion and culture: 'If a person who had been deeply moved by the mosaics of Ravenna, the ceiling paintings of the Sistine Chapel, or the portraits of the older Rembrandt, were asked whether his experience had been religious or cultural, he would find the question difficult to answer. It might be correct to say that the experience is cultural in form and religious in substance. It is cultural because it is not attached to a specific ritual act; but it is religious because it touches on the question of the Absolute and the limits of human existence.' And Tillich continues: 'This is as true of music, poetry, philosophy and science as it is of painting. And whatever is true in this intuition and understanding of the world remains true in the practical work of shaping laws and customs, in morality and education, in community and state. Culture is religious wherever human existence is subjected to ultimate questions and thus transcended; and wherever unconditional meaning becomes visible in works that have only conditioned meaning in themselves.'

Tillich wishes neither that culture should have a heteronomous form imposed upon it from outside through a religious law, nor that it should live autonomously without any link with an ultimate ground and meaning, but that it should recognise in itself, theonomously, its unconditional divine meaning, in the ground of its own being. Where this happens, and where profane spheres, such as the State, philosophy, science and the arts, penetrate to their own ground and meaning, without having recourse to any specifically religious ideas, they are no longer profane, but attain, even without 'ecclesiastical authorisation', the dimension of the religious. Where this does not happen, and where the profane spheres consciously break or forget their link with the unconditional, cultural life becomes empty and without spirit. But when religion is separated from culture, it becomes 'primitive'.

In conscious opposition to Barth, who, during his 'dialectic period' at least, tore apart heaven and earth, God and the world, religion and culture, Tillich has always endeavoured from the very beginning of his writing and teaching to bridge over the cleavage between religion and culture, even though as a result he was bound to arouse the suspicion that he was not a theologian but a philosopher of culture – something which since the First World War and the collapse of liberal cultural Protestantism has been an insult to a theologian. But here Tillich is in constant opposition to the Reformed tradition, and stands in the 'German Lutheran tradition', in line with Luther, Schleiermacher and Hegel.

In all this, Paul Tillich has rediscovered *profaneness* as an essential element in Christianity, and especially in Protestantism. For if something holy and unconditional lies in the depth of every historical situation and phenomenon and can break through at any moment, and if religious thought and activity is only the visible representation of what is suddenly present in profane thought and activity, then the separation between a sacred and a profane sphere is in principle abolished: 'In the presence of the Unconditioned (the Majesty of God in the traditional language of Christianity), there is no preferred sphere. There are no persons, scriptures, communities, institutions, or actions that are holy in themselves, nor are there any that are profane in themselves. The profane can profess the quality of holiness, and the holy does not cease to be profane. The priest is a layman, and the layman can become a priest at any time.' This was for Tillich not only an expression of a theological perception, but also an attitude he maintained practically and personally. He says of himself: 'As a clergyman and theologian, I cannot be anything other than a layman and philosopher who has tried to say something about the limits of human existence. Nor have I any intention of concealing my theological endeavours. On the contrary, I have aired them where, for example, in my work as a professor of philosophy they could easily have been concealed. But I did not want to develop a theological habitude that would set me apart from profane life and earn me the label "religious". . . . To think of the clergyman as a man whose faith is a professional requirement borders on blasphemy.'[66]

For Tillich, Protestantism is 'radical laicism': everything in the world is 'secular' and every secular thing is 'essentially religious'. Every person, every place and every action is qualified by this association with the unconditional; it penetrates every moment of daily life and sanctifies it: 'The universe is God's sanctuary. Every work day is a day of the Lord, every supper a Lord's supper, every work a fulfilment of the divine task, every joy a joy in God. In all preliminary concerns, ultimate concern is present, consecrating them.'[67]

But Tillich goes even further than this. If God is a name for that which concerns us unconditionally, and is therefore present everywhere where man is unconditionally challenged, then the traditional religious lines of battle become strangely confused and altered. For it is possible for God, in the Church, to become a finite concern, one object among others, and therefore no longer something which is an unconditional concern, while at the same time a religious element can be concealed in a profane or even anti-religious and anti-Christian movement, because the people involved in it have an infinite concern, something that concerns them unconditionally, something holy in secular clothing. This was the reason why Tillich joined the 'Religious Socialists' after the First World War and shared in the founding of their movement in Germany. The 'fathers of Continental religious socialism' recognised that the Church had lost its true nature and that in its place a secular group or movement could become one of the 'bearers of grace' – 'though latently'. Thus through democratic socialism, which was non-religious, and indeed at that time even atheistic, God had spoken more powerfully and revealed more of his will than through most of the activities of the Church and most ecclesiastical piety at the same period. Tillich was aware that in this judgement he was in agreement with Karl Barth.[68]

The same understanding which led Tillich after the First World War to make his unconventional judgement upon the religious situation can also assist us now, after the Second World War, to come to a clearer understanding of our own religious situation, and to draw the lines of battle elsewhere than is required by ecclesiastical convention. The decisive dividing line in religion today does not run between Christians and non-Christians, but between those who are self-complacent and those who are disturbed, between the indifferent and the vigilant, between those who are content and those who doubt, between those who ask and those who no longer ask. Here it is quite possible for Christians and non-Christians to be on the same side. There are Christians and non-Christians, both of whom in their own way have 'finished' with God. And there are both Christians and non-Christians who are still in no sense finished with God, who are ceaselessly disturbed by the question whether what they received yesterday as the truth about God is still the truth about God today; who seek and inquire whether what they have hitherto believed, or alternatively have not believed, to be true of God, is in fact so; and who constantly feel themselves threatened in their faith by unbelief, and in their unbelief by faith, and by the very intensity of their questioning and doubt bear witness to God as a living God.

Tillich systematised these experiences in his distinction between the *manifest* and *latent*, the revealed and hidden Church. What seems to him to make such a distinction urgent is 'the existence of a Christian humanism outside the Christian Church'. Therefore, Tillich uses the concept of the 'latent Church' not as has usually been the case in Church history, in order to restrict the Church to true believers, but on the contrary to extend it to those who apparently are no longer believers, that is, to that 'ninety-five per cent' of whom it is customary today to make the uncharitable assertion that they have simply forgotten to break with the Church. Tillich pleads on their behalf: 'It is not permissible to designate as "unchurched" those who have become alienated from organised denominations and traditional creeds. In living among these groups for half a generation I learned how much of the latent Church there is within them. I encountered the experience of the finite character of human existence, the quest for the eternal and unconditioned, an absolute devotion to justice and love, a hope that lies beyond any Utopia, an appreciation of Christian values and a very sensitive recognition of the ideological misuse of Christianity in the interpenetration of Church and State. It has often seemed to me that the "latent Church", as I call what I found among these groups, was a truer church than the organised denominations, if only because its members did not presume to possess the truth. . . . The latent Church has neither the religious nor the organisational weapons necessary for this struggle. . . .

The concept of the latent Church is a concept of the boundary on which countless Protestants in our day are fated to stand.'[69]

But the question now arises: If all phenomena and things in the world, cultural movements as well as the Churches, the latent Church as well as the manifest Church, represent something unconditional and religious, one merely in a hidden and mediated way, and the others in an open and unmediated way – why is there still any distinction between them?

Tillich's answer is as follows: Because the kingdom of God has still not come, because God is not yet all in all – 'If we could see the holy in every reality, we should be in the kingdom of God.' The proof that we do not yet live in the kingdom of God is the fact that although everything in the world has a connection with the unconditional, religion nevertheless still exists as a separate sphere within the world. For Tillich, religion is the most convincing proof of the fall of man. It owes its 'origin to need': its existence is due to the fact that man is separated from his true being and lives in the state of estrangement. The New Being which appeared in Jesus Christ has done away with this separation in principle, but not yet in practice. And for this reason religion still exists in the world, and with it the division it brings: 'A religious culture beside a secular culture, a temple beside a town hall, a Lord's Supper beside a daily supper, prayer beside work, meditation beside research, *caritas* beside *eros*.' Tillich knows that this 'duality' can never be overcome in time and space, that is, within history. But it makes a difference to him 'whether the duality is deepened into a bridgeless gap . . . or whether it is recognised as something which should not be and which is overcome fragmentarily by anticipation, so to speak'.[70] Tillich would prefer to overcome the duality by anticipation. Here we find ourselves once again face to face with the basic motive of his theology, the ultimate impulse of his theological thought.

Christian universalism

Deep down in Tillich's theology there is a powerful and indeed dangerous impulse to do away with the distance between God and the world, and thereby, not perhaps to remove the cleavage between religion and civilisation, temple and town hall, prayer and work, meditation and research, but as far as possible to bridge over it. His belief-ful realism presses on towards unity, almost to the point of becoming a new Christian monism. The fragmentation and estrangement in the world causes Tillich suffering, and fills him with an insatiable longing to win back its lost unity. He would like to join, unite, heal and reconcile. He 'hungers and thirsts' for a unified meaning for the world; he seeks for it and finds it. Looking back upon his student days in Berlin, Heinz-Dietrich Wendland recalls Tillich's lectures: 'What fascinated us and often almost overwhelmed us was the dynamism and the unifying power of his thought: this was not specialist theology remote from the world, but an attempt to pursue every movement of the stormy years of the 1920's, every mode of human existence, every form of society right down to its ultimate foundation in the ground and abyss of being, and in everything to find the One which concerns us *unconditionally*.'[71]

But at this point a considerable danger threatens Tillich's theology. It lies in the fact that Tillich finds the Christian revelation everywhere in the world, and in this way erodes away its distinctiveness. This is the charge which throughout his life Karl Barth has raised against him. As early as 1923 he accuses Tillich of 'making much too sweeping generalisations', of 'a too facile universalism'. In reading Tillich's writings, he perceives everywhere a 'large steamroller of faith and revelation' which carries him over everything, over houses, men and animals, as though it could be taken for granted that judgement and grace prevailed everywhere, as though everything could simply be drawn into the paradox of the revelation in Christ. In Barth's view it is not possible to speak in this way of God's revelation. What takes place in it is not a general 'It is' and 'There is', but a unique event and happening, the imparting of a gift. The young Barth would have nothing to do with such a 'theology of the tower of Babel', and neither will he in his old age. In the last lecture which he gave in Basle, Barth once again explicitly mentioned Tillich. He regards his idea of philosophical theology or theological philosophy as 'pure wishful thinking, "too good to be true"'. Certainly, in Barth's view it is relatively simple for anyone with a certain talent and appetite for speculative thought to create such a synthesis, but this would be to reduce to a unity and to a reciprocal cancelling out of things which in this world either *de iure* or *de facto* are *dual*. And therefore Barth can only cry: 'What solutions! What prospects! "Would that we were there!"'[72] The philosopher Wilhelm Weischedel raises the same objections against Paul Tillich as the theologian Karl Barth. In his 'respectful disagreement' with Tillich he shows how by the aid of his theologically exaggerated concept of being Tillich brings philosophy and theology so close to one another that both seem to coalesce into one. And therefore Weischedel asks the same question of Tillich as Barth: 'Does everything not merge together as a result into an undifferentiated oneness?'[73]

In fact there is in Tillich's theology and religious feeling something undifferentiated, indefinite and vague. The boundary between the reality of God and the reality of the world threatens to become confused. God seems to become so worldly, and the world so divine, that both begin to lose their outline, God his deity and the world its worldliness. Thus it was possible, at the annual meeting of the American Philosophical Association in Chicago in May 1960, for three prominent philosophers to discuss in all seriousness the question: 'Is Tillich an atheist?' The journal *The Christian Century* wrote about this discussion at the time: 'The problem presented in such a provocative way was not merely whether America's most eminent theologian was actually advocating atheism, but whether his statements about God do or do not affirm the reality of a Being worthy to be made the object of religious devotion. . . .'[74] Tillich's desire to bring God into the world and to reconcile everything that is separated leads him to the point where there is a risk of God's losing his personal being, and where the concrete features of his countenance begin to fade. It is no accident that when Tillich speaks of God he prefers impersonal expressions: 'being', 'the divine', 'the unconditional' (and uses the neuter gender in German: *das Sein, das Göttliche*, etc.).

But the risk of confusing distinctions and obscuring clear patterns is only the shadow cast by a bright light. This bright light which shines in Tillich's theology is his loving and almost pastoral concern to help his contemporaries to look for God not beyond their history, not above and outside the world, nor in some remote foreign land or some remote alien period, but in the reality of the world and their lives, as their ultimate true reality. Tillich's theological purpose can be summed up in a single sentence: 'The profoundest demand of all is that we learn to speak of God in such a way that he appears not as an object above all other objects, nor as a mere symbol, but as the really real in everything that claims reality.'[75]

One might almost say of the great Protestant theologians of the twentieth century that they will be known by their prepositions! The strength and the weakness of the theology of each one can be seen in the preposition which is predominant in his case. In Karl Barth's case, this is 'above': God is *above* the world. Barth's strength is that he has rediscovered the deity of God, and that he has discovered it as love; while the obverse of his strength is that he places him too high in heaven and as a result loses sight of concrete history. In Bultmann's case, the dominating preposition is 'opposite': man stands *opposite* God, faced with a decision. Bultmann's strength is that he understands the Christian kerygma as a call to existential decision and therefore brings it into the present day, while the obverse of his strength is that in this process the gospel loses its relationship to reality, and instead of a gift becomes a demand. In Tillich, the preposition which dominates is 'in'; we encounter the reality of God *in* the reality of the world, as its ultimate true reality. Tillich's strength is that in his work man really encounters God in the world, in everything that exists, not as an alien law imposed upon him from outside or above, but as something which concerns him directly and unconditionally, and happens in the midst of us; the obverse of his strength is that God and the world are so interwoven that man can no longer tell the world from God, and can no longer tell God from the world. But wherever the presence of God in the world and his nearness to man is taken as seriously as Tillich takes it, it is never possible to avoid a tinge of pantheism or mysticism.

It is characteristic of Tillich's theological approach that he chose as a text for his examination sermon as a candidate Paul's statement: 'All things are yours; and you are Christ's; and Christ is God's' (1 Cor. 3:22 f.). In the last analysis, Tillich's whole theology from beginning to end is nothing other than an exegesis of this text: 'The whole world is yours, he [Paul] says, the whole life, present and future, not parts of it. These important words speak of scientific knowledge and its passion, artistic beauty and its excitement, politics and their use of power, eating and drinking and their joy, sexual love and its ecstasy, family life and its warmth and friendship with its intimacy, justice with its clarity, nature with its might and restfulness, the man-made world above nature, the technical world and its fascination, philosophy . . . with its profundity – daring to ask ultimate questions. In all of these things is wisdom of this world and power of this world and all these things are ours. They belong to us and we belong to them; we create them, and they fulfil us.'[76]

The right to describe such a vast sphere and to draw 'everything', the reality of the whole world, into Christian faith and Christian theology, is possible for Tillich only because of the continuation of Paul's saying: 'And you are Christ's.' In Jesus the Christ, a New Being has appeared, and it is the New Being which gives Tillich authority for his philosophical theology, which forms the tacit and rarely uttered assumption of everything which he says about God and the world, and which gives his theology its christological unity and cosmic universality. In Tillich's work there is a 'christological universalism' similar to that in Barth, but it is more deeply rooted in concrete history, and is therefore more concealed.

When Paul Tillich returned to Germany after the war as a guest lecturer, one theologian said that his theology was like a 'late flowering' of the Western mind. A year later, another theologian, on the occasion of another lecture, exclaimed: 'This man was born one hundred years too soon!' Which of them was right? Both statements apply to Tillich. In his theology he reaped the harvest of the spirit of antiquity and of the Christian West. But he did not gather it in and store it up, he milled it and turned it into bread for men today and tomorrow. He 'stored up' the past in view of the future. And the future is stronger for him than the past, the vision of what is becoming more powerful than the taking stock of what has been.

CHAPTER TEN

THE END OF THE PROTESTANT ERA?

A new interpretation of the doctrine of justification

No other twentieth-century Protestant theologian has given such fundamental consideration to the future of Protestantism and so honestly posed the question of its possible end as Paul Tillich. For this reason, it is proper for our stocktaking of Protestant theology in the present century to conclude with him. He has thought out the essential ideas and doctrines of Protestantism to their logical end, to the point at which they are shown to have finally come to an end, or else are transformed. Tillich was driven to this intensive critical consideration of the fate of Protestantism not by the objective interest of a neutral observer, but by the personal involvement of one who was intimately concerned himself. Throughout his life he has felt himself to belong in a special way to Protestantism, and within Protestantism, to Lutheranism.

In the autobiographical sketch which was written in 1936, three years after his emigration from Germany, and in which, in order to introduce himself to his new readers and hearers in America, he described how his thoughts had developed out of his life, Tillich writes: 'I am a Lutheran by birth, education, religious experience and theological reflection. . . . The substance of my religion is and remains Lutheran. . . . My philosophical thinking also expresses this unique content.' Tillich lists numerous elements of this 'Lutheran substance': 'a consciousness of the "corruption" of existence, a repudiation of every kind of social Utopia (including the metaphysics of progressivism), an awareness of the irrational and demonic nature of existence, an appreciation of the mystical element in religion, and a rejection of Puritanical legalism in private and corporal life.' But the principal element in Tillich's Lutheran substance is the *doctrine of justification*, Luther's doctrine of the justification of man in the sight of God through faith alone. It is this – under the influence of his master Martin Kähler in Halle – which formed the starting-point of his theological thinking and which throughout his life remained the hidden centre of his theological and religious existence.[1] The doctrine of justification also forms the basis of his conception of Protestantism. Everything that Tillich says about the nature and destiny

of Protestantism originates and has its enduring foundation in this
doctrine.

Tillich's attitude to the Reformation doctrine of justification is
determined by a twofold realisation. He is firmly convinced that the
essence of the doctrine of justification is of as much concern to us today
as it was to the men of the sixteenth century. But he is equally sure that
the form in which the doctrine of justification has been handed down is
no longer intelligible and acceptable to us today: 'This idea is strange to
the man of today and even to Protestant people in the churches; indeed
it is so strange . . . that there is scarcely any way of making it intelligible
to him. . . . This whole complex of ideas which for more than a century –
not so very long ago – was discussed in every household and workshop,
in every market and country inn of Germany, is now scarcely understandable even to our most intelligent scholars. We have here a break-
ing-down of tradition that has few parallels. And we should not imagine
that it will be possible in some simple fashion to leap over this gulf and
resume our connection with the Reformation again.' Consequently,
Tillich also regards the rediscovery of Luther's theology, which has
come to be known as the 'Luther Renaissance', as inadequate for our
own time. It remains too much within the framework of mere historical
repetition, and is consequently of more significance for academic study
than for practical religion. If the doctrine of justification is really to
have power and meaning for us once again, then we have no choice but
to reinterpret for ourselves the religious reality which it once implied,
and which is still the same at the present day, and to express it in new
words for contemporary man.[2]

Tillich's concern in the renewal of the doctrine of justification is not
with a single article of dogma, but with the basis of all belief in God.
For not merely the doctrine of justification, but all concrete elements of
Christian preaching, even its most central doctrines, such as those of
God, Christ, the Church and revelation, have been called into question
for the men of our time. Tillich in consequence sees his task as that of
making the content of the Lutheran doctrine of justification a force for
our time in a new way, but without proclaiming the concrete religious
statements associated with it. According to Tillich, our guiding principle
in the new interpretation of the doctrine of justification must be 'the
search for God beyond what we usually call "God", the search for God
who is the ground which sustains everything that has a particular
existence of its own, and would therefore also sustain a God who himself was a particular existent'.[3] Consequently, for Tillich the renewal of

the doctrine of justification is identical with the overcoming of super-naturalism or theism in theology. This is the sense in which he has undertaken to reinterpret the Reformation doctrine of justification for our own time. One could regard his argument as taking place in three steps, in each of which it becomes more radical and universal, but at the same time more abstract.

In his *new interpretation of the doctrine of justification* Tillich begins with the 'situation', as required by his 'method of correlation'.[4] He sees the situation as determined by the fact that today autonomous culture has collapsed. This collapse of autonomous culture has made modern man realise once again that his existence is unconditionally threatened, and has therefore made him receptive again to the doctrine of justification. The central content of the doctrine of justification is the radical procla-mation of the 'human boundary situation', and the experience which modern man has had in the collapse of autonomous culture corresponds to this: he has once again become aware that his existence is totally threatened by non-being. From this situation, the question of certainty in life arises: What is it that gives certainty to our lives? What can we base ourselves on? What is the foundation of our existence?

This is the question which the doctrine of justification must answer today. According to Tillich, this answer is twofold. It consists first of all in the radical recognition of the human boundary situation, in an unconditional *No* to every attempt on the part of man to secure himself against the total threat to his existence and to escape it. There is no security for man – 'neither through his submerging himself in the vital life-process, through intellectual or spiritual activity, through sacra-ments, through mysticism and asceticism, through right belief or strenuous piety'. Everything that man undertakes in order to create certainty for himself, and to give his life an ultimate firm basis, is con-demned to failure. It is a concealed form of man's autocratic tendencies which raises what is relative to an absolute and so tries to create for him the certainty which he desires, thus basing his life upon him-self.[5]

But this denial is merely the other side of the unconditional *Yes* to man which is contained in the doctrine of justification: '*You are accepted*, accepted by that which is greater than you, and the name of which you do not know. Do not ask for the name now; perhaps you will find it later. Do not try to do anything now; perhaps later you will do much. Do not seek for anything; do not perform anything; do not intend anything. *Simply accept the fact that you are accepted!* If that happens to us, we experience grace. After such an experience, we may not be better than before, and we may not believe more than before. But everything is transformed. In that moment, grace conquers sin, and reconciliation bridges the gulf of estrangement. And nothing is demanded of this experience, no religious or moral or intellectual presupposition, nothing but *acceptance*.' The unconditional Yes to man is based on the taking possession of man by the power of the New Being which has appeared in Jesus Christ, and holds him and sustains him before he knows it, before he has even begun to ask, to doubt and to despair. This Yes sounds through all Tillich's sermons like a bell, ringing out over the questions, doubts and despairs of man. One cannot preach grace more unconditionally, more radically and more universally than Tillich does. Nothing is demanded of man here: no moral endeavour, no intellectual achievement, not even the acceptance of a concrete religious statement, not even the knowledge of the presupposition of divine grace, not even the naming of the name of God. Man must only accept that he is accepted: 'He must accept acceptance.'[6]

But Tillich goes even further in his reinterpretation of the Reformation doctrine of justification, and it is here that he takes the decisive step: he applies the principle of justification by faith not merely to the religious aspect of moral life, but also to the *intellectual life of religion*: not merely the sinner, but also the doubter is justified by faith. Tillich sees faith hidden at the bottom of every serious doubt, that is, faith that there is truth. Anyone who doubts the truth thereby proclaims his infinite passion for truth. And so the doubter remains within the truth, even though his sole truth is his very lack of truth; and the sceptic partakes of faith, even though his faith has no concrete content. Wherever the situation of doubt is experienced in its most extreme radical form there the certainty emerges that the truth which the doubter seeks and the meaning of life for which he who is in despair wrestles, is not the goal but the prerequisite of all doubt and despair. Consequently, the doubter, with his doubt, and he who despairs, with his despair, testify that they are in the truth and therefore in unity with God – and thus they are 'justified' in their thinking. Tillich concludes this argument with the statement: 'So the paradox got hold of me that he who seriously denies God, affirms him.'[7]

Here we have the application of the doctrine of justification to intellectual *thought*, justification not merely of the sinner, but also of the *doubter*! Just as no moral works justify man in the sight of God, neither do any works of the intellect: neither correct thought as a 'work' nor the renunciation of all thought can lead to God. The revelation of truth can no more become a possession than the forgiveness of sins. Just as no one can boast of possessing love, so no one – no believer and no Church – can boast of possessing truth. 'Orthodoxy is intellectual pharisaism.'[8] Tillich can even go so far in his application of the doctrine of justification to intellectual thought, and therefore in his warning against every kind of heteronomy, as to praise Pilate because he doubted the existence of the truth: 'Let me do something unusual from a Christian standpoint, namely, to express the praise of Pilate – not the unjust judge, but the cynic and sceptic; and of all those among us in whom Pilate's question is alive. For in the depth of every serious doubt and every despair of truth, the passion for truth is still at work. Don't give in too quickly to those who want to alleviate your anxiety about truth. Don't be seduced into a truth which is not really *your* truth, even if the seducer is your Church, or your party, or your parental tradition. Go with Pilate, if you cannot go with Jesus; but go in seriousness with him!'[9]

The discovery that not merely the sinner but also the doubter is justified by faith brought Tillich 'a strong feeling of relief'. Through this discovery, as he tells us, he became a 'conscious Protestant', and in fact it was this alone which made it possible for him to remain a theologian. The personal and theological consequences of this discovery were 'immense' for him.[10]

By extending justification to intellectual thought and therefore to the doubter, Tillich comes to see Christianity as a gospel for all men, not merely for believers, but also for unbelievers, for those who despair of the meaning of life and so feel that it is impossible for them to believe in God. This radical and universal understanding of the doctrine of justification makes it possible for Tillich to perceive God even where the name 'God' is no longer heard. If this interpretation of justification is correct, then there is 'no possible atheism', and atheism is an 'impossibility' and an 'illusion'. And it is this which Paul Tillich, like Karl Barth, in fact asserts. He cannot amass sufficient paradoxes to express this conclusion: doubt about the meaning of life is an expression of its meaning and the experience of being separated from God an expression of his presence; God is present in every act of faith, even if the act of faith includes the denial of God; the wish that there should be no God is one of the 'genuine elements of profound religion'; we can only deny God because he impels us to do so; the very protest against God is a hidden demonstration on behalf of God. For God himself is the presupposition of the question about God and of doubt about him.[11]

But Tillich has expressed the idea of justification for contemporary man even more radically, understanding it as a result more universally, but at the same time in a more abstract form. The fear that dominates our age is the 'fear of doubt and meaninglessness'. It is the fear of losing the meaning of one's own existence or of having already lost it. Consequently, the most important and at the same time the most disturbing question is that which is posed to faith. In Tillich's previous exposition of the doctrine of justification, particularly in his application of justification to intellectual thought, truth is still present as a presupposition in the doubt of the doubter, and in the despair of him who despairs in the meaning of life. But what happens if meaninglessness becomes absolute and swallows everything, if life is as meaningless as death, guilt as doubtful as perfection, and being no more meaningful than non-being? How can faith then endure?

In his book *The Courage to Be* (1952), and especially in its last chapter, Tillich gives to this radical question an equally radical answer.[12] There he attempts to give a new interpretation of the expression 'faith', which has become unintelligible, by an analysis of 'courage'. As Tillich once asserted in a personal conversation, he wrote this book for men who are 'possessed by radical doubt' – 'and this is the reason for the philosophical mode of argument, the philosophical language and attitude'.[13]

What kind of courage is able to take non-being into itself in the form of doubt and meaninglessness? What kind of faith can endure together with doubt and meaninglessness? It is this question with which Tillich deals here. The answer must remain within the 'situation': it must accept the state of meaninglessness as a given fact. It would be no answer if it demanded that this state should be done away with – for this is the very thing which is impossible. It must be an answer which looks doubt and meaninglessness in the face and therefore a courage or faith which can endure doubt and meaninglessness.

By identifying the possible answer Tillich has already given the actual answer: the courage which looks despair in the face already *is* faith, and the act of taking meaninglessness on oneself is a meaningful act. Tillich substantiates this by the following argument. In the situation of meaninglessness the meaning of life is reduced to doubt concerning the meaning of life. But this doubt is itself an act of life; it is something positive – in spite of its negative content. Every radical negation lives from the fact that it must affirm itself as a living act in order to be capable of a radical denial. At every moment in which we doubt the meaning of life, this meaning is affirmed by us: 'The negative lives from the positive it negates.'

The self-affirmation which is concealed in every radical negation is not a human achievement. Rather, it is an expression of the self-affirmation of being itself. The courage to be is rooted in the ground of being. Here Tillich relates his argument to his ontology. He conceives of being as the 'power of being'. This means that being has non-being within itself, and constantly overcomes it. Thus being itself has the character of self-affirmation, and man partakes in this self-affirmation. In every act of the courage to be, the power of being itself is at work, whether man recognises it or not; in every act of faith, the ground of being is manifested, however questionable the concrete content of the act of faith may be. There are no valid proofs of the existence of God, but there are acts of courage or faith in which, as for example when we look despair in the face or take meaninglessness upon ourselves, we affirm the power of being and thereby bear witness to the presence of God in all that exists. Tillich seeks to overcome the fear of doubt and meaning-lessness through a kind of mysticism of being: through the mystical participation of all that exists in self-affirming being itself.

This faith, which takes doubt and meaninglessness into itself without appealing to a special divine revelation, Tillich calls *absolute faith*. The expression signifies that this faith no longer has any concrete content: 'It is simply faith – undirected, absolute.' It is the mere experience of being accepted: who or what it is that accepts cannot be defined, because all definitions are broken down by doubt and meaninglessness.

The content of absolute faith, if one can speak here of a 'content' at all, is the *God above God*, that is, the God who lies beyond the symbol 'God', who transcends all conceptions of God, who is not a person and has no name and cannot be expressed in any image. Here 'theism', which conceives of God as one being alongside other beings, and one person beside other persons, is transcended: 'The God above God cannot be described.' Consequently, absolute faith is 'without the safety of words and concepts, it is without a name, a Church, a cult, a theology. But it is moving in the depth of all of them.'

In what he says about absolute faith and the God above God, Tillich's thought has gone to an extreme which is only permissible for a theolo-gian if he is impelled towards it not by a delight in speculation but by love for his fellow men. Tillich himself has said of his book *The Courage to Be* that he let the conclusion 'come to a point like a needle', and that this needle point 'is meant to prick'.[14]

And prick it does, unbelievers lightly, but theologians painfully. It is Tillich's intention to give those who do not believe the courage to believe, by showing them that their doubt and despair contains an act of self-affirmation, which does not come from their own heart, but in which the power of being is at work. As far as theologians are concerned, Tillich points out to them that in the face of radical doubt and total meaninglessness, purely personal categories such as 'encounter', 'subject-object', 'I and thou', are inadequate, and instead 'personalism with respect to God is balanced by a trans-personal presence of the divine'. This requirement is in accordance with the paradoxical way in which the Bible speaks of God: God forgives sin, and it is at the same time he who brings about the acceptance of forgiveness in man; God is spoken to in prayer as 'Thou', and is at the same time closer to man than he is to himself. It is paradoxes of this kind which constantly drive faith towards the God above the God of theism. This is something which the Church must learn in its preaching. It should not give up the concrete and personal symbols in which it speaks of God, but it should know and admit that they are symbols, and look in them for the power of being itself.

Tillich's *The Courage to Be* is a rescue attempt undertaken with the courage of despair: Tillich seeks to save man's faith by refining the idea of God to an extreme abstraction. He does the same as Herbert Braun: the cargo is thrown overboard so that at least the ship may remain afloat. But does Tillich really succeed in rescuing faith in this way? He himself says of his absolute faith that 'it is not a place where one can live'. It is only the 'needle point', the uttermost extreme of theological utterance.

The Protestant principle

The radical and universal interpretation of the Protestant doctrine of justification provides Paul Tillich with the key for his judgement upon Protestantism. It is from this that he derives what he calls the *Protestant principle*.[15] With the aid of this principle, Tillich leads Protestantism out of the ecclesiastical and denominational cul-de-sac into which it has wandered through its own fault and by historical destiny, and gives it back the wide scope of a far-reaching spiritual movement. But he also uses it to submit Protestantism as an historical phenomenon to a theological criticism, and examines its possibilities and future tasks.

The Protestant principle is 'the unfathomable basis in Protestantism', 'the critical and dynamic source of all Protestant realisations', 'the ultimate criterion of all religious and all spiritual experiences'. It is the expression of the true relationship between the unconditional and the conditional, or in religious terms, between God and man. Both the 'ground' of our existence and the 'judgement' upon our existence are revealed in it, together with the Yes and No which are contained in the human boundary situation as proclaimed by the Protestant doctrine of justification.

What is at work in the Protestant principle is the creative ground of all being, which is continuously pressing towards a new realisation in history, and in which there is as it were a holy urge towards historical realisation. In contrast to the 'inclination to intellectualisation' which is to be found elsewhere in Protestantism, Tillich regards it as of great importance that the Protestant principle is not merely an 'idea', but is realised in a concrete way in 'positive formative power'. The forms in which this positive formative power appear are called by Tillich *Gestalten*, 'embodiments in a concrete form', of grace. For example, the word of God is spoken to us from beyond our being; but if it is received, it is no longer only transcendent, it is also immanent, and creates a 'divine structure of reality': it brings about faith as the formative power of personal life or of a community and Church. Thus, according to Tillich, grace chooses finite forms in order to appear in them: human form in Christ, verbal form in the Bible, material form in the sacraments, and in the weakness of the Church. But it must be noted that divine grace only *appears* in a finite form, and is not changed into it. Wherever a finite form is changed into a divine form, it is idolatry, and man is always making himself idols.

A protest then arises against such idolatry, and it was this which gave the Protestant principle its name. It is the 'prophetic protest' against any attempt to declare something conditional to be unconditional, to exalt something finite into the infinite, whether it is the structure of a state, a world view, a system of society, a social class, but also a hierarchy, a Church, a denomination, a dogma or the Bible itself. The Protestant principle attacks all sanctified authorities, powers, traditions, doctrines and institutions, and subjects them to criticism. It fights against every objectivisation of God, and will not tolerate any sacred places, persons, actions and times. No one can tie the divine down to time and place. Tillich's theology attains an almost prophetic ardour in its passionate protest against any attempt to reduce God to finite proportions. It culminates in the statement that there is no unconditional truth of faith –

except one, that no man possesses any such truth. Christianity's symbol for this is the cross of Christ: the 'Son of God' was not slain by the irreligious, because they were against divine truth, but by the devout, who believed that they possessed divine truth. Consequently, the cross signifies the judgement upon every human claim to unconditional truth and authority.

Thus in the Protestant principle affirmation and denial, positive formative power and critical protest, are united. This union brings to light the 'ambiguous significance' of all religion: wherever men accept God, they do so in a religious form, and this religious form is the business of the priest. But wherever men accept God, they 'unavoidably' make an idol of him, and the prophet then makes his protest. Thus the priestly and the prophetic elements, formative power and protest, are in conflict, and yet the one derives from the other. This unresolved tension forms the 'eternal problem' of religion, namely that God is present, but not present as an object. And it is this which the Protestant principle expresses with its affirmation and denial.

The Protestant principle is not necessarily linked with Protestantism as an historical phenomenon. It is of universal significance, present in all periods of history, and its possibilities are never exhausted, neither in the Reformation, nor in primitive Christianity, nor in any other form of Christianity. The prophets of Israel proclaimed it, and it can be seen in the picture of Jesus as the Christ; it forms the basis of the Reformation Churches, and it is no stranger even to Catholicism. It is not even limited to Christianity, but can also be found in all other great religions, and indeed not only in other religions, but in all other intellectual movements. It can also be proclaimed by secular movements, by individuals and groups who without Protestant symbols express the true human situation in the face of the ultimate and unconditional; and if these movements, individuals and groups do this better and with greater authority than the Protestant Churches, then it is they and not the Protestant Churches which represent the Protestant principle.

Consequently, Tillich distinguishes between Protestantism as a *reality* and as a *principle*. As an historical reality, Protestantism is limited and transitory like any other historical reality, but as a principle it is as unlimited and enduring as the experience of the unconditional in the world. As an historical phenomenon, Protestantism is subject to its own principles, which means that the protest of the Protestant principle is also directed against any absolute claim on the part of Protestantism. The Protestant principle is also the judge of the affairs of Protestantism.

Tillich considers that this may possibly even be the way in which the Protestant principle must be asserted today. He asks whether the *end of the Protestant era* may not perhaps have come at the present time, and this he regards as by no means a purely rhetorical question.

The post-Protestant era

While Tillich regards religion as in general more powerful than before the First World War, at least in men's feeling and longings, he considers that the power of Protestantism has at the same time declined: 'Protestantism now faces the most difficult struggle of all the occidental religions and denominations in the present world situation.'[16] Tillich sees the reason for this weakening of Protestantism in its lack of synchronisation: the historical development is contrary to Protestantism, and the relationship between the times and the values of Protestantism has changed. What Protestantism once affirmed seems today to have become uncertain, and what it denies, men today are longing for. The freedom and moral responsibility of the individual, personal decision, spiritual independence, intellectual honesty, rational clarity – all these were once the great affirmations of Protestantism, for which it took up arms; spiritual dependence, subjection to outside authority, heteronomy, conformity, and collectivism were what it denied and fought against. But today we see its affirmations becoming negations and its negations affirmations. We live in a period in which the universal loss of the meaning of existence also threatens to break down every personal life, in which individuals are determined by the motives of others, in which everyone is somebody else, and no one is any longer himself. Thus we are faced today not so much with the task of giving rein to the free personality, but rather that of ordering the masses anew and therefore of giving a place, not, as formerly, to the individual, but to the collective. But this situation creates an intellectual and emotional climate in which authoritarian and totalitarian tendencies flourish with great ease. It is as though men, and particularly the younger generation, are weary of their autonomy, as though they can no longer bear the fearful burden of having to make their own independent intellectual and moral decisions, and as though they want to be as free as they can be. What they desire is security. They prefer security to freedom. Consequently, each looks for a new authority, which is expressed in ordered forms of life and easily accessible symbols. There is a longing for a new collective order, a preference for living in a safe abode, even in a safe abode of faith. But

this whole development is completely contrary to the spirit of Protestantism. As a result, hardly anyone today still seriously believes that the
forces which will restore the unity of future society can come from the
great Protestant Churches.

The very situation which is unfavourable to Protestantism creates a
new opportunity for Roman Catholicism today. Catholicism is
attuned to man's need of security and authority at the end of the
modern age, in the same way as Protestantism was attuned to his
demand for freedom at the beginning of the modern age. It seems to
offer what modern man longs for: a thorough-going heteronomy,
freedom from the burden of autonomous responsibility, an unbroken
tradition and authority, an ancient and enduring life of its own. Consequently, Catholicism exercises 'a great attraction' upon modern man,
where Protestantism can only defend itself with difficulty.

Today's situation manifests not merely a temporary but a fundamental weakness of Protestantism, or rather, the obverse of a strength which
Protestantism has had from its origin, and which very soon after it came
into being became a danger to it.[17] Tillich describes this danger as
follows: 'One of the earliest experiences I had with Protestant preaching
was its moralistic character or, more exactly, its tendency to over-
burden the personal centre and to make the relation to God dependent
upon continuous, conscious decisions and experiences.' The impression
of Protestant preaching which Tillich describes here can be summed
up in the terms 'individualisation', 'intellectualisation', 'spiritualisation'. Whenever Tillich speaks of the future of Protestantism, he
mentions this threefold danger, which is basically a single danger: its
origin lies in the centre of Protestantism, at its strongest point, and consists of the excessive moral and intellectual demand made upon the
individual.

Protestant preaching concentrates the religious life upon the individual act of justification, and draws many graces into this one grace.
Thus it turns to the centre of the personality, the conscience, and forces
it to a decision: every Protestant Christian must undergo the original
religious experience of Martin Luther. It demands 'the radicalism of the
heroic age of Protestantism as the permanent attitude of everybody'.
At the same time, everything is based upon the word. Sacraments and
symbols are replaced by rational arguments, so that man has scarcely
anything visible left to take hold of. The mystery of religion disappears.
In this way, Protestantism became a 'highly intellectualised religion'.
Tillich sees the visible sign of this in the gown of the Protestant minister.

It is the medieval professorial gown, and thus it symbolises the fact that ultimate authority within the Protestant Churches is represented by the faculties of theology. But professors are authorities in the first instance not because of their religious charisma, but because of their skill in logical and academic argumentation.

As a result of this one-sided emphasis on intellectual understanding and moral decision, Protestantism created a 'theology of consciousness'; that is, religion was largely limited to the sphere of the rational consciousness. The unconscious levels remained untouched, empty and suppressed, in a state of religious atrophy, while at the same time the conscious levels of the mind were overloaded by the constant demand for understanding and the obligation to make a decision. But the suppressed vital and emotional forces reacted against the dictatorship of the rational consciousness in a chaotic and destructive eruption. The consequence has been an increase of mental illness, in Protestant countries in particular – a fact to which Tillich frequently refers.

The form of the Protestant Church is also in accordance with this intellectualisation of religion. Either it gives an organisational form to the Protestant principle and makes it the guardian of 'pure doctrine', enshrined in the letters of the Bible and supervised by the ministry of the Church, or else, in an eternal protest against every concrete religious content, it becomes 'an almost formless group' of persons, 'of secular persons without any sacramental quality, in which from one generation to another the consciousness of the human boundary situation has been handed down'. The more spiritual the Protestant Church has become, the more it has created a vacuum for other forces which have crowded into the areas of life it has left empty. The final result has been the complete secularisation of the world and the end of religion. Protestantism has well understood how to form individual religious personalities, but it has failed in the education of the masses. The damage done by Protestantism is coming to light today in man's industrial society.

The future of Protestantism will depend on how far it becomes able, by the power of its own Protestant principle, to transform itself and adapt itself to the new situation. Tillich is certain that the Protestant era in the form it has taken hitherto is at an end, and that Protestantism must seek a new synthesis. It is not yet possible to describe exactly what the era that is to come will be like. All that can be said is that it will be neither a return to the Catholic era, nor a repetition of primitive Christianity, nor an advance to a new form of secularisation: 'It is something beyond all these forms, a new form of Christianity, to be expected and prepared for, but not yet to be named.' Nevertheless, a consideration of the demands of the situation and the content of the Christian message makes it possible even today to enumerate some of the elements which will certainly form part of it. And therefore Tillich ventures to give not a complete picture, but a preliminary and hasty sketch of the *post-Protestant era*. He mentions in general three elements as 'requirements for the future'.[18]

Even in the post-Protestant era the *prophetic Protestant principle* must be maintained.[19] The protest against any power which claims for itself an absolute or divine character, whether it is a state, a leader, a party, or a Church, is even more necessary today than it used to be, for under the pressure of modern collectivism new totalitarian powers and authorities are everywhere asserting themselves. But at the present hour the Protestant principle ought only to take the form of a corrective, and not of a basic and constituent element of the Church. Since the critical and divisive power of the Protestant principle has prevailed for so long, it is now important to emphasise its constructive and unifying power.

This leads to Tillich's second and most important requirement for a future Protestantism, and one which demands the greatest change in today's Protestant Church. It can be summed up by saying: Renewal of form through *sacraments* and *symbols*.[20] Mere formless preaching, through the word which is addressed to the intellect and appeals to the will, and which therefore makes the Church into a school or a humanitarian society, must be complemented by living and concrete 'embodiments' of grace. It is this which Tillich hopes for from the renewal of sacramental and symbolic thought in Protestantism. Sacraments and symbols take hold of the whole man, not only his conscious being, but also his unconscious being. They are an expression of the fact that being comes before obligation, the sacred reality before the moral demand, grace before faith, and the Church before the devotion of the individual – in short, that Christianity is a religion and not a morality. It is the presence of God, represented through the symbols themselves. Consequently, for Tillich 'mysticism' is one of the requirements he lays down for a future Protestantism: 'A Protestantism in which meditation and contemplation, ecstasy and "mystic union" have no longer a place has ceased to be a religion; it has become an intellectual and formal system in traditional religious concepts.'

With regard to the challenge posed to the Church by industrial mass society, Tillich sees here a 'fateful question' for Protestantism: 'The

masses that are disintegrated need symbols that are immediately understandable without the mediation of intellect.' Whether Protestantism will
exist in the future or not will depend largely upon whether Protestantism
succeeds in obtaining such new symbols. Tillich, however, is perfectly
aware that he is asking for something beyond human control. But he
trusts the grace of God to realise itself in ever new embodiments.

However, the renewal of sacramental and symbolic thought does not
signify a new separation between the sacred and profane spheres.
Profaneness remains an obligation for the Protestantism of the future.
Thus Tillich explicitly mentions profaneness as his second requirement.[21]
So for the post-Protestant or trans-Protestant era everything that
Tillich has said about 'belief-ful realism', 'religion' and the relation
between 'religion and culture' remains valid: the unconditional must be
experienced in the conditional, and the transcendent in this world, so
that the reality of God is not to be sought and found above or outside
the reality of the world, but in the reality of the world, as its ultimate
true reality.

Thus according to Tillich the most important structural elements of a
new pattern of Christian religious belief and practice, and of the Church,
ought to be prophetic criticism, sacramental mysticism and secular
universalism: 'With the realisation of these demands a new era of
Christianity would begin, which would not be non-Protestant, but
post-Protestant.' Tillich describes this new Christianity as an 'evangelical
Catholicism'.[22] The expression signifies that what he has in mind is not
a repetition of medieval Catholicism, but a new Catholicism, which
contains within itself medieval Catholicism together with Protestantism
and humanism, but will go beyond all three. Tillich obviously is not
thinking of a new united Church, but rather of an ecumenical kind of
religion which is at home in all Churches. This is indicated also by the
manner in which he conceives the coming about of post-Protestant
Christianity. It must be sustained by an '*avant-garde* group' which,
keeping its distance from the great Protestant Churches, takes the sociological form of a closed movement, an order or fellowship, which by
religious, political and intellectual means prepares the structure of what
is to come: 'If there were such a movement, the end of the Protestant
era would not yet have arrived!' The idea of 'an order or fellowship' repeatedly recurs in Tillich's work when he is considering the
future of Protestantism.[23] It strikes one as a mixture of resignation and
Utopianism: as though Tillich no longer believed in any large-scale
change, and was therefore taking refuge in a small circle, as though he

had forgotten that the small circle of 'religious socialists' after the First World War did not achieve any large-scale historical effect.

But even if the end of Protestantism had come, in Tillich's view this would not signify the end of the Protestant principle. On the contrary, it would be an effect of the Protestant principle, a consequence of its prophetic protest, and therefore the herald of a new manifestation of its truth and power. In this sense, Tillich shares Schleiermacher's view: 'The Reformation still continues.'[24]

The 'kairos'

Tillich's consideration of the future of Protestantism has gone beyond the mere concerns of the Church and theology, and has increasingly attained the level of an interpretation of the spiritual and religious situation of twentieth-century mankind. Tillich has become more and more a Protestant interpreter of history and a prophetic commentator upon his age. Driven on by his love for his contemporaries, and guided by his method of correlation, which asks about the historical 'situation', in order to give the answer of the eternal gospel concerning it, he has repeatedly turned to consider, speak and write about the destiny of man in our own time. As he has gone on, his judgement has become more and more gloomy, critical and profound, but at the same time, his hope has become more and more universal and radical, and, one may almost say, more desperate. This can be seen from a comparison between his assessments of the spiritual and religious situation after the First World War and again after the second. Such a comparison throws a great deal of light on the course followed by Protestant theology during this period.

In his different interpretations of the spiritual and religious situation after the First World War and after the second, Tillich is guided by his concept of the *kairos*, which is the most characteristic expression of his Protestant view of history.[25] In accordance with Greek usage, Tillich distinguishes between *chronos*, time which can be measured by clocks and which is governed by the regular movement of the heavenly bodies, and *kairos*, the single historical moment determined by destiny; and he fills the concept of the *kairos* with prophetic and Christian content. *Kairos* is 'the fullness of time', the moment in which the eternal breaks into the temporal, shatters and transforms it and prepares it to receive the eternal; the moment in which the conditional cancels itself out and makes itself the instrument of the unconditional. In the *kairos* crisis and creation take place together – crisis, by the attacking and breaking down of an ancient structure of reality which has become demonic; and creation, by the preparation and coming into being of a new, redeemed structure of reality. For Christian faith, the archetype of every *kairos* is the appearance of Jesus as the Christ. This forms the 'centre of history', at which the 'formative principle' which gives meaning to the whole of history, from the beginning to the end, is visible in a concrete form. That which happened in this unique, particular and universal *kairos* is repeated 'in derived form' at every turning-point in history, bringing into being 'centres' of lesser importance, which serve as dividing marks for the periodicity of history. In every *kairos* 'the kingdom of God is at hand', for in every *kairos* there takes place an unrepeatable and unique decision for or against the unconditional. Such a *kairos* does not need to be an age of special outward devotion, but it is an age which faces the unconditional and is open to it, which is permeated and guided by the consciousness of the presence of the unconditional in all cultural forms and functions; in short, it is a 'period of theonomy', characterised by a direct turning towards the divine and an openness to the divine.

Tillich interpreted and experienced the period after the *First World War* as a *kairos*.[26] This was 'an historical moment of fulfilment', 'pregnant with creative possibilities'. It gave Tillich and his friends the impetus to found the religious socialist movement. *Religious socialism* was understood as 'the attempt at interpreting and shaping socialism from the viewpoint of theonomy, from the vision of the *kairos*'. More radical and revolutionary than political socialism, it sought to carry the criticism of the existing state of affairs to the depth and to the point where the unconditional brings forth the crisis and the *kairos* enters awareness. The religious socialists hoped for a new 'era of theonomy'. The occasion for this hope was the collapse of bourgeois idealist culture and of the alliance which the Protestant Church had made with it. This seemed to provide the possibility of closing the profound gulf between the social and political revolution and the tradition of the Church, and in general between secular culture and religion. But the enterprise failed. History has shown that it was too late for such an attempt. In the political and social sphere it turned out to be impossible to break down the materialism of the working-class parties: 'The Old Guard prevailed against us and against the youth of their own movement.' And in the religious sphere a 'neo-orthodoxy' was formed, in the guise of dialectic theology.

But does this mean that the religious socialists were deluded in their belief that after the First World War they experienced a *kairos*, a 'fullness of time'? To this question Tillich gives the paradoxical answer: 'We were wrong and we were not wrong.' The message of the *kairos* is 'always an error', because it sees as immediately present 'what from the idealist point of view never becomes reality and from the realistic point of view is fulfilled over long periods of time'; and the message of the *kairos* is 'never an error', because whoever proclaims it is already taken hold of by the *kairos* and the *kairos* is therefore already present.

After the *Second World War* Tillich did not have the same 'ecstatic experience' as after the First World War. The darkness was greater than the light, and 'Utopian hope' was replaced by 'cynical realism'. But in addition to this, there was a new and decisive element: *the experience of the end*. Looking back upon the period after the First World War, Tillich writes: 'We looked at the beginning of the new more than at the end of the old. We did not realise the price that mankind has to pay for the coming of a new theonomy; we still believed in transitions without catastrophes. We did not see the possibility of final catastrophes as the true prophets, the prophets of doom, announced them. Therefore, our theonomous interpretation of history had a slight tinge of romanticism. . . . This has come to an end because the end itself has appeared like a flash of lightning before our eyes. . . . While after the First World War the mood of a new beginning prevailed, after the Second World War a mood of the end prevails.'[27]

What was borne in upon Tillich everywhere after the Second World War was the *experience of emptiness*, a lack of ultimate validity and absoluteness in all spheres of human existence, in language and education, in politics and philosophy, in the development of personalities and in the life of societies. Tillich sees the reason for the experience of the 'end' and of 'emptiness' in the 'loss of the dimension of depth'.

But for this very reason Tillich considers that the possibility of the new *kairos* is present. The end itself can be transformed into a new beginning, and emptiness itself can contain a promise. Emptiness can become a 'holy emptiness', a vacuum, out of which a new creation becomes possible, like the original creation from nothing. The realisation that we have lost the dimension of depth can already signify a turning towards it: 'Anyone who understands that he is separated from the ground and meaning of his life, is in a certain sense united with it by this understanding.' Nothing is more necessary for us than a radical understanding of our religious situation, resisting the temptation of covering it up by false hopes and Utopias, and of allowing ourselves to be deceived by some increase in Church attendance or some similar growth of ecclesiastical activity. Such outward successes on the part of the Church could be a confirmation of the fact that we have lost touch with the true dimension of religion. If today, after the Second World War, the possibility of a *kairos* exists at all, then it lies in the recognition of the 'end' and of 'emptiness'.[28]

It was in this sense that Tillich preached on the *absence of God* in our time during his last session as a visiting lecturer in the summer term of 1961 in Hamburg: 'We live in a period in which the God we know is the absent God.' What is the reason for this? First of all Tillich lists the usual reasons for the absence of God: our resistance, our indifference, our lack of seriousness, our honest or dishonest questioning, our genuine or cynical doubt. But the final and true answer to the question why God is absent is different: 'The final answer to the question as to who makes God absent is God himself! It is the work of the Spirit that removes God from our sight, not only for some men, but sometimes for many in a particular period. . . . The Spirit of God hides God from our sight.' But in the very fact that God hides himself from us may lie the possibility of a turning-point and therefore of a new *kairos*: 'But in knowing God as the absent God, we *know* of him; we feel his absence as the empty space that is left by something or someone that once belonged to us and has now vanished from our view. . . . And then the absent one may return and take the space that belongs to him, and the Spiritual Presence may break again into our consciousness, awakening us to recognise what we are, shaking and transforming us.'[29]

This experience of the 'absence of God' must be present in the preaching and activity of the Church at the present day. Every religion has two directions, the vertical and the horizontal; it must proclaim eternal meaning and also the realisation in time of eternal meaning. For a long time religion – as exemplified by liberal cultural Protestantism in Europe or the social gospel movement in America – has chiefly devoted its power to the horizontal direction, and in the process has almost forgotten the vertical; and it continues to do so, in part even with renewed efforts, to the present day. It gives political, economic, social and cultural advice, but runs the risk of forgetting its true message, the one thing that is needful: the New Being, the eternal and unconditional. It is true that religion must speak to our contemporary situation, but what it says must be a message from outside; today the vertical is more important than the horizontal: 'If religion had only the word everybody has – every newspaper, every radio, every speaker – if religion simply followed the general trend of public opinion, it would have no word at all worth listening to. If religion gave only a little more enthusiasm, a little more certainty, a little more dignity to something that would be done anyhow, with or without religion, then religion would have no significance at all for the present situation or any other situation. If religion ceased to be the spiritual sword, cutting through all human enthusiasms and certainties and dignities, judging them, transforming them, transcending them – then religion would be swallowed up by the general process of civilisation and should disappear as soon as possible as a useless and disturbing nuisance.'[30]

The question which is usually asked today is 'What shall we do?' But this usual question must be answered by an unusual question: 'Whence can we receive?' Men must once again learn to understand that one can do and give nothing if one has received nothing. And the Church too must learn this again, if it is to have any message for contemporary men: 'Religion is, first, an open hand to receive a gift and, second, an acting hand to distribute gifts.'[31]

But if in the first instance religion is an open hand to receive gifts, then this hand must above all be empty, and Christians too must be ready to give up their entire knowledge of God, which they think they possess, and wait for God. But nothing comes so hard to men as to wait for God. They are always busy making themselves an image of God, instead of waiting for him as he is, and waiting for him to come: 'Our religious life is characterised more by that kind of creation than anything else. I think of the theologian who does not wait for God, because he possesses Him, enclosed within a doctrine. I think of the biblical student who does not wait for God because he possesses Him, enclosed in a book. I think of the churchman who does not wait for God, because he possesses Him, enclosed in an institution. I think of the believer who does not wait for God because he possesses Him, enclosed within his own experience. It is not easy to endure this not having God, this waiting for God. It is not easy to preach, Sunday after Sunday, without convincing ourselves and others that we *have* God, and can dispose of Him. It is not easy to proclaim God to children and pagans, sceptics and secularists, and at the same time to make clear to them that we ourselves do not possess God, that we too wait for Him. I am convinced that much of the rebellion against Christianity is due to the overt or veiled claim of the Christians to possess God, and therefore, also, to the loss of this element of waiting. . . . We are stronger when we wait than when we possess.'[32]

Not to possess God, but to wait upon God; to have even Christianity as though one did not have it – this is the culmination of Paul Tillich's theology; it is at the same time the unrest in the whole of Protestant theology in the twentieth century. Numerous men in our time – theologians and non-theologians – have been ready to confront their traditional knowledge of God with the changed reality of the world, to abandon it and to wait upon God, and this is the reason why there has been more upheaval in Protestant theology since the First World War than in any other academic discipline, apart from the natural sciences. Here we have set out upon the way, and we do not know where it leads. If one had told people at the end of the Middle Ages, who likewise were looking for a new way of speaking about God, that Martin Luther's Reformation would end in this way, they would have put their hands over their ears in horror and cried: 'Anything but that!' The same will be true of us.

Every new way of speaking of God in the present age is no more than a tentative experiment. But even if theology were to succeed in giving a new answer to the question our age asks about God, this in its turn would be no more than a temporary answer. For only the gospel is eternal, and theology is temporal; it must always translate the eternal gospel anew for the changing times. Consequently, the cathedral which theologians are building is never finished, nor may it ever be finished if it is genuinely to be a cathedral in which God is preached and worshipped. Here again, it is true that 'God does not dwell in temples made with hands'. Or again, 'You shall not make any image or likeness of God.' The keystone of the arch may not be placed in position if heaven is to look through (W. von Loewenich). But because the keystone which bears and sustains the arch may never be put in place, the arch constantly falls in, and so all theology is always condemned to failure. The reason for the failure of theology is the greatness of its object. Yet it is a task which we can never cease to carry out, and which we may not cease to carry out. We must always begin to build once again, and we must always dare once again to do the unheard of thing, which consists of men, sinful, finite, imperfect and mortal men, daring to speak in human words about God. Here too it is God's grace alone which can make good what in every case man does badly. God must also forgive us our theology, our theology perhaps most of all.

NOTES

CHAPTER ONE

1. Karl Barth, 'Evangelical Theology in the Nineteenth Century', in *The Humanity of God*, Collins, London, 1961, and John Knox Press, Richmond, 1963, p. 14. Also available in Fontana Library, 1967.

2. Eduard Thurneysen, *Revolutionary Theology in the Making*, Epworth Press, London, and John Knox Press, Richmond, 1964, p. 12. – Karl Barth, *Epistle to the Romans*, Oxford University Press, London and New York, 1933, p. 9.

3. For this and the following, cf. esp. Karl Barth, 'Das Wort Gottes als Aufgabe der Theologie', in *Anfänge der dialektischen Theologie* I, ed. Jürgen Moltmann, Munich, 1962, pp. 197 ff.

4. Ibid., p. 199.

5. This and other passages from the correspondence between Barth and Thurneysen are given by E. Thurneysen, op. cit., pp. 26 ff.

6. Cf. for this and the following the Preface to the 2nd ed. of the *Epistle to the Romans*, p. 9.

7. Karl Barth, *The Word of God and the Word of Man*, Hodder and Stoughton, London, and Harper, New York, 1929, p. 43.

8. Recounted by Georg Merz, *Wege und Wandlungen*, Munich, 1961, p. 212.

9. 'Biblische Fragen, Einsichten und Ausblicke', 1920, in *Anfänge der dialektischen Theologie* I, pp. 55 ff.

10. Cf. for the whole the Prefaces to successive editions of the *Epistle to the Romans* and 'Biblische Fragen, Einsichten und Ausblicke', esp. p. 55.

11. E. Thurneysen, op. cit., p. 36.

12. 'Biblische Fragen, Einsichten und Ausblicke', p. 55; the *Epistle to the Romans*, p. 12.

13. The *Epistle to the Romans*, p. 1.

14. Ibid., p. 8.

15. *Anfänge der dialektischen Theologie* I, pp. 119 ff.

16. The *Epistle to the Romans*, p. 10.

17. Ibid., pp. 330 f.

18. pp. 37, 40, 114.

19. Hans Urs von Balthasar, *Karl Barth, Darstellung und Deutung seiner Theologie*, Cologne, 1961, p. 182.

20. Friedrich Gogarten, *Der Zerfall des Humanismus und die Gottesfrage*, Stuttgart, 1937, pp. 13 ff.

21. Gustaf Wingren, *Die Methodenfrage der Theologie,* Göttingen, 1957, esp. pp. 114 f.

22. G. C. Berkouwer, *Der Triumph der Gnade in der Theologie Karl Barths,* Neukirchen, 1957, pp. 14 ff.

23. *Kirchenblatt f. d. ref. Schweiz,* 1940, p. 100.

24. The *Epistle to the Romans,* pp. 311 ff.

25. *Anfänge der dialektischen Theologie* I, pp. 205 f.

26. 'Dank und Reverenz', *Ev. Theol.,* Vol. 23, 1963, pp. 137 ff.

27. Cf. on what follows the *Epistle to the Romans,* pp. 29 f., 38 f., 85, 92, 97 f., 110, 129, 137, 147, 159, 196, 203, 206, 234; *Das Wort Gottes und die Theologie, Gesammelte Aufsätze* (Collected Essays) I, Munich, 1924, pp. 99–205.

28. The *Epistle to the Romans,* pp. 260 f.

29. *Ges. Aufsätze* I, p. 342. Cf. ibid., pp. 82 ff.; *Anfänge der dialektischen Theologie* I, pp. 9 ff., 212 ff., 216 f.; The *Epistle to the Romans,* pp. 176 ff., 502 ff.

30. Urs von Balthasar, op. cit., p. 91.

31. Paul Tillich, *Kritisches und positives Paradox. Eine Auseinandersetzung mit K. Barth und F. Gogarten,* 1923; repr. in *Ges. Werke* VIII, Stuttgart, 1962, pp. 216 ff.; cf. also P. Tillich, 'Kairos and Logos', in *The Interpretation of History,* Scribner's, New York, 1936, pp. 137 f.

32. The *Epistle to the Romans,* pp. 79, 94 f.

33. *Ges. Aufsätze* I, p. 59.

34. On 'faith' cf. the *Epistle to the Romans,* pp. 33 f., 39, 41 f., 57, 94, 100, 150, 180, 225, 255 f., 292, 296, 315; *Anfänge der dialektischen Theologie* I, pp. 65 f.

35. On 'ethics' cf. the *Epistle to the Romans,* pp. 292, 424–75, esp. 431 ff., 434, 462 ff., 467–71.

36. On the following cf. the *Epistle to the Romans,* pp. 475–92, esp. 477 f., 480–85, 486–92, 492 f., 502.

37. On the following cf. the *Epistle to the Romans,* pp. 49 f., 136, 168, 174, 209, 231 ff., 240 ff., 253, 266 f., 368, 409.

38. On the following cf. the *Epistle to the Romans,* pp. 129 f., 183 ff., 247 f., 252 f., 266 ff., 269.

39. On the following cf. the *Epistle to the Romans,* pp. 332 ff., 368, 373 f., 378, 387 f., 391, 405; *Anfänge der dialektischen Theologie* I, p. 51.

40. On the following cf. the *Epistle to the Romans,* pp. 129, 333 ff., 336 ff., 341 f., 344 f., 375, 393; *Anfänge der dialektischen Theologie* I, p. 62.

41. Karl Barth, *From Rousseau to Ritschl,* SCM Press, London, 1959, p. 308.

42. Ibid., p. 307.

43. Urs von Balthasar, op. cit., p. 210.

44. Cf. Agnes von Zahn-Harnack, *Adol, von Harnack,* Berlin, 1936, pp. 531 ff.

45. Repr. in Karl Barth, *Theologische Fragen und Antworten. Ges. Vorträge* III, Zollikon, Zürich, 1957, pp. 7 ff.

46. Eduard Thurneysen, 'Abschied von "Zwischen den Zeiten"', in *Anfänge der dialektischen Theologie* II, p. 322.

47. *Römerbrief*, reprint, p. xxv.

48. *Anfänge der dialektischen Theologie* II, pp. 95 ff.

49. *Anfänge der dialektischen Theologie* II, p. 335; I, p. 319; Rudolf Bultmann, *Glauben und Verstehen, Ges. Aufsätze* I, Tübingen, 1933, p. 2; *Anfänge der dialektischen Theologie* II, pp. 289 f.

50. *Anfänge der dialektischen Theologie* I, pp. 268 f.; II, p. 110; Rudolf Bultmann, *Glauben und Verstehen* I, p. 118.

51. Friedrich Gogarten, *Die religiöse Entscheidung*, 1921, p. 20; *Anfänge der dialektischen Theologie* I, pp. 269 f.; II, p. 281.

52. *Anfänge der dialektischen Theologie* I, p. 262; II, p. 120; Rudolf Bultmann, *Glauben und Verstehen* I, p. 15.

53. Friedrich Gogarten, 1921, in an open letter to Emil Fuchs, *Anfänge der dialektischen Theologie* II, p. 124.

54. Eduard Thurneysen, 'Die Anfänge', in *Festschrift zu Karl Barths 70. Geburtstag*, p. 858; Georg Merz, *Wege und Wandlungen*, p. 244.

55. Friedrich Gogarten, 'Zur Geisteslage des Theologen. Noch eine Antwort an Paul Tillich', in Tillich, *Ges. Werke* VII, p. 246.

56. *Anfänge der dialektischen Theologie* II, pp. 101 ff.

57. Quoted by Jürgen Moltmann, *Anfänge der dialektischen Theologie* II, p. 94.

58. *Anfänge der dialektischen Theologie* II, pp. 134 ff.

59. Klaus Scholder, 'Neuere deutsche Geschichte und protestantische Theologie', in *Ev. Theol.* 23, 1963, pp. 510 ff.

60. Friedrich Gogarten, *Gericht oder Skepsis. Eine Streitschrift gegen Karl Barth*, Jena, 1937, p. 13.

61. Rudolf Otto, *The Idea of the Holy*, Oxford University Press, London, 2nd ed., 1950, p. 82.

62. Ibid., pp. 97, 98, 108.

63. p. 18.

64. pp. 99, 102.

65. p. 136.

66. Cf. Heinz Zahrnt, *The Historical Jesus*, Collins, London, and Harper, New York, 1963, pp. 43 ff.

67. Rudolf Bultmann, *Jesus Christ and Mythology*, SCM Press, London, 1960, and Scribner's, New York, 1958, p. 13.

68. Cf. Heinz Zahrnt, op. cit., pp. 74 ff.

69. A. von Harnack and H. Lietzmann, *Karl Holl †, Zwei Gedächtnisreden*, Bonn, 1926, p. 4.

70. Ibid., p. 5.

CHAPTER TWO

1. For the following cf. Karl Barth, *Theological Existence Today*, Hodder and Stoughton, London, 1933, pp. 9, 12, 13, 31, 46, 81.

364   THE QUESTION OF GOD

2. The Protestants who, during the Hitler régime, tried to bring about a synthesis between Nazism and Christianity. (Ed.)

3. Karl Barth, 'Abschied von "Zwischen den Zeiten"', in Anfänge der dialektischen Theologie II, p. 316.

4. As early as 1922 in a letter to E. Thurneysen; Revolutionary Theology in the Making, p. 122.

5. Anfänge der dialektischen Theologie II, pp. 316, 318.

6. 7th September, 1922 to Thurneysen; op. cit., p. 110.

7. Friedrich Gogarten, 'Historismus', in Zwischen den Zeiten, Vol. 2, 1924, n. 8, pp. 7 ff.

8. Anfänge der dialektischen Theologie II, pp. 315, 317.

9. Ibid., pp. 321 ff.

10. Emil Brunner, Natural Theology, Geoffrey Bles, London, 1946, p. 16.

11. Emil Brunner, 'Die Grenzen der Humanität', 1922, in Anfänge der dialektischen Theologie I, p. 272.

12. Emil Brunner, Die Mystik und das Wort, Tübingen, 1924, p. 10.

13. Emil Brunner, Natural Theology, p. 25.

14. Ibid., p. 23.

15. p. 58.

16. p. 59.

17. Quoted by Wenzel Lohff, 'Paul Althaus', in Theologen unserer Zeit, Leonhard Reinisch, Munich, 1960, pp. 65 f.

18. Paul Althaus, Grundriss der Dogmatik, Vol. 1, 2nd ed., 1936, p. 13.

19. Ibid., pp. 28, 30.

20. pp. 17 f.

21. Karl Barth, 'Nein! Antwort an Emil Brunner', Theologische Existenz heute, n. 14, Munich, 1934, pp. 12–13; translated in Natural Theology, p. 76.

22. Ibid., p. 127.

23. Karl Barth, 'Die Not der evangelischen Kirche', in Der Götze wackelt, ed. Karl Kupisch, Berlin, 1961, pp. 61 f.

24. Ibid., p. 56.

CHAPTER THREE

1. Emil Brunner, 'Autobiographische Skizze', in Reformatio, Vol. 12, 1963, p. 642.

2. Ibid.

3. Quoted by Wenzel Lohff, 'Emil Brunner', in Theologen unserer Zeit, Munich, 1960, p. 42.

4. 'Autobiographische Skizze', p. 639.

5. Emil Brunner, Man in Revolt, Lutterworth Press, London, and Westminster Press, Philadelphia, 1947, pp. 17 ff., 24, 140.

6. Ibid., pp. 9 (mistranslated there), 51 f.

7. pp. 180, 237 ff.

8. Emil Brunner, *Truth as Encounter*, SCM Press, London, and Westminster Press, Philadelphia, 1964, p. 165.

9. Ibid., p. 164.

10. p. 167.

11. p. 15.

12. p. 114; Emil Brunner, *The Misunderstanding of the Church*, Lutterworth Press, London, and Westminster Press, Philadelphia, 1953, p. 13.

13. *The Misunderstanding of the Church*, p. 83.

14. Ibid., p. 111.

15. *Truth as Encounter*, p. 188.

16. *The Misunderstanding of the Church*, p. 112.

17. *Truth as Encounter*, p. 42.

CHAPTER FOUR

1. Karl Barth, *The Humanity of God*, pp. 35–66.

2. Ibid., pp. 42 f.

3. p. 38.

4. pp. 45 f.

5. pp. 45, 55.

6. 'Evangelical Theology in the Nineteenth Century', in *The Humanity of God*, p. 11.

7. *Church Dogmatics* III. 4, T. and T. Clark, Edinburgh, Vols. I–IV published 1936–62, Preface, p. xiii; 'Parergon. Karl Barth über sich selbst', in *Ev. Theol.*, Vol. 8, 1948–49, pp. 268 ff.; 'Brechen und Bauen. Eine Diskussion 1947', in *Der Götze wackelt*, ed. Karl Kupisch, Berlin, 1961, pp. 112 f.; 'Dank und Reverenz', in *Ev. Theol.*, Vol. 23, 1963, pp. 337 ff.

8. *Der Götze wackelt*, p. 113.

9. Karl Barth, *Evangelical Theology*, London, 1963, pp. 8, 92 ff.

10. 'Parergon', p. 272.

11. Hans Urs von Balthasar, op. cit., p. 50.

12. *Church Dogmatics* I. 1, p. ix.

13. Gerhard Gloege, 'Karl Barth', in *Religion in Geschichte und Gegenwart*, Vol. I, 3rd ed., col. 895; Regin Prenter, 'Glauben und Erkennen bei Karl Barth', in *Kerygma und Dogma*, Vol. 2, 1956, p. 178.

14. Emil Brunner, 'Der neue Barth', in *Zeitschr. f. Theol. u. Kirche*, Vol. 48, 1951, p. 91.

15. 'Parergon', pp. 272 f.

16. *Junge Kirche*, Vol. 25, 1964, p. 702.

17. 'Parergon', pp. 268 f.

18. *Church Dogmatics* III. 1, p. 81; cf. I. 1, pp. 119, 127, 244 f., 255.

19. *Evangelical Theology*, pp. 31 f.

20. *Church Dogmatics* IV. 3 (second half), p. 677; *Dogmatics in Outline*, SCM Press, London, and Harper, New York, 1949, p. 15.

21. *Church Dogmatics* I. 2, pp. 299 f., cf. pp. 301 ff.

22. *Church Dogmatics* IV. 1, p. 45; II. 1, p. 444; *Dogmatics in Outline*, p. 36.

23. *Church Dogmatics* II. 1, p. 444.

24. *Church Dogmatics* I. 2, pp. 191 f.; *Dogmatics in Outline*, p. 99.

25. *Church Dogmatics* II. 2, pp. 52 ff.; cf. II. 2, pp. 180 f., III. 4, pp. 480 f., IV. 1, p. 186; *Dogmatics in Outline*, p. 90.

26. 'Parergon', p. 272.

27. *Church Dogmatics* II. 2, pp. 53 f.

28. *Church Dogmatics* IV. 1, p. 81.

29. *Church Dogmatics* III. 1, pp. 44, 59, 231; *Dogmatics in Outline*, pp. 39 f., 58.

30. *Dogmatics in Outline*, pp. 58, 63; *Church Dogmatics* III. 2, p. 76.

31. *Church Dogmatics* III. 1, p. 44, cf. p. 76; IV. 3 (first half), p. 137.

32. *Church Dogmatics* III. 1, p. 231, IV. 1, pp. 9 f., II. 1, pp. 18 ff.; *Der Götze wackelt*, p. 109.

33. *Dogmatics in Outline*, p. 58; *Church Dogmatics* IV. 3 (first half), p. 153; cf. pp. 137, 151.

34. *Dogmatics in Outline*, p. 58; *Church Dogmatics* III. 1, p. 351.

35. Karl Barth, *Evangelium und Gesetz*, 3rd ed., Munich, 1935; *Theologische Existenz heute*, Vol. 50, 1961, pp. 6 f., 11 f., 13; *Church Dogmatics* II. 2, p. 511.

36. Hans Urs von Balthasar, op. cit., p. 210.

37. *Church Dogmatics* III. 3, pp. 50 f.

38. *Church Dogmatics* I. 1, p. x.

39. *Church Dogmatics* II. 1, pp. 74, 83, 188, 243.

40. *Church Dogmatics* III. 3, p. 186.

41. *Dogmatics in Outline*, p. 64.

42. Correspondence between Barth and Thurneysen, op. cit., p. 107 (letter of 20th March, 1924).

43. *Church Dogmatics* III. 2, p. 220; IV. 2, p. 346; *Dogmatics in Outline*, pp. 31 f., 42 f., 52; *Church Dogmatics* III. 1, pp. 185 ff.; III. 4, pp. 150 ff.

44. *Church Dogmatics* III. 2, pp. 41, 43 f.; III. 4, p. 42; III. 2, pp. 133 ff.

45. *Church Dogmatics* III. 2, p. 136.

46. Barth in 1947 in a discussion (*Der Götze wackelt*, p. 119).

47. *The Humanity of God*, pp. 52 f.

48. Karl Barth, 'Humanismus', in *Theol. Studien*, Vol. 28, Zollikon, Zürich, 1950, pp. 5, 6, 8 f., 11, 22.

49. *Church Dogmatics* III. 3, p. 87.

50. *The Humanity of God*, p. 49.

51. 'Parergon', p. 272.

52. Regin Prenter, 'Glauben und Erkennen bei K. Barth', in *Kerygma und Dogma*, Vol. 2, 1956, p. 189.

53. *Church Dogmatics* IV. 1, p. 293.

54. *Dogmatics in Outline*, p. 104.

55. *Church Dogmatics* II. 2, p. 93.

56. Hans Urs von Balthasar, *Karl Barth*, p. 187.

57. *Church Dogmatics* II. 2, pp. 146 f. (the phrase in brackets is not translated).

58. *Church Dogmatics* II. 2, pp. 13 f., 15, 91, 92 f.; 'Gottes Gnadenwahl', *Theol. Existenz heute*, Vol. 47, 1936, pp. 6, 19.

59. *Church Dogmatics* II. 2, pp. 58 f., 116, 157.

60. Ibid., II. 2, pp. 50 f., 94, 133, 163, 168, 170, 318 f., 351 ff.; 'Gottes Gnadenwahl', pp. 20 ff.

61. 'Gottes Gnadenwahl', p. 8; *Church Dogmatics* II. 2, pp. 89, 92 f.

62. *Church Dogmatics* II. 2, pp. 319, 326, 349; IV. 1, p. 312; III. 1, p. 189.

63. *Church Dogmatics* II. 2, pp. 421 f.

64. *Church Dogmatics* II. 2, pp. 323 f., 325 f., 477, 480.

65. Karl Barth, *The Humanity of God*, pp. 61 f.; O. Weber, W. Kreck, E. Wolf, 'Die Predigt von der Gnadenwahl', *Theol. Existenz heute*, Vol. 28, Munich, 1951, p. 7; K. Barth, 'Die Botschaft von der freien Gnade', *Theol. Studien*, Vol. 23, Zollikon, Zürich, 1947, p. 6.

66. Helmut Thielicke, *Theologische Ethik* I, 2nd ed., Tübingen, 1958, § 596 c.

67. Ibid., p. 583.

68. *Church Dogmatics* III. 1, pp. 108 ff.; III. 3, pp. 327 ff., 351 ff., 360 f.; IV. 3 (first half), p. 177; *Dogmatics in Outline*, p. 57.

69. *Church Dogmatics* IV. 1, p. 48; III. 3, p. 363; III. 1, p. 108.

70. Urs von Balthasar, op. cit., pp. 225 f., 380.

71. Helmut Thielicke, op. cit., p. 596.

72. Gustaf Wingren, *Die Methodenfrage der Theologie*, Göttingen, 1957, pp. 53 f.

73. *Church Dogmatics* I. 1, p. 91.

74. In *Junge Kirche*, Vol. 25, 1964, p. 700.

75. *Church Dogmatics* I. 2, p. 793.

76. *Evangelical Theology*, p. 183; *Church Dogmatics* III. 4, p. 419; IV. 1, p. 18.

77. *The Humanity of God*, p. 59; *Evangelical Theology*, pp. 38 f., 183.

78. *Church Dogmatics* IV. 1, pp. 288 f., 292.

79. Dietrich Bonhoeffer, *Letters and Papers from Prison*, SCM Press, London, and Macmillan Co., New York, 3rd revised and enlarged edition, 1967, p. 156, cf. pp. 153, 181, 182.

80. Paul Tillich, *On the Boundary*, Collins, London, 1967, and Scribner's, New York, 1966, p. 41.

81. Cf. Regin Prenter, *Mündige Welt* III, Munich, 1960, pp. 17, 21.

82. 'Amsterdamer Fragen und Antworten', in *Theol. Existenz heute*. N.S. no. 15, Munich, 1949, pp. 3 f., 7.

83. Ibid., pp. 25 ff., 29.

84. pp. 8, 28.

85. *Die Lehre vom Worte Gottes. Prolegomena zur Christlichen Dogmatik*, Munich, 1927, Preface, p. ix.

CHAPTER FIVE

1. Friedrich Nietzsche, Complete Works, ed. Oscar Levy, Vol. 10, *The Joyful Wisdom*, J. N. Foulis, Edinburgh, 1910, and Macmillan Co., New York, 1925, pp. 167 ff.

2. Jean Paul, *Sämtl. Werke*, Pt. I, Vol. 6, ed. Kurt Schreinert, Weimar, 1928, pp. 247 ff.

3. Martin Heidegger, 'Nietzsches Wort "Gott ist tot"', in *Holzwege*, Frankfurt-am-Main, 1950, pp. 199 ff. Cf. also Rudolf Bultmann, 'Der Gottesgedanke und der moderne Mensch', in *Zeitschr. f. Theol. u. Kirche*, Vol. 60, 1963, pp. 335 ff.

4. Werner Heisenberg in a lecture in Munich in 1954; repr. in *Sonntagsblatt*, Hamburg, 1954, no. 24.

5. Quoted by Reinhold Niebuhr, *Faith and History*, Nisbet, London, and Scribner's, New York, 1949, p. 98. Cf. B. Russell, *The Scientific Outlook*, Allen and Unwin, London, and Norton Co., New York, 1931, pp. 155 f.

6. Viktor von Weizsäcker, *Am Anfang schuf Gott Himmel und Erde. Grundfragen der Naturphilosophie*, Göttingen, 1954, p. 26.

7. Friedrich Gogarten, *Verhängnis und Hoffnung der Neuzeit. Die Säkularisierung als theologisches Problem*, Stuttgart, 1953, p. 103.

8. Dietrich Bonhoeffer, *Letters and Papers from Prison*, pp. 152, 180.

9. Martin Heidegger, *Holzwege*, p. 103.

10. Friedrich Gogarten, *Der Mensch zwischen Gott und Welt*, Heidelberg, 1952, p. 419.

11. Dietrich Bonhoeffer, op. cit., p. 152.

12. Op. cit., p. 185.

13. p. 196. For the whole theme cf. pp. 155, 174 f., 179, 196 ff.

14. C. F. von Weizsäcker, *The Relevance of Science*, Collins, London, and Harper, New York, 1964, p. 121.

15. Dietrich Bonhoeffer, op. cit., pp. 153, 179, 188 f., 190 f.

16. pp. 189 ff.

17. pp. 153, 179.

18. p. 179.

19. pp. 192 f.

20. Gerhard Ebeling, 'Non-religious Interpretation of Biblical Concepts', in *Word and Faith*, SCM Press, London, and Fortress Press, Philadelphia, 1963, p. 131.

21. Friedrich Gogarten, *Was ist Christentum?*, Göttingen, 1956, p. 73; *Verhängnis und Hoffnung der Neuzeit*, pp. 8, 98 f., 102; *Der Mensch zwischen Gott und Welt*, p. 118.

22. Friedrich Gogarten, *Der Mensch zwischen Gott und Welt*, pp. 9 ff., 249 f.; *Verhängnis und Hoffnung der Neuzeit*, pp. 25 ff., 71.

23. *Verhängnis und Hoffnung der Neuzeit*, p. 69.

24. *Der Mensch zwischen Gott und Welt*, pp. 12 ff., 146 ff., 317; *Verhängnis und Hoffnung der Neuzeit*, pp. 13 ff., 20 ff.; *Demythologising and History*, SCM Press, London, and Scribner's, New York, 1955, p. 21.

25. *Der Mensch zwischen Gott und Welt*, p. 28.

26. *Verhängnis und Hoffnung der Neuzeit*, p. 94.

27. *Der Mensch zwischen Gott und Welt*, pp. 360 f.

28. C. F. von Weizsäcker, *The Relevance of Science*, pp. 50 f.; cf. pp. 26, 49, 178.

29. F. Gogarten, *Der Mensch zwischen Gott und Welt*, pp. 12 ff., 23 f., 317 ff., 419; *Was ist Christentum?*, p. 66 f., 73.

30. *Der Mensch zwischen Gott und Welt*, p. 117.

31. Luther's Works, Weimar Edition XXX. 2, p. 565; XXVII, p. 418; XIV, p. 553.

32. *Der Mensch zwischen Gott und Welt*, p. 231.

33. C. F. von Weizsäcker, *The Relevance of Science*, p. 162.

34. F. Gogarten, *Der Mensch zwischen Gott und Welt*, pp. 25, 180.

35. Ibid., pp. 158 f.

36. p. 419.

37. p. 334.

38. p. 341.

39. *Verhängnis und Hoffnung der Neuzeit*, p. 103.

40. C. F. von Weizsäcker, *The Relevance of Science*, p. 179.

41. *Letters and Papers from Prison*, pp. 97, 154.

42. G. Ebeling, 'Non-religious Interpretation of Biblical Concepts', loc. cit., p. 125; W. Jetter, 'Elementare Predigt', in *Zeitschr. f. Theol. u. Kirche*, Vol. 59, 1962, p. 346.

43. Dietrich Bonhoeffer, *The Cost of Discipleship*, SCM Press, London, and Macmillan Co., New York, 1948, pp. 29 f.

44. *Letters and Papers from Prison*, pp. 152 ff.

45. Ibid., pp. 177 f., 195.

46. pp. 196 ff.

47. pp. 198 f., 209 f.

48. Gerhard Ebeling, op. cit., p. 160, n. 1.

49. Dietrich Bonhoeffer, *Ges. Schriften II*, ed. Eberhard Bethge, Munich, 1959, pp. 420 f.

50. *Letters and Papers from Prison*, p. 201.

51. Ibid., pp. 201 f.

52. pp. 155, 175, 201.

53. pp. 185 f.

54. p. 156.

55. p. 111.

56. On the following cf. Dietrich Bonhoeffer, *Ethics*, SCM Press, London, and Macmillan Co., New York, 1955, pp. 62 ff.

57. *Letters and Papers from Prison*, pp. 18, 165 ff., esp. p. 172.

58. Ibid., p. 78.

59. Told by Otto Dudzus in *I Knew Dietrich Bonhoeffer*, Collins, London, and Harper, New York, 1960, p. 82.

60. Ibid., p. 232.

61. Cf. Gerhard Ebeling, op. cit., pp. 158 ff.

62. Gerhard Ebeling, 'Theology and Reality', in *Word and Faith*, p. 196.

CHAPTER SIX

1. Karl Barth, *Church and State*, SCM Press, London, 1939, pp. 3 ff.

2. Karl Barth, *Eine Schweizer Stimme 1938–45*, 2nd ed., Zollikon, Zürich, 1948, pp. 113, 121 f.

3. *Church and State*, p. 33.

4. Ibid., pp. 13–22; *Dogmatics in Outline*, pp. 110 f.

5. *Church and State*, pp. 29, 36, 48; 'The Christian Community and the Civil Community', in *Against the Stream*, SCM Press, London, and Philosophical Library, New York, 1954, p. 21.

6. 'The Christian Community and the Civil Community', loc. cit., pp. 32 ff.

7. Ibid., pp. 34–42.

8. *Church and State*, pp. 77 ff.; 'The Christian Community and the Civil Community', loc. cit., p. 44; *Der Götze wackelt*, p. 114.

9. Helmut Thielicke, *Theologische Ethik* I, Tübingen, 1951, pp. 411 f.; II. 2, 1958, p. 717.

10. Helmut Thielicke, *Theologische Ethik* II. 2, p. 452.

11. Helmut Thielicke, *Einführung in die christliche Ethik*, Munich, 1963, p. 7; *Theologische Ethik* II. 1, Tübingen, 1955, pp. 1 ff.

12. *Einführung*, pp. 10 f.

13. *Theologische Ethik* II. 2, pp. 757 f.

14. *Einführung*, p. 12.

15. Helmut Thielicke, *Theologische Ethik* III, Tübingen, 1964, p. x.

16. *Theol. Ethik* II. 1, pp. 1, 274.

17. *Theol. Ethik* I, p. 712; II. 2, pp. 762 f.

18. Cf. on all this *Theol. Ethik* I, pp. 701 f.; II. 1, pp. 190 ff.; II. 2, pp. 547 ff., 572 ff.

19. Cf. *Theol. Ethik* II. 1, pp. 56 ff., 62 ff., 80 ff., 191 ff., 220 ff.

20. For the doctrine of the two kingdoms in Thielicke cf. *Theol. Ethik* I, pp. 9 ff., 583–604; II. 1, pp. 314 ff., 371 ff., 380 f., 534 ff., 542 ff.; II. 2, pp. 5 ff., 295 ff., 452 ff., 551 f., 565 ff., 572 ff., 699 ff.

21. Jürgen Moltmann, *The Theology of Hope*, SCM Press, London, and Harper, New York, 1967, p. 16.

22. Ibid., pp. 15 ff., 37, 137.

23. pp. 17, 33 ff., 84.

24. pp. 287 ff.

25. pp. 304 f., 324 ff., 330 ff.

26. Karl Jaspers, *The Future of Mankind*, University of Chicago Press, 1961, pp. 258, 259.

CHAPTER SEVEN

1. Rudolf Bultmann, 'Die liberale Theologie und die jüngste theologische Bewegung', 1924, in *Glauben und Verstehen, Ges. Aufsätze* (Collected Essays) I, Tübingen, 1933, pp. 2 f.

2. Rudolf Bultmann, 'Bultmann Replies to his Critics', in *Kerygma and Myth*, Vol. I, Society for the Promotion of Christian Knowledge, London, 1953, pp. 210 f.; *Jesus Christ and Mythology*, p. 84; 'What Sense is there to speak of God', *The Christian Scholar*, XLIII, 3, 1960, pp. 213–22.

3. Rudolf Bultmann, 'The New Testament and Mythology', *Kerygma and Myth*, Vol. I, pp. 42 f.; 'Der Begriff des Wortes Gottes im Neuen Testament', 1931, in *Glauben und Verstehen* I, pp. 282 ff.; 'Zur Frage der Christologie', 1927, in *Glauben und Verstehen* I, pp. 91 f.

4. *Glauben und Verstehen* I, pp. 91 f.; *Kerygma und Mythos* II, pp. 188, 190; *Jesus Christ and Mythology*, p. 32.

5. Karl Jaspers and Rudolf Bultmann, *Kerygma and Myth*, Vol. II, p. 179.

6. James M. Robinson, *A New Quest of the Historical Jesus*, SCM Press, London, and Allenson, Naperville (Ill.), 1959, p. 10.

7. Friedrich Gogarten, 'Theologie und Geschichte', in *Zeitschr. f. Theol. u. Kirche*, Vol. 50, 1953, p. 340.

8. 25th March 1942 to Winifred Krause; published in *Bonhoeffer Auswahl*, ed. Richard Grunow, Munich, 1964, p. 537.

9. *Kerygma and Myth*, Vol. I, p. 45.

10. Otto Küster, *Glauben müssen? Theologische Essays*, Stuttgart, 1963, p. 30.

11. Friedrich Gogarten, *Demythologising and History*, p. 10.

12. Otto Küster, *Glauben müssen?*, p. 29.

13. 'The New Testament and Mythology', *Kerygma and Myth*, Vol. I, pp. 5, 120.

14. *Kerygma and Myth*, Vol. II, p. 181.

15. *Kerygma and Myth*, Vol. I, p. 10.

16. *Kerygma and Myth*, Vol. II, p. 185; *Jesus Christ and Mythology*, pp. 18, 45; 'Zum Problem der Entmythologisierung', 1963, in *Glauben und Verstehen, Ges. Aufsätze* IV, Tübingen, 1965, p. 130.

17. *Kerygma and Myth*, Vol. I, p. 15.

18. Rudolf Bultmann, 'The Problem of Hermeneutics', in *Essays*, London, 1955, p. 256.

19. Rudolf Bultmann, 'Die Bedeutung der "dialektischen Theologie" für die neutestamentliche Wissenschaft', 1928, in *Glauben und Verstehen* I, p. 133.

20. *Jesus Christ and Mythology*, pp. 54 ff.; *Kerygma and Myth*, Vol. II, p. 193.

21. *Kerygma and Myth*, Vol. II, p. 193; *Jesus Christ and Mythology*, p. 56.

22. Friedrich Hegel, *Philosophy of Right*, Oxford University Press, London and New York, 1942, p. 13.

23. Reinhard Wittram, *Das Interesse an der Geschichte*, Göttingen, 1958, pp. 15 f.

24. Martin Heidegger, 'Die Zeit des Weltbildes', in *Holzwege*, p. 87.

25. On the whole matter cf. Friedrich Gogarten, *Verhängnis und Hoffnung der Neuzeit*; and in particular *Demythologising and History*, pp. 49 ff.

26. Martin Heidegger, *Being and Time*, SCM Press, London, and Harper, New York, 1962, p. 447.

27. Rudolf Bultmann, *Jesus and the Word*, 1934, repr. Scribner's, New York, 1958, London, Fontana Library, 1962, pp. 11, 16.

28. The *Epistle to the Romans*, p. 7.

29. *Protestantische Theologie im 19. Jahrhundert*, pp. 1 ff.

30. Rudolf Bultmann, 'Kirche und Lehre in Neuen Testament', 1929, in *Glauben und Verstehen* I, p. 159; *Wissenschaft und Existenz*, 1955, in *Glauben und Verstehen* III, Tübingen, 1960, p. 116.

31. Cf. 'Zum Problem der Entmythologisierung', in *Glauben und Verstehen* IV, pp. 131 ff.; 'Antwort an Ernst Käsemann', ibid., pp. 192 f.

32. 'Die Bedeutung der "dialektischen Theologie", etc.', in *Glauben und Verstehen* I, pp. 126 f.

33. 'The Problem of Hermeneutics', in *Essays*, pp. 246, 252 f.; 'Antwort an Ernst Käsemann', in *Glauben und Verstehen* IV, p. 193; *History and Eschatology* (Gifford Lectures), Edinburgh University Press, and Harper, New York, 1957, pp. 110 ff.

34. 'Die Bedeutung der "dialektischen Theologie", etc.', in *Glauben und Verstehen* I, p. 128; 'The Problem of Hermeneutics', in *Essays*, pp. 240 ff., 245, 252 ff.; *History and Eschatology*, p. 113.

35. 'Kirche und Lehre im Neuen Testament', in *Glauben und Verstehen* I, p. 161; 'Die Bedeutung der "dialektischen Theologie", etc.', in *Glauben und Verstehen* I, pp. 125 f.

36. 'The Problem of Hermeneutics', in *Essays*, p. 257; *Jesus Christ and Mythology*, p. 52.

37. *Jesus Christ and Mythology*, p. 53; 'The Question of Natural Revelation', in *Essays*, pp. 94 ff.

38. 'Points of Contact and Conflict', in *Essays*, pp. 135 ff.; 'The Question of Natural Revelation', in *Essays*, p. 98.

39. *Jesus Christ and Mythology*, p. 53.

40. *Kerygma and Myth*, Vol. I, pp. 17 ff.; *History and Eschatology*, pp. 96 f., 140 ff.; 'Die liberale Theologie und die jüngste theologische Bewegung', 1924, in *Glauben und Verstehen* I, p. 19.

41. *Kerygma and Myth*, Vol. I, p. 20; *History and Eschatology*, pp. 149 ff.

42. *Kerygma and Myth*, Vol. I, p. 25.

43. On the following cf. *Kerygma and Myth*, Vol. I, pp. 26 f.

44. 'Revelation in the New Testament', in *Existence and Faith*, Hodder and Stoughton, London, and Meridian Books, New York, 1961, and Fontana Library, 1964, p. 100.

45. *Kerygma and Myth*, Vol. I, pp. 28 f.; *History and Eschatology*, pp. 149 ff.

46. *Kerygma and Myth*, Vol. I, pp. 31 ff.

47. Ibid., Vol. I, pp. 34 f.

48. On the following cf. *Kerygma and Myth*, Vol. I, pp. 35–43.

49. Ibid., pp. 41 f.

50. Rudolf Bultmann, 'Das Verhältnis der urchristlichen Christusbotschaft zum historischen Jesus', in *Sitzungsberichte der Heidelberger Akademie d. Wissenschaften*, *Philos.-hist. Klasse*, 1960, Pt. 3, 2nd ed., Heidelberg, 1961, p. 27.

51. Rudolf Bultmann, 'Revelation in the New Testament', in *Existence and Faith*, p. 91.

52. 'What sense is there to speak of God', *The Christian Scholar*, XLIII, 3, 1960, pp. 213–22; 'Die liberale Theologie, etc.', in *Glauben und Verstehen* I, p. 25; *Kerygma and Myth*, Vol. I, p. 196; 'A Reply to Thesis of J. Schniewind', *Kerygma and Myth*, Vol. I, p. 107.

53. *Kerygma and Myth*, Vol. I, p. 147.

54. Rudolf Bultmann, 'The Crisis in Belief', in *Essays*, p. 1.

55. Rudolf Bultmann, 'Die Bedeutung des geschichtlichen Jesus für die Theologie des Paulus', 1929, in *Glauben und Verstehen* I, p. 208; 'Revelation in the New Testament', in *Existence and Faith*, p. 87.

56. 'Zur Frage der Christologie', in *Glauben und Verstehen* I, pp. 88 f.; *Jesus Christ and Mythology*, p. 71; 'Points of Contact and Conflict', in *Essays*, p. 134.

57. *Kerygma and Myth*, Vol. II, pp. 184 f.; 'Die Frage der "dialektischen" Theologie', 1926, in *Anfänge der dialektischen Theologie* II, pp. 86 f.

58. Heinrich Ott, 'Existentiale Interpretation und anonyme Christlichkeit', in *Zeit und Geschichte (Bultmann-Festschrift)*, Tübingen, 1964, p. 376.

59. *Kerygma and Myth*, Vol. II, p. 204; *Jesus Christ and Mythology*, p. 76.

60. *Kerygma and Myth*, Vol. I, p. 41; *Theology of the New Testament*, SCM Press, London, and Scribner's, New York, 1952–55, Vol. I, p. 301, cf. *Kerygma and Myth*, Vol. I, p. 115; *Glauben und Verstehen* I, pp. 37, 107, 282; III, pp. 22 f.

61. 'Die Bedeutung des geschichtlichen Jesus, etc.', in *Glauben und Verstehen* I, p. 208; cf. *Kerygma and Myth*, Vol. I, pp. 42 f.

62. *Kerygma and Myth*, Vol. I, p. 43.

63. *Jesus Christ and Mythology*, pp. 61 f., 79 ff.; 'Zum Problem der Entmythologisierung', in *Glauben und Verstehen* IV, pp. 136 f.; *Kerygma and Myth*, Vol. I, p. 44; *History and Eschatology*, pp. 152 ff.

64. Rudolf Bultmann, 'Der Gottesgedanke und der modern Mensch', 1963, in *Glauben und Verstehen* IV, pp. 124 f.; cf. pp. 120 ff.

65. Karl Barth, *Christliche Dogmatik*, pp. 404 ff.; 'Rudolf Bultmann. Ein Versuch, ihn zu verstehen', *Kerygma and Myth*, Vol. II, p. 121.

66. Jürgen Moltmann, 'Exegese und Eschatologie der Geschichte', in *Ev. Theol.*, Vol. 22, 1962, pp. 45, 52 f.; *The Theology of Hope*, p. 271.

67. *History and Eschatology*, p. 155.

68. *Geschichte und Eschatologie im Neuen Testament*, 1954, in *Glauben und Verstehen* III, p. 102.

69. Rudolf Bohren, 'Die Krise der Predigt als Frage an die Exegese', in *Ev. Theol.*, Vol. 22, 1962, p. 83.

70. Cf. Ernst Käsemann, 'Die Anfänge christlicher Theologie', in *Zeitschr. f. Theol. u. Kirche*, Vol. 57, 1960, p. 175.

71. *Marburger Predigten*, Tübingen, 1956, p. 226.

72. *The Theology of Hope*, p. 65.

73. Cf. Heinz Zahrnt, *The Historical Jesus*, p. 91.

74. Carl Friedrich von Weizsäcker, *Zum Weltbild der Physik*, 10th ed., Stuttgart, 1963, p. 263.

75. *Glauben müssen?*, p. 149.

76. *Kerygma and Myth*, Vol. I, p. 117; 'Der Begriff des Wortes Gottes im Neuen Testament', in *Glauben und Verstehen* I, p. 292; 'Die Bedeutung des geschichtlichen Jesus für die Theologie des Paulus', in *Glauben und Verstehen* I, pp. 205 ff., 211; 'Das Verhältnis der urchristlichen Botschaft zum historischen Jesus', p. 10.

77. *Theology of the New Testament*, Vol. II, p. 60.

78. *Jesus and the Word*, p. 14.

79. 'Die Christologie des Neuen Testaments', in *Glauben und Verstehen* I, pp. 250 f.; *Die Erforschung der synoptischen Evangelien*, 3rd ed., Berlin, 1960, p. 42.

80. 'Die liberale Theologie und die jüngste theologische Bewegung', in *Glauben und Verstehen* I, p. 3.

81. Ernst Lohmeyer in a review, quoted from Werner Georg Kümmel, *Das Neue Testament. Geschichte der Erforschung seiner Probleme*, Freiburg and Munich, 1958, p. 483.

82. 'The Crisis in Belief', in *Essays*, p. 18.

83. 'Zur Frage der Christologie', in *Glauben und Verstehen* I, p. 101.

84. Ibid., pp. 99 f.

85. Rudolf Bohren, *Die Krise der Predigt als Frage an die Exegese*, pp. 73 f.

86. Walter Künneth, *Glauben an Jesus? Die Begegnung der Christologie mit der modernen Existenz*, Hamburg, 1962, p. 97.

87. Karl Barth, 'Rudolf Bultmann, etc.', in *Kerygma and Myth*, Vol. II, p. 111.

88. N. A. Dahl, 'Der historische Jesus als geschichtswissenschaftliches und theologisches Problem', in *Kerygma und Dogma*, Vol. I, 1955, p. 126.

89. Karl Barth, 'Rudolf Bultmann, etc.', in *Kerygma and Myth*, Vol. II, pp. 99 f.

90. Otto Küster, *Glauben müssen?*, p. 116.

NOTES TO PAGES 242–62

91. Karl Jaspers and Rudolf Bultmann, 'Can the event of Jesus Christ be demythologised', in *Kerygma and Myth*, Vol. II, p. 178.

92. Karl Barth, 'Rudolf Bultmann, etc.', *Kerygma and Myth*, Vol. II, p. 117.

CHAPTER EIGHT

1. Ernst Käsemann, 'Probleme neutestamentlicher Arbeit in Deutschland', in *Die Freiheit des Evangeliums und die Ordnung der Gesellschaft*, 1952, p. 151.

2. Ernst Käsemann, 'Sackgassen im Streit um den historischen Jesus', in *Exegetische Versuche und Besinnungen* II, Göttingen, 1964, p. 42.

3. Ibid., p. 37.

4. Ernst Käsemann, 'Theologie', in *Theologie für Nichttheologen*, 4th series, Stuttgart, 1965, p. 52.

5. Ernst Käsemann, 'Neutestamentliche Fragen von heute', 1957, in *Exegetische Versuche und Besinnungen* II, p. 20.

6. Käsemann, 'Sackgassen', loc. cit., p. 52.

7. Ibid., p. 53.

8. Günther Bornkamm, *Jesus of Nazareth*, Hodder and Stoughton, London, and Harper, New York, 1960, pp. 9, 22; Gerhard Ebeling, 'Jesus und Glaube', 1958, in *Wort und Glaube*, Tübingen, 1960, p. 207; *Theology and Proclamation*, Collins, London, and Fortress Press, Philadelphia, 1966, pp. 64 f.

9. Gerhard Ebeling, 'Jesus und Glaube', loc. cit., p. 208; *The Nature of Faith*, Collins, London, and Fortress Press, Philadelphia, 1961, p. 46.

10. Ernst Käsemann, 'Das Problem des historischen Jesus', 1954, in *Exegetische Versuche und Besinnungen* I, Göttingen, 1960, pp. 192 f., 195 ff., 201 f.; 'Die Anfänge christlicher Theologie', 1960, in *Exegetische Versuche und Besinnungen* II, p. 95; 'Sackgassen', loc. cit., pp. 46 f.

11. Günther Bornkamm, *Jesus of Nazareth*, p. 23.

12. Ibid., p. 21.

13. Willi Marxsen, *Anfangsprobleme der Christologie*, Gütersloh, 1960, p. 18.

14. Gerhard Ebeling, *Theology and Proclamation*, p. 76.

15. Ulrich Wilckens, 'Das Offenbarungsverständnis in der Geschichte des Urchristentums', in *Offenbarung als Geschichte*, ed. Wolfhart Pannenberg, Göttingen, 1961, p. 60.

16. Rudolf Bultmann, *Jesus and the Word*, p. 14; Günther Bornkamm, *Jesus of Nazareth*, pp. 24 ff.; Ernst Käsemann, 'Das Problem des historischen Jesus', loc. cit., p. 213.

17. On the following cf. Ernst Käsemann, 'Das Problem des historischen Jesus', loc. cit., pp. 206–12.

18. On the following cf. Ernst Fuchs, 'Die Frage nach dem historischen Jesus', 1956, in *Zur Frage nach dem historischen Jesus, Ges. Aufsätze* (Collected Essays) II, Tübingen, 1960, pp. 152 ff.; 'Glaube und Geschichte im Blick auf die Frage nach dem historischen Jesus', 1957; ibid., pp. 168 ff.; 'Die Theologie des Neuen Testaments und der historische Jesus', 1960, ibid., pp. 377 ff.

19. On the following cf. Gerhard Ebeling, 'Jesus und Glaube', 1958, in *Wort und Glaube*, Tübingen, 1960, pp. 203 ff., esp. 238 ff.; 'Die Frage nach dem historischen Jesus und das Problem der Christologie', 1959, ibid., p. 300, esp. pp. 302 ff., 308 ff., 311; *The Nature of Faith*, pp. 44 ff.; *Theology and Proclamation*, pp. 54 ff.

20. On the following cf. Heinz Zahrnt, *The Historical Jesus*, pp. 110 ff.

21. Günther Bornkamm, *Jesus of Nazareth*, pp. 169 ff.

22. Ernst Käsemann, 'Das Problem des historischen Jesus', loc. cit., p. 211.

23. Günther Bornkamm, *Jesus of Nazareth*, p. 178.

24. Paul Althaus, *Das sogenannte Kerygma und der historische Jesus*, Gütersloh, 1958, p. 43; Ernst Käsemann, 'Das Problem des historischen Jesus', loc. cit., p. 206; Rudolf Bultmann, 'Die Christologie des Neuen Testaments', in *Glauben und Verstehen* I, pp. 265 f.

25. E. Käsemann, 'Sackgassen im Streit um den historischen Jesus', loc. cit., p. 56.

26. Ernst Fuchs, *Zur Frage nach dem historischen Jesus*, Preface.

27. Gerhard Ebeling, 'Historischer Jesus und Christologie', loc. cit., p. 311.

28. Ibid., p. 305.

29. For the whole cf. Ernst Käsemann, 'Neutestamentliche Fragen von heute', 1957, in *Exegetische Versuche und Besinnungen* II, pp. 23 ff.; *Die Anfänge christlicher Theologie*, 1960, ibid., pp. 82 ff.; 'Zum Thema der urchristlichen Apokalyptik', 1962, ibid., pp. 105 ff.

30. On the following cf. Herbert Braun, 'Der Sinn der neutestamentlichen Christologie', in *Zeitschr. f. Theol. u. Kirche*, Vol. 54, 1957, pp. 344 ff.

31. Ibid., pp. 347 ff.

32. p. 368.

33. p. 377.

34. pp. 371 ff.

35. p. 377; 'Die Problematik einer Theologie des Neuen Testaments', in *Zeitschr. f. Theol. u. Kirche*, Vol. 58, 1961, Supp. 2, pp. 12 ff.

36. Herbert Braun, 'Die Problematik einer Theologie des Neuen Testaments', pp. 3 ff.

37. Ibid., pp. 8 ff.

38. pp. 12 ff.

39. pp. 17 ff.

40. Helmut Gollwitzer, *Die Existenz Gottes im Bekenntnis des Glaubens*, Munich, 1963, p. 39.

41. Ibid., pp. 49 f.

42. p. 73.

43. p. 32.

44. p. 103.

45. p. 173.

46. Herbert Braun, 'Gottes Existenz und meine Geschichtlichkeit im Neuen Testament. Eine Antwort an H. Gollwitzer', in *Zeit und Geschichte. Dankgabe an Rudolf Bultmann zum 80. Geburtstag*, Tübingen, 1964, pp. 399 ff.

47. Ibid., pp. 407 f.

48. pp. 417 ff.

49. pp. 419 ff.

50. Ernst Käsemann, 'Sackgassen im Streit um den historischen Jesus', loc. cit., p. 51.

51. Wolfhart Pannenberg, 'Heilgeschehen und Geschichte', in *Kerygma und Dogma*, Vol. 5, 1959, p. 218.

52. Friedrich Hegel, *Philosophy of Right*, p. 13.

53. Wolfhart Pannenberg, 'Heilsgeschehen und Geschichte', loc. cit., p. 259.

54. Ibid., p. 286.

55. *Offenbarung als Geschichte*, ed. Wolfhart Pannenberg, Göttingen, 1961, pp. 103 f.

56. Wolfhart Pannenberg, 'Hermeneutik und Universalgeschichte', in *Zeitschr. f. Theol. u. Kirche*, Vol. 60, 1963, p. 116.

57. Wolfhart Pannenberg, 'Heilsgeschehen und Geschichte', loc. cit., p. 287; *Offenbarung als Geschichte*, pp. 98 ff., 112 ff.

58. Wolfhart Pannenberg, 'Heilsgeschehen und Geschichte', loc. cit., pp. 275, 278 f.

59. Ibid., pp. 246 ff.

60. Hans Conzelmann, 'Randbemerkungen zur Lage im Neuen Testament', in *Ev. Theol.*, Vol. 22, 1962, p. 228.

61. Hans-Georg Geyer, 'Geschichte als theologisches Problem', in *Ev. Theol.*, Vol. 22, 1962, pp. 101 f.; Lothar Steiger, 'Offenbarungsgeschichtliche und theologische Vernunft. Zur Theologie W. Pannenbergs', in *Zeitschr. f. Theol. u. Kirche*, Vol. 59, 1962, p. 96.

62. Jürgen Moltmann, *Theology of Hope*, p. 78.

63. Walter Künneth, *Glauben an Jesus?*, Hamburg, 1962, p. 74.

64. Martin Seils, 'Zur sprachphilosophischen und worttheologischen Problematik der Auseinandersetzung zwischen Existenztheologie und Geschichtstheologie', in *Neue Zeitschr. f. syst. Theol. u. Religionsphilosophie*, Vol. 7, 1965, pp. 1 ff.

65. Repr. in *Stimme der Gemeinde*, Vol. 16, 1964, col. 680.

66. Manfred Mezger, 'Redliche Predigt', in *Zeit und Geschichte. Dankgabe an Rudolf Bultmann zum 80. Geburtstag*, Tübingen, 1964, pp. 426 ff.

67. Manfred Mezger, 'Die geschichtliche Wahrheit als Vollmacht der Predigt', in *Ev. Theol.*, Vol. 22, 1962, p. 492.

68. Heinrich Vogel, *Jesus Christus und der religionslose Mensch*, Berlin, 1955, pp. 11 f.; Heinz Zahrnt, *The Historical Jesus*, p. 91.

CHAPTER NINE

1. Paul Tillich, 'Ethics in a Changing World', in *Religion and the Modern World*, Philadelphia, 1941; repr. in *The Protestant Era*, Nisbet, London, 1951, p. 167, and University of Chicago Press, 1948, p. 150; 'Storms of our Times', in *Anglican Theological Review*, Vol. 25, 1943; repr. in *The Protestant Era*, p. 260, Am. ed., p. 237.

2. 'Storms of our Times', loc. cit., pp. 260 ff.; Am. ed., pp. 237 ff.; 'Das Christliche Menschenbild im 20. Jahrhundert', 1955, in *Auf der Grenze. Aus dem Lebenswerk Paul Tillichs*, Stuttgart, 1962, pp. 127 ff.

3. 'On the Boundary', in *The Interpretation of History*, p. 52, cf. Hans Fischer-Barnicol in an NDR broadcast, 25th April 1964.

4. 'Das Christliche Menschenbild im 20. Jahrhundert', loc. cit., pp. 128 ff.

5. *The Protestant Era*, Preface, p. xxxii; Am. ed., p. xvii.

6. 'Philosophy and Fate', in *The Protestant Era*, pp. 15 ff.; Am ed., pp. 3 ff.

7. 'Realism and Faith', in *The Protestant Era*, p. 91; Am. ed., p. 81.

8. 'The Protestant Message and the Man of Today', in *The Protestant Era*, pp. 190 ff., 200 f.; *The New Being* (Sermons), SCM Press, London, and Scribner's, New York, 1963, pp. 122 f.

9. From a sermon (duplicated), quoted by William W. Bartley, *The Retreat to Commitment*, New York, 1962, p. 73.

10. *On the Boundary*, p. 65; 'The Lost Dimension in Religion', *Saturday Evening Post*, Philadelphia, 14th June, 1958, pp. 29, 76, 78–79; *Systematic Theology* II, London, 1957, pp. 123 ff.; Am. ed., pp. 115 ff.; *The Eternal Now* (Sermons), SCM Press, London, 1967, and Scribner's, New York, 1963.

11. *The Protestant Era*, Preface, p. xxiv.

12. Communicated by Helmut Thielicke, 'Paul Tillich, Wanderer zwischen zwei Welten', in *Der Spannungsbogen. Festgabe für Paul Tillich zum 75. Geburtstag*, Stuttgart, 1961, p. 20.

13. 'Kritisches und positives Paradox. Eine Auseinandersetzung mit K. Barth und F. Gogarten', 1923; repr. in *Gesammelte Werke* VII, p. 241.

14. *Systematic Theology* II, Preface.

15. *Systematic Theology* I, Nisbet, London, 1953, p. 4, and University of Chicago Press, 1951.

16. *The Protestant Era*, Preface, p. xxvii; Am. ed., p. xiii.

17. Ibid.

18. Open letter to Lücke, *Werke*, Pt. I, Vol. V, p. 614.

19. *The Protestant Era*, Preface, pp. xlii f.; Am. ed., pp. xxvi f.

20. *Theology of Culture*, Oxford University Press, New York, 1959, p. v.

21. *On the Boundary*, p. 13.

22. 'Philosophy and Theology', in *Religion and Life*, Vol. 10, 1941; repr. in *The Protestant Era*, p. 93; Am. ed., p. 83; *Biblical Religion and the Search for Ultimate Reality*, Nisbet, London, and University of Chicago Press, 1944, p. 85.

23. *Systematic Theology* I, pp. 68 ff.; Am. ed., pp. 60 ff.; *Biblical Religion, etc.*, p. 29.

24. For the following cf. *Biblical Religion, etc.*, pp. 1 ff.; *Systematic Theology* I, pp. 35, 152; Am. ed., pp. 26, 144 ff.; II, pp. 93 ff.; Am. ed., pp. 85 f.; 'What is wrong with "Dialectical Theology"?', in *Journal of Religion* (Chicago) XV, 1935, 2, pp. 127–45.

25. *Systematic Theology* I, pp. 69 f.; Am. ed., pp. 61 f.

26. Ibid., p. 69; Am. ed., p. 61.

27. On the following cf. *Systematic Theology* II, p. 30; Am. ed., p. 27; 'Aspects of a Religious Analysis of Culture', in *Theology of Culture*, pp. 48 f.; 'Existential Analysis and Religious Symbols', in *Contemporary Problems in Religion*, ed. H. A. Basilius, Detroit, 1956, pp. 35–55; *The Interpretation of History*, pp. 39 f.

28. *Systematic Theology* I, p. 72; Am. ed., p. 60; II, pp. 16 ff.; Am ed., pp. 19 ff.

29. *Systematic Theology* I, p. 72; Am. ed., p. 64.

30. Ibid., pp. 6 ff., 35 f.; Am. ed., pp. 6 ff., 26 f.

31. *Biblical Religion and the Search for Ultimate Reality*, pp. 7 f., 10; 'Philosophy and Theology', in *The Protestant Era*, pp. 93 ff.; Am. ed., pp. 83 ff.

32. *Biblical Religion, etc.*, pp. 6, 56 f.; *Systematic Theology* I, pp. 21 ff.; Am. ed., pp. 20 ff.; 'Philosophy and Theology', pp. 95 ff.; Am. ed., pp. 85 f.

33. *Biblical Religion, etc.*, p. 83.

34. Ibid., pp. 11 ff., 51; 'Philosophy and Theology', p. 95; Am. ed., p. 85; *The Courage to Be*, Nisbet, London, 1953, pp. 30 ff., and Yale University Press, 1952, 1959; Fontana Library, 1962.

35. *The Shaking of the Foundations* (Sermons), SCM Press, London, and Scribner's, New York, 1949, pp. 55 ff. Also available in Pelican, 1962.

36. *Biblical Religion, etc.*, p. 13; 'Existential Analysis and Religious Symbols', in *Contemporary Problems in Religion*, ed. H. A. Basilius, Detroit, 1956, pp. 35–55; *Systematic Theology*, II, p. 39; Am. ed., p. 32; 'The Protestant Message and the Man of Today', 1929.

37. *The Shaking of the Foundations*, p. 94.

38. Ibid., pp. 65 ff., 108 ff.

39. On the following cf. *Systematic Theology* II, pp. 33–50; Am. ed., pp. 29–44.

40. On the following cf. *Systematic Theology* II, pp. 51–68; Am. ed., pp. 44–59; *Biblical Religion, etc.*; *The Shaking of the Foundations*, pp. 154 f., 158 ff.; 'Existential Analysis and Religious Symbols', in *Contemporary Problems in Religion*, pp. 35–55.

41. *Systematic Theology* I, p. 69; Am. ed., p. 61; II, pp. 14 f., 26; Am. ed., pp. 6 f., 21 f.

42. *The Shaking of the Foundations*, p. 57.

43. 'The Formative Power of Protestantism', in *The Protestant Era*, p. 215; Am. ed., p. 206.

44. *Eschatologie und Geschichte*, 1927, *Gesammelte Werke* VI, pp. 72 f.; 'Wesen und Wandel des Glaubens', in *Weltperspektiven* VIII, Berlin, 1961, pp. 19 f.

45. *Systematic Theology* II, pp. 5 ff.; *The Courage to Be*, pp. 174 ff.; *Biblical Religion, etc.*, p. 81; 'Wesen und Wandel des Glaubens', loc. cit., pp. 58 f.; 'Realism in Faith', in *The Protestant Era*, p. 92; Am. ed., p. 69; 'The Recovery of the Prophetic Tradition in the Reformation' (three lectures, 1950), Christianity and Modern Man Publications, Washington, D.C. (duplicated); *Christianity and the Encounter of World Religions*, Columbia University Press, 1963, pp. 89 ff.; 'Religion as a Dimension in Man's Spiritual Life', in *Theology of Culture*, p. 8 f.; 'Dimensionen, Schichten und die Einheit des Seins', 1959, *Gesammelte Werke*, pp. 125 ff.

46. On the following cf. *On the Boundary*, pp. 36 ff.; 'Auseinandersetzung mit Karl Barth und Friedrich Gogarten', 1923, *Gesammelte Werke* VII, pp. 240 ff.; 'Kairos', in *The Protestant Era*, pp. 50 ff.; Am. ed., pp. 32 ff.; *The Protestant Era*, Preface, p. xxx; Am. ed., pp. xix f.; *Kairos und Utopia*, 1959, *Gesammelte Werke* VI, pp. 155 f.

47. On the following cf. *Systematic Theology* II, pp. 9 ff., 125 ff., 134; Am. ed., pp. 9 ff., 108 ff., 115; 'Wesen und Wandel des Glaubens', loc. cit., pp. 53 ff., 62 ff.; 'Recht und Bedeutung religiöser Symbole', 1961, *Gesammelte Werke* V, pp. 237 ff.; 'The Lost Dimension in Religion', *Saturday Evening Post*, Philadelphia, 14th June, 1958, pp. 29, 76, 78–79; 'The Nature of Religious Language', in *Theology of Culture*, pp. 53 ff.; 'Religion and Secular Culture', 1946, in *The Protestant Era*, pp. 68 f.; Am. ed., pp. 55 ff.

48. Wilhelm Weischedel, 'Paul Tillichs philosophische Theologie. Ein ehrerbietiger Widerspruch', in *Der Spannungsbogen*, p. 35.

49. *Systematic Theology* I, p. 19; Am. ed., p. 17; 'Wesen und Wandel des Glaubens', loc. cit., p. 11; 'Kairos', in *The Protestant Era*, pp. 41 ff.

50. On the following cf. *Systematic Theology* I, pp. 21 ff., 25 ff.; Am. ed., pp. 18 ff., 22 ff.; *The Protestant Era*, Preface, p. xlii; Am. ed., p. xxvi; 'Philosophy and Theology', 1941, in *The Protestant Era*, pp. 93 ff.; Am. ed., pp. 83 ff.; *Biblical Religion, etc.*, p. 61; *On the Boundary*, pp. 51 ff.

51. W. Weischedel, op. cit., p. 44.

52. *The Courage to Be*, pp. 37 ff.; cf. pp. 135 ff.

53. *Systematic Theology* I, p. 55; Am. ed., p. 49; cf. 'The Lost Dimension in Religion' (n. 10); 'Das Christliche Menschenbild im 20. Jahrhundert', 1955; 'Das Christliche Verständnis des modernen Menschen', in *Auf der Grenze, Aus dem Lebenswerk Paul Tillichs*, Stuttgart, 1962, pp. 132 ff.

54. 'Das Christliche Verständnis des modernen Menschen', loc. cit., p. 139; 'Spiritual Problems of Postwar Reconstruction', in *The Protestant Era*, p. 288; Am. ed., p. 261.

55. For Tillich's christology cf. esp. *Systematic Theology* I, pp. 18 ff., 150; Am. ed., pp. 16 ff., 142; II, pp. 112–90; Am. ed., pp. 97–173; *Biblical Religion, etc.*, pp. 37 ff.

56. *Systematic Theology* II, pp. 154 f.; Am. ed., pp. 134 f.

57. *Systematic Theology* I, pp. 55 f.; Am. ed., pp. 49 f.; II, pp. 136 ff., 191 ff.; Am. ed., pp. 114 ff., 173 ff.

58. *The New Being*, pp. 15 ff.; cf. *The Shaking of the Foundations*, pp. 101 ff.

59. 'The Protestant Message and the Man of Today', in *The Protestant Era*, p. 203; Am. ed., p. 192.

60. On the following cf. 'Realism and Faith', in *The Protestant Era*, pp. 74 ff., esp. pp. 82 ff., 85 ff., 89 ff.; Am. ed., pp. 67 ff.; 'The Formative Power of Protestantism', in *The Protestant Era*, pp. 205 ff., esp. pp. 214 ff.; Am. ed., pp. 201 ff., esp. pp. 214 ff.

61. *The Shaking of the Foundations*, pp. 79 ff.

62. *The New Being*, p. 47.

63. *Systematic Theology* I, pp. 108 ff.; *The Courage to Be*, pp. 77 f.; 'Wesen und Wandel des Glaubens', loc. cit., pp. 12 ff.; 'Realism and Faith', in *The Protestant Era*, pp. 76 ff.; Am. ed., pp. 69 ff.; *Systematic Theology* I, p. 19; Am. ed., p. 9; 'Wesen und Wandel des Glaubens', loc. cit., p. 11; 'Kairos', in *The Protestant Era*, pp. 41 f.; Am. ed., pp. 43 f.; 'The Idea and the Ideal of Personality', in *The Protestant Era*, pp. 147 ff.; Am. ed., pp. 115 ff.

64. *Gesammelte Werke* I, Preface; 'Religion as a Dimension in Man's Spiritual Life', in *Theology of Culture*, pp. 7 f.; 'Our Protestant Principles', in *The Protestant* (New York) IV. 7th August 1942, pp. 8–14; *The New Being*, pp. 155 f.; *The Protestant Era*, Preface, p. xxx; Am. ed., p. xvii; 'Vertical and Horizontal Thinking', in *American Scholar* (New York) XV. 1, 1945–46, pp. 102–05, 110–12.

65. *On the Boundary*, p. 68; 'Religion and Secular Culture', in *The Protestant Era*, pp. 61 ff.; Am. ed., pp. 55 ff.; 'Our Protestant Principles', loc. cit.; 'Auseinandersetzung mit Karl Barth und Friedrich Gogarten', in *Gesammelte Werke* VII, pp. 240 ff.; *Systematic Theology* I, p. 45; Am. ed., pp. 38 f.

66. *On the Boundary*, pp. 71 f.

67. 'The Protestant Principle and the Proletarian Situation', in *The Protestant Era*, pp. 251 ff.; Am. ed., pp. 174 ff.; 'Aspects of a Religious Analysis of Culture', in *Theology of Culture*, p. 41.

68. 'Religion and Secular Culture', in *The Protestant Era*, pp. 61 ff.; Am. ed., pp. 55 ff.; 'The Formative Power of Protestantism', ibid., p. 213; 'What is Wrong with "Dialectical Theology"?', in *Journal of Religion* (Chicago) XV, 1935, no. 2, pp. 127–45.

69. *On the Boundary*, pp. 67 f.

70. 'Religion and Secular Culture', in *The Protestant Era*, p. 66; Am. ed., p. 59; 'Religion as a Dimension of Man's Spiritual Life', in *Theology of Culture*, p. 12; 'Religion and Culture', in 'The Lost Dimension in Religion' (cf. n. 10); 'Nature and Sacrament', in *The Protestant Era*, p. 123; Am. ed., pp. 110 f.

71. Heinz-Dietrich Wendland, 'Zu Tillichs 75. Geburtstag', *Sonntagsblatt* (Hamburg), 20th August, 1961.

72. Karl Barth, 'Antworten und Fragen an Paul Tillich', in Tillich's *Gesammelte Werke* VII, pp. 226 ff., esp. pp. 232 ff.; *Evangelical Theology*, London, 1963, p. 113.

73. W. Weischedel, 'Paul Tillichs philosophische Theologie', loc. cit., pp. 32 f.

74. Issue of 31st May, 1961.

75. 'The Formative Power of Protestantism', in *The Protestant Era*, p. 218; Am. ed., pp. 217 f.

76. *The New Being*, p. 111.

CHAPTER TEN

1. *On the Boundary*, pp. 47 f., 74 f.

2. 'The Protestant Message and the Man of Today', in *The Protestant Era*, pp. 193 ff.; Am. ed., pp. 196 ff.

3. 'The Recovery of the Prophetic Tradition in the Reformation' (three lectures, 1950), Christianity and Modern Man Publications (duplicated).

4. 'The Protestant Message and the Man of Today', in *The Protestant Era*, p. 189; Am. ed., pp. 193 f.

5. Ibid., pp. 192 ff., esp. pp. 196 ff., 201 ff.; Am. ed., pp. 201 ff.

6. Ibid., pp. 202 f.; Am. ed., pp. 203 ff.; *The Shaking of the Foundations*, p. 162; *Systematic Theology* II, p. 207; Am. ed., p. 179.

7. 'Rechtfertigung und Zweifel', *Vorträge der theol. Konferenz zu Giessen*, 39th series, Giessen, 1924, pp. 24 ff.; *The Protestant Era*, Preface, p. xxix; Am. ed., p. xv; 'Wesen und Wandel des Glaubens', loc. cit., pp. 25 ff.

8. *The Protestant Era*, Preface, pp. xxix f.; Am. ed., pp. xv f.; *On the Boundary*, pp. 50 f.

9. *The New Being*, pp. 67 f.

10. *The Protestant Era*, Preface, pp. xxix f.; Am. ed., pp. xiv f.

11. Ibid.; 'Wesen und Wandel des Glaubens', loc. cit., p. 57; *The Shaking of the Foundations*, pp. 40, 44 f., 47.

12. For the following cf. *The Courage to Be*, pp. 147 ff.

13. Quoted by Christoph Rhein, *Paul Tillich, Philosoph und Theologe. Eine Einführung in sein Denken*, Stuttgart, 1957, p. 111, n. 27.

14. Ibid.

15. *The Protestant Era*, Preface, pp. xxvi f., xxxi f., xxxvii f.; Am. ed., pp. xii f., xvi f., xxi f.; 'The Formative Power of Protestantism', loc. cit., pp. 205 ff.; Am. ed., pp. 214 ff.; 'Our Protestant Principles', in *The Protestant* (New York) IV, 7th August, 1942, pp. 8–14; 'The Protestant Principle and the Proletarian Situation', in *The Protestant Era*, pp. 237 ff.; Am. ed., pp. 161 ff.; 'The Protestant Message and the Man of Today', loc. cit., pp. 204 ff.; Am. ed., pp. 201 ff.; 'The End of the Protestant Era?', in *The Protestant Era*, pp. 222 ff.; Am. ed., pp. 226 ff.; 'Wesen und Wandel des Glaubens', loc. cit., pp. 114, 143; *The Eternal Now*, pp. 122 ff.

16. *The Protestant Era*, Preface, pp. xxxvii, xliv f.; Am. ed., pp. xxi, xxviii f.; 'The End of the Protestant Era?', loc. cit., pp. 222 ff.; Am. ed., pp. 222 ff.; 'The Protestant Message and the Man of Today', loc. cit., p. 191; Am. ed., p. 200; 'Die bleibende Bedeutung der katholischen Kirche für den Protestantismus', in *Gesammelte Werke* VII, pp. 124 ff.; *The Courage to Be*, pp. 91 ff., 111 ff.

17. *The Protestant Era*, Preface, pp. xxxvi, xxxix; Am. ed., pp. xxiii, xxv; 'The End of the Protestant Era?', loc. cit., pp. 226 f.; Am. ed., pp. 226 f.; 'The Protestant Principle and the Proletarian Situation', loc. cit., pp. 257 f.; 'The Protestant Message and the Man of Today', loc. cit., p. 198; Am. ed., p. 199; 'Our Protestant Principles', loc. cit., pp. 8–14; 'The Recovery of the Prophetic Tradition in the Reformation' (three lectures, 1950), Christianity and Modern Man Publications (duplicated); 'The Idea and the Ideal of Personality', loc. cit., pp. 148 f.; Am. ed., pp. 132 f.; 'Nature and Sacrament', loc. cit., pp. 105 ff.; Am. ed., pp. 94 ff.

18. *The Protestant Era*, Preface, pp. xxxvii f., xlv; Am. ed., pp. xxiii f., xxviii f.

19. 'The End of the Protestant Era?', loc. cit., pp. 223 f.; Am. ed., p. 230; 'Die bleibende Bedeutung der katholischen Kirche für den Protestantismus', loc. cit., p. 129.

20. *The Protestant Era*, Preface, pp. xxxviii f.; Am. ed., pp. xxii f.; 'The End of the Protestant Era?', loc. cit., pp. 228 f.; Am. ed., pp. 229 f.; 'Ende der Protestantischen Ära?' I, in *Gesammelte Werke* VII, p. 157; 'Die bleibende Bedeutung der katholischen Kirche für den Protestantismus', loc. cit., pp. 126 ff., 131; 'The Formative Power of Protestantism', loc. cit., p. 218; Am. ed., pp. 211 f.; 'Nature and Sacrament', loc. cit., pp. 105 ff., 122 ff.; Am. ed., pp. 94 ff., 110 ff.; 'The Recovery of the Prophetic Tradition in the Reformation' (three lectures, 1950), Christianity and Modern Man Publications (duplicated); *The Shaking of the Foundations*, p. 86.

21. 'The End of the Protestant Era?', loc. cit., p. 230; Am. ed., p. 230.

22. 'Ende der protestantischen Ära?' I, in *Gesammelte Werke* VII, pp. 152, 157.

23. 'The End of the Protestant Era?', loc. cit., pp. 233 f.; Am. ed., pp. 232 f.; 'Ende der Protestantischen Ära?' I, *Gesammelte Werke* VII, p. 158; 'Spiritual Problems of post-war Reconstruction', in *The Protestant Era*, pp. 293 ff.; Am. ed., pp. 267 ff.; *The Interpretation of History*, p. 63.

24. *The Protestant Era*, Preface, p. xxvi; Am. ed., p. xii; 'Die bleibende Bedeutung der katholischen Kirche für den Protestantismus', loc. cit., p. 125.

25. *The Protestant Era*, Preface, pp. xxxiv f.; Am. ed., pp. xix f.; 'Kairos', in *The Protestant Era*, pp. 38 ff.; Am. ed., pp. 32 ff.; 'Kairos and Logos', in *The Interpretation of History*, pp. 123 ff.; 'Kairos' III, 1958, *Gesammelte Werke* VI, pp. 137 ff.; 'Ethics in a Changing World', in *The Protestant Era*, p. 173; Am. ed., pp. 155 f.; 'Kairos und Utopie', *Gesammelte Werke* VI, pp. 149 ff.; 'Christologie und Geschichtsdeutung', ibid., pp. 83 ff.; 'Victory in Defeat: the Meaning of History in the Light of the Christian Prophetism', in *Interpretation* (Richmond), VI, January 1955, pp. 17–28; *The Shaking of the Foundations*, pp. 34 ff.; *The Eternal Now*, pp. 103 ff.

26. *The Protestant Era*, Preface, pp. xxxi ff.; Am. ed., pp. xix f.; 'Kairos', loc cit., pp. 55 f.; Am. ed., p. 48; 'Kairos' III, 1958, *Gesammelte Werke* VI, p. 139; 'Kairos und Utopie', ibid., pp. 149 f.; 'Religion and Secular Culture', in *The Protestant Era*, pp. 61 ff.; Am. ed., pp. 59 ff.

27. *The Protestant Era*, Preface, p. xlv; Am. ed., p. xxviii; 'Religion and Secular Culture', loc. cit., p. 66; Am. ed., p. 60.

28. 'The Lost Dimension in Religion', loc. cit.

29. Sermon, 'The Divine Reality', in *The Eternal Now*, pp. 65 ff.

30. 'Vertical and Horizontal Thinking', in *The American Scholar* (New York) XV, 1, 1945–46; 'The Word of Religion', in *The Protestant Era*, p. 181; Am. ed., p. 185.

31. 'The Word of Religion', loc. cit., p. 185; Am. ed., p. 188.

32. *The Shaking of the Foundations*, pp. 150 ff.

ACKNOWLEDGEMENTS

The translator and publishers wish to acknowledge their indebtedness for permission to reproduce copyright material as follows: from *Church Dogmatics* (Vols. I–IV) by Karl Barth, translated by G. T. Thompson, etc. and published by T. & T. Clark, Edinburgh; from *Dogmatics in Outline* by Karl Barth, translated by G. T. Thompson and published by SCM Press, London, and Harper & Row, New York; from *The Epistle to the Romans*, 1933, by Karl Barth, translated by E. C. Hoskyns and published by Oxford University Press; from 'The Humanity of God' by Karl Barth, which first appeared in the *Scottish Journal of Theology Occasional Papers*, No. 8, translated by J. S. McNab and published by Oliver & Boyd Ltd., Edinburgh, also translated by John Newton Thomas and Thomas Wieser and published in book form by the John Knox Press, Richmond, Virginia; from *Revolutionary Theology in the Making: Barth-Thurneysen Correspondence, 1914–1925*, translated by James D. Smart and published by Epworth Press, London, and John Knox Press, Richmond, Virginia; from *Cost of Discipleship* by Dietrich Bonhoeffer, translated by R. H. Fuller, second edition © by SCM Press Ltd., 1959, reprinted with permission of SCM Press Ltd., London, and The Macmillan Company, New York; from *Letters and Papers from Prison*, Revised Edition by Dietrich Bonhoeffer, translated by R. H. Fuller, Frank Clark, etc., copyright 1953 by The Macmillan Company, copyright © by SCM Press Ltd., 1967, reprinted with permission of SCM Press Ltd., London, and The Macmillan Company, New York; from *Jesus of Nazareth* by Günther Bornkamm, translated by I. and F. McLuskey with James Robinson and published by Hodder & Stoughton, London, and Harper & Row, New York; from *Man in Revolt* by Emil Brunner, translated by Olive Wyon and published by Lutterworth Press, London, and The Westminster Press, Philadelphia, copyright 1947, W. L. Jenkins; from *The Misunderstanding of the Church* by Emil Brunner, translated by Harold Knight and published by Lutterworth Press, London, and The Westminster Press, Philadelphia, copyright 1953 by W. L. Jenkins; from *Truth as Encounter* by Emil Brunner, translated by D. Cairns and T. H. L. Parker and published by SCM Press, London, and The Westminster Press, Philadelphia, © 1943 by The Westminster Press and 1964 by W. L. Jenkins; from *Essays* by Rudolf Bultmann, © 1955 by Rudolf Bultmann, reprinted with permission of The Macmillan Company, New York; from *History and Eschatology* by Rudolf Bultmann, published by Edinburgh University Press and by Harper & Row, New York; from *Jesus Christ and Mythology* by Rudolf Bultmann, published by SCM Press, London, and Scribner's, New York; from 'What sense is there to speak of God' by Rudolf Bultmann in *The Christian Scholar*, XLIII, 3, 1960, New York; from *Existence and Faith* by Rudolf Bultmann, translated by Schubert M. Ogden and published by Hodder & Stoughton, London, and the World Publishing Company, New York; from *Kerygma and Myth*, edited by H. W. Bartsch, translated by R. H. Fuller and published by S.P.C.K., London, and Alec R. Allenson, Inc., Naperville, Illinois; from 'Is Modern Theology

INDEX

INDEX

Church and State, 176 ff.

civilisation, 32 f., 40 f., 43, 44 f., 46, 151, 303, 334, 358. *See* culture

clericalism, 80

Cohen, Hermann, 27

collective, 349, 352

commandment of love, 174, 175, 182 f., 190, 192, 194, 200

compromise, 190 ff., 200

Confessing Church, 56, 68, 119, 131, 164, 173

confession of faith, 279

conscience, 62, 134, 350

consciousness; religious, 32, 38; theology of, 19

conservatism, 34, 189

Constantine the Great, 79, 81

Conzelmann, Hans, 254, 267, 290, 291

Copernicus, 37

corporeality, *see* body

correlation, method of, 305 ff., 341, 354

cosmos, 105, 142, 149, 197, 269

Council of the Protestant Church in Germany, 171 f.

Courage to be, 298

covenant of God, 86, 95 ff.

creation, 29, 94, 97, 100, 107, 319 *et passim*; and covenant, 95 f., 108; fallen, 190; and justification, 141 ff.; new, 325; order of, 96 ff.; and revelation, 61

creator, 72, 100, 117

credo quia absurdum, 31

creed, objective and subjective, 69, 92

crisis, 11, 23, 24, 26, 30, 44, 45, 46, 47, 297, 354 f. *See* theology of crisis

cross, 28, 115, 158, 218, 251, 348; and resurrection, 112, 234, 259

crusades, 27

'cultural Protestantism', 32, 162, 330, 357

culture, 46, 303, 322, 329 f., 341, 355. *See* civilisation

damnation, 322

death, 26, 29, 64, 161, 218, 226 f., 230, 290, 297, 314, 322

dechristianisation, 69. *See* secularisation

Decline of the West, 26

Deissmann, Adolf, 16

democracy, 180 f., 182

demythologisation, 214 ff., 225, 229, 233, 238, 241, 246, 250, 252, 276, 283, 319. *See* existentialist interpretation, myth

denomination, 332, 349

depth, 301, 315, 356

Descartes, René, 224

desecularisation, 231

De servo arbitrio, 50

despair, 296, 322, 346; 'theology of', 26. *See* doubt

destiny, 322, 354

dialectic; Barth's dialectic method, 29 ff.; 'dialectic theology', 29 ff., 41, 45, 47, 54, 63, 210 f., 215 f., 248, 302, 355

Dibelius, Martin, 67

Dibelius, Otto, 52

Dilthey, Wilhelm, 74, 243, 286

'disparity' of New Testament statements, 273 ff.

doctrine, pure, 73, 77, 78, 119, 173, 214, 351

dogma, 73 f., 78

dogmatic theology, 32, 117, 184. *See* Church Dogmatics

Dohnanyi, Hans von, 159

Dostoievsky, F. M., 11, 27, 37, 130

doubt, 297, 342 f., 344, 345, 346

Droysen, J. G., 207

dualism; Bultmann's methodological, 249 f.; cosmic, 206; Gogarten's, 47

Easter, 234, 235, 253, 257, 264; event, 267, 268; faith, 256, 260. *See* resurrection

Ebeling, Gerhard, 139, 154, 159, 169, 254, 256, 257, 263, 264, 267, 268, 269, 291

Ebner, Ferdinand, 58, 70, 242

Eckhart, 327

ecstasy, 328, 352

ecumenism, 81 f., 353

Einstein, Albert, 74

ekklesia, 76 ff., 156. *See* Church

election, 94, 107; of Israel, 235